Reading the Fire

READING
the FIRE

The Traditional Indian Literatures of America

JAROLD RAMSEY

Revised and Expanded

University of Washington Press

Seattle & London

This University of Washington Press publication is a
revised and expanded version of READING THE FIRE: ESSAYS IN THE
TRADITIONAL INDIAN LITERATURES OF THE FAR WEST,
published in 1983 by the University of Nebraska Press. It includes
four new essays along with the eleven original essays.

Library of Congress Cataloging-in-Publication Data
Ramsey, Jarold, 1937–
Reading the fire : the traditional Indian literatures of America /
Jarold Ramsey. — Rev. and expanded.
p.   cm.
Includes bibliographical references.
ISBN 0-295-97787-6
1. Folk literature, Indian—West (U.S.)—History and criticism.
2. Indian Literature—West (U.S.)—History and criticism.
I. Title.
PM155.R35   1999
398.2'089'97—dc21   99-13656
CIP

For *my mother,*
Wilma Mendenhall Ramsey,
and in memory of my father,
A. S. Ramsey

mahsie, mahsie

CONTENTS

VII

PREFACE

IN THE FIFTEEN YEARS SINCE THIS BOOK FIRST AP‹ peared, the domain of traditional and modern American Indian literatures has grown rapidly and in many directions. For one thing, a brilliant new generation of Native writers is in circulation now, taking their place alongside their still-active "elders" in the on-going American Indian literary renaissance. That new works by N. Scott Momaday *and* Sherman Alexie, Leslie Silko *and* Elizabeth Woody, James Welch *and* David Treuer are being published in the same time-frame is proof positive that the Native literary impulse has vitality, range, depth, and what Whitman liked to call "vista."

For another thing, the critical study of both traditional and modern Indian verbal art has flourished since 1983, becoming a well-defined and lively academic field, with its own journals, conferences, landmark publications, theoretical factions, and internal quarrels. It has even acquired an international dimension, with European scholars—especially in Italy and Germany—making important contributions. Traditional stories and poems and the works of Indian writers are being taught widely, not just in "Native American Literature" courses (which have proliferated), but also in mainstream American literature courses—indicating that this nation's first and oldest literary heritage is at long last being recognized in the canonical scheme of American Literature.

My own work since 1983 has in the main carried on with the pre-occupations that led to the eleven essays that made up the first edition of *Reading the Fire*—that is, with the oral/traditional narratives of western tribes and with the continuities linking them with modern Indian writing. Hence the three-part format of the 1983 edition is retained here, only expanded and more formally marked: first, essays on basic elements of the traditional literature—creation and origin myths, tricksters and their stories, and the verbal art of Native ceremony and ritual; then a range of close readings of individual stories, illustrating the difficulties and rewards of engaging their kind literarily, and offering (I hope) models of how to overcome these difficulties; and, thirdly, a section of essays exploring the fascinating (and still neglected) subject of Native literary adaptation and assimilation of Anglo materials and forms, and looking on into the interplay of tradition and individual talent in modern Indian writing. In addition to adding four new essays (3, 8, 13, and 14), I have "corrected" and updated but not extensively revised the original eleven essays, except for the final piece (essay 15 in this edition), which has been expanded to bring into view work by new Indian authors and permit a fuller treatment of the theoretical dimensions of such work in relation to the traditional repertories.

I'm grateful to the University of Washington Press for the opportunity to thus consolidate twenty-five years of work in an emergent field; and I am especially grateful to colleagues who have forthrightly identified strengths and weaknesses in the original book, as they have found them. Over the last two decades, literary *theory* has "arrived" in Indian studies, in a variety of modes—deconstruction, ethnographic theory, feminist theory, orality theory, ethnopoetics in various formats—and overall our collective purchase on our difficult subject has been greatly fortified and made more accountable thereby. Certainly some of the new essays in this edition benefit, or so I think, from theoretical moves and strategies that were unknown to me twenty years ago. Theory has been teaching us to be ever more self-critical of our editorial and interpretive engagements with traditional Indian texts, more alert to lurking Eurocentric biases in our viewpoints, more open to and respectful of perhaps unmitigable differences between the verbal art of a Clackamas Chinook or Navajo narrative and the art of a story by James Joyce.

And yet it seems important now for literary theory in our field to recognize its limits, its points-of-diminishing returns, its obligations. To generate high-powered theory about oral/traditional texts without offering practical guidance and patient exemplification of method in terms of particular texts is to beg the question of theory's usefulness in the first place. To relentlessly problematize the task of understanding Native oral materials as literary art, dismissing earlier editors and commentators for not seeing or for misconstruing the problems, can be a disservice both to the oral repertories themselves and to interested readers for whom critical theory should be, finally, enabling as well as admonitory.

In these terms, Dell Hymes's study, "*In Vain I Tried to Tell You*": *Essays in Native American Ethnopoetics,* has been for many a source and a model of enabling theory-and-application since its publication in 1982. Certainly it has been indispensable to both editions of *this* book. And it is heartening as to the future of our field to see both the ongoing progress of Hymes's own monumental ethnopoetics project since "*In Vain*" appeared and the recent publication of a book like William Clements's *Native American Verbal Art* (University of Arizona Press, 1996). Clements's book is a meticulous and historically rich study of the ways we have tried over three centuries to make printable, readable texts out of an oral art. Very much in the spirit of Hymes's work, Clements's clear-headed and patient examination of the ways we have appropriated and distorted Indian stories and songs and misunderstood them is certainly cautionary—but it is also encouraging, respectful both of Indian oral literature and of readers' imaginations, and certain to be useful.

I hope for the same in this new edition of *Reading the Fire.*

Madras/Rochester
January 1999

ACKNOWLEDGMENTS

THE DEFECTS AND SHORTCOMINGS OF THIS BOOK
are mine, all mine; but whatever its virtues, its indebtedness is a pleasure
to itemize, because in doing so I can set down here the names of many wise
and generous friends from whom I have learned, or should have learned,
much. My gratitude to them equals that of the mouthless citizens of Ni-
mishxa'ya on the Columbia, when Coyote gave them all mouths, or that of
the first married couple in another Chinookan story, when Coyote taught
them how to perform the act of love.

In particular I want to name the following: Dell Hymes, Karl Kroeber, and Barre Toelken—mentors and fellow travelers; and the late Row-
land Collins, for his generous encouragement and support, as chairman of
the University of Rochester Department of English, early in this work.

And among friends, colleagues, and students who have listened,
objected, countered, humored, pointed out, and sometimes even agreed,
these especially: Randy Bouchard, Lori Burlingame, David Day, Rob
Evans, Larry Evers, the late Alice Florendo, the late George Ford, Grace
and Al Harris, Howard Horsford, Virginia Hymes, David Jeffrey, Bruce

Johnson, Frank Kermode, Chris Koch, Karl Kroeber, Merrill Lewis, W. S. Merwin, Lee Mitchell, Russell Peck, Fitzjohn Porter Poole, John Purdy, Bill Robbins, LaVonne Ruoff, Frank Shuffelton, Kim Stafford, William Stafford, Brian Swann, Otto and Rick Thaler, Roger Weaver, Mary Young, and the members of English 557 (Spring 1982) and of NEH Summer Seminars in 1985 and 1988; Jane Dever and Helen Craven, typists extraordinaire; and my Sweathouse Council and Secret Society—Dorothy, John, Kate, Sophia.

Parts of the following essays have previously been published in somewhat different form but with the exception of essay 15, under the same titles. They are reprinted here with the permission of the publishers: essay 3 from *Literature and Medicine* 8 (1989), pp. 78–99; essay 4 from *Western American Literature* 13, no. 2 (August 1978); essay 5 from *Smoothing the Ground: Essays on Native American Literature,* ed. Brian Swann (Berkeley and Los Angeles: University of California Press, 1983, © the Regents of the University of California); essay 6 from *PMLA* 92 (1977); essay 8 from *Oral Tradition,* vol.10, no. 2 (1995–96), pp. 263–81; essay 9 from *Sound Heritage* 5, no. 3 (1976), pp. 9–13; essay 12 from *Journal of American Folklore* 90, no. 358 (1977), pp. 442–54; essay 13 from *The Native in Literature,* ed. King, Calvert, and Hoy (Toronto: ECW Press, 1987), pp. 206–24; essay 14 from *Boundary 2,* vol. 2, no. 3 (Fall 1992), pp. 180–96, reprinted in *American Indian Persistence and Resurgence,* ed. Karl Kroeber (Durham: Duke University Press, 1994), pp. 181–97; essay 15 as "The Teacher of Modern American Indian Writing as Ethnographer and Critic," in *College English* 41, pt. 2 (October 1979), pp. 163–69.

The following publishers have generously given permission to use extended quotations from copyrighted works: From Melville Jacobs, *Kalapuya Texts,* University of Washington Publications in Anthropology, vol. 11 (1945), p. 91, presented here as it appeared in Dell Hymes's verse version in the *Journal of the Folklore Institute* (1981), pp. 148–49, and reprinted courtesy of Dell Hymes. Also from Melville Jacobs, *Clackamas Chinook Texts,* pt. 1, Indiana University Research Center in Anthropology, Folklore, and Linguistics, pub. 11, pp. 359–60. From Pamela Munro, "Two Stories by Nellie Brown," *in Yuman Texts,* ed. Margaret Langdon, *International Journal of American Linguistics,* North American Texts Series, vol. 1, no. 3 (1976), p. 48. From Melville Jacobs, *The People Are Coming Soon* (Seattle: University of Washington Press, 1960), pp. 52, 176, 179, 180, 359–60. From

Elizabeth Jacobs, "Wild Woman," *Nehalem Tillamook Tales* (Eugene: University of Oregon Books, 1959), text no. 14, pp. 45–54. From *The Letters and Journals of Simon Fraser, 1806–8,* ed. W. Kaye Lamb (Canada: Macmillan Co., 1960), pp. 89–92; reprinted courtesy of W. Kaye Lamb. From Morris Swadesh, "Cayuse Interlinear Texts," MS film 373.1, reel 48, Boas Collection, American Philosophical Society, Philadelphia. From L. V. McWhorter, *Hear Me My Chiefs: Nez Perce History and Legend* (Caldwell, Idaho: Caxton Press, 1952). From "The Trip to the Moon," narrator Annie York, recorded in the Thompson (Interior Salish) language (November 1973), translated by Mamie Henry and edited by Randy Bouchard and Dorothy Kennedy for the British Columbia Indian Language Project, Victoria, B.C.; courtesy of Randy Bouchard, BCILP Director. From Duane Niatum, "Raven and the Fear of Growing White," *Songs for the Harvester of Dreams* (Seattle: University of Washington Press, 1981), p. 29. From John Bierhorst, ed., *Four Masterworks of American Indian Literature* (Tucson: University of Arizona Press, 1984), excerpts from "Night Chant" and "Condolence Ritual." From Elizabeth Woody, excerpts from *Luminaries of the Humble* (Tucson: University of Arizona Press, 1994) and *Seven Hands Seven Hearts* (Portland: Eighth Mountain Press, 1994).

We are reading the fire. It is <u>this</u> fire burning before us here and now;

and it is also every fire that ever flared and flickered before gleaming eyes,

anywhere. When we face the fire, the stories begin

—IN THE SPIRIT OF BACHELARD

INTRODUCTION

THESE ESSAYS HAVE GROWN OUT OF TWENTY-FIVE years of research, writing, and teaching in a new field of American literary study, and I hope that they contribute something to the continuing growth of that field and make for new possibilities for other writers. And I hope, too, that they convey something of the excitement that those of us who work with Native American literature feel about the prospect of its receiving serious recognition *as* literary art, specifically as "American Literature," and part of our collective imaginative heritage.

Such recognition and the interpretive study that would justify it have been long in coming. Well more than seventy-five years ago, the foundation for both was laid down during what has been aptly called the Heroic Age of American Indian studies, in the fieldwork of Franz Boas and his colleagues and students, who raced against the foreclosings of history to learn the Native languages and record literary samples of them, at least, for study. The urgency and farsightedness of this effort can be illustrated in the work Boas did in 1890–91 and 1894 with one Chinookan informant, Charles Cultee. What Boas discovered in Cultee, born in 1850, was not only a linguistic informant fluent in two Chinookan languages thought to be extinct, Lower Chinook and Kathlamet, but also a gifted and enthusiastic recitalist, a literary scholar, and an artist in his own right. On three visits to Cultee's home in Bay Center, Washington, Boas managed to learn enough of the languages to transcribe and translate sixty-six narrative and ethnographic texts—all that now survive in them. *Chinook Texts* was published in 1894, and *Kathlamet Texts* in 1901, but by then the indefatigable Boas was at work elsewhere, and within a few years Charles Cultee and the traditional literatures that found their last clear voice in him were gone—except for Boas's texts.[1]

Despite such now-or-never urgencies in their work as transcribers, Boas and his colleagues managed to give some attention in those early years to the task of interpreting their collections as literature. In particular they jointly undertook to refute recent attempts by European scholars, most of them German followers of Max Müller, to use the newly recorded American Indian narratives to validate Müller's general theory that all mythology must be understood as the product of a universal impulse to "explain" celestial phenomena—the sun, moon, and stars. Singling out recent publications by Paul Ehrenreich for special refutation, Boas, T. T. Waterman, Robert Lowie, Paul Radin, and others wrote a series of formidably detailed and rigorous monographs showing that the Native mythologies are what they are because of a complex of factors, cultural, social, and literary, as well as etiological; and that, in Waterman's terse summation of his case against Ehrenreich and the solar-myth thesis, "folk-tales in their present form do not show any trace of having taken shape from the contemplation of the heavenly bodies. Even where nature does enter into mythologies, the desire for *explaining* does not seem to be the moving factor."[2]

However wacky the solar-myth theories of Ehrenreich and others of his persuasion seem today, there is cause to be grateful that they provoked such work in interpretive refutation by Boas and his school. For never before or since has there been such comprehensive and systematic knowledge of the details of Indian myth-literature operating in American scholarship. Waterman's argument against "the explanatory element," for example, cites texts (most of them published no more than fifteen years before he wrote) from fifty-eight different tribes and groups. The literary methods and assumptions in this cross-tribal scholarship were often very naive, and in general, the early work is clearer on what Native literature *is not* than on what it *is;* but for its attempt at an accountable comprehensiveness—before computers—it points the way, I think, to the truly systematic treatment the surviving traditional Native repertories deserve, and may someday receive.

Certainly the early work helped make possible the few substantial literary studies of Indian texts to appear between the 1920s and the 1960s, a period when American anthropology and linguistics turned to other pursuits and the literary establishment learned to affect a New Critical disdain for the provincial and the Native. The work of Paul Radin, Stith Thompson, A. L. Kroeber, Gladys Reichard, Melville Jacobs, and a few others notably continued what Boas and his coworkers had begun, but for the most part they had to labor in the face of general academic and literary indifference.[3]

Now the academies and the literati are showing new interest in the American Indian heritage, and while there is certainly a trendy component to this interest, there is also something real in it—manifested on the one hand by books, publications in scholarly journals, and the creation of professional societies, and on the other hand by a more-than-passing interest in the traditional literatures on the part of many American writers (including new generations of talented Indian poets and novelists).[4] For myself, I was first drawn to the Western mythologies as a poet looking for new ways to imagine the American land, and what I found was the oldest way, whereby the Paiutes and the Blackfeet and the Tillamooks storied their lands as home. Perhaps Theodore Roethke prophesied such Native discoveries in those lines *pace* Eliot in the *North American Sequence:*

> Old men should be explorers?
> I'd be an Indian.
> Ogalala?
> Iroquois.[5]

The essays in this book do not aim at comprehensiveness; I have not attempted to write a "survey" or a "guide" to the study and appreciation of traditional Native literatures on a national scale, or lay down a theoretical foundation for doing so. Far short of that, I have tried to write some exemplary essays about representative Native works from a range of Indian communities across the country, concentrating on the Far West, the region whose Indian and Anglo culture and history I know best. In this respect, *Reading the Fire* is a sequel and a companion volume to my anthology of traditional Indian literature from the Oregon country, *Coyote Was Going There.*[6] A number of the texts I discuss at length here were first reprinted in *Coyote;* I have tried to follow up my anthology choices with interpretation. Here, as in the anthology, I have been attentive to what I have called "the ecological imagination" and the profound sense of place it sustains in the Native literature of the West; but where *Coyote Was Going There* was centered on the Oregon country, in this book, reflecting the course of my studies since then, I have expanded the scope to include some Southwest, Rocky Mountain, North Coast, and Northeast materials. Again, "coverage" is not the aim, but I do hope that serious readers will be able to move across my gaps and perhaps fill some of them in by extension or suggestion from the topics I do cover.

The essays gathered here can be read separately (indeed, more than half of them were first written for individual publication), but they are in this format interrelated, and they do follow a certain order. That is, they move from general accountings of creation and origin myth-narratives and ceremonial literature and one crucial mythic character type (the Trickster) into a central section consisting of five detailed "practical" interpretations of individual narratives. I chose to undertake readings of these particular texts, not because they together amount to anything like a formal or thematic representation of traditional Native narrative art, but rather because they seem to me to exhibit, diversely, something of the richness and artistic astuteness of this literature. (They also exemplify some of the difficulties inherent in interpreting such materials.) Then, in the last sequence of seven essays, I take up the neglected but important question of how the Native literary imagination has responded to contact with Anglo culture; how it has carried on against and indeed within that culture, in the form of prophetic narratives, mythic assimilations of real events, Biblical adaptations, and (in the final essay) in the remarkable creative adaptations of Native traditions to Anglo literary forms and modern realities by Indian poets and writers over the last twenty-five years.

I referred at the beginning to growth and excitement in the field of Indian literary study. To a large extent that condition is currently energized by the work of some gifted scholars who are worthy inheritors of the Boas-Radin-Jacobs tradition in being fluent in one or more native languages and in attempting to bring this all-too-rare linguistic knowledge to bear on literary interpretation and appreciation of the repertories. Among these seminal writers are Dell Hymes, J. Barre Toelken, and Dennis Tedlock; what they and others have contributed already to the recognition of Native literary art speaks for itself, and it is to be hoped that through their writing and teaching, new generations of students (including Native Americans) will be drawn into the ongoing work—perhaps attracted to the study of Indian languages in order to come to terms with their literatures, as Edmund Wilson eventually mastered Russian so as to read Tolstoy and Dostoevsky on their own terms. In particular, the further development of "ethnopoetics" as a unified interpretive methodology is to be hoped for and encouraged.[7]

None of the essays in this book benefits directly from the linguistic knowledge of a Native language that so informs, say, Hymes's studies of Chinookan texts, or Archie Phinney's and Ella Deloria's editions of tales in their own languages (Nez Perce and Dakota, respectively). Like most of my probable readers, I do not command an Indian language, and the commentary here must begin, and end, with what I can discover in English-language texts, mostly the work of Boas-era scholars and their Indian collaborators. Along with the perennial charge that dealing with oral narrative as "literature" is a contradiction in terms (so much then for Homer, *Beowulf,* and the *Kalevala?*), two less obvious and more serious objections might be leveled against such an interpretive venture as this: (1) that languages, literatures, and translations being what they are, interpretation based on translated texts is prima facie suspect, and probably illegitimate; (2) that, in particular, translations based on transcriptions made chiefly for ethnographic and linguistic purposes (as in the Boas era) are likely to be so devoid of crucial literary-performance features as to be virtually worthless—hence our efforts should be wholly directed toward transcribing, translating, and interpreting the Indian literatures as they are *currently* being performed.

To the first objection, it should be answered categorically that, if conducted within specific limits, interpretations of translated works for which the translations are linguistically accurate can be legitimate and can be worthwhile—witness the achievements in the field of "comparative literature." More pragmatically, if I wish that I and my readers could read and "hear" the Englished texts presented here in their original Native force (and I do), I am so convinced of their literary merit *as they exist,* in their scholarly translations, that I have no misgivings about trying to elucidate them. A number of these texts, in fact, now survive for Anglos and Native speakers alike *only* in English translations—for example, the Joshua "Genesis" narrative in essay 1, the Nez Perce "Orpheus" story discussed in essay 4, the Wasco ecological story taken up in essay 5, and the Tillamook drama of incest given in essay 7. These are, as they stand, wise and compelling works of imaginative literature: shall we ignore them because we cannot retranslate them according to modern techniques? Or because our delight in them is not seconded by knowledge of the original language in which they lived? [8]

Several answers to the second objection are in order. One lies in the simple unhappy fact that if ethnopoetic retranscription and retranslation of the literatures are desirable where possible (as in the Southwest and British Columbia), they are often not possible, owing to the loss of the repertories and the circumstances that once sustained their regular recitation. And shall we then deliberately ignore the neglected wealth of texts from the Boas era because, although linguistically sound for the most part, they lack the special dimensions of performance and translation done for literary purposes? No, surely not—and, in fact, a method has been developed whereby the reconstruction and retranslation of the old native-language texts along ethnopoetic lines can be undertaken; for this as for much else we are indebted to Dell Hymes. [9]

All in all, such reclamation of existing texts should go hand-in-hand with renewed efforts, as called for by Dennis Tedlock, to record and publish Indian literary performances now, where possible; indeed the two kinds of work depend on each other and must go forward together with a third pursuit if the common goal of establishing a credible American Indian literary scholarship is to be realized. That third pursuit, centering on literary theory, close formal analysis of the translated texts as examples of literary art, and the use of ethnographic data, is I hope represented by these essays.

What I have tried to bring to bear on the Native literature is a willingness to play their strangeness as texts (and the ethnographic information, always incomplete, that helps mitigate such strangeness) off against our critical competence in "our own" literature, culturally framed as *it* is. How very strange these stories are, undeniably, alongside comparable works in non-Native fictional and dramatic repertories! If we try to align, say, the Nez Perce Orpheus story with modern narratives dramatizing that universal theme—say, Cocteau's *Orphée*—we must notice, on the score of provenience and modus operandi alone, certain profound differences:

— the Nez Perce story is oral, traditional, anonymous (as to "author"; its teller is known to be a Nez Perce woman, Wayi'latpu), and tribal;
— it originally existed in dramatic performances and shared memories thereof, not in print; it was therefore, no matter how old, always "one generation from vanishing";
— it would be well known to all adults, who probably could not remember when as children they first heard versions of it; hence the outcome of the story would be assumed by raconteur and audience together;
— its characters and episodes are to some extent conventional and interchangeable with those in other stories in the repertory, and the story itself would be perceived by raconteur and audience as part of the shared repertory or "myth-body" of the tribe;
— its plot contains "magical" repetitions and other ritualesque narrative elements, and in general its meanings and dramatic effect for a Native audience would be implicated with the rituals and sacraments of the tribe;
— as an artistic property, it belonged to the group and was not conceived of as being the idiosyncratic creation and self-expression of an individual "author";
— rather, it was expected to speak to and for the consensus of the group, including children as well as grownups, and to provide an imaginative "centering" of the group's values, purposes, and pleasures.

Such alien premises must be confronted squarely lest we do this literature the disservice, compounded by a show of scholarship, that has been done to it for so long in popular culture—that is, co-opt it, anglicize it, make it conform to Anglo literary conventions and tastes, as Longfellow converted the Ojibwa trickster-transformer Manabozho into a plausible hero he called, courtesy of the Iroquois, Hiawatha. Or (to take a famous reverse case) as the elders of the Tiv tribe utterly transmogrified the meaning of *Hamlet* according to their customs, when Laura Bohannon told them the story one day in the Nigerian bush.[10] There is no use any longer trying to deny or minimize the difficulties attendant on interpreting the verbal arts of other cultures; but perhaps, if these difficulties are patiently confronted, in a spirit of theoretical accountability, Native-traditional imagination can speak to Anglo-modern imagination after all, and what appears to be hopelessly inaccessible (as some of our theorists have been telling us recently) *can* be painstakingly worked out and understood. I think so, at any rate, and I like to think that in the process our ethnocentrism stands to diminish and our literacy to increase. Not only are we perforce learning that the impulses and strategies of literary art can and do manifest themselves in forms and for purposes not dreamed of in the philosophies of Percy Lubbock, I. A. Richards, and Wellek and Warren, but we are also in a position to see our own literary conventions and assumptions, and the works they have achieved, more keenly, more appreciatively.

I have not given up Shakespeare, my first and major literary passion, to write these essays, but in the discovery of certain odd parallels, between, say, *The Winter's Tale* and a Tillamook incest story, or between an aspect of tragic characterization in Shakespeare and a strategy of portrayal in a Clackamas Chinook story, I have come to feel that each literary pursuit enriches the other, Shakespeare profiting from the Tillamook and Clackamas as well as vice versa.[11]

In the preface to his edition of *Nez Perce Texts,* which consists of narratives he took down in Nez Perce Sahaptin from his own mother, Archie Phinney urged his readers to cultivate a certain kind of imaginative attention in reading the stories as stories: "Any substantial appreciation of these tales must come not from the simple elements of drama unfolded but from vivid feelings within oneself, feeling as a moving current all the figures and the relationships that belong to the whole myth-body."[12] Despite all the decentralized diversity, the centripetal and often anarchic energy of our literature (especially in this century), doesn't Phinney's formula ring true for us, too, narrative art being what it is, and our imaginations of life being what they are? How else but with this dilated awareness do we properly read Shakespeare's or Chaucer's or Yeats's or Faulkner's "myth-body"?

In a little Wishram Chinookan story from along Coyote's journey up the Columbia River, a Myth-age woman chief tells Coyote (before he uncharitably turns her into a petroglyph) that as chief of her people she is "teaching them how to live well and to build good houses."[13] Such, as I hope to show in these essays, are leading purposes, beyond amusement, of traditional Indian literature, although they are realized with more art and much less of "the primitive" than we have been used to think. But consider—"how to live well and to build good houses": surely these represent imaginative purposes foreign neither to the characters in many of our *own* masterworks nor to their readers, you and me, who turn for delight and instruction to the formal play of our own language—like the Wascos and Nez Perces, and all the other Native peoples of the American West.

PART ONE

1 / Creations and Origins

There was no land, only a great lake. Kamukamts came from the north in a canoe. It floated along. It stopped. He shook it, but could not move it. He looked down, and in the water he saw the roof of a house. It was the house of Pocket Gopher. Gopher looked up. Then Kamukamts went down into the house, and they talked.

Kamukamts said, "You had better be thinking of what is the best thing to do."

"Yes, I am thinking of that now," replied Gopher.

"If you can plan anything better than I can do, you shall be the elder brother," promised Kamukamts. "What kind of food are we going to have?"

Gopher opened his mouth to yawn, and fish, roots, and berries came forth.

"It seems that you will be the elder brother," said Kamukamts.[1]

THE GREAT MAJORITY OF READERS TODAY, IF THEY have had any contact with traditional American Indian narratives, have gotten it first through reading—probably in childhood—versions of Native creation and origin myths. These are not bad entrees into the traditional literature, and I would propose to take them up first here even if they weren't the most familiar category of Indian stories to begin with, but that very familiarity has its problems, and I want to scout two in particular.

First, if our general knowledge of the traditional literatures of the American Indian is compromised by a longstanding reliance on corrupted and unauthentic texts, this unhappy state of affairs is especially true for creation and origin myths. Every form of textual debasement known can be illustrated, I think, in the fate of these stories at the hands of Anglo writers and editors over the years, many of them well intended but working in the presumptions of ignorance, others merely careless or exploitive, or both. There has always been a pronounced tendency, for example, to render Native cosmogonies as versions of the Judeo-Christian Genesis, leaving out much that is distinctively "Indian," so as to call attention, a la comparative mythology, to the fact that the Indians also had Eden myths, flood myths, Babel myths, and so on. In particular, editors and redactors have been guilty of cultural bias in silently eliminating the erotic, bawdy, and playful elements of Indian creation stories, giving the wrong impression that, like our Genesis text (itself, it now appears, a severely edited palimpsest), the Native creations are all remote, grand, teleologically rigorous affairs, full of what has been called "the perfection of origins."[2]

A less obvious difficulty with the relative familiarity of Native creation stories is that such familiarity usually comes with ignorance of two facts: (1) such stories constitute only a small portion of the surviving traditional literatures; (2) such stories, engaging and accessible as they often are, are not especially representative of these literatures. Readers who grew up, as I did, encountering Plains and Far West creation and origin narratives in schoolbooks, Boy Scout materials, and so forth, have understandably concluded that "How the Earth Was Formed" and "How the Chipmunk Got Its Stripes" and "The Fight Between the Mountains" illustrate the thematic and emotional range and artistry of Indian narrative.

Nothing could be farther from the truth, as I hope to show in these essays. The etiological motive, as T. T. Waterman demonstrated seventy years ago in his monumental and neglected study, "The Explanatory Element in the Folktales of the North American Indians,"[3] is only one generic motive among many at work in the Native literature and rarely appears as an exclusive motive; yet the general conception of myth that Waterman, Franz Boas, Robert Lowie, Paul Radin, and other pioneers undertook to refute—that it fundamentally expresses a human impulse to *explain* natural phenomena, especially solar and lunar—is still very much alive today, in the popular view of what Indian stories are and what they mean. Native narratives given to "explaining" conspicuous natural features and above all capable of being understood with a minimum of knowledge about the cultures they reflect are still what the general reading public in America knows, and favors. A regrettable state of affairs: as if we were to deny artistic value and significance to the traditional literature of India except for its *Just So* stories.

The fact is that the traditional repertory of any well-transcribed American Indian group contains a rich diversity of imaginative motives and literary forms, some corresponding to the motives and forms of our literature, and some not. Besides cosmogonies and origin myths, we will find—if we look—cycles of trickster stories exploring the world in a spirit of "anything possible," rather like picaresque novels; didactic and pedagogical narratives, not so much "explaining" as chartering customs and rituals; stories of realistic bent; "problem" stories that engage and clarify pressing conflicts between social norms and personal impulses; hero stories, like epic episodes; songs (often integral to narratives, like dramatic lyrics); prophecies; ceremonial texts; and mythopoetic syntheses of Native and Anglo materials, with many of the characteristics of romance.

Nonetheless, having identified these misunderstandings, we can profitably begin with a consideration of a few representative Western Indian myths of creation and origins. But—what is a myth? As Percy Cohen has pointed out, none of the standard ways of formulating the subject—etiological, cultural, psychoanalytical, structural, and so on—seems to be wholly adequate to the task of accounting for the mythic impulse and its manifestations, and none of them is probably without some merit in carrying out that formidable task.[4]

I want to propose, therefore, an eclectic working definition, one that favors inclusiveness rather than exclusiveness, and that allows for recognition of multiple, simultaneous, and complementary lines of meaning in a given myth. In the history of any culture, it appears that certain central institutions come to accept a variety of purposes; people expect more and more of them as vital agencies. So—to mention a not inappropriate analogue for myth—in our culture the school has evolved into a bewilderment of social, political, economic, and psychological, as well as pedagogical purposes; and so, by the same process of centralizing of functions, the mythologies of tribal societies seem to have evolved toward functional complexity. Bronislaw Malinowski's perception about what a myth-narrative means to a Melanesian tribesman is valid, I think, for our Western American context as well: a myth is "not an idle tale, but a hard-working active force."[5] In our attempts to engage myth-texts on literary grounds, then, as imaginative verbal constructs, we must be prepared to deal with this "hardworking" aspect by recognizing that they may in fact be structured to "perform" a number of functions all at once.

Myths are sacred traditional stories whose shaping function is to tell the people who know them who they are; how, through what origins and transformations, they have come to possess their particular world; and how they should live in that world, and with each other.

Notice that this definition replaces the simplistic *why* of a purely etiological formulation of myth with questions of *who* and *how;* that is, it focuses attention upon the relationships between a group's myth-repertory and its sense of collective identity in relation to origins, welfare, and destiny. Therefore, it stresses the importance of ethnography to interpretation. And this emphasis on mythic fabulation of collective experience does not preclude speculation, at least, on the ways in which myth can be both medium and mediator of deeply personal, individual meanings. From the evidence of the Native American literatures, I would venture to guess on this score that if the individuals forming the first Indian communities had somehow found a way to achieve social solidarity and order without affronting individuality, they wouldn't have created for themselves the richly imaginative accommodations to tribal living that we now attempt to understand as "Indian mythology." They wouldn't have needed what myth as we have it provides.

One extreme of myth interpretation, notably encouraged by Claude Lévi-Strauss and followed by some of his disciples, conceives of mythology as being so remote from the individual minds that have known it, transmitted it, perhaps re-created it, that it is best seen as a sort of grand natural process, just going its own glacial way, according to its own laws: in Dell Hymes's witty phrase, an "imperturbable self-transmogrification."[6] That mythic stories *do* "story" themselves systematically over time is, I think, undeniable; but unless we can also learn as readers to attend to evidence of historical and individual human "perturbation" and deliberate artistic "transmogrification" in them, we cannot really hope to claim them as imaginative literature. I think the claim can and should be made, because the evidence of artistic control and of personalized content, expressing such personal factors as gender (see essays 6 and 8) is certainly there. If for most traditional narratives the identity of the "individual talent" working on the "tradition" is irrecoverable, that shouldn't preclude our engaging as best we can the artistic achievements of that talent, whosoever it belonged to.

Now let's turn back to some representative Western Indian creation and origin stories in which such difficult questions of personal content are, conveniently for our purposes, unimportant—these are, it would appear, very old stories, well worn, "imperturbable," and impersonal. Return to the Klamath story with which we began—Kamukamts and Pocket Gopher, remember, have begun a sort of creative competition, to see who can earn the title "Elder Brother."

That night Gopher caused his companion to sleep, and he burrowed under the bottom of the lake and made it bulge up into hills and mountains, which raised their tops above the surface. In the morning he said, "You had better go up and look around!" When Kamukamts went out he was astonished. Gopher asked what should become of his house, and Kamukamts replied, "It will always remain as the oldest mountain [Modoc Point]."

"What will our children have for amusement?" asked Kamukamts. They played the game of throwing spears at a mark. They threw them, and their targets were hills. Kamukamts's spear knocked off the top of Bare Island, and so it is today. Then they invented all the other games.

Gopher asked, "What will live on the mountains?"

"Mountain lions, bears, elk, deer." Kamukamts named all the animals, both beasts and birds.

"What will grow in the mountains?" asked Gopher.

"I will walk over the earth and see what I can do," replied Kamukamts. So he went about and selected homes for the different tribes, and in each territory he placed something which was to characterize that particular tribe, such as obsidian in the Paiute country, marble in the Shasta country, and tules in the Klamath country. Then he looked about and saw smoke. Kamukamts said, "What is the matter, I wonder? I see smoke here and there."

And Gopher replied, "You have beaten me. You are the elder brother." For he knew that the smoke was from the fires of people brought into being by

Kamukamts. They listened, and heard the sound of people talking and of children laughing and playing. The people increased very rapidly, and the animals and plants on the mountains multiplied.[7]

Obviously such a narrative of beginnings does not conform to modern Judeo-Christian conventions of the genre! What we witness here is far short of a real cosmogony, comparable to the first chapters of Genesis. However it happened, the world has already gotten itself primally created, though not properly organized, and the adventures of Kamukamts and Pocket Gopher are considerably ex post facto what our modern "Big Bang" cosmologists call "the first three minutes." Furthermore, it is clear that what is at stake here etiologically speaking is not the globe at large anyway, but only the Klamath world in southwest Oregon and northern California—its distinctive features and boundaries, centering on Klamath Lake. And whereas our Judeo-Christian narrative is resonant with a sense of what Mircea Eliade has called the power, prestige, and perfection of origins, literally *God's Story*, the tone of the Klamath story as we have it is remarkably casual and lighthearted . . . an amiable tale, then, rather than an overwhelmingly majestic one.[8]

On all three counts, "The Klamath Creation" is representative of Western Indian creation narratives, at least in the form in which they now exist. With some notable exceptions—the Cheyenne, Maidu, Navajo, and several of the Pueblo cosmogonies are as philosophically systematic and grand as any cosmologist could wish[9]—such stories are, like this one, indifferent to global beginnings, concentrating instead on the creation and ordering of the immediate environs of the people who know the story, and investing the action of the story with a sense of casual improvisation, or so it seems to us, expecting something different.

But, like Genesis, such stories do establish priorities and ultimate values; creation myths are ipso facto teleological formulations as well. Thus, as with our tradition, the Klamath narrative leads up to the appearance in the world of the human race; man appears to be the final cause in Aristotelian terms. But of course it is a teleology alien to us in which the world takes its shape according to a friendly competition between two demi-urges as to who will be called "Elder Brother"; and as for specific priorities, it is noteworthy that Kamukamts (the Klamath progenitor per se) and Pocket Gopher decide to invent sports and amusements immediately after they have created gathering-foods and solid land, and indeed *be-fore* creating the game animals. At the end, Gopher concedes the contest to Kamukamts (who has been in control all along, evidently, but has genially hidden his advantage) on the grounds that communities of people with campfires have arrived on the Klamath scene at Kamukamts's instigation—the ultimate show, it seems, of creative prowess.

Etiologically, one might well ask, "What is 'explained' here, really?" In truth, very little—in moral terms, certainly, neither the awesome perfections of a divine plan nor the origins of evil in some human violation of such a plan. Keeping to our working definition of myth, the story's emphasis is not so much on why as on *how*—specifically how, under what circumstances, the Klamaths came into possession of their world and their distinctive cultural "way." Both world and way are initiated here under imaginative premises not of divine perfection but rather of this life's essential bounty and goodness . . . life looks to be eminently possible. Whereas God pauses in the cosmic silence to declare that His work is good, Kamukamts and Gopher merely observe the vivid human evidence of how well, really, creation is turning out for the Klamaths—"They listened, and heard the sound of people talking and of children laughing and playing. The people increased very rapidly, and the animals and plants on the mountains multiplied."

The fact that the Klamaths lost their ancestral lands in the 1950s through the bureaucratic atrocity known as "termination," despite the imaginative authority of their mythological charter to these lands, is one of the cruelest ironies in recent Native American history. But of course it must be assumed that every Indian nation to lose its domain from the sixteenth century on possessed such a mythic charter, which government officials at treaty-making sessions invariably dismissed whenever Native participants tried to introduce the testimony of tribal myth.[10]

A similar combination of casual tone, improvised action, ethnocentric focus, and affirmation of the essential goodness of human life in situ can be seen in the "Old Man" creation cycle of the Blackfeet Indians of Montana.[11] "Old Man," Na'pi, analogous as a transformer to Kamukamts, travels north across the Blackfeet lands "fixing things up" in what is to be their final order—the essentials of life but also the pleasant inessentials, as when he slides down a steep hill and creates what the Blackfeet know as "Old Man's Sliding Ground." True to type, the creation cycle ends abruptly at the edge of the Blackfeet world: "This is as far as the Blackfeet followed Old Man. The Cree know what he did farther north."

Again, Old Man's transforming work proceeds on a trial-and-error basis rather than according to some divine cosmogonic plan. He stumbles over a knoll and to commemorate the accident raises two buttes, forever to be known as "The Knees"; on the plains he engenders trees, grass, and edibles ("camas, wild carrots, wild turnips, sweet-root, bitter-root, sarvis berries, bull berries, cherries, plums, and rosebuds"); and he creates the animals, but not without difficulty as to their proper habitats. He tries to place the bighorn sheep on the prairie, but it does poorly there, so he takes it up into the mountains, where it thrives, being so agile. While he is in the mountains he makes the antelope and turns it loose among the rocks. It runs so fast that it falls down and hurts itself, so he removes it to the plains, where it can run free.

After this, Na'pi determines, apparently in the order of things, to create human life, a woman and a child.

So he formed them both—the woman and the child, her son—of clay. After he had moulded the clay in human shape, he said to the clay, "You must be people," and then he covered it up and left it, and went away. The next morning he went to the place and took the covering off and saw that the clay shapes had changed a little. The second morning there was still more change, and the third still more. The fourth morning he went to the place, took the covering off, looked at the images, and told them to rise and walk; and they did so. They walked down to the river with their maker, and then he told them that his name was Na'pi, Old Man.[12]

Now at this point in the Blackfeet genesis, as so often in these Western Indian accounts of creation, the first human death occurs, and with it is broached, and significantly lost, the possibility of a natural return to life after dying. Again, the emphasis in the narrative of these grave doings is not so much etiological as imaginative and interpretive—a story is given that seems calculated to render death and its finality imaginable, even acceptable according to our knowledge of human strengths and failings. And from a symbolic perspective, how wonderfully fitting—art, not accident, surely—that it should all commence as the first humans stand gazing, with Old Man, at a *river*.

As they were standing by the river, the woman said to him, "How is it? Will we always live, will there be no end to it?" He said, "I have never thought of that. We will have to decide it. I will take this buffalo chip and throw it in the river. If it floats, when people die, in four days they will become alive again; they will die for only four days. But if it sinks, there will be an end to them." He threw the chip into the river, and it floated. The woman turned and picked up a stone, and said, "No, I will throw this stone in the river; if it floats we will always live, if it sinks people must die, that they may always be sorry for each other." The woman threw the stone into the water, and it sank. "There," said Old Man, "you have chosen. There will be an end to them."

It was not many nights after this that the woman's child died, and she cried a great deal for it. She said to Old Man, "Let us change this. The law that you first made, let that be a law." He said, "Not so. What is made law must be a law. We will undo nothing that we have done. People will have to die."

That is how we came to be people. It was he who made us.

To approach this mythic episode as a *Just So* story about the origin of death is to miss its subtlety and power altogether. The question "why do we have permanent death" is not really to be answered, except on a rather brutal causal basis, "Because the first woman foolishly and most regrettably opted for it." This is what happens, of course, but it is not what the story seems to say about the relationship of human nature and life and death. Consider the details. The woman, gazing at the endless flow of the river, wonders if human life will be like that, and she appears to conclude that it must not be, to be properly "human"; it must instead be limited by death. And as she competes with Old Man in the throwing contest, in which the sinking of her lifeless stone is to be decisive, "in the nature of things," over the floating of Old Man's organic buffalo chip, she gives a most compelling reason for establishing death as a condition of life: "People must die," she says, "that they may always be sorry for each other." Is it not true in all cultures that the knowledge of our shared human mortality, our inevitably fatal weakness, is the basis of all ethics, all compassion, charity, solidarity of kind? First Woman resolutely throws her stone, which will sink beneath the river's surface even as each of us will ultimately sink from life—and in doing so she establishes precisely what Shakespeare's Macbeth guiltily calls "that great bond / Which keeps me pale" (3.2.49–50): the inviolable racial bond, that is, of humans bound to each other in their common mortality, and therefore capable of being "sorry for each other." [13]

Now, it is a conventional feature of most Western myth-narratives on this theme that an actor (most commonly it is Coyote) theoretically opts for universal death, as here, the usual reason being that if there were to be no end to life, the world would soon become overcrowded.[14] But what an imaginative difference between this straightforward and rather positivistic "ecological" sanctioning of mortality and the Blackfeet First Woman's richly ambiguous *moral* postulation of death's value-to-come!

But her choice, however resonant of the future, is still hypothetical, "expert beyond experience" so to speak; and what happens next is characteristic of the subtle and unsentimental wisdom of such narratives. Having deliberately set the precedent for death in order to establish a compelling if abstract moral principle for all time to come, First Woman (like her counterparts in most such stories) then in fact suffers the first death—that of her son—and immediately asks Old Man to revoke the mortal law she has just ordained! Perhaps there is a measure of justice to be seen in this turn of events, given what she has just done; but mostly, I think, there is a poignant revelation of First Woman as *one of us,* a fellow mortal: capable of noble proposals and all-too-human lapses; capable of theoretical certitude and experiential regret; susceptible to helpless grief and a familiar feckless wish that "the laws could be changed" when we are personally affected by them. Mortality has now come terribly into the world, but not without human significance, and First Woman is learning the condition of her mortality, and ours: death is not explained, per se (how could it be, really?), but rather the purpose of the myth is to effect an imaginative accommodation of the fact of death to the condition of living. The last lines of the story sum up its accommodative and consolatory power as a myth with memorable simplicity: "That is how we came to be people."[15]

(Subsequently, Old Man gives the first people [how the dead son is replaced and how the people at large are engendered are not explained] their proper foods, tools, hunting techniques, ceremonies, and other lore. But it is understood that the first article in their charter as "people" is that they are mortal, and therefore moral, beings.)

Samuel Beckett's plays have justly been admired for their "mythic" quality—specifically for their rigorous concentration on just a few details, motives, actions, and words, as if these were all that really mattered in human existence. *Act without words I,* for example (originally staged as a sort of coda to *End Game*), brilliantly "stages" the first minutes of its mute hero's life in a manner suggestive of creation myths—he is summoned on stage dramatically, and in his various pratfalls and unavailing attempts to rationally order and control his environment, he, like the Blackfeet First Woman in her initial actions, poignantly expresses a human *essence* very much at odds with the terms of his existence, both natural and supernatural.[16] (It is important to notice that in myth, the Existentialist principle "Existence Precedes Essence" is reversed.) Perhaps Beckett's little expressionist masterpiece only means to show us "how it is" fundamentally in any given life—"what we're up against"—but then this is precisely what myths show us, too: "how it is" in terms of the first instances of birth, error, evil, loss, death, grief, and so on.

But here, of course, the comparison breaks down—instructively, I think. If the style of Beckett's play is mythic, the substance is certainly *not*. It appears that, however poignantly he symbolizes our basic predicaments, Beckett's Everyman is setting no mythic precedents for us to inherit in the fullness of time. Whereas the Blackfeet First Woman ordains death and human solidarity, and then must be the first of us to suffer what she has ordained, Everyman's climactic act is a nihilistic triumph of unilateral renunciation. His "looking at his hands" while in a fetal position, oblivious to the offstage cues that have tormented him heretofore, certainly speaks to our modern frustrations and is, I think, a kind of endgame victory; but the sense of a "future collective," which myth invariably creates in its audience, is missing. Which is to say that Beckett's mythic mime-play and our Blackfeet narrative are eschatological opposites: the myth evokes a mood of self-conscious expectancy; the play leads through futile actions to a condition of isolated waiting for an end.

Like Beckett's *Act*, the Klamath and Blackfeet myths have an imaginative resonance beyond their size. The terseness and concentration of these texts become less striking, perhaps, when we remember that Genesis 1–3 itself, divested of the enormous "midrash" it now supports in our minds, runs to only eighty verses—but still the texts are brief as measured against other narratives from their respective tribes. It may be that these texts and others like them are traditional summaries rather than full recitals of the sort that might have been given on special ceremonial occasions, but if so, we can now never know for sure; nothing more complete or more fully textured has survived from these people.[17]

I want to turn now to a third Far Western creation narrative, in part because it is a more leisurely told and much more generously detailed story; its texture is unusually rich in expressive details, and one can at least speculate that it is the record of a full-scale recitation. But in fact we don't know: all we know is that the story was told to Livingston Farrand in 1900 by one Charlie Depoe, a surviving member of a small group of Athapascan-speaking Indians on the southwest Oregon coast known locally as the "Joshuas," and later edited for publication by Leo J. Frachtenberg.[18] The provenience could hardly be more stark: Farrand took down only four Joshua stories besides this one, and Charlie Depoe's culture, virtually extinct by 1915, is only fragmentarily recorded. Yet, as with the Klamath and Blackfeet creation stories, the evidence is unmistakable of a well-made story, a narrative of one world's beginnings worthy to stand alongside other such narratives as a mythic accommodation to life as we know and suffer it.

Given the fact that Charlie Depoe's telling languished in utter obscurity for over sixty years before re-publication and study, it seems right to provide the full text here. The first part amounts to an unusually full cosmogony (at least for Western Indians), and the second part, in establishing the first human family, seems to take on something of the quality of a romance—slow paced and dreamlike. Or so it seems to me as I reread it, and I am reminded of a similar shift in effect in our own Genesis, from the strenuous events of the cosmogony itself to the Edenic idyll of Adam and Eve, before the serpent enters the story "and all that woe." But in most respects, Genesis is not a useful analogue to Charlie Depoe's story—and let us turn to it now without further comparison or commentary:

In the beginning there was no land. There was nothing but the sky, some fog, and water. The water was still; there were no breakers. A sweat-house stood on the water, and in it there lived two men—The Giver and his companion. The Giver's companion had tobacco. He usually stayed outside watching, while The Giver remained in the sweat-house.

One day it seemed to the watcher as if daylight were coming. He went inside and told The Giver that he saw something strange coming. Soon there appeared something that looked like land, and on it two trees were growing. The man kept on looking, and soon was able to distinguish that the object that was approaching was white land. Then the ocean began to move, bringing the land nearer. Its eastern portion was dark. The western part kept on moving until it struck the sweat-house, where it stopped. It began to stretch to the north and to the south. The land was white like snow. There was no grass on it. It expanded like the waves of the ocean. Then the fog began to disappear and the watcher could look far away.

He went into the sweat-house, and asked, "Giver, are you ready?" and The Giver said, "Is the land solid?—"Not quite," replied the man. Then The Giver took some tobacco and began to smoke. He blew the smoke on the land, and the land became motionless. Only two trees were growing at that time, redwood to the south, and ash to the north. Five times The Giver smoked, while discussing with his companion various means of creating the world and the people. Then night came, and after that daylight appeared again. Four days The Giver worked; and trees began to bud, and [buds] fell like drops of water upon the ground. Grass came up, and leaves appeared on the trees. The Giver walked around the piece of land that had stopped near his sweat-house, commanding the ocean to withdraw and to be calm.

Then The Giver made five cakes of mud. Of the first cake he made a stone and dropped it into the water, telling it to make a noise and to expand, as soon as it hit the bottom. After a long while he heard a faint noise and knew then that the water was very deep. He waited some time before dropping the second cake. This time he heard the noise sooner, and knew that the land was coming nearer to the surface. After he had dropped the third cake, the land reached almost to the surface of the water. So he went into the sweat-house and opened a new sack of tobacco. Soon his companion shouted from outside. "It looks as if breakers are coming!" The Giver was glad, because he knew now that the land was coming up from the bottom of the ocean. After the sixth wave the water receded, and The Giver scattered tobacco all over. Sand appeared. More breakers came in, receding farther and farther and farther westward. Thus the land and the world were created. To the west, to the north, and to the south there was tide-water; to the east the land was dry. The new land was soft and looked like sand. The Giver stepped on it and said, "I am going to see if the great land has come"; and as he stepped, the land grew hard.

Then The Giver looked at the sand and saw a man's tracks. They seemed to have come from the north, disappearing in the water on the south. He wondered what that could mean, and was very much worried. He went back to his first piece of land, and told the water to overflow the land he had created out of the five cakes of mud. Some time afterward he ordered the water to recede, and looked again. This time he saw the tracks coming from the west and returning to the water on the north side. He was puzzled and ordered the water to cover up his new land once more. Five times he repeated this process. At last he became discouraged and said, "This is going to make trouble in the future!" and since then there has always been trouble in the world.

Then The Giver began to wonder how he could make people. First he took some grass, mixed it with mud, and rubbed it in his hands. Then he ordered a house to appear, gave the two mud figures to his companion, and told him to put them into the house. After four days two dogs—a male and a bitch—appeared. They watched the dogs, and twelve days later the bitch gave birth to pups. The Giver then made food for the dogs. All kinds of dogs were born in that litter of pups. They were all howling. After a while The Giver went to work again. He took some white sand from the new land, and made two figures in the same way as before. He gave the figures to his companion, and ordered a house for them. Then he warned the dogs not to go to the new house, as it was intended for the new people. After thirteen days The Giver heard a great hissing, and a big snake came out of the house, followed by a female snake and many small snakes. The Giver felt bad when he saw this and went to his companion, telling him that this trouble was due to the tracks that had first appeared in the world. Soon the land became full of snakes, which, not having seen The Giver, wondered how everything had come about. The world was inhabited by dogs and snakes only.

One day The Giver wished three baskets to appear, gave them to his companion, and told him to fill them partly with fresh water and partly with salt water. Then he put ten of the biggest snakes into the baskets, crushed them, and threw them into the ocean. Two bad snakes got away from him; and all snake-like animals that live today come from these snakes. The Giver said to these two snakes, "You two will live and surround the world like a belt, so that it won't break!" Then he crushed five bad dogs in the same way, made a great ditch with his finger, and threw the dogs into the ditch. These dogs became water-monsters. All animals that raise their heads above the water and smell, and then disappear quickly under the water, came from these five dogs.

Pretty soon The Giver began to think again, "How can I make people? I have failed twice!" Now, for the first time his companion spoke. He said, "Let me smoke tonight, and see if people will not come out of the smoke." For three days he smoked, at the end of which a house appeared with smoke coming out of it. The man told The Giver, "There is a house!" After a while a beautiful woman came out of the house, carrying a water-basket. Then The Giver was glad and said, "Now we shall have no more trouble in creating people." The woman did not see The Giver and his companion, as they were watching her. After nine days the woman became sad, and wondered who her father and relatives were. She had plenty of food.

One day The Giver said to his companion, "Stay here and take this woman for your wife! You shall have children and be the father of all the people. I am leaving this world. Everything on it shall belong to you." And the man answered, "It is well; but, perchance, I too may have troubles." Then The Giver asked him, "How are you going to be troubled?" So the man said, "Do you make this woman sleep, so that I can go to her without her seeing me." The woman found life in the house very easy. Whenever she wished for anything, it appeared at once. About noon she felt sleepy for the first time. When night came, she prepared her bed and lay down. As soon as she was sound asleep, the man went in to her. She was not aware of this, but dreamed that a handsome man was with her. This was an entirely new dream to her. At daybreak she woke up and looked into the blanket. No one was there, although she was sure that someone had been with her. She wished to know who had been with her that night. So next evening she prepared her bed again, hoping that the same thing would happen; but no one came to her. She did the same every night without any one coming near her.

Soon the woman became pregnant. The Giver and his companion were still on the land, watching her; but she could not see them, because they were invisible to her. After a while the child was born. It was a boy. He grew very fast. The young woman made a cradle for him. After six months the boy could talk. The woman still wanted to know who the father of her child was. So one day she wrapped the child in blankets, and said, "I will neglect the boy and let him cry, and, perchance, his father may come. I will go and look at the country."

She started south, carrying the baby on her back. She traveled for ten years, seeing no one and never looking at the child. After a long time she could hear only a faint sound coming from behind. Nothing remained of the boy but skin and bones. Finally she stopped at Salomä [a camas prairie far up the Coquille River] and here for the first time she took the child from her back and looked at it. Its eyes were sunken and hollow; the boy was a mere skeleton. The woman felt bad and began to cry. She took the boy out of the cradle and went to the river to bathe. After she had put on her clothes, she felt of the child's heart. It was still beating!

The boy urinated, and was dirty all over. His body was covered with maggots, and he had acquired various diseases. The woman took him to the water and washed his body. She had no milk with which to feed him; so she sang a medicine song, and milk came to her. She gave the breast to the child, but it was too weak to suck: hence she had to feed it gradually. As the days went by the boy grew stronger. After three days his eyes were better. Then they went back to their house, where they found plenty of food. The boy grew soon into a strong and handsome young man, and was helping his mother with her work. One day he asked her, "Mother, where is your husband?" and she replied, "I only dreamed of my husband." Then she told him all that had happened before he was born; and the boy said, "Oh! Maybe my father may turn up some day."

Then The Giver said to his companion, "The woman is home now." That night the woman longed for her husband. She had been dreaming all the time that he was a handsome man and that her boy looked just like him. At dusk it seemed to her as if someone were coming. Her heart began to beat. Soon she heard footsteps. The door opened, and her boy exclaimed, "Oh, my father has come!" She looked and saw the man in her dreams. At first she was ashamed and bashful. The man told her all that had happened before and claimed her as his wife.

One day The Giver told the man that all the world had been made for him. Then he instructed him how to act at all times and under all conditions. He also admonished him to have more children, and the man had sixteen children. The first one was a boy, then came a girl, then another boy, and so on. Half of his children went to live north of the Rogue River, while the other half settled down south of the river. The Giver told the man that hereafter he would obtain everything by wishing. Then he straightened out the world, made it flat, and placed the waters. He created all sorts of animals, and cautioned the man not to cut down more trees or kill more animals than he needed. And after all this had been done, he bade him farewell and went up to the sky. "You and your wife and your children shall speak different languages. You shall be the progenitors of all the different tribes."

In principio: the initial scene is of an embryonic maritime world— only sky, fog, motionless water; no breakers, no land, no life, nothing "coming" as yet. The world remains to be born (cosmogony means "birth of the world," in fact), and the cosmogonists on hand are "on-stage" (in contrast to Beckett's play) and are well equipped in Native terms for the task in that they dwell in a sweat-house, in times to come the place of spiritual as well as physical perfection, and possess that potent vehicle of the spirit, tobacco. From the outset, the sacred meaning of their work is emphasized through the repetition of actions according to "pattern-numbers," a quite unusual variety of them in fact—fives, threes, fours, and multiples, as if number itself in some Pythagorean sense were central to creation.[19]

"The Giver," who smokes, is in charge; but in a doubling of parts, widespread in Indian myth (consider the Klamath and Blackfeet stories already discussed), he is assisted in his labors by a secondary figure, less divinely gifted but more recognizably human, whose crucial change of role through the story is expressed by a shift of appellation, from The Giver's "companion" to simply "the man." As companion and protoman, this figure seems to mediate between The Giver and the world-in-progress: he watches, reports, discusses with The Giver "various means of creating the world and the people," takes custody of the first animals—and eventually, as we will see, actually takes his turn at smoking, and creates woman, after The Giver has failed twice. Clearly, the story aims to invest Creation with (as jargon would have it) an "on-site" human perspective.[20]

With the mainland established, and vegetation (redwood in what is now northern California, ash in what is now southwest Oregon—the botanical limits of the Joshua world), The Giver undertakes—crucially, for a coastal people—to create the littoral and the shore. To do so, he employs a variant of what is probably the most widespread and therefore probably the oldest story-motif in Native American literature, the so-called "Earth Diver" episode, which figures in creation narratives from the Micmacs and Penobscots of the northeastern coast to the Indians of the Pacific coast.[21] Here there is no team of animal divers attempting to bring up earth from the seabottom; The Giver simply drops five mudcakes one after the other until the appearance of breakers tells him that, in effect, the land and the ocean are now "connected."

At this point, the narrative seems to turn, unlike the Klamath and Blackfeet stories, toward *theodicy*. No sooner has The Giver stepped out on the new land, then he sees "a man's tracks" coming from the north. A magical five times The Giver erases these mysterious footprints with water: each time they reappear, and at last he gives up with the gnomic warning: "This is going to make trouble in the future." What, according to our working conception of myth, does this mean? Clearly it serves to indicate that, here again, the Creator's powers are sharply limited; he cannot remove the ominous footprints, he can only interpret them as spelling trouble to come. Specifically, *human* trouble, it appears; trouble for and between people. It may be that the northern origins of the tracks refer specifically to a traditional enmity between the Joshuas and their northern neighbors, the Penutian-speaking Coos. If so the detail has a general mythic meaning as well, not etiological but narrative, to the effect that "trouble came at the very beginning, even before people, despite The Giver's efforts to remove it—and it left human footprints." In terms of theodicy, a divine "way" is not being justified here; instead the episode merely initiates "the way it is" on the score of evil. And the theoretical association of trouble with human life is of course dramatized in subsequent episodes, beginning with the next one, which concerns the rather bizarre trouble The Giver has with the task of making people in the first place.[22]

Trial gives way to error, and to his dismay the world is soon full of dogs and snakes only. The Giver can only correct part of the problem: he turns some of the dogs into seals, otters, and the like, and he manages to encircle the earth with two of the snakes, securing it belt-wise like the Midgard Serpent or *Jörmungander* of Nordic mythology.[23] Significantly, it remains for the human companion to try his hand at making people. For the first time *he* smokes, and for a wonder he creates a house "with smoke coming out of it—that is, a real domestic house, manmade as it were, out of which steps a beautiful woman, already carrying a waterbasket.

The Giver's response to his assistant's achievement is wonderful, both exultant and droll: "Now we shall have no more trouble in creating people." Procreation is, he sees, a human achievement in this first instance, albeit with special spirit assistance; and so it will be henceforth, he prophesies, now that the world is sexualized. Acting on this certainty, The Giver orders his companion to marry the woman and people the world. But the man has his own peculiarly human foresight and responds: "It is well, but perchance I too may have troubles." No doubt this rather winning hesitation on the threshold of human life refers generally to the discovery that "trouble" is already abroad, and likely to beset the man as he enters the world—but specifically it seems to refer to the mixed prospects of procreation and family life. "Male and female created he them." All well and good for The Giver to exult, "Now we shall have no more trouble in creating people"; on his part the man seems to anticipate inevitable sexual and familial miseries to come, and in bashfully persuading The Giver to let him visit the woman in a dream—as a demon lover, as it were—he in effect ironically ensures that the woman and their son will have their share of trouble indeed because of his domestic absenteeism.

At this point, with the plot thickening markedly, we can recognize what, thematically, the story is "about," beyond cosmogenesis. It might be said that all creation myths are formulations of the desire to know our progenitors, our first parents—but that theme is especially prominent in Charlie Depoe's narrative; in effect it organizes the story. All of the creatures brought to life by The Giver and his companion inquire after their parentage. First the dogs, who howl, as Farrand explains for his narrator in a footnote, just as "every dog to-day howls looking up to the sky, because he is crying for his first father, whom he never knew."[24] Then the snakes, "which, not having seen The Giver, wondered how everything had come about." Then the first woman, who "after nine days became sad, and wondered who her father and relatives were." And finally, the boy, who asks his mother about his paternity, and prepares for the story's climactic scene of recognition by saying, wistfully, "Oh! Maybe my father may turn up some day."

One thinks here of Lévi-Strauss's discovery through synchronic analysis that the Oedipus myth is really a formulation of two conflicting views of man's origins: are they autochthonous, or are they sexual? Have we sprung from the earth like plants, or were we engendered? "Born from one, or born from two?"[25] In mentioning this celebrated essay I am not proposing that our Joshua myth effects anything comparable to the subtle and profound mediation between irreconcilable opposites that Lévi-Strauss finds in the Oedipus story—but there *is* a dramatic opposition to be seen here, at least, between what the first animals and human characters want to know about their origins, and what we as audience know, through the story, about the labors of The Giver and his companion. The effect of this opposition seems to be to heighten our self-consciousness: we are, that is, the People—descended from such fathers, who know the story of creation and man's parentage, as these first people and creatures did not. As I hope to show in subsequent discussions of individual texts, such cultivation of forms of imaginative self-consciousness in the audience is central to the artistry of traditional Western Indian narratives.

A second line of opposition—again, commonplace, and perhaps inherent in creation stories generally—takes the form of emphasis on the process of actualization, from dream-states, emblematic of spirituality, to reality.[26] On the cosmogonic level, of course, the substantial world emerges from the reveries of The Giver and his companion, specifically from their smoking (even as the substance of the myth may be said to emerge from the shared "dreaming" of the teller and his listeners). On the human level, in the second part of the story the action likewise proceeds from dreams to realities, to "responsibilities" as Yeats put it—the woman first experiences sexual intercourse and love memorably as "an entirely new dream," and, having significantly put aside her initial curiosity about her father, she goes out to search for "the man in her dreams"—that is, the father of her child.[27] Their son in his turn has only his mother's report of these dreams to satisfy his paternal curiosity, until the final scene in which recognition seems to take the form of an awakening.

The search for husband and father constitutes a ten-year odyssey in which the woman illustrates the "trouble" now footprinted in the world by deliberately abusing her child in order to find her dream-husband. Her priorities are all wrong, it appears. When she guiltily "wakes up" at length to the child's condition, he is nearly dead from disease and neglect, and the afflictions his mother has brought upon him will now be part of the human story, mythically speaking; as Farrand explains in a note from Charlie Depoe: "As she washed him, the diseases dropped to the ground and have remained in the world ever since." [28]

But with the mother's discovery of her proper responsibilities to her boy, the real product of a "dream," he is able to grow to young manhood and make inquiries about his absent father. The Homeric associations here are inevitable and should not be resisted but rather examined for possible interpretive value. The basic circumstances that give Odysseus's homecoming as father and spouse so much emotional power are present here, too, albeit most oddly rearranged: in the aftermath of a long, troubled journey (but by a wife), we have the wife whose memory of her husband is dreamlike; the son, who only knows what he has been told about his paternity, but who is first to recognize the father figure when he actually comes; the initial bashfulness of the wife; the man's long narrative, joining past to present, of "all that had happened before." When Telemachus says of his father in Book One, "My mother says indeed I am his. I for my part / do not know. Nobody really knows his own father," [29] Homer yokes together the "ontogenetic" and the "phylogenetic" and the mythic dimensions of his story. Telemachus's doubts simultaneously apply to his individual case, and also to all human cases, given the terms of human procreation and consciousness; and also, by a metaphorical extension, to the general case of humans in quest of a creator. In The Odyssey this last dimension is, I think, undeveloped, "free-floating" in the poem's epic context; in the Indian story, which is after all a creation myth, it is explicit.

Thus in the final scene of primal concord and recognition, a mythological equation is completed, between the happy outcome of the quest for progenitors on the part of the characters in the myth, and the foregone happy outcome of the quest for origins and progenitors which has, amongst the Joshua Indians, given rise to the myth itself. "Nobody really knows his father." But on the contrary, as the first son ultimately comes to know his father, and as his mother is rewarded for her belated success at mothering by knowing "the man of her dreams," both "father" and husband, so the Joshuas would know again the identity of all their progenitors, these members of the first human family, and also, of course, the now absent instigator of it all, "The Giver."

To sum up, what would the Klamath, Blackfeet, and Joshua audiences have understood in creation and origin narratives like these? What would adults, hearing the stories once again, have remembered and reaffirmed in their imaginations, and what would they have expected their children to learn from the recitations, beyond specific kinds of lore?[30] Given the limits and uncertainties of our knowledge about traditional Indian cultures, these are perhaps presumptuous questions, but I will venture a few tentative and general answers.

First, that in their different ways these stories must have conveyed an affirmative impression of human life, that *from the beginning* it has been, if not ever perfect or prelapserian, essentially good, "sweet," "open," stable, and commodious, and spiritually accessible.

Second, that although the world was created under less-than-perfect, in some cases under "all-too-human" auspices, and indeed those imperfect beings who live in it are certain to experience what Charlie Depoe calls "trouble"—nonetheless there have been from the beginning powerful mitigations of evil and misfortune according to a principle of human solidarity—"feeling sorry for each other," in the Blackfeet formula.

And third, that this solidarity is specifically ethnocentric, relating to the way in which myth-narratives like these confirmed in their audiences the conviction that they were consolidated as the People, for better and for worse the proud and rightful inheritors of a distinctive world and cultural way, and above all the possessors of ritualized sacred stories about how that world and way began, and are to be continued.

At the very end of the Joshua narrative, The Giver tells the man in this spirit that "all the world had been made for him." What is meant is, "all the world that is worth caring about"—half of the first children, we are told, disperse to live north of the mouth of the Rogue River and half go to live across the river to the south: corresponding exactly to the two main Joshua communities in historical times.[31]

Then, after chartering the Joshua world, The Giver is reported to have instructed the man "how to act at all times and under all conditions," specifically licensing the seeking of ultimate goods by "wishing" (even as the world itself has been wished and dreamed into actuality), and cautioning the man "not to cut down more trees or kill more animals" than necessary. The rules, limits, and sanctions of a way of life—really, just the idea of such mythic legislation—are thus laid down, and it is typical of creation and origin narratives that, as here, the complexities of the Native way thus established are left undeveloped. For the full drama of these complexities, and for an understanding of the social, psychological, and ultimately the artistic value of the Native literature about them, we need to move beyond the creation and origin myths to the full traditional repertories to which they stand rather as antechambers. But we have made, I hope, our beginning.

2 / Coyote and Friends
An Experiment in
Interpretive Bricolage

IN FORMULATING A WORKING DEFINITION OF MYTH at the beginning of the previous essay, I argued that in general, Indian myth-narratives seem to be carrying out a *plurality* of significant and interrelated functions simultaneously, and that an ideal form of interpretation would undertake to recognize such plurality within the unity of a given narrative.[1] Certainly our own Anglo literary works—for example, a short story by William Faulkner—often appear to be "doing several things at once," working on a number of different levels, as we say. Most readers are willing to grant the legitimacy of a multiplex approach, one that would engage, say, "theological" as well as "psychological" currents, or "documentary" as well as "theological," or "mythic" as well as "documentary," or all of these currents together. Why then should myth-narratives, the imaginative properties of whole diverse cultures, not of particular authors, be denied such a pluralistic study?

Nowhere is the capacity of traditional Native American literature to do several things at once more obvious, or more perplexing, than in trickster narratives. Although to square the Native literature according to a trickster-story rule would be as misleading in its way as to square it according to a rule of creation stories only, the importance of Coyote and his kind and their stories can hardly be over emphasized, I think. The trickster figure is ubiquitous in Native literature and, as I hope to show, is conceptually central to it; it has obvious and important affinities with types of characters in our own literature, notably in this century, and therefore represents at least one genuine intersection of print-based and oral-tribal literary interests for study. On the other hand, as a traditional "type" among the Indians it corresponds to a compelling folklore figure of global distribution: Shakespeare's Autolycus, Ted Hughes's Crow, Ken Kesey's Randal McMurphy, Ralph Ellison's Rinehart, and Faulkner's Flem Snopes; Anansi, Ture, Loki, Hermes, Tyll Eulenspiegel, and Chu; and Coyote, Blue Jay, Wakdjunkaga, Nanabush (the Hare), and Raven—to understand something of the literary functioning of the last-named group of Indian tricksters is, perhaps, to understand something about the other two groups as well.

Again, it would be a gross distortion to deal exclusively with tricksters, as if they were the only Native characterological type worth considering. Ideally, we should have a thorough study of each tribal repertory according to its main figures and types and their accustomed roles and interrelationships—what, in fact, Melville Jacobs has given us for Clackamas Chinook, in *The Content and Style of an Oral Literature,* under the heading of "Personalities."[2] But for the special purposes of this essay, I want to dwell on the one Native type whose protean nature seems capable of subsuming all other possible types sooner or later—that is, "all man's epitome," the Trickster. And I want to proceed along pluralistic lines of interpretation, at the risk, as the reader may as well be warned, of seeming to follow a trail as devious as that followed by our subject.

For the Indians of America, a trickster gazetteer would look something like this:

COYOTE: Plateau, Great Basin, and Rocky Mountain groups, but also some transitional coastal areas, and most of California—Chinookan, Sahaptin, Interior Salish, Navajo, Karok, Maidu, Mohave, and so on

RAVEN: North coast groups of British Columbia and Alaska—Haida, Nootka, Tsimshian, Kwakiutl, and so on

BLUE JAY: some Northwest Chinookan groups

RACCOON: Columbia River Chinookan; Wabanaki

DRAGONFLY (Daldal): Takelma (Oregon Athapaskan)

SOUTH WIND (As'ai'yahahl): peculiar to the Salish-speaking Oregon Tillamooks

KAMUKAMTS: Klamath and Modoc

IKTOMI (Spider): Sioux

GLUSKAP: Algonquian

MANABOZHO: Ojibwa

HARE: Menominee, Winnebago

"OLD MAN" (Na'pi): Blackfeet, Crow

WAKDJUNKAGA: Winnebago

Of what is a trickster capable? Anything, it appears from the evidence; anything, that is, that does not express consistent restraint or altruistic, responsibly domestic, or executive motives. The Chinookan and Sahaptin Coyote, for example, wanders around, masquerades, lies, steals, attempts to defraud, hoards, gorges himself, commits rape, masturbates, schemes to commit incest, seeks unwarranted revenges, wastes natural resources, plays malicious tricks, is dismembered, swallowed whole, expelled, publicly humiliated—all the while inventing important rituals, naming and placing the tribes, chartering fishing rights, laying down laws of marriage, warfare, and so on, and establishing the permanence of death.[3]

Defining such a various creature is a little like trying to juggle hummingbirds or arm wrestle Proteus. Does one proceed deductively by positing a category, for which examples can be found, or inductively, moving from putative examples to a concept which generalizes their features? And in literary terms, is the quintessence of tricksterhood to be sought in an actor's *character* or in his role? Without meaning to plead a trickster's logical license myself, my provisional answer is "both": the following definition is both inductive and deductive, and attentive to character features and to role. (Necessarily, such a definition glosses over distinctions, as between different trickster-animal characteristics, that are carefully observed in the traditions of individual Indian communities.[4])

The Trickster is an imaginary hyperbolic figure of the human, irrepressibly energetic and apparently unkillable, whose episodic career is based upon hostility to domesticity, maturity, good citizenship, modesty, and fidelity of any kind; who in Freudian terms is mostly id, a little ego, and no superego;

who is given to playful disguises and shape-changing; and who in his clever self-seeking may accomplish important mythic transformations of reality, both in terms of creating possibility and in terms of setting human limits. From a structural standpoint, tricksters are important mediative figures.

Now as we will see, there are Native tricksters who, in fact, possess other qualities in addition to these—but these amount, I think, to an identifiable core. Again, we are confronted with what appears to be a jarring contradiction between the Trickster's full-time role as a fool and rascal, a source of amusement, and his intermittent role as a mythic transformer of reality. But in order to resolve this contradiction, we must first deal with the range of meanings he is capable of creating as a trickster per se.

First, from a purely literary standpoint, the Trickster is clearly indispensable to Native repertories as an inexhaustible creator of situations and episodes. He is always "coming along," "going there," not in the sense of a purposeful journey from X to Y, of course, but rather in the picaresque sense of being capable of turning up when the narrative needs him and in the fund of comic possibility he carries. When the Trickster does turn up, he generally dominates the story through sheer force of character ("animal magnetism," one is tempted to say), and we perceive it as another "trickster tale," one of a subgenre of stories that Indians themselves have recognized as such.

But in some repertories, at least, Coyote, or his tricksterish equivalent, is capable of serving subordinate literary purposes, either as an undeveloped and incidental plot agent or as a foil to other, more central characters. In the well-known Clackamas story "Seal and Her Younger Brother Lived There," for example, Seal's brother is murdered in bed by a sinister "wife," apparently a man in female disguise, who disappears after the murder. Dell Hymes and others have argued that the murder is only a narrative pretext to the real concern of the story, which is the contrasting responses of Seal and her little daughter to the calamity, and the murderer is presumably what Hymes has recently called a "neutralized" trickster figure, adapted for the special purposes of the Clackamas plot from other versions of the story in which he plays a more active role.[5]

As for tricksters who serve as foils, such a strategy occurs most frequently in stories centering on young emerging human heroes, with the Trickster's buffoonery and lack of discipline setting off the heroic virtues of the protagonist. For example, in the Okanagan story "Dirty Boy," all the young men compete in various tests for the prize of the chief's daughters, and the triumphs of "Dirty Boy" (really "Sun" in disguise) are amusingly counterpointed with the utter failures of Coyote, who ignores the rules of the tests, tries to cheat, tries too hard to win, is revealed as a bad sport, and so on. Perhaps the fullest and most sophisticated range of exploitations of tricksters in these terms appears in Ella Deloria's great collection, *Dakota Texts,* in which from story to story Iktomi, the humanoid Sioux Trickster, appears now as protagonist, and now as a secondary character, a foil or plot thickener.[6] But in general, Western tricksters are much less flexibly employed.

Such technical storytelling advantages are important and have been neglected in most discussions, but it might be fairly objected that they *could* be and in fact are sometimes obtained in character types other than the trickster— in the fool or the villain, for example. The functional essence of Trickster, his literary raison d'être, lies elsewhere, I think: it lies in his predilection, one might say his genius, for always being in the middle, in all kinds of middles, in muddles. One of Lévi-Strauss's major contributions to the understanding of traditional narratives is his recognition that tricksters are exemplars of the *mediative* process out of which, according to structuralism, myth is generated. "[L]ike Ash-Boy and Cinderella, the trickster is a mediator. Since his mediating function occupies a position between two polar terms, he must retain something of that duality—namely, an ambiguous and equivocal character."[7]

(Lest the term "mediation" assume here, as it too often does in structuralist writings, a magical instrumentality, like The Clown's all-purpose courtly reply in *All's Well That Ends Well,* "O Lord, sir," let me suggest that it means a dynamic interposing of the mind between polar opposites, allowing it to hold onto both opposites, as if affirming "either/and"— exactly what W. B. Yeats claimed for the symbolic geometry of his *Vision,* that it allowed him to "hold in a single thought reality and justice."[8] Mediation does not mean "compromise or reconciliation" or a Hegelian middle term: if I understand Lévi-Strauss, it is a continuing process of the mind, not a transitional step toward some conclusion.)

So, as Lévi-Strauss points out in speculating about the cultural origins of the figure, it is surely no accident that the two most popular and widespread animal tricksters among Western tribes are Coyote and Raven, who as scavengers and omnivores occupy an obvious mediating position in the ecological scheme between the herbivores and the carnivores. One might object that there are notable humanoid tricksters—the Winnebago Wakdjunkaga and the Klamath Kamukamts, for example—but of course we humans are notorious omnivores ourselves! In that, we are close kin to Coyote and Raven. Our identity likewise involves being "in between" in terms of strategies of subsistence, to begin with, and on the plane of existential consciousness, it involves being uncomfortably "in between" in lots of other respects, too—as the antics of such figures can symbolically reveal. The world through which the Indian tricksters wander seems to bristle with inherent polarities and conceptual oppositions (what Shakespeare's Timon calls "confounding contraries"), rather suggestive of Blake's world view or Yeats's lifelong antithetical vision of "the old antinomies of day and night."[9] But where Blake and Yeats as Romantics committed the poetic imagination to a lonely and sternly heroic engagement, part battle and part dance, with the polarities of modern life, and no doubt would bridle at the very concept of "mediation," the Indians and other tribal peoples seem to have relied on an age-old collective figure, unselfconscious and distinctly unheroic, to hold together indifferently well the various polarities of their experience, lest things seem to pull apart for the lack of a mediating center. Let's examine what Coyote and his kind accomplish in their stories, as casual all-purpose mediators. The trail is a fascinating tangle of psychological, environmental, cultural, historical, and theological as well as literary elements: it is veritably "Trickster's Trail."

First, as Lévi-Strauss's theory about the original "type-casting" of the omnivorous and scavenging animals as tricksters suggests, their kind of story seems to function crucially as a way of mediating between the realm of human society and the realm of nature, effecting imaginative accommodations of the former to the latter and vice versa without blurring or weakening the distinctions whereby "the People" maintain their identity *as* people, one distinctive form of life in a variously living world. To the extent that, as I claimed earlier, myths in general tell their understanders who they are, trickster stories seem calculated to provide important human identifications through the adventures of an ambiguous creature who is somehow intermediate between human and nonhuman. As the poet Ted Hughes has aptly said about his own composite modern Trickster, "Crow," "He's a man to correct man but of course he's not a man, he's a crow."[10]

Again and again, Western tricksters appear to be at odds, like their human protégés to come, with the nonhuman natural order: they abuse and in turn are scorned by other creatures; they unnaturally but "all too humanly" waste natural goods, are greedy, "perverse," and so on, often in pursuit of recognizable human goods like status and esteem; above all, they are capable of exercising cognitive intelligence, although they rarely do, in fact, except in the form of the shortsighted selfish schemes for which they are famous. On the other, nonhuman side of the ledger, they are capable of a whole battery of deeds that are not allowable according to the canons of idealized "human nature," but are natural among animals—incest, for example. And in general the partial animality of the Trickster expresses itself in his basic intolerance of domesticity in any form: he is, like one of his sly animal totems, essentially a self-reliant loner, a potentially disruptive outsider in his appetites and capacities even when he is temporarily domiciled.

The capital instance of a trickster plying between Nature and Society is the career of the Winnebago Wakdjunkaga, in Paul Radin's classic texts. Wakdjunkaga actually begins the cycle as a human chief, with a community to govern, but after violating the rules of chiefhood, he drops out of human society altogether and enters nature, where he understands and is understood by all creatures (he calls them "little brothers"). He plays tricks on his animal kin, and is himself tricked and humiliated. Eventually he gravitates back toward society, first in an outrageous sexual disguise as the bride of a chief's son, and then after another stint in nature, as a legitimate husband and father (albeit still subject to tricksterish lapses).

To an unusual degree, Wakdjunkaga actually evolves as a character, according to his partial reacquisition of a socialized human identity. His concerns change from those of an utterly deracinated human thing, nameless, purposeless, homeless, all but swallowed up (more than once) by the natural order, to those of an individuated "citizen": envy of his neighbors, greed, desire to be "a big man." In total his adventures vividly delineate both the boundaries and the points of mutual access between the human world and the natural—and one of his earliest companions on his trail back to society, a fox, sums up pithily what the whole cycle is about in these terms: "The world," says Fox, "is going to be a difficult place in which to live, and I am trying to find some clean place in which to dwell." [11] One recalls here again Tsagiglálal's view of her purpose as a Wasco chief, to teach people "how to live well and to build good houses." That is, finding one's proper station (and therefore one's identity) in a world of polarized entities like Nature and Society *is* difficult: Wakdjunkaga's misadventures betwixt and between animal and human experience render the difficulty less mysterious, at least, through a kind of comic mediation, characteristic of Indian tricksters in general.

Beyond the Trickster's services as a courier in the no-man's-land between human and animal, there is his obvious value as mediator between the antinomies of tribal good citizenship and individual self-fulfillment. All evidence (our modern sentimentalists of Indian life often ignore it) indicates that traditional Native cultures were sternly normative, ruled by custom and its executive agency, group opinion, with morality enforced in the individual by the prospect of public exposure, and "shame" before one's fellows, rather than by the prospect of "guilt" in the sight of some all-seeing deity. Life in such "shame-cultures" can be mightily repressive, as everybody knows who has run afoul of customary opinion in a small town: a bad conscience can be eased, or even put aside, but a morality based upon fear of social castigation is unrelenting; it provides for no appeal on behalf of the way of the individual as against the way of the People.

Enter Trickster as mediator. His outrageous sexual antics, his thorough selfishness, his general irresponsibility, his polymorphous dedication to the perverse in the stories must have allowed the "good citizens" of the tribe to affirm the system of prohibitions and punishments that Trickster chronically runs afoul of—at the same time that they could vicariously delight and find release in his irresponsible individualism. My point is that through the mediation of the Trickster, the people could in effect have their traditional morality both ways, at least in the imagination—familiar with his stories, they knew that his reckless hedonistic conduct would come to no good end, according to tribal values—but before those ends arrived, episodically, they could richly enjoy themselves, as if on holiday! Indeed, the saturnalian spirit of these stories offers yet another literary illustration, I think, of Freud's theory of wit and the comic, whereby it is supposed that the psychic energy we customarily employ in maintaining repressions can, under certain circumstances, be released and redirected to the cause of celebration.[12]

Perhaps it is not too farfetched to recall here also Freud's related observation about the culture-preserving function of all art: "Art offers substitutive satisfactions for the oldest and still most deeply felt cultural renunciations, and for that it serves as nothing else does to reconcile a man to the sacrifices he has made on behalf of civilization." [13] Now, the Trickster is by definition not one to make such sacrifices, and that is just the point: *both* his self-indulgences and his embarrassments must have made the tribal audiences feel better about *their* personal renunciations on behalf of tribal order. Is it otherwise with us and certain of our most memorable literary figures, after all: in our delight in Falstaff's roguery, while it lasts, and our grudging recognition of the civic rightness of his exposure and rejection, when they inevitably come? The trouble with Falstaff as a trickster-variant is that Shakespeare allows him to grow old and infirm, and thus subject to our sentimentality, and eventually to die—true trickster narratives never allow this, although there is poignancy in the concluding episodes of some cycles, in which the heroes leave Earth and are translated forever beyond earthly trouble—and thus beyond further narrative interest. [14]

That there is a satirical, antiheroic potential in this function of the trickster figure has been amply demonstrated by Radin in his discussion of Wakdjunkaga's career. Wakdjunkaga commits what would be sacrileges in Winnebago terms at every other step, it appears—especially against political and religious ceremonies and heroical codes and customs in warfare, major details of which come in for burlesque one by one, in a manner too persistent to be other than deliberately satirical. [15] Again, the overall effect of such episodes would be that of release, and a comic reassessment, perhaps, of the lofty claims of tribal custom and ceremony in relation to the sanctions of one's own commonsensical selfish life. No doubt we could identify many more instances of trickster satire if we had a better grasp of the sacrosanct and heroic elements of the traditional tribal cultures. As it is, the trickster-as-false-shaman is so common a motif in Western repertories that a persistent satirical impulse against the excesses and abuses of shamanism, if not against the institution itself, is not to be doubted. And such stories tend to invalidate the currently popular notion that certain of our new Anglo poets and writers are somehow "shamans," or are at least writing in a "shamanistic" tradition. [16] Not only were Indian narrative artists not shamans, their trickster stories suggest a degree of skepticism about the latter's activities and privileges, or at least an awareness of the possibilities of false shamanism.

Now it might be objected, as against the uniqueness of the set of functions that I am claiming for the trickster figure, that there are other characters in the Native literature equally capable of effecting this kind of psycho-social mediation villains, for example, like the violent and orgiastic Grizzly people and "Wild Women" in Chinookan and Tillamook stories, respectively. Couldn't Native listeners have vicariously experienced the unnatural gratifications of such monstrous figures, too, and perhaps sublimated them according to the norms of the tribe? I doubt that this happened to a significant extent. Without denying that we are always capable of lending villains our dreams, as E. M. Forster once said of lovers in novels,[17] the villainous type as it figures in Western Indian literature appears to be too starkly vicious, too alien a character to be subject to sublimative responses. When we rightly say of Coyote as he disguises himself as an infant so as to ravish a group of young women and is ultimately exposed and mutilated, that he is a "horrible example," we mean that what he does is, however repugnant, imaginable as human conduct, and that judging from other stories about him, he might have known better, and indeed sometimes does. That is to say, as a horrible example he still has mediative validity—as the truly villainous Native characters do not; as their equivalents in our literary-cultural system—Iago for example—likewise do not.

In this connection, it is worth repeating what Barre Toelken's Navajo informant and collaborator Yellowman said in reply to three questions about Navajo Coyote stories. "Why tell the stories?"—"If my children hear the stories, they will grow up to be good people; if they don't hear them, they will turn out to be bad."—"Why tell them to adults?"—"Through the stories everything is made possible."—"Why does Coyote do all those things, foolish on one occasion, good on another, terrible on another?"— "If he did not do all those things, then those things would not be possible in the world."[18] In Navajo thought, according to Toelken, the telling of a story amounts to the actual creation or re-creation of a reality. Hence, I understand Yellowman to be saying that before actions can be understood (as by a child) or reconfirmed (as by an adult) as morally "impossible," they must be enacted as realities in a story and thus seen as "possible" to commit, even to enjoy in the imagination. Thus, by amorally trying everything, up to but not beyond the point of monstrousness, Coyote makes the morality of the Navajo world fictively possible—and intelligible to the imagination.

Géza Róheim and others have argued that, from a psychoanalytic standpoint, the typical Indian trickster is in fact a perfect "culture-hero," given the rigidity and repressiveness of Native cultures. "Why is Coyote the really popular hero?" Róheim asks. "Why is there such a strong element of the obscene, of the unpermissable, or contrary in these beings? And why the vicarious pleasure in these narratives? The answer is that North American Indians have a very strong superego, and the representative of the Id as hero is a counterbalance to social pressure. . . . No wonder then that the real hero of their mythology is the Id—although to preserve the integrity of the ego they pretend to deride their hero." [19]

Now this makes good applied-Freudian sense along the lines we have been following, and indeed it is hard to think of another literary or folklore figure more richly expressive of what we call the Id—"primal libidinous energy"—than the trickster. But to claim the theoretical value of Róheim's argument, we must rescue it from its considerable oversimplifications. First, most sophisticated Indians I know emphatically reject the notion that their traditional trickster figure represents a "culture hero," and there is literary as well as ethnographic evidence to support their objections. Many Western tribes have, in fact, one or more well-developed, authentic, all-purpose literary heroes: the Yuman and Mohave figure "Cane," for example, and in Chinookan mythologies, admirable figures like Eagle, who often exhibits culture-heroic qualities while in the contrasting company of Coyote.

Then, too, Trickster as we have him in Indian tradition simply resists in his utter variousness the label Róheim would give him. If he is typically expressive of, and often willy-nilly subject to the Id, he is *not* simply that entity in unmixed literary form. To the extent that he schemes and deceives, and often shows sensitivity to his selfhood in the form of envy, pride, and vindictiveness, and is sometimes capable of effecting permanent mythic alterations in reality, is he not also, however unstably, expressive of the Ego? Again, the idea of mediator serves our analysis better than the idea of "culture hero": indisputably linked to—fueled by—the Id, tricksters may be said to mediate as unstable ego-formations between Id and Superego, according to the general psychosocial function already discussed.[20]

One startling fact about the formal recitation of trickster tales is that in all Western Indian groups, small children were expected to be in the audience and to listen attentively to the tellings, no matter how violent or bawdy. Earlier I spoke of the social value of tricksters as "horrible examples" of unrestrained appetite, selfishness, and other forms of inappropriate behavior, and no doubt such vivid examples constituted a major part of the early moral education of Native children, as Yellowman's remarks to Toelken indicate. But what about the psycho-dynamics of such instruction? Were preadolescents in danger of being traumatized in following Coyote from masturbation to rape to incest, and on to bizarre sexual encounters with female monsters, as in stories based on the *vagina dentata* motif?

Apparently not—on the contrary, it appears likely that public performance of such stories effectively mediated between the developing child and his fears and uncertainties about himself. Toward the beginning of his distinguished career, the psychologist Erik Erikson studied the Yurok people of northern California and gave special attention to Yurok methods of childrearing and to the developmental significance of communal dances, ceremonies, and myth-recitals. Far from noting evidence of trauma, Erikson asserts that

only he who has seen Indian children sitting through a night of dances can understand the possibility that rituals and myths, by acknowledging unspeakable feelings in more than verbal representations, take care of the impulses and fears of a period of childhood where our children still fight their lonely battles with the Oedipal provocations of an every-family-for-itself culture.[21]

This ontogenetic function is memorably illustrated in the early adventures of the Winnebago Wakdjunkaga. Not only is he desocialized in these episodes, he exhibits an utterly infantile, undifferentiated consciousness; he is like a great lubberly baby. Lacking the proprioceptive faculties of an ego, he literally does not know how the parts of his body "hook up" as components of one articulated and controllable organism: his left hand fights with his right, he assigns his rectum to sentry duty and severely punishes it when it fails to alert him to trouble, and so on. One inevitably thinks in these episodes of any child's intense discovery in infancy of its bodily parts; and its long-drawn-out and uneasy education through childhood and adolescence as to the proper functions of these parts. In particular,

Wakdjunkaga in this part of the cycle seems to follow precisely the basic Freudian ontogenetic sequence, orality-anality-genitality: first stuffing himself with soup, then becoming maniacally preoccupied with his anus and its functions as noted above, and then awakening one morning to find that his penis (which is so long he must carry it coiled in a box) has erected itself and is flying his blanket like a chief's banner![22] (With this episode, his active sexual career begins.)

Wakdjunkaga is, again, a special case, in that his stories are subsumed in a clearly developmental "plot," unlike the trickster episodes in most other repertories as we have them.[23] But if generally unconnected by plot, these episodes often do dramatize infantile conduct and somatic perceptions—to take just one example, the universal Western story of Coyote getting trapped inside a tree and escaping by dismantling himself and throwing the parts one by one out through a knothole, with the result that his eyes are stolen and must be trickily retrieved.[24] And in more general terms, the bizarre bodily metamorphoses to which Coyote and his kind frequently resort—into babies, into animals large and small, into trees and stones—seem especially calculated to appeal to children along lines of somatic self-consciousness.

In summary, then, given the prominent place of juveniles in myth-audiences and the well-documented Native emphasis on education through myth,[25] we can conclude that another of the trickster's interlocking mediative functions is to "get between" children and their unverbalized fears and preoccupations about themselves, especially about their growing bodies in relation to their developing selves, and render such anxieties harmless or at least subject to normative laughter, and not a furtive amusement, either, but shared openly with the adults of the tribe.

Such orthogenic functions are, after all, much like what Bruno Bettelheim has persuasively claimed for fairy stories in our culture: "While it entertains the child, the fairy tale enlightens him about himself, and fosters his personality development. . . . Fairy stories represent in imaginative form what the process of healthy human development consists of."[26]

Much of what Bettelheim observes about the value for anxious children of, say, "The Frog King" and "Cinderella" sheds light, I think, on trickster narratives, but cultural differences limit the comparison, two in particular: (1) no figures in the Grimms' marchen (at least in the form in which we know them) exhibit the wild range of conduct of which Indian tricksters are routinely capable, and (2) whereas in our culture fairy tales are customarily transmitted from parents or other elders to children under intimate "bedtime" circumstances, Indian children were exposed, as in Erikson's account, to dramatic performances of trickster stories as part of a heterogeneous audience.

If, as I have been suggesting, the trickster serves the cause of ontogenetic awareness, through depictions of childhood "at its worst" (and, following Bettelheim's concept, Native hero stories often show it at its "best"), then doesn't a figure like Coyote also simultaneously serve the cause of *phylogenetic* awareness?—that is, promote the tribal group's sense of itself as an evolved entity with a distinctive history? Yes—hence the peculiar importance of trickster stories in fulfilling the mythic function of "telling the people who they are." Or, to exploit yet once again for literary purposes the evolutionist's dictum: "ontogeny recapitulates phylogeny." What happens to the trickster is inevitably part of the early history of each human being, generation by generation: and at the same time it serves by analogy as a way of conceiving part of the early history of the race, or the tribal group itself.

Most scholars of the trickster figure in North America and elsewhere have concluded that the figure is very old indeed, a literary survival from very ancient times.[27] Paul Radin asks, rhetorically, "Are we dealing here with the workings of the mythopoeic imagination, common to all mankind, which, at a certain period in man's history, gives us his picture of the world of himself? Is this a *speculum mentis* wherein is depicted man's struggle with himself and with a world into which he had been thrust without his volition and consent?"[28] Radin does not pursue his implication here, but we can, to the effect that not only anthropologists and their Anglo readers but, more crucially, Native listeners would perceive the trickster as a *speculum mentis* in these terms, a giver of depth to human history. As mirrors of a hypothesized primitive mind and condition, then, as well as of infantile minds, tricksters would seem to function as sources of a kind of tribal historical perspective. As if to say: "Here's how uncouth and infantile it was around here at the beginning"—and of course to point back to primitive beginnings in this way is also to point forward with a kind of evolutionary pride to the sophisticated present, occupied by "the People," who have such stories as evidence of their evolved status ("progress" as such is not at issue). And for confirmation of how it was in mythic times, as represented in trickster episodes, they need only observe how it is with children!

Perhaps Victor Turner's theories of liminality can be cited here to mark our trail a little further. In the course of several studies (but not to my knowledge in a separate treatise) Turner has identified the trickster as a special kind of liminal figure, a permanent indicator, as it were, of "threshold" experiences, rites of passage wherein our reliance on "structure" breaks down and ambiguity for a time prevails. Liminal figures exist in a state of "outsiderhood," and may in fact come to share in an "outsider's" modality which Turner calls "communitas," as set off from society at large.[29]

Now it is hard to see how any North American trickster may be said to participate in a true communitas, as Turner defines it—but it does seem to me that the basic concept of liminality can be applied to both the ontogenetic and the phylogenetic trickster functions we have been examining. Childhood can thus be seen as a series of "thresholds," over which one passes as "initiand" toward full adult identity, just as the race itself may be conceived as once standing on the mere threshold of human significance. A trickster like Wakdjunkaga vividly marks both kinds of self-consciousness, one might say, and, in fact, connects and mediates between them.

At any rate, it is worth noting that narrators of Myth Age stories in the Western literatures frequently comment in these terms on the foolishness, fecklessness, and general childlike lack of good sense of the Myth Age characters, including Coyote. Radin, for example, quotes from the beginning of a Gros Ventre creation story: "The people before the present people were wild. They did not know how to do anything."[30] And such stories often end, as they do in Clackamas Chinook, with a prophecy to the effect that "The People" (that is, the real grown-up Indians, with all their distinctive identity and know-how) "are coming soon." The kind of historical self-consciousness that trickster stories may have promoted is not all that different, perhaps, from what Aeschylus' audience must have felt about their place in the world's story upon hearing Prometheus' haunting lines about those "creatures of a day," their primitive ancestors:

For men had eyes but saw to no purpose; they had ears but did not hear. Like the shapes of dreams they dragged through their long lives and handled all things in bewilderment and confusion. They did not know of building houses with bricks to face the sun; they did not know how to work in wood. They lived like swarming ants in holes in the ground, in the sunless caves of the earth.[31]

But here, not inappropriately (Turner has observed that liminal figures are haunters of crossroads), we come to a fork in our Trickster's Trail—if not an impasse. Whereas Prometheus as a titan stands apart from and above the protohumans he elects to aid, tricksters like Wakdjunkaga and Coyote are, as we have seen, first amongst Myth Age equals in exhibiting primitive, rudimentary human qualities. Yet, if distinctly less than "titanic" in mentality and motives, most Far Western tricksters do intermittently exercise promethean powers in effecting radical and permanent transformations of the world. As writers from Daniel Brinton on have asked, how can one character be both Trickster and Transformer?[32] And we must ask, having come this far in our study of trickster functions per se, how can all these mediative functions be reconciled with such a unilaterally heroic role?

Not, certainly, according to Hellenic literary typologies and categories. As Franz Boas first pointed out, what Far Western tricksters do as transformers they do not do from lofty promethean motives; rather, they characteristically fix up reality by whim or accident (as with their supererogatory powers) or in the pursuit of selfish not altruistic ends, and certainly not in a spirit of self-sacrifice. If in their functioning as transformers they sometimes exhibit a sense of "mythic fitness" in proclaiming what "the people who are coming soon" (the real Indians) will need in the finished world, their actions are still inextricably bound up in their careers as tricksters. The North Coast Raven brings sunlight to the world because he "thought it would be hard for him to obtain his food if it were always dark";[33] Kamukamts transforms the Klamath country, as we have seen, in a genial competition with Gopher to see who deserves the honorific title of "Elder Brother."[34]

It may well be, as Radin and others have argued, that the trickster figure evolved first, serving functional needs like those discussed above, and eventually acquired, through some principle of mythological evolution not understood, the role of transformer. But the archaeology of the figure will not, I think, satisfactorily explain the composite significance it has in Western Indian narratives, and which Indians still accept without a sense of contradiction.[35]

Perhaps at least a partial explanation is already before us. Just as the trickster's dual role cannot be understood in terms of comparisons with Prometheus and other heroic benefactors in Western culture, so it cannot be understood in terms of Judeo-Christian ideas of "perfect origins," divine cosmogonies, and the like. Both the traditional literature and the Native commentary upon it seem to validate, for Western tribes at least, Lévi-Strauss's conception of the trickster-transformer as a *bricoleur,* a sort of mythic handy-man who "cobbles" reality in the form of a *bricolage* out of the available material, and with something distinctly less transcendent than a divine plan or teleology to guide him—namely, his own impressionable, wayward, *avid* mind.[36] To believe that the world as we have it is largely the work of a trickster is, in a mode of thought unfamiliar to our culture, to know and accept it *on its own terms,* neither postlapserian nor millennial: as if to say, "Well, now, the world is not perfect; how could it be, given its original artisan, our trickster ancestor—but it's pretty good, considering; good enough, anyway. It's a world: ours." Or, in this judicious appraisal by a Thompson River Indian: "Coyote taught the people how to eat, how to wear clothes, make houses, hunt, fish, etc. Coyote did a great deal of good, but he did not finish everything properly. Sometimes he made mistakes, and although he was wise and powerful, he did many foolish things. He was too fond of playing tricks for his own amusement. He was also selfish, boastful, and vain."[37]

As we have seen, one of the distinguishing properties of tricksters is their sheer vitality. Speaking of his long traffic as a poet with Coyote lore, Gary Snyder has remarked that "the first thing that excited me about Coyote tales was the delightful Dadaistic energy, leaping somehow into a modern frame of reference."[38] That tricksters are overcharged with biological energy is dramatized of course in their overt actions as imaginative characters, given to trying *anything,* and it is also frequently expressed in casual supererogatory transformations of parts of their bodies into foodstuffs for the sustenance of the people to come. The feces of the Tillamook character "South Wind," for example, are turned into salmon-berries; portions of Wakdjunkaga's penis, when it is finally cut down to proper size, become staple roots and berries for the Winnebagos.[39]

Tricksters are also, as we have noticed in passing, unkillable. They may suffer bad luck or just retribution in the form of starvation, poisoning, dismemberment, ingestion by monsters, incineration, drowning, fatal falls, and so on—but, as we would have it, it is a universal convention that they revive (either in explicit, generally formulaic episodes of revival, or implicitly, between one story and another), and go blithely on their way. They are mythic survivors, "hot for the world" (as Charles Olson once said of the Mayans[40]) in a way that signifies, *per speculum mentis,* both the persistence in us of the unreconstructed Id, and the sheer avid amoral persistence of the human race itself. Trickster's lesson on this point is that the two things are profoundly interrelated.

In Coyote's or Raven's adventures we are, I think, in imaginative contact with a primal vitality that is understood as running from the mythic beginnings of the world up to the present human moment and beyond. Once made, this contact can be (at least I find it so) irresistible, and even uncanny—quite beyond the broad comedy that is its official tonality. As Radin memorably says about Trickster, "If we laugh at him, he grins at us. What happens to him, happens to us."[41] We may indeed laugh scornfully at Trickster's pranks and pratfalls, and hopefully learn from his stories why and how we should maintain the social order he defies—but we ignore or deny his vital, anarchic claim on us only at our individual and collective peril. In this sense, then, there is no contradiction but rather an organic rightness in the transformer's role the Indians have given him. He was here at the first, uniquely endowed with the sheer charge of life if not with the human gifts of directing it beyond survival—and who else then could have shaped the world's possibilities and limits for us, but him?

Can so many functions be performed by one literary figure? Yes, and I hope I have suggested how, given their peculiar interrelationships, they may well be operating simultaneously in a given trickster story, as a kind of gestalt, all the while the story carries out its promise of amusement. Perhaps I should say "may well have been operating" in deference to our historical and ethnological remoteness from such stories, but I would rather proceed here and throughout on the assumption that what "operated" in these stories for their traditional Native audiences may at least intersect with what we can now discern in them as imaginative constructs.

I think that in their various incarnations Indian tricksters must have served the strong needs of their audience, living in monistic and highly centralized cultures, for *plurality.*[42] Tricksters make things possible, both fictively and morally (the two forms of enablement are never unrelated), and they effect complex mediations whereby human polarities are imaginatively held together and indeed in a fashion integrated—Nature as against Society, social collectivity as against individuality, "Id" as against "Superego," Childhood as against Adulthood and the individual's experience as against that of the race, prehistory as against "history," and, finally, on the level of mythic transformations, what could have been in the world as against what is.

Having been forced up to now to consider bits and pieces of trickster stories for illustration, rather than whole delicious texts, the reader is invited to test these propositions on the following little Coyote narratives—three Western trickster stories amongst thousands, conveying neither sweetness nor light, perhaps, but functionally very wise in the peculiar way of their kind.

The News Precedes Coyote (Santiam Kalapuya)

Coyote was going along [down the Willamette],
   he wanted to go to the [Oregon City] falls here.
Now then he made camp,
   now then it became morning,
      now then he went on again.

Now then it became dark,
   now then he camped again,
      now then at morning he went on again.

Now then it was dark,
   now then he camped again,
      now then at morning he went on again.

Now then at dark he camped again,
   now then he slept in a sweathouse.
      Now then in the sweathouse he made it rock.

Now then he was licking his penis,
   now then he came out:
      "This sweathouse will be a rock."

Now then he went along.
　　Now then he was going along,
　　　　now then he saw a lot of people in a canoe.

Now then Coyote called out,
　　"What's the news?"
Again he called out,
　　"What's the news?"
　　"What's the news?"

Now then one of those people said,
　　"What can be calling out?
　　Oh it is that Coyote!"
Now then that person called back to him,
　　"Hello!"

Coyote said,
　　"What news is there?"

Now then that person said,
　　"There is no news at all,
　　"The only news [is] Coyote was sucking his penis."

"Ah! Wonder where the one who saw me was standing?
　　"Ohhh, I will go back.
　　"I will see where he could have been standing, I wonder."

Now then he went back,
Now then he got to the sweathouse here,
　　Now then he examined his sweathouse
now then he saw
　　where the rock had been cracked apart

"Ohhhhh! I suppose this is where the news came out from it.
　　"That is how it is going to be,
　　　　"That is the way it will always be,
　　"Nothing will ever be hidden,
　　　　"That is the way it will always be."

Old-Man-Coyote's Visit to the Crow-Indians (Crow)

When the Crow camp had increased to a considerable size, Old-Man-Coyote paid his first visit there. The women were busy getting bark from the cottonwoods and were drinking the sap. Old-Man-Coyote said, "I'll visit the Crow Indians whom I made." A mountain-goat was eating before him, he made a white horse out of it and painted it so that it appeared as a pinto with red ears; it was a pretty horse with a yellow rump. He rode it, bidding it prance in lively fashion. He put his legs up tight. The horse said, "What do you want me to do?"—"Paw the ground and neigh aloud." After a while he made his horse stand quiet. He took the bark used by women and from it made feather trappings for his horse. He fashioned a fancy bridle out of bark; he took the biggest leaves to be found and stretched them together for a mountain-lion-skin saddlecloth. He made red and green flannel out of leaves for his horse, also some fancy breast ornament. He stood a little ways from his horse and thought its decoration was fine. Then he took dirt and painted himself. He made a switch decorated with porcupine work. He looked at himself in a glass and thought he looked fine. His leggings and other garments were fine. He had prettily beaded moccasins. He had braids down to his waist, with bells on them. He saw his outfit was complete. He took an old buffalo shoulderblade and made an eagle-tail fan out of it.

When the sun was low, he said, "I'll go into camp." He was so fully decorated that he could hardly move. "I'll have the Crow imitate me." He went a little ways, then tightened his hold on the horse which would then paw and neigh. The Crow were playing the hoop game. . . . Old-Man-Coyote approached. He appeared, not noticing anyone. All stopped and looked. "Who is this Crow? There's no one like him." The women ran out to look at the handsome man. The women were having a plum-seed game. He would watch them, then he would tighten his hold on the horse, which acted according to his instructions. He was also holding a coupstick. He went to where they could all watch him. All gathered around to see his dress. He would make his horse paw and neigh. The horse was shy. When he came up and they cheered the winner in the ring game, the noise frightened the horse. It shied and Old-Man-Coyote tumbled off with his finery. All shouted. His horse ran away and turned back into a brush-deer again, and escaped to the brush. All recognized him then. They cried, "Catch him." All tried to hold him in order to get his advice. All ran for him. His finery fell off. He turned into a wolf, and ran off barking. His decorations were strung along the road. They looked at all his finery, but when they picked it up, it was nothing but bark. Hereafter all adopted the kind of dress seen on Old-Man-Coyote.

A *Warning about* Coyote (*Mohave*)

My grandson was coming. He just came to the house. So I asked him, "Do you know anything?"

"Yes, I know things—this one here tells me things." He meant the book.

"Do you know?" ["Can you read it?"]

"A little, yes," he said.

So I said, "It's an animal book. There are different things in it. There's a coyote standing there. This one is a coyote. "

A long time ago the Indians said, "When you've been walking far, you might meet Coyote." They'd say that to a little boy. "If you meet him, what will you say?" That one says, "Child, won't you follow me and eat *tadiichhavaso* [a corn dish]?" "Yes, I'll go with you," he says. "I'll sit on your back; I'm going. I'm coming along," he says.

"I've heard that."

(They'd say that to scare them. They didn't want them to go too far.)[43]

3 / The Poetry and Drama of Healing: The Iroquoian Condolence Ritual and the Navajo Night Chant

ONE OF THE CENTRAL IMPULSES OF NATIVE AMERI‑ can traditional literature is the impulse to summon and direct the powers of *healing*. This employment of verbal art for therapeutic purposes ranges in the tribal repertories from short lyrical incantations, like this Modoc shaman's song, "What do I suck out? / The disease I suck out,"[1] to elabo‑ rate rituals of healing taking hours or even days to perform and involving the participation of whole teams of ritualists and the concentrated atten‑ tion of onlookers. Of the latter undertakings, two of the most powerful and impressive in literary terms to have been transcribed for reading are the *Condolence Ritual* of the Iroquois Nations and the *Night Chant* of the Navajos.

John Bierhorst has aptly identified the *Condolence Ritual* and the *Night Chant* as "masterworks" of Native American literature.[2] They are both poetic and dramatic liturgies; as will be seen, they are in form and content very different from one another, but they have in common the purpose of restoring the well-being and vitality of a patient or subject, and beyond this, the reaffirmation of the fundamental unity and balance of life, according to the Iroquois or Navajo scheme of things. Underlying the conceptual and verbal design of each is a profoundly *holistic* idea of healing—an idea largely unfamiliar to modern Anglo medical practice but characteristic of Native American medicine. Everything is seen as interconnected and interdependent, part of the great hoop of life (to use a widespread traditional Indian figure).[3] What in Anglo terms are discrete human, natural, and supernatural realms are in Native terms interpenetrating and mutual, for better and for worse; indeed, the hard-and-fast Anglo distinction between *natural* and *supernatural* does not apply in most Native conceptions of reality.

In Indian healing, physical afflictions invariably have spiritual implications, and vice versa: treatment of the body or of the spirit alone, then, would not suffice. Likewise, in terms of the "politics" of healing, Indian praxis recognizes that the illness and debilitation of one person diminishes, and perhaps threatens, the whole community, human and otherwise, and conversely his or her restoration to physical and mental health enhances the health and good order of the community. "One for all, and all for one," as we say: with a literal and unblinking confidence, Native healers assume that the sun, the moon, the stars, the rain, the corn, and all the rest of the living order are profoundly implicated in the cure of one human individual's afflictions, and must be, as it were, brought into consultation for the curing to be successful. And its success adds something to the balance of powers and forces that constitutes the general good.[4]

A passage in Leslie Silko's novel *Ceremony* expresses this traditional Indian concept of holistic healing very exactly—and also underscores the profound difference between the Indian concept and the way of modern medical practice, with its exclusive focus on the individual patient and his or her complaints. Silko's hero, a Pueblo Indian named Tayo, who has returned from World War II with physical and psychological afflictions that have been diagnosed by military doctors and psychiatrists as "battle fatigue," at first doubts whether the traditional healers of his own people can heal him:

He wanted to yell at the medicine man, to yell the things the white doctors had yelled at him—that he had to think only of himself, and not about the others, that he would never get well as long as he used words like "we" and "us." But he had known the answer all along, even while the white doctors were telling him he could get well and he was trying to believe them: medicine didn't work that way, because the world didn't work that way. His sickness was only part of something larger, and his cure would be found only in something great and inclusive of everything.[5]

This last sentence goes to the heart of both the *Condolence Ritual* and the *Night Chant* as healing rituals "inclusive of everything"—and perhaps it will serve to suggest why and how the essential medium of each is a highly charged poetic language, in which imagery, metaphor (especially synecdoche), symbol, and syntactical patterning all contribute to the overall effect of what might crudely be called "word-magic." In Native American traditional literature (and for that matter in the writings of contemporary Indian poets and writers), words are understood to have, if used properly, a magical instrumentality—*they can make things happen.*[6] In rhetorical terms, the use of words in Native liturgical and ceremonial texts like the *Condolence Ritual* and the *Night Chant* seeks two related affective goals: *invocation,* of forces and powers outside of but contingent upon human affairs; and *evocation,* of feelings of well-being in the patient and his or her well-wishers. In both works, words and ritual actions are organized with a force and concentration such that, despite the double translation from the Native language into English and out of their cultural frame and into ours, and despite the reduction in presentational mode from performance to reading, a truly awesome effect of expressive power is often achieved in them, as if some great process in nature were being reenacted in words.

Experiencing this effect, one is forcibly reminded of the insignificant role played by expressive language and indeed by the imagination in Western medical practice. In our culture, patients may—if lucky—hearken to the cheering but usually incidental words of a doctor's "bedside manner"; more likely, we are only left to ponder in silence the rather mythic-sounding names on the prescription bottle label: Ornade, Tetracycline, Tagamet, Inderol, Librium . . . But let us return to our examination of the Iroquois and Navajo healing ceremonies, and take up each work in detail for comparative analysis, beginning with the *Condolence Ritual.*

The *Condolence Ritual* has been, probably for four centuries, the supreme political and spiritual ceremony of the League of the Iroquois, or *Ho-de-no-sau-nee.* From the legendary time of its founder, Hiawatha, the League has consisted of five nations, speaking more or less mutually intelligible dialects of the Iroquoian language: the Senecas, Cayugas, Oneidas, Onondagas, and Mohawks.[7] As Lewis Henry Morgan was the first to observe in detail, the League is basically organized into two moieties—the "Elder Brothers," consisting of the Mohawks, the Onondagas, and the Senecas; and the "Younger Brothers," the Cayugas and the Oneidas.[8] The commanding image of the Iroquois in American history and folklore reflects the great power and influence they exerted over three centuries on British, French, and American endeavors in the Eastern Great Lakes region (to say nothing of their sway over their fellow Indians from New England to Illinois), but in fact, behind the fearsome impression of unity of purpose that it conveyed to the outside world, the League appears to have been a rather unstable political entity, constantly subject to internal stresses and strains between its moieties, and within them.

Some historians, in fact, suggest that the great achievement of the League was not its unity of purpose and action per se, but rather the creation in the minds of its real and possible adversaries of the *impression* of unity and omnipotence.[9] Be that as it may, the history of the League makes it clear that its members were constantly in need of reaffirming on a political, and beyond that on a spiritual, basis their basic solidarity.

An obvious opportunity for such collective reaffirmation would come upon the death of any one of the League's fifty great chiefs, or sachems: and this is, in fact, the origin and one of the ongoing purposes of the *Condolence Ritual.* On an occasion of sorrow and perhaps uncertainty for one of the nations in the League, and for the moiety with which it is affiliated, the performance of the *Ritual* by representatives of the entire League is calculated to dramatize its solidarity and to guarantee symbolically its continuity by leading the participants from grief and mourning over the death of a chief to joy and renewed confidence in the revelation at the end of the ceremony, of his successor, who perpetuates his name.

At least in the form in which it is now preserved (dating mostly from nineteenth-century transcriptions), the *Condolence Ritual* is not as closely affiliated with the mythology of its Iroquoian tribes as is generally the case with Native American ceremonial literature.[10] As we will see, the Navajo *Night Chant* is explicitly "chartered" in Navajo myth, which gives accounts of its origins and detailed directions as to its correct performance. This sort of mythic *subtext* seems to be lacking in the *Condolence Ritual.* Instead, it is full of reverent references to the semihistorical founding of the Great League and to its legendary founders; and in particular one legend concerning Hiawatha seems to haunt the *Ritual* like a dire prophecy that its purpose of renewing and reconsolidating the League might someday fail. In this story Iroquoian life before the League is depicted as a Hobbesian utter anarchy, nations and individuals pitted against each other senselessly and brutally. Hiawatha's wife and children have been murdered in this chaotic time, and he has gone into the woods to live as a cannibal! One day he spies his reflection in a pond and is struck that the intelligent and humane visage he sees is not that of a cannibalistic savage. In fact, it is the face of Hiawatha's angelic alter ego Dekanawideh, who inspires him to change his own inhuman ways and then set about organizing the Great League. This he does, after heroic difficulties, and the *Condolence Ritual* is the great continuing monument to the vision of unity upon which Hiawatha and the other founders built the League—but the image of its opposite, Hiawatha's earlier life in a brutish state of nature, underlies the grand rhetoric of the *Ritual* as a stern warning of a once and possibly future condition of the Iroquoian people.[11]

I have been examining the *Condolence Ritual* as a ceremony of political succession and reaffirmation, but first of all it is a rite of *condolence,* of physical and emotional healing of grief; its immediate purpose in these terms is to bring mourners back from their obsessive misery of loss into active participation in life. The symbolic focus of the *Ritual* is doubled, in a way that reflects the structure of Iroquoian society. Most of the time the "you" being addressed in concern and sympathy is specifically identifiable as the surviving sachems of the dead man's moiety; but overall it is clear that the mourning moiety, and indeed the whole Iroquoian confederacy, is symbolically conceived of as a mourning widow, upon whose return to active good health and sanity the very welfare of the League depends. This latter figure of a grieving woman expresses, of course, the profoundly matriarchal basis of Iroquoian society—women were the farmers, the property owners, and the selectors (and if need be, the deposers) of the male sachems.[12] In the words of the *Ritual,* Woman

> shall
> have the care of all that is planted by which life
> is sustained and supported, and so the power to

breathe is fortified; and . . . the
warriors shall be her assistants. (*CR*, 159)

In the course of the ceremony, Death—a horrific force identified as "the Great Destroyer"—must once again be driven out of the human community and back into the Upstate wilderness where he will lurk until another fatal occasion (the polar opposition between "forest" and "village" is prominent throughout the *Ritual*). But more important than exorcism per se is the effort to deal with the mourners' possible fixation on death, and therefore their withdrawal from the ongoing collective business of life. This is a common motif in Native American mythology, often appearing at the conclusion of myths giving the origins of death, and also in Orpheus myths, which establish the finality of death. In a Clackamas Chinook Orphic narrative, for example, Coyote tries and fails to bring his dead children back to life and then, having mourned at length and on a grand scale, he comes to his senses and ordains that there shall be a formal limit to mourning of ten days, after which the mourner will return to his or her proper tribal pursuits.[13] The implication here, and in the *Condolence Ritual,* is that the private course of grief must be limited, both for the good of the griever and for the greater good of the community, whose well-being has been doubly diminished, permanently by the death of the victim and at least temporarily by the withdrawing into helpless grief of his loved ones.

As a ritual of healing in these terms, the *Condolence Ritual* is a very shrewd and systematic and psychologically astute course of treatment of the physical and psychosocial condition of deep grief. As several observers have noted, its procedure is authentically *clinical,* as it moves in a style that is both methodical and imaginative, from grief's physical symptoms to its ultimate social and spiritual consequences.[14] According to the basic scenario, the moiety that has not lost a sachem to death comes as the "clearminded" to the stricken moiety and undertakes to condole with its members. The ceremony begins with a roll call of the legendary founders of the League and an invocation of their powers against the League's present state of crisis over the death of one of the founders' successors. Then the clearminded turn to their task of healing, taking up fifteen "Articles" of condolence (sometimes the whole set is called the "Requickening Oration") and in the process moving from overtly physical symptoms of mourning to psychological symptoms and finally to social and political considerations. The treatment thus proceeds from *inside*—that is, concern with the state of individual mourners—to *outside,* concern with the state of the whole League. One thinks of Shakespeare's adaptation of the "Body Politic" trope in plays like Part Two of *Henry IV,* in which the ill health of individuals like King Henry and Falstaff is dramatized both literally and symbolically—representing, that is, the uncertain state of health of the whole realm. But of course Shakespeare is using the trope in the creation of historical drama, whereas the *Condolence Ritual* uses it to express the Iroquoian concept of interconnectedness, which the entire ritual is working to affirm as part of its therapeutic purpose.

In brief, Article One of the Requickening Oration fixes on the eyes of the mourner, blinded with tears, to which the clearminded respond, "'now, we wipe away the tears from thy / face, using the white fawnskin of pity'" (*CR,* 131). In Article Two, the mourner's ears are found to be deaf with grief:

> now thou hearest nothing of
> the sounds made by mankind . . .
>
> .   .   .   .
>
> so we proceed to restore thy
> person by removing the obstacles obstructing
> the passages of thy ears. (*CR,* 133)

And in Three, it is the mourner's throat that must be cleared of the constrictions of grief that have prevented proper breathing and speaking:

> where the
> Great Destroyer has been harshly cruel, . . . the
> throat of the flesh-body becomes sorely
> obstructed, so that then it is plainly to be seen
> that the vitality of the person's life has become
> lessened, also that of the mind of that person. (*CR,* 134) [15]

Article Four concludes this first section of specifically somatic treatment by offering "Water-of-pity" to soothe the mourner's congested heart and other organs (*CR,* 145).

Articles Five through Ten take up the affective symptoms of grief and distress over loss; the orator of the clearminded now addresses himself to the task of healing the *emotions* of the bereaved. Article Five directly acknowledges the bloody husk-mat bed of the late chief and verbally wipes the bloodstains away with "the skin of the spotted fawn, *the words / of pity and comfort*" (*CR*, 148). In Articles Six, Seven, and Eight, the mourner's inability or unwillingness to look around with comprehension (despite the physical cleansing of the eyes in Article One) is noted and ministered to. In Six, the "darkness of grief" is driven away: "'Now therefore, we make it daylight again for / thee'" (*CR*, 149–50); in Seven, it is the mourner's "loss of the sky" that the clearminded attend to—his or her persistence in looking down rather than up: "'Now, then, we beautify / again the sky for you. It shall now continue to / be beautiful'" (*CR*, 151). And, logically enough, in Eight the sun itself, having been lost to the dead chief's widow and comrades, is restored to view, so that "around thy person rays or haloes of / light will abundantly appear" (*CR*, 152).

Concluding this *affective* series, Article Nine directly images the collective mind of the mourners as a heap of clay "on the grave of the / one whom thou didst trust," and firmly separates the living from the dead by smoothing the grave soil and entombing the corpse under a wooden slab. "And so the bones of him on / whom thou didst fondly trust shall rest / peacefully and undisturbed" (*CR*, 154)—with the reflexive implication that the living should now get on with the pleasure and business of life. And Article Ten reminds the mourners that if they are wrathfully contemplating revenge, in the belief that their chief was a victim of murder, the Law of the League prohibits revenge, requiring instead a blood payment of twenty strings of wampum to the survivors.

The final five articles carry the effort of condoling and healing further outward from the individual mourners and their physical and emotional afflictions, to the symbolic mind and body of the whole Iroquoian League. Article Eleven, "The Council Fire," reminds the entire assembly of the sacred importance of the council fire, from the founding of the League to the present moment, and vividly depicts Death as the enemy of the fire and all that it represents, socially and politically:

> that Being of Darkness, lying
> hard by the lodges where it is black night, yea,
> that Being which here at the very tops of our
> heads, goes about menacing with its couched
> weapon—(*CR*, 156)

Death having once again scattered the council fire and distracted those who govern the people around it, the clearminded ritually "gather again the / scattered Firebrands, *thy Chiefs,* and now, indeed, / do we rekindle the Council Fire for thee" (*CR,* 157). This summary action is followed in Twelve by an eloquent hymn of praise to women, reaffirming the primary role of womankind in the Iroquoian matriarchal scheme: "and moreover / . . . the / warriors shall be her assistants" (*CR,* 159). In a telling apocalyptic allusion to the Iroquoian creation myth, in which the First Woman falls from her home in the sky onto "Turtle Island," which becomes our Earth, the orator in Twelve warns his listeners that unless women are respected and sexual harmony prevails, "the time is near in which the feet of thy people / will hang over the abyss of the sundered earth" (*CR,* 160).

In effect, Article Thirteen concludes and summarizes the whole sequence of ritual acts of condolence and healing by confronting, now directly, the possibility that unrestrained grief may lead to insanity: the mourners are bluntly enjoined against such self-indulgence—"'We forbid thee in this / matter'" (*CR,* 161). And then, as the seven-hour-long *Ritual* reaches its political climax, Article Fourteen reaffirms the mutuality of the flame whereby "the Torch of Notification" shall always be lit to initiate any ritual of condolence in the League; and finally, in Article Fifteen, having healed the grief of the dead chief's people, the clearminded ask them to identify his successor. Before that intensely dramatic moment is reached, however, the mourners sing the "Condoling Hymn," a sacred Iroquois anthem already sung to them by the clearminded (after the conclusion of the Roll Call of the Founding Fathers [*CR,* 140–41]), but now *they* sing it, somewhat reworded from its original form so that it appears to be the dead chief who is singing, in gratitude and benediction, and in affirmation of the League's continuation:

> The League has come again to greet me;
> [regular form: "I come again to greet and thank the League"]
> The kindred come again to greet me;
> The warriors come again to greet me;
> The women come again to greet me.
> My forefathers—what they established—
> My forefathers—hearken to them! (*CR,* 165–66)

Then, at last, the new chief is identified and invested with the name and power of his predecessors, and the ceremony concludes with the now-restored mourning moiety calling for a feast, dancing, and indulgence in an entertainment the Iroquois set great store by, the telling of one's dreams (itself not without therapeutic value!).[16]

A passage from Article Eleven, "The Council Fire," clearly illustrates the extraordinary astuteness and power of the *Condolence Ritual,* in uniting in one grand rhetorical design private grief and political anxiety, literal individual condolence and the symbolic affirmation of the "clearmindedness," mutuality, and well-being of the entire League:

> Thou sittest there now with bowed head; thou
> no longer dost meditate on anything whatsoever
> of thy former affairs—wherein thou wast laboring
> for thy niece and for thy nephew, *for the men*
> *and the women of thy people;* yea, for thy
> children, and also for thy grandchildren, who run
> about thy sides, and for these also who are still
> swathed to cradleboards, and also for those
> children who, still unborn, whose faces, still
> underground, are coming toward thee; yea, for
> these warriors and for these women; that is the
> extent, indeed, of the solicitude and vigilant care
> which were in the hands of him, thy uncle—*thy*
> *mother's brother*—who has departed, while he
> labored for their daily welfare, and who at this
> moment is floating away far homeward.
>
> . . . .
>
> Now, again, indeed, we raise thee up to full
> stature, erect among thy people. We also cheer
> up thy mind. More than this, we again set thee
> in order around the place where we have
> rekindled the Fire for thee, my offspring. (*CR,* 157–58)

The Navajos are famous for their extensive repertory of colorful ceremonies and "chants"—*Blessingway, Beautyway, Enemyway, Mountain Chant, Red Ant Way,* and so on, a total, according to one survey, of fifty-eight distinct ceremonials.[17] Of these, the *Night Chant* corresponds most closely in sacred importance to the Iroquois *Condolence Ritual.*[18] As John

Bierhorst has aptly observed, the *Night Chant* "epitomizes the mythos of Navajoism and gives expression to its ideals."[19]

Whereas the *Condolence Ritual* occupies one afternoon and evening, the *Night Chant* covers no less than nine days and nights, always in winter. Its specific therapeutic purpose is to restore to health a single "patient" who is suffering from some disorder connecting the body and the mind: blindness, deafness, dizziness, headaches, paralytic strokes, and so on. What we would call the "psychosomatic" power of the ceremony is assumed by the Navajos to be double-edged—potentially dangerous as well as benefi-cent. The great nineteenth-century Navajo scholar Washington Matthews thought his painstaking transcription and translation of the text of the *Night Chant* his best achievement, but when he developed some of the very neurological ailments that the ceremony is supposed to cure, many Nava-jos concluded that he was paying the price of delving too deeply into their religious affairs, without proper safeguards.[20]

The *Night Chant* lacks the direct political emphasis of its Iroquoian counterpart; its focus is correspondingly more overtly religious and spiri-tual. But still, its ceremonial design, like that of the *Condolence Ritual,* is based on the idea that the welfare of one individual implicates the welfare of everybody, and that, in fact, the Navajo "Body Politic" will benefit if the afflicted body and mind of one of its members are restored to health.

In format, the *Night Chant* is a bona fide "multimedia" production, consisting by turns (and sometimes simultaneously) of recitation; singing, both solo and choral; ritual per se, involving the manipulation of a vari-ety of symbolic properties, notably *kethawns* (prayer-sticks that can be smoked); symbolic drama, in which major Navajo deities are imperson-ated; dancing; sand painting; and even rites of passage for Navajo children.[21] The length and complexity of the ceremony must have made it always very costly to mount, and reports attest to recent performances centering more on the desire of wealthy Navajos for status and consolidation of good for-tune, than on their afflictions.[22]

But in Washington Matthews's superb text, the governing purpose of the *Night Chant* is clearly to heal and revitalize. What it endeavors to make, in a complex liturgy of words, music, images, and ritual actions is nothing less than a symbolic re-creation of the whole Navajo universe, around the patient, with him or her as its focal point. The Navajo concept of order is denoted by a virtually untranslatable word, *hozho,* meaning "balance," "symmetry," "equilibrium of many parts," "ideal order," "beauty." . . . Health is a manifestation of hozho in all these aspects; illness is taken to indicate that, for the patient, things have gotten out of their proper balance, because he or she has in some way acted in excess, or violated a taboo, or fallen victim to witchcraft. Navajo traditional healing, then, from the level of "household remedies" to the grand exercises of the *Night Chant,* aims at restoring balance and harmony, both within the patient and between the patient and the rest of the natural order.[23] At the very outset of the ceremony, the chief Navajo god Hastshéyalti, "Talking God," is reported to be saying to the patient, " 'Your body is holy' " (*NC,* 293). And the *Night Chant's* concluding benediction, "Thus walk in beauty" (*NC,* 332), expresses the hope that the patient has been restored to the holiness of his or her body, and that his or her relationship with the rest of the world is one of hozho, ideal order.

As in the *Condolence Ritual,* the affective appeal of the *Night Chant* is double. It involves invocation of supernatural powers to restore the patient's wellness, and evocation in the patient and in everyone else engaged in the ceremony—actors and well-wishers alike—of feelings of harmony with creation and vital balance. The *rhetoric* of the ceremony, as John Bierhorst was first to point out, is organized around two opposing but complementary ideas of healing: exorcism and blessing—the expulsion from the patient of evil things, or things that are bad in excess, and the summoning of good, health-producing things.[24] In the typical formula of Matthews's text, a particular Navajo deity may be asked to "take away" some spell afflicting the patient and also be implored to "restore" some element of the patient's proper health. To illustrate, here is the initial appearance of this formula, in a prayer to Owl on the First Day:

> My feet restore for me.
> My legs restore for me.
> My body restore for me.
> My mind restore for me.
> My voice restore for me.
> Today take out your spell for me.
> Today your spell for me is removed. (*NC,* 294–95)

Bierhorst's careful analysis of the exorcism/blessing scheme reveals that "the tension created by the two opposing ideas operates at every level and may be looked upon as the ceremony's organizing principle."[25] Individual passages may be chiefly expulsive or attractive, but—as in the example just given—rarely is the *Night Chant's* rhetoric one thing or the other for long without crossing over to its complementary opposite, as if to maintain a proper rhetorical balance for healing. Indeed, in Bierhorst's analysis, the structure of the entire ceremony appears to be organized according to this principle into three units: Part One, Days 1–4, "Purification," predominantly exorcistic; Part Two, Days 5–8, "Healing," predominantly concerned with attraction of good powers and restoration; and Part Three, Day 9, "Reprise," in which, Bierhorst suggests, the accumulated tension between negative and positive, driving out and calling in, exorcism and blessing, discharges (one thinks of ionized rainclouds!) climactically into a night of singing (hence the title, *Night Chant*), in which the necessary opposites of the ceremony are ecstatically resolved and joined in the patient's recovery of health.[26]

The ritual nonverbal action of the *Night Chant* leading up to this grand finale also reflects, moment by moment, the ceremony's dual program of casting out evil/attracting good. At the beginning of the Day 4, for example, the actor impersonating the god Hastshéyalti plants a green sapling in the floor of the lodge and then, bending its tip toward the patient, ties it to a mask affixed to the patient's face. When Hastshéyalti releases the bent sapling, it jerks the mask away, drawing harmful powers away from the patient as it goes (*NC,* 310). On the other hand (as in the scene following this one), the *Night Chant's* rituals extensively use *pollen* as both the most sacred of foods and the most potent of medicines. Like other Indian groups, the Navajos identify pollen with the sun and with the primal forces of life: often in the *Night Chant* it is given to the patient, the ceremonialists, and the audience to eat, as a kind of collective sacrament; elsewhere it is sprinkled on the patient and on ritual paraphernalia as a potent charm.

The most spectacular positive events in the *Night Chant* are the performances of three sand paintings on the evenings of the fifth, sixth, and seventh days.[27] In each performance, after the chanter and his assistants have re-created the required traditional design depicting Navajo gods literally grain by grain, it is destroyed so that the sand, now potent with the power of the completed picture, can be applied as medicine to the patient.

Eyewitnesses of these sand-painting sessions have reported the palpable intensity that builds up in the lodge as the sacred images are made to appear, over several hours, on the hogan floor—and even a cursory reading of the *Night Chant* text will suggest how in language and action the entire ceremony builds in power and tension throughout until the release of the final night and dawn. Line by line, moment by moment, the pluses and minuses of the patient's cure must be balanced out, kept in a dynamic equilibrium; the traditional words and melodies must be spoken and sung "just so"—the whole incredibly elaborate effort to regain the proper balance of life for the patient and to restore his or her place in the cosmos must proceed word by careful word, grain by anxious grain, with no lapses on any level, with dangers increasing as the whole ceremonial edifice rises around the patient, until at last he or she can receive its full curative effect.

Such an imaginatively charged setting recalls Leslie Silko's idea, referred to earlier, of a cure that could be "found only in something great and inclusive of everything"—and it also invites comparison with the accustomed setting and focus of Anglo medical care. The *Night Chant* endeavors, as we have seen, to restore its patients to the full spectrum of harmonized relationships that constitute well-being to the Navajos—with their bodies, with the human community, with the natural and divine order. And the ceremony's therapeutic purpose is couched in powerful language—in words both invocative of beneficial powers and evocative of feelings of assurance in the patients and their well-wishers. One is struck forcibly by how different it is with doctors and patients in our own culture! When in standard medical practice today is a physician likely to emphasize to a patient the idea that one or several communities have a stake in his or her recovery? And where—either in medical education or in practice—is the affective power of language likely to be brought into play?

In his *Anatomy of an Illness* and more recently in *The Healing Heart*, Norman Cousins has emphasized both the beneficial and the deleterious effects of the words doctors offer their patients; in the latter book, in particular, he calls for professional recognition of the crucial place of language in the art of medicine:

In health care, the words used by the physician have a profound effect on the well-being of the patient.

Words, when used by the doctor, can be gate-openers or gate-slammers. . . . The right words can potentiate a patient, mobilize the will to live, and provide a congenial environment for heroic response. The wrong words can produce despair and defeat or hinder the usefulness of whatever treatment is prescribed.[28]

It is hard to think of a verbal passage from any culture that illustrates what Cousins calls "the right words" for the purposes of healing better than the *Night Chant.* Not that anyone seriously wants physicians nowadays to take on official shamanistic obligations, but knowing something about how poetic language has served the cause of health amongst the Navajos, or for that matter the Iroquois, might in Cousins's terms be useful knowledge for today's practitioners.

Here, perhaps, we should look from the *Night Chant* back to the *Condolence Ritual,* in order to take some measure of their similarities and differences as liturgies of healing. Again, a primary difference—albeit one of degree not kind—is the overt political emphasis in the *Ritual,* its concern with the health of the Iroquoian people as constituting a political entity. The *Night Chant* is certainly concerned with the well-being of the whole human community, as symbolized by the individual patient—but whereas in the Iroquoian rite the complex "you" addressed as mourning "patient" is clearly being identified and ministered to in political terms, as widow-of-sachem, fellow sachem, member-of-moiety, and so on, in the *Night Chant* the patient (male or female) is simply addressed as one individual, and presumably representative, Navajo.

This fundamental difference—which reflects the differences in political systems between the highly politicized Iroquois and the individualistic and decentralized Navajos—is interestingly borne out in the relationship of each work to tribal mythology. In the *Condolence Ritual,* as we have already seen, Iroquoian mythology is hardly implicated at all (despite the fact that the nations of the League held their myths largely in common); in place of creation and origin myths per se, the *Ritual* appears to derive its imaginative charter from the semihistorical legends of the League's political creation.

In the *Night Chant,* on the other hand, Navajo mythology, especially the stories of the "Fourth World" (the stage of creation from which the people emerged into this world) underlies and authorizes the ceremony at every point, and accounts, etiologically, for the Navajos' auspicious claim on the supernatural order through the *Chant*. Katherine Spencer has identified the two main *Night Chant* narratives as the stories of "The Visionary" and "The Stricken Twins."[29] Briefly, in both narratives the protagonists, mediators between the human and supernatural communities, suffer social rejection and physical affliction in their dogged pursuit of divine knowledge and recognition. At length, after many tribulations, the Visionary and the Twins are accepted by the supernaturals and cured of their ailments, whereupon they return home to the human realm and teach the people how to perform the *Night Chant*. In the case of "the Visionary," the hero actually suffers in the course of his mission from a series of complaints— paralysis, fainting spells, and so on—which constitute precisely the diseases for which the *Night Chant* will become the appropriate treatment. The Visionary's tutor throughout, and eventually the chief ceremonialist of his cure, is Hastshéyalti, Talking God, who as we have seen, presides over the *Night Chant* as the latter-day Navajos enact it.

Hastshéyalti is also the benevolent sponsor of the Stricken Twins in *their* mission; having been abandoned by their family, they are seeking a cure for their blindness and deafness. Their acceptance by the gods and the actual course of their healing treatment are interrupted repeatedly by blunders and all-too-human lapses on their part. These establish the *Night Chant*'s main taboos—against talking during the ceremony, for example—and its main practical requirements, such as the fee that must be paid to the ceremonialists.

Another notable difference between these two liturgical masterpieces is in the conception of space and territory each embodies. Again, the Iroquoian political-historical perspective expresses itself in the longhouse setup of the participating groups, which mirrors exactly the actual geopolitical location of the nations relative to one another—the Mohawks to the east ("keepers of the eastern door"), the Senecas to the west ("keepers of the western door"), the Onondagas in between ("the firekeepers"); and for the junior moiety, south of their elders in the longhouse as in reality, the Cayugas to the west, the Oneidas to the east.[30] And when at the beginning a roll call of ancient Iroquoian villages is added to the roll call of the League's founders, the names of the villages are given according to their affiliations with three ancient political groups of clans: Wolf, Tortoise, and Bear (*CR*, 128–29).

In contrast, space in the *Night Chant* is marked out very methodically according to spiritual coordinates; what is paramount in the ceremony's persistent reference to directions and locations is an effort to get the patient "centered" in his or her life again, and indeed centered symbolically in the whole order of creation. The Navajo compass is "boxed" on the patient's behalf in every conceivable way: the first four days of the ceremony are oriented, respectively, to the East, South, West, and North; the four sacred Navajo mountains are invoked around the patient—Tsisnadzhini (east), Tsotsil (south), Dokoslid (west), and Depentas (north); sacred "central" locations like the "White House" ruins of the Anasazi in Canyon de Chelly are frequently named, as if to further position the patient in the center of the world. On the most fundamental level of verbal structure the following formula appears in virtually every episode in one variation or another:

> May it be happy *before* me.
> May it be happy *behind* me.
> May it be happy *below* me.
> May it be happy *above* me.
> With it happy *all around* me, may I walk.
> (*NC*, 295; italics mine)

Finally, there is the question of the patient's own role in each ceremony. In the *Condolence Ritual*, as befits its political approach to the task of healing grief, the success of the clearmindeds' efforts is not signaled until, following the Articles of Requickening, the mourning moiety sings the Iroquoian "Great Hymn" as if they were the dead sachem bidding his colleagues hail and farewell. Then the mourners dramatize their recovery and that of the whole League by installing the dead sachem's successor and welcoming all present to a feast and a dance.

In the *Night Chant*, the patient's role, passive at first, grows more and more active as the ceremony's days and nights pass, dramatically affirming his or her recovery. At the end of the eighth day, for example, it is the patient who presents *kethawns* to the impersonated gods who are in attendance, rather than vice versa, as has been the case before now (*NC*, 324).

In the central prayer of the ninth day, a beautifully elaborated restatement of the whole verbal structure of the *Night Chant,* the patient recites the prayer's more than three hundred lines after the chanter, three times. No mean feat of performance, one would think! When this strenuous recitation is concluded, the chanter explicitly affirms the patient's restoration by speaking for Hastshéyalti just as he did at the beginning: "'Your body is strong, / Your body is holy now,' he says" (*NC,* 330).

And then, at the end of the tumultuous free-form singing-until-dawn of songs from within the ceremonial lodge alternating with songs from well-wishers outside that concludes the entire ceremony, comes the simple, eloquently affirmative action toward which the whole nine days of tense activity have been building. In Bierhorst's stage direction: *"The patient, facing east, inhales the breath of dawn"* (*NC,* 332).[31]

Just before this wonderful moment, as noted above, the patient has shown him- or herself sufficiently recovered to recite with the chanter a summary prayer that is, surely, the poetic climax of the *Night Chant.* It is also one of the great landmarks of Native American traditional literary art. Like the whole ceremony (and, for that matter, like the *Condolence Ritual*), this concluding prayer moves through language with the incremental majesty and inexorable pace of a natural process—like the coming-on of a rainstorm or the ripening of a field of corn. Nothing pertaining to the human and natural well-being of the patient, it seems, can be left out, as the Navajo cosmos is verbally re-created one more time with the patient as its focal point; the patient's solidarity with the weather, with the growth of plants, and with the human generations now and in the past and future is confidently asserted.

If healing is not just a *topic* of literature, but potentially, as Norman Cousins and others have been suggesting, a human good that the varieties of literary art can actually promote, then surely this final prayer of the *Night Chant* and the Articles of Requickening in the *Condolence Ritual* embody such a beneficent poetic power—even in translation, even out of cultural context, as read in a study rather than heard and seen in an Iroquoian longhouse or a Navajo medicine lodge. I have been able here to deal with each work only fragmentarily; each deserves at the least a full continuous reading, aloud and in good company if possible. For all their ethnological and rhetorical differences, both represent the American Indians' great collective achievement in coming to a sacred understanding of their lives; and both testify equally to the Indian conviction that poetic language—words used just so—was, and is, crucial to that great understanding, including the recovery and preservation of good health. How much, then, do we lose in modern society by largely ignoring the powers of our own language to heal, to restore, to speak to and for the body in its afflictions?

> Happily I recover.
> Happily my interior becomes cool.
> Happily my eyes regain their power.
> Happily my head becomes cool.
> Happily my limbs regain their power.
> Happily I hear again.
> Happily for me the *spell* is taken off.
> Happily may I walk.
> Impervious to pain, may I walk.
> Feeling light within, may I walk.
> With lively feelings, may I walk.
> Happily abundant dark clouds I desire.
> Happily abundant dark mists I desire.
> Happily abundant passing showers I desire.
> Happily an abundance of vegetation I desire.
> Happily an abundance of pollen I desire.
> Happily abundant dew I desire.
> Happily may fair white corn, to the ends of the earth, come with you.
> Happily may fair yellow corn, to the ends of the earth, come with you.
>
> .   .   .   .
>
> Thus happily you accomplish your tasks.
> Happily the old men will regard you.
> Happily the old women will regard you.
> Happily the young men will regard you.
> Happily the young women will regard you.
> Happily the boys will regard you.
> Happily the girls will regard you.
> Happily the children will regard you.
> Happily the chiefs will regard you.
> Happily, as they scatter in different directions, they will regard you.
> Happily, as they approach their homes, they will regard you.
> Happily may their roads home be on the trail of pollen.
> Happily may they all get back.

In beauty I walk.
With beauty before me, I walk.
With beauty behind me, I walk.
With beauty below me, I walk.
With beauty above me, I walk.
With beauty all around me, I walk.
It is finished in beauty,
It is finished in beauty,
It is finished in beauty,
It is finished in beauty. (*NC,* 328–30)

PART TWO

4 / From Mythic to Fictive
in a Nez Perce Orpheus Myth

THE ORPHIC STORY, OF A HERO'S UNSUCCESSFUL
quest to bring back a loved one from the Land of the Dead, is apparently
universal among American Indian tribes.[1] In its permutations, the story
has a powerful intrinsic appeal that transcends cultural barriers, speaking
to us all as mortal humans; and when looked at as oral literature, many of
the Indian Orpheus stories reveal, even at the double remove of transcription into print and translation, a striking degree of narrative artistry, as if
their anonymous creators were conscious of rising to the occasion of a
great theme.

Of such myths, surely one of the most compelling is the Nez Perce
"Coyote and the Shadow People," recorded and translated by Archie Phinney in Lapwai, Idaho, in 1929. Now, Phinney's texts are of special value
in the study of traditional Western Indian literature because they were collected and edited under nearly perfect conditions. Phinney was a Nez Perce
himself, educated at Columbia University and trained in ethnography and
linguistics by Franz Boas; and when he returned to the Lapwai Reservation,
he took as his sole informant his own mother, Wayilatpu, a gifted story-

teller who spoke no English and whose knowledge of her repertory, Phinney tells us, extended back three generations and therefore "beyond the time when the influences of new intertribal contacts and of wholesale myth-trading at non-reservation Indian schools became apparent in Nez Perce mythology."[2]

In terms of classical Boasian scholarship, then, it would be hard to improve upon Phinney's circumstances—they are probably unique among Far Western Indians—and it is clear from his textual work that he brought to it an unusual combination of editorial rigor and literary sensitivity. His translations aim at the more-than-literal re-creation in English of stylistic features in the original narratives; there is a kind of elegance to them, which, to be sure, now and then does strike a somewhat stilted Latinate note, but which, overall, seems appropriate to stories as rich as these. One of Phinney's great virtues, I think, is his constant awareness of what can be lost in transforming the drama of oral narrative into print-lines on a page. He complained in a letter to Boas of the "loss of spirit"—the fascination furnished by the peculiar Indian vocal tradition for humor—in the recording of these animal stories. Indians were better storytellers than whites, he observed, adding that when he read his story mechanically, he found "only the cold corpse."[3]

Beyond question Phinney's complaint was and is well founded—for us to read a Nez Perce narrative now involves, inescapably, a loss of dramatic power in transcription from performance to text, loss of denotative and evocative power through translation, and loss of imaginative context through the isolating of one story from the whole Native repertory, or "mythbody" as Phinney calls it.[4] Yet, surely much expressive vitality and meaning remain if we are careful in our reading. Let's turn to the story, with Phinney's remarks as a challenge not a deterrent.

Coyote and the Shadow People

Coyote and his wife were dwelling there. His wife became ill. She died.
Then Coyote became very, very lonely. He did nothing but weep for his wife.

There the death spirit came to him and said, "Coyote, do you pine for your wife?"—"Yes, friend, I long for her . . ." replied Coyote. "I could take you to the place where your wife has gone, but, I tell you, you must do everything just exactly as I say; not once are you to disregard my commands and do something else."—"Yes," replied Coyote, "yes, friend, and what else could I do? I will do everything you say." Then the ghost told him, "Yes. Now let us go." Coyote added, "Yes, let it be so that we are going."

They went. There he said to Coyote again, "You must do whatever I say. Do not disobey."—"Yes, yes, friend. I have been pining so deeply, and why should I not heed you?" Coyote could not see the spirit clearly. He appeared to be only a shadow. They started and went along over a plain. "Oh, there are many horses; it looks like a round-up," exclaimed the ghost. "Yes," replied Coyote, though he really saw none, "yes, there are many horses."

They had arrived now near the place of the dead. The ghost knew that Coyote could see nothing but he said, "Oh look, such quantities of service berries! Let us pick some to eat. Now when you see me reach up you too will reach up and when I bend the limb down you too will pull your hands down."— "Yes," Coyote said to him, "so be it, thus I will do." The ghost reached up and bent the branch down and Coyote did the same. Although he could see no berries he imitated the ghost in putting his hand to and from his mouth in the manner of eating. Thus they picked and ate berries. Coyote watched him carefully and imitated every action. When the ghost would put his hand into his mouth Coyote would do the same. "Such good service berries these are," commented the ghost. "Yes, friend, it is good that we have found them," agreed Coyote. "Now let us go." And they went on.

"We are about to arrive," the ghost told him. "There is a long, very, very long lodge. Your wife is in there somewhere. Just wait and let me ask someone." In a little while the ghost returned and said to Coyote, "Yes, they have told me where your wife is. We are coming to a door through which we will enter. You will do in every way exactly what you see me do. I will take hold of the door flap, raise it up, and bending low, will enter. Then you too will take hold of the door flap and do the same." They proceeded now in this manner to enter.

It happened that Coyote's wife was sitting right near the entrance. The ghost said to Coyote, "Sit here beside your wife." They both sat. The ghost added, "Your wife is now going to prepare food for us." Coyote could see nothing, except that he was sitting there on an open prairie where nothing was in sight; yet he could feel the presence of the shadow. "Now she has prepared our food. Let us eat." The ghost reached down and then brought his hand to his mouth. Coyote could see nothing but the prairie dust. They ate. Coyote imitated all the movements of his companion. When they had finished and the woman had apparently put the food away, the ghost said to Coyote, "You stay here. I must go around to see some people."

He went out but returned soon. "Here we have conditions different from those you have in the land of the living. When it gets dark here it has dawned in your land and when it dawns for us it is growing dark for you." And now it began to grow dark and Coyote seemed to hear people whispering, talking in faint tones, all around him. Then darkness set in. Oh, Coyote saw many fires in a longhouse. He saw that he was in a very, very large lodge and there were many fires burning. He saw the various people. They seemed to have shadowlike forms but he was able to recognize different persons. He saw his wife sitting by his side.

He was overjoyed, and he joyfully greeted all his old friends who had died long ago. How happy he was! He would march down the aisles between the fires, going here and there, and talk with the people. He did this throughout the night. Now he could see the doorway through which he and his friend had entered. At last it began to dawn and his friend came to him and said, "Coyote, our night is falling and in a little while you will not see us. But you must stay right here. Do not go anywhere at all. Stay right here and then in the evening you will see all these people again." "Yes, friend. Where could I possibly go? I will spend the day here."

The dawn came and Coyote found himself alone sitting there in the middle of the prairie. He spent the day there, just dying from the heat, parching from the heat, thirsting from the heat. Coyote stayed here several days. He would suffer through the day, but always at night he would make merry in the great lodge.

One day his ghost friend came to him and said, "Tomorrow you will go home. You will take your wife with you."—"Yes, friend, but I like it here so much, I am having a good time and I should like to remain here." "Yes," the ghost replied, "nevertheless you will go tomorrow, and you must guard against your inclination to do foolish things. Do not yield to any queer notions. I will advise you now what you are to do. There are five mountains. You will travel for five days. Your wife will be with you but you must never, never touch her. Do not let any strange impulses possess you. You may talk to her but never touch her. Only after you have crossed and descended from the fifth mountain you may do whatever you like."—"Yes, friend," replied Coyote.

When dawn came again, Coyote and his wife started. At first it seemed to him as if he were going alone, yet he was dimly aware of his wife's presence as she walked along behind. They crossed one mountain, and, now, Coyote could feel more definitely the presence of his wife; like a shadow she seemed. They went on and crossed the second mountain. They camped at night at the foot of each mountain. They had a little conical lodge which they would set up each time. Coyote's wife would sit on one side of the fire and he on the other. Her form appeared clearer and clearer.

The death spirit, who had sent them, now began to count the days and to figure the distance Coyote and his wife had covered. "I hope that he will do everything right and take his wife through to the world beyond," he kept saying to himself.

Here Coyote and his wife were spending their last night, their fourth camping, and on the morrow she would again assume fully the character of a living person. They were camping for the last time and Coyote could see her very clearly as if she were a real person who sat opposite him. He could see her face and body very clearly, but only looked and dared not touch her.

But suddenly a joyous impulse seized him; the joy of having his wife again overwhelmed him. He jumped to his feet, and rushed over to embrace her. His wife cried out, "Stop! Stop! Coyote! Do not touch me. Stop!" Her warning had no effect. Coyote rushed over to his wife and just as he touched her body she vanished. She disappeared—returned to the shadow-land.

When the death-spirit learned of Coyote's folly he became deeply angry. "You inveterate doer of this kind of thing! I told you not to do anything foolish. You, Coyote, were about to establish the practice of returning from death. Only a short time away the human race is coming, but you have spoiled everything and established for them death as it is."

Here Coyote wept and wept. He decided, "Tomorrow I shall return to see them again." He started back the following morning and as he went along he began to recognize the places where he and his spirit friend had passed before. He found the place where the ghost had seen the herd of horses, and now he began to do the same things they had done on their way to the shadow-land. "Oh, look at the horses; it looks like a round-up." He went on until he came to the place where the ghost had found the service berries. "Oh, such choice service berries! Let us pick and eat some." He went through the motions of picking and eating berries.

He went on and finally came to the place where the lodge had stood. He said to himself, "Now when I take hold of the door flap and raise it up you must do the same." Coyote remembered all the little things his friend had done. He saw the spot where he had sat before. He went there, sat down, and said, "Now, your wife has brought us food. Let us eat." He went through the motions of eating again. Darkness fell, and now Coyote listened for the voices, and he looked all around. He looked here and there, but nothing appeared. Coyote sat there in the middle of the prairie. He sat there all night but the lodge didn't appear again nor did the ghost ever return to him.[5]

More than most of the other narratives in *Nez Perce Texts*, "Coyote and the Shadow People" is intelligible without extensive ethnographic commentary, but it is helpful to know that the hero, Coyote, *itsayáya,* is usually a wily but reckless, self-seeking trickster and adventurer in Nez Perce myths, much given to opportunistic deceptions (often for sex) that usually backfire outrageously. His classical mythic name in this role as *the* (or *that*) Coyote, according to Phinney, is *nasáwaylu.*[6] But like the Trickster in other Western Indian mythologies, Coyote is also the Nez Perce "transformer," the Myth Age personage who "travels about" transforming the unfinished world and its inhabitants and setting precedents (for better and for worse) that create reality as the latter-day Indians knew it. So, in this Orphic story, the awesome mythic powers and options in Coyote's complex role are emphasized, and to some extent he is made to seem capable of heroically living up to this role and behaving along exemplary human lines of conduct, as in his love and sustained grief for his wife and his persistence in seeking her. Such a humanized portrayal of Coyote or any trickster is rare in Native literature: but even as he invests his protagonist with a measure of dignity and fellow-feeling, the narrator clearly reminds us of Coyote's reputation as a trickster, *nasáwaylu,* in the spirit guide's repeated warnings against doing "foolish things" and of course in his denunciation of Coyote near the end.

The mysterious "lodge of shadows" where Coyote finds his wife presumably had its real-life counterpart in the long pole-and-mat structures of the Nez Perces, pitched like tipis side by side with a continuous ridgepole; such a lodge, over one hundred feet long, was erected to house the death feast of the great Nez Perce leader Joseph at Nespelem, Washington, in 1904.[7] Conceptually, the lodge reflects a widespread Western Indian view of the afterlife as a remote condition of the spirit in which the basic circumstances of early life are inverted: the night of the living is the daytime of the dead and vice versa, what is tangible to them is intangible to us (and the reverse), and so on. A morally neutral location—there is no alternative destination for the sinful—the Indian spirit-place seems to be at best a kind of eschatological afterthought, a "lodge of shadows" indeed where the surviving spirits exist not unpleasantly but without the raw immediacy and sweetness of mortal life. Early missionaries among the Nez Perces and other Great Plateau tribes were baffled by this conception of the essential goodness of earthly life set off by contrast with images of a shadowy, static afterlife; one of them, the Catholic Father Blanchet, complained that his Native subjects "were surprised and provoked when I explained to them the blessedness of heaven; they appeared to like better the sojourn on this earth than to go away to enjoy celestial bliss."[8]

The narrative and dramatic strategies of "Coyote and the Shadow People" are conventional in Native terms, and typical of Western Indian literature; and yet they seem, as they combine in this story, to achieve an imaginative power that is remarkable. In common with most Orphic stories, Indian and otherwise, the structure is highly symmetrical, details from before Coyote's arrival at the lodge corresponding to those coming afterward—a Journey In and a Journey Out. Thus, the death of his wife, his mourning, and the initial appearance of the spirit guide are balanced by the final loss of his wife, his second mourning, and the final appearance of the spirit guide; his initial ritualized journey to the "lodge of shadows" is paralleled by the ritual stages of his journey back with his wife. In this symmetrical structure, only two main events are singular, set off by themselves—his joyful reunion with his dead wife and his solitary second journey to the lodge—and the special significance of their being isolated as single actions we will see in a moment.

Of all the narrative strategies employed in Indian myth, foreshadowing appears most frequently, and with the widest latitude of effects. This has everything to do, of course, with the fact that the stories were well known in outline to tribal audiences; with the outcome of a given story foreknown, the recitalist had a built-in condition of dramatic irony to exploit.[9] In the case of a story like "Coyote and the Shadow People," the ironic foreshadowing carries over beyond what only a Nez Perce listener would have recognized: we *all* know, after all, with varying degrees of conviction, that death is irrevocable, and final. Thus in a sense everything Coyote does in his quest foreshadows his failure, both for himself and his wife and for the great precedent of returning from death that he (as the death spirit's unknowing instrument) might establish. And yet, true to its genre (and to human nature), the story does set our unresigned human imaginations against our mortal knowledge of death's finality. We consign to Coyote our Orphic dreams.

Specific prefigurements occur at every turn. There is the spirit guide's initial stern demand that Coyote—of all people, the Nez Perce Trickster!—must follow his instructions exactly, unquestioningly. The strange ritual en route involving invisible horses, a tent flap, and a meal are clearly tests of Coyote's imagination and will; he is rewarded for his unaccustomed self-control by seeing his wife and dead associates, but in the daytime, ominously, he loses all sight of them and must "suffer through the day," "sitting there in the middle of a prairie"—the latter phrase almost a verbatim anticipation of the story's final narrative line. His complacent wish to prolong the idyll in the lodge instead of returning home with his wife evidently contradicts the purposes of the spirit guide, both for Coyote and his wife and for the human race to come. And it, too, foreshadows the end, as does the spirit guide's unexplained injunction against touching his wife on the return trip: like all such taboos, it implies its own eventual tragic violation.

As for their journey back, the landscape through which Coyote and his wife travel is ritualized and programmatic, the five mountains serving as checkpoints for Coyote's tense progress: the brief appearance of the spirit guide at this point in the story, worrying about his protégé, notably heightens the tension. (Such intrusions are in fact uncommon in Western Indian narratives.) The fact that Coyote's wife grows day by day more tangible and real to him, of course, dramatizes the progressive heroic success of his quest to him—at the same time that it brings him, all too human, closer and closer to the forbidden but irresistible embrace, in a kind of vectoring of encouragement and temptation.

The climax, by the time it comes, is wholly foreshadowed; as usual, according to the *dramatic* premises of Indian narrative, its enactment is stark, tacit, "dramatic." We must imagine for ourselves the emotional reality evoked so economically by Coyote's impulsive gesture and his wife's cry—her one speech in the story.[10] That Coyote's loss of his wife, and indeed his unknowing forfeiture of the Orphic dream, should hinge on his inability to resist *touching* her rather than looking back at her, as in the Greek prototypes and many Indian versions, seems to me to be beautifully calculated to express the tragic paradox in Coyote's situation. He has been seeing his dead wife for some time, but now that she appears to be fully tangible, seeing is not enough. To return to life again is to touch and be touched, ultimately in a sexual sense; Coyote would not "foolishly" violate the taboo and lose her if he did not love and desire her so much. To put the paradox another way, in terms of literary effect: if he could "take the long view" and restrain himself, the reality of his feelings for his wife would surely be suspect. The story asks its unblinking mythic question of us, Coyote's mortal inheritors: Would we be able to do otherwise? Well, at the level on which the story speaks to us as good citizens, obeyers of laws and keepers of taboos, I suppose we do answer, "Oh yes, we'd better do otherwise!" But to answer, on the heart's own level, "No, probably not," as I think we must, is to feel the peculiar mood of this myth—chastened, instructed, consoled. People die, we are reminded, and we cannot bring them back because they—and we—are in the nature of things imperfect, shortsighted, alive chiefly in the present moment; that is to say, we are mortal. The "truth" of all mythology is, finally, tautological.

Before taking up the story's final episode, I want to digress briefly on some parallels to this moment of climax and reversal in other Native Orpheus stories from the Oregon Country, so as to at least point toward the imaginative diversity and psychological subtlety inherent in this kind of narrative. In the Wasco and Wishram Chinookan versions, as told along the Columbia River, Coyote and Eagle (a wise headman) both lose their wives; and after Eagle leads them on a highly complicated raid on the Lodge of Spirits and they are headed home again with a box containing the spirits of their wives and everyone else who has died, as well as samples of deciduous plants, Coyote begins to hear his wife's voice from within the box. Unable to wait until they reach home—there is no taboo as such— Coyote tricks Eagle into letting him carry the box and seizes the first opportunity to unfasten the lid—whereupon all the spirits, including his wife, fly off in a great swarm, leaving only the plant samples in the box. Eagle denounces Coyote for his impatience, explaining that if they had gotten the box home intact, all people, as well as the trees and grasses, would die only for a season, and then return to life.[11]

In Melville Jacobs's great collection of Clackamas Chinook stories, there is an Orphic variant titled "Badger and Coyote Were Neighbors."[12] When Coyote's five children are killed trying to steal a wonderful ball from another village (as their ambitious and greedy father has urged them to do), Coyote first attempts suicide by fire, water, and knife, and then, in the following spring, undertakes to collect his children's bones and carry them home in such a magical way that they will be reanimated. Day by day he carries them homeward in his basket, very, very carefully, so slowly and deliberately does he move that on the fourth night he can look back and see his previous night's campfire. By now he can hear his children talking to one another. On the fifth and final day, however, an insect of some sort, "maybe a centipede," appears in Coyote's path and taunts him by sniffing the air and declaring that "Coyote is carrying dead persons along!" At first

Coyote controls himself but at last loses his temper and chases after the insect—with the result that his nearly revived children are jostled and they die again, and with them all hope of bringing loved ones back, "just so," from death. It is left for Coyote, sadder and wiser, to invent the customs of mourning, whereby a mourner's grief will be limited in deference to the welfare of the tribe.

A few comparisons. In all three stories, Coyote takes his fatal hasty step in ignorance of the great human precedent he is throwing away: given his chronic self-centeredness and preoccupation with the moment, perhaps the point is being made that such grave knowledge would be irrelevant to him anyway, as a guide to action. He is inconstant and fallible: like us. The Wishram and Clackamas stories seem to have a wider etiological scope than the Nez Perce in that they couple the lost human precedent of returning from death with the achieved precedent of seasonal revivals among plants, as in the Persephone myth; the Nez Perce Coyote is denied even that Wordsworthian consolation. As for the moment of truth itself: you can take your pick from among three wonderfully vivid dramatizations, each having its own fix on human frailty and desire—the Wishram Coyote singling his wife's voice out of all the buzzing in the spirit-box, "like a great swarm of flies"; or the marvelous psychological projection of the Clackamas Coyote's internal doubts and impatience on a mocking insect in his path; or, again, the stark detail of the Nez Perce Coyote's seeing his wife's living body again, across the fire. Do we really want to call this kind of art "primitive"?

Now to carry on with the structure of the Nez Perce story. Before, we noticed that two of its events are structurally singular and unbalanced—Coyote's reunion with his wife and his second quest for her by himself. The reunion stands alone, of course, because the return to life and home it is to be an initial stage of, is doomed. As for Coyote's second quest, begun after the final meaning of his Orphic failure has been emphatically spelled out to him, it is virtually unique in North American Native literature. [13] In this surprising final episode, the narrative seems to move beyond the modus and logic of myth per se, assuming a status more like that of fiction—as if Coyote has now entered our kind of reality.

At the end of many Indian Orpheus stories, the failed quester wants to go back after his lost loved one, but will not or cannot oppose the precedent he has just established. In Phinney's other Orpheus story, for example, after Coyote has "looked back" and thus lost his chance to carry his daughter all the way back from death, he pleads, "Let me follow you back and I will bring you again"; but the offer is refused and after a little weeping, he wanders off.[14] But here, on some level of consciousness at least, Coyote actually does set out again, as if moving beyond the finalized terms of his own myth, as explained to him by the spirit guide. Now "playing" both himself and the spirit guide, he carefully and self-consciously repeats the actions which structured his initial successful trip to the lodge—he "sees horses," "picks and eats service berries," "lifts the tent-flap," "eats his unseen wife's cooking." But whereas the initial trip reaches its happy outcome with its *fifth* episode, "meets wife' [*five* being, again, the Nez Perce cult-number), the sequence of this second trip terminates in effect after only four events, or rather the structural parallel of the second sequence with the first breaks down with the narration of a fifth event that is mundane rather than magical, and anticlimactic rather than climactic: just Coyote sitting there, alone.

Now it is possible that Coyote's second quest would have struck Nez Perce listeners as a kind of ironic analogue to the solitary and highly ritualized visionary quests on which all Native religions in the Far West were founded—Coyote, having had genuine commerce with the spirit world and having violated its terms, can now only go through the motions, as if in a dream. Indeed, it may be that behind many of the weird journeys and heroic ordeals in Nez Perce and other Western repertories, there stands, ultimately, the cultural archetype of the spirit quest.[15]

But this is extracurricular speculation, and I think a more helpful literary parallel to the episode of Coyote's attempted return can be found in myths, from a variety of tribes, which dramatize the origin of death itself. Typically, a Myth Age person decrees that, according to some abstract philanthropical principle—the danger of overcrowding and famine, for example—people will have to die. Then the decreer in fact suffers the first mortal loss (often it is a child who dies) and, humanlike, pleads unavailingly with the creator for a repeal or postponement of the new law. In the Blackfeet "Old Man" cycle, for instance (as we saw in essay 1), First Woman opts for universal human mortality for a compelling but highly abstract reason: "so people will be sorry for one another."[16] But when her son dies soon afterward, she rejects this wisdom and begs "Old Man," unsuccessfully, to change the Way. Like Coyote in his second return, First Woman appears to move beyond her mythic situation per se into the common tragic experience of mortality; she and Coyote both actively "suffer," as if in a fictive work, their own myths, as we do in real life who follow them.[17]

Where before Coyote is, as we say, "all too human" in wanting to touch his wife so ardently in a moment that he loses her forever, so here, in this post-Orphic sequel, he is shown to be poignantly, definitively human in his confidence that his own unaided imagination and desire, supplemented by a little ceremonial knowledge, will suffice to carry him back to the lodge of the shadow people and his wife, despite the mythic precedent he has just set. His actions in retracing his steps and playing both himself and the spirit guide "just so" are at once heroic and ridiculous; here he becomes most fully integrated as himself, Coyote *itsayáya* and *nasáwaylu*. The end of his quest, with Coyote sitting alone "there in the middle of the prairie," has an affective resonance and finality beyond any other Orpheus story I know.

Wayilatpu's Nez Perce narrative gives us Coyote as an image of human loss, mythically speaking the first in a long, unbroken line of unresigned mourners who again and again wake up from their Orphic dreams into what Yeats called "the desolation of reality." [18] But it is a desolation for which, through the story, we have words and a human image.

5 / "The Hunter Who Had an Elk for a Guardian Spirit," and the Ecological Imagination

IT IS ALTOGETHER TOO EASY TO SENTIMENTALIZE the American Indians and their traditional literature on the score of environmental wisdom, as a glance at recent reviews of and dust-jacket blurbs about books by Indians and about Native American culture will reveal. The Noble Savage stereotype, always an accurate mirror of our fears and guilts, is being recast nowadays as Aboriginal Ecologist, full of "PNW" (Profound Natural Wisdom[1]) and given to shedding silent tears on television over our botched landscapes, courtesy of the American Advertising Council and participating stations.

Yet our ecological crisis is real, however we may misrepresent it, and we clearly need, as the saying goes, all the help we can get. In particular we need, beyond the political and economic incentives to clean up our land, air, and water, to find ways to cultivate an imaginative awareness of man's beholden place in the natural order. Ecological science is not enough, I think, to bring us around to the simple but radical recognition that we belong to the biosphere more than it belongs to us. We must find ways to institutionalize the sense of that relationship in our very imaginations. And, all stereotypes and smarmy commercials aside, the American Indians have always had such ways to "reconcile / the people and the stones," as William Carlos Williams once put it ("A Sort of a Song");[2] and if there are sharp practical limits, given the enormous differences between the circumstances of their traditional world and those we live with today, to what we can learn from Indians on the basis of practices, we should nonetheless be looking closely at what they have done to inculcate in themselves the full awareness of ecological interdependence. Before the coming of the whites, at least, it was strictly a matter of daily life or death, this rapport with the rest of nature; and so it is becoming for us. "In imagination begins practicality"; we must imagine our survival on the earth.

Among Western Indian groups, the winter spirit-power ceremonials seem to have served (along with other purposes) to emphasize and renew the people's sense of participatory solidarity with the rest of creation. For example, the Wasco and Wishram Indians, closely related Chinookan people who lived on both sides of the Columbia River near what is now The Dalles, Oregon, generally bestowed public names on their young people in the winter season. The recipient was given the name of some long-dead but well-remembered ancestor, and in the course of the ceremony he or she would be identified as a named human being in the presence of the intermingled human, natural, and supernatural communities of life. A ritual leader would speak to the assembly of family and tribespeople, and it would respond in unison:

> This person will be [Spédis].
> *A-xi*
> This name used to belong to [Spédis] a long time ago.
> *A-xi*
> We want the mountains, creeks, rivers, bluffs, timber to know
> that this person is now named [Spédis].
> *A-xi*
> We want to let the fishes, birds, winds, snow, rain, sun, moon, stars
> to know that [Spédis] has the same as become alive again.
> His name will be heard again when this person is called.
> *A-xi*[3]

Those who spoke *a-xi* on behalf of the child being named must have been sharply aware, once again, of their responsible human connections with the "mountains, rivers, timber, fishes, winds," and so on; in a special sense they and the ritual's leader were speaking to these entities. The same concern continues to this day in the seasonal "preharvest" festivals of the Wascos and Wishrams on the Warm Springs and Yakima reservations. In the Warm Springs longhouse, for example, the onset of the huckleberry season in late August is marked by several nights of ceremony, one highlight of which is an oration by a tribal leader, traditional in content and form, but delivered in English for the special benefit of children. Customarily the orator begins by observing how the people have once again met for "the dedication of a new food that's coming on this 19–," and goes on to stress how the lore of the huckleberry has been handed down since the beginning of time, according to the faith of the old people that each young generation would observe the traditional ways "as long as they are Indians."[4]

Similar ceremonies are currently observed (in some cases are being revived) in the Northwest and elsewhere on the occasion of a boy's first killing of a deer.[5] The emphasis in such rites is upon recognition of the hunter's new prowess in balance with traditional respect and gratitude for the deer and for the bounties of the land in general—bounties which, it is assumed, have a spiritual basis and are subject to human propitiation or (as the case may be) alienation and loss.

The spiritual basis of human survival in nature is widely and insistently dramatized, of course, in the traditional oral literatures of Western Indians, as can be seen most clearly when one moves past sentimental Anglo retellings and examines accurately transcribed and translated texts. In 1885, the pioneer ethnologist Jeremiah Curtin wintered on the Warm Springs Reservation and, in the course of mastering the Wasco Chinook language, recorded a range of myths and tales from Charlie Pitt and Donald McKay. One of Curtin's tales, as edited by Edward Sapir and included in his *Wishram Texts* (1909),[6] is a small masterpiece of Western Indian oral narrative art, marvelously concise and dramatic; and it imaginatively embodies the Indians' belief in the supreme importance of maintaining proper rapport with the rest of nature, better than any other narrative I know of. To identify the story as simply an "ecological fable" for our times would be a misrepresentation, given its considerable literary sophistication and the differences between the Wascos' "ecological" concerns and ours, but even though we do not hunt for our daily meat and tend to find our guardian spirits—if any—in the media, it is a story worth knowing, one to put an edge on the imagination.

The Hunter Who Had an Elk for a Guardian Spirit

There was a man at Dog River [Hood River] in days gone by, whose wife was with child. Pretty soon she gave birth to a boy. While she was sick, the man carried wood, and one day a piece of bark fell on his forehead and cut him. When the boy was large enough to shoot, he killed birds and squirrels; he was a good shot. One day, however, his father said to him, "You don't do as I used to. I am ashamed to own you. When I was of your age, I used to catch young elks. One day when I killed a young elk, the old one attacked me and made this scar you see on my forehead."

Then the boy had a visit from an elk, and the Elk said, "If you will serve me and hear what I say, I will be your master and will help you in every necessity. You must not be proud. You must not kill too many of any animal. I will be your guardian spirit."

So the young man became a great hunter, knew where every animal was—elk, bear, deer. He killed what he needed for himself, and no more. The old man, his father, said to him, "You are not doing enough. At your age I used to do much more." The young man was grieved at his father's scolding. The Elk, the young man's helper, was very angry at the old man. At last [he] [7] helped the young man to kill five whole herds of elk. He killed all except his own spirit elk, though he tried without knowing it to kill even [that one]. This elk went to a lake and pretended to be dead; the young man went into the water to draw the elk out, but as soon as he touched it, both sank.

After touching bottom, the young man woke as from a sleep, and saw bears, deer, and elks without number, and they were all persons. Those that he killed were there too, and they groaned. A voice called, "Draw him in." Each time the voice was heard, he was drawn nearer his master, the Elk, until he was at his side. Then the great Elk said, "Why did you go beyond what I commanded? Your father required more of you than he himself ever did. Do you see our people on both sides? These are they whom you have killed. You have inflicted many needless wounds on our people. Your father lied to you. He never saw my father, as he falsely told you, saying that my father had met him. He also told you that my father gave him a scar. That is not true; he was carrying firewood when you were born, and a piece of bark fell on him and cut him. Now I shall leave you, and never be your guardian spirit again."

When the Elk had finished, a voice was heard saying five times, "Cast him out." The young man went home. The old man was talking, feeling well. The young man told his two wives to fix a bed for him. They did so. He lay there five days and nights, and then told his wives, "Heat water to wash me, also call my friends so that I may talk to them. Bring five elk skins." All this was done. The people came together, and he told them, "My father was dissatisfied because, as he said, I did not do as he had done. What my father wanted grieved the guardian spirit which visited and aided me. My father deceived me. He said that he had been scarred on the head by a great elk while taking the young elk away. He said that I was a disgrace to him. He wanted me to kill more than was needed. He lied. The spirit has left me, and I die."

Even by the standards of Indian traditional literature, the story is strikingly compact; none of its details, it seems, is wasted, and none but contributes forcibly to the terse unity of the whole. For most Anglo readers it should be, overall, an *accessible* story—but it is well, nonetheless, to begin interpretation by aligning its elements with Chinookan ethnology.[8] Ethnographic commentary in this instance should provide not so much revelations of esoteric meanings as a deepening of perceived meanings and, at the same time, a set of valid limits to such perceptions.

The story centers its drama, then, on a major premise of Wasco-Chinookan culture: the highly desirable acquisition of spirit-power, or *yuhlmah,* and specifically the acquisition of a guardian spirit.[9] Like most other Western groups, the Wascos viewed their world animistically and held that the shape and quality of an individual's life after childhood was largely determined, apart from family connections, by his secret personal commerce with animistic spirits. In particular, one was expected to go forth in childhood and adolescence in active quest for one or more guardian spirits; under conditions of physical and psychological duress (fatigue from a long solitary journey, fasting, isolation, and so forth), a spirit might manifest itself to the quester and offer, under certain conditions (notably secrecy and obedience), to serve as guardian and tutor for the rest of his life.

Occasionally the affinities between spirit and young candidate would be so strong and auspicious that the former would appear to the latter irrespective of the formal spirit quest—as, apparently, in the story at hand.

But however attained, identification with a particular spirit meant that one's interests, aptitudes, and opportunities were accordingly channeled by the identification. To put it in socioeconomic terms, there was a spirit power "division of labor," such that, for example, those who received deer or elk guardians were in general supposed to be efficacious hunters, as in our story.

But, although an individual's kin and associates might infer his spiritual connection from his proclivities and accomplishments (and also from his singing and dancing during the midwinter "power" festivities), it could not be more than a kind of "open secret" during life; and only at death, or under circumstances of mortal danger, was it to be openly revealed. So, in a historical memoir of a battle between Wishrams and Northern Paiutes in the 1860s, when a Wishram man was wounded, apparently mortally, a wolf's backbone was displayed to represent his guardian spirit, and he revealed that, consequent to his boyhood wolf-vision, he saw certain strange weather signs which, if he were to recover now, would reappear. They did, and he recovered.[10] The display of the wolf's backbone on behalf of the dying soldier is analogous to the request on behalf of the young hunter in our story for "five elk skins" to be brought forward (five being, in Chinookan culture generally, the cult or spirit-pattern number indicative of magical happenings). According to Spier and Sapir, the custom held that "the dying man called for some article connected with his spirit [and] told how he came by his power."[11]

To summarize: when a Chinookan anticipated imminent death, only then did he divulge "the greatest secret of his life,"[12] the implication being that through divulgence came release of the guardian, now no longer to be needed. What is special about our Wasco story, of course, is that the young hero dies because he has earlier alienated and lost his guardian spirit; what in normal circumstances would be a symptom of approaching death, the deliberate separation from one's guardian, here becomes under distressing circumstances the unwilled cause of death: "The spirit has left me, and I die." A terrible fate, indeed, to be rejected by the very source of one's accustomed psychic vitality, well-being, and social identity—analogous in Christian terms to loss of the soul and in psychological terms to loss of ego.

The tensions and uncertainties of living according to the cultivation of acquired or conferred spirit-power are often neglected by ethnographers, but they are vividly manifested in traditional narratives like the

Wasco story at hand. Melville Jacobs justly observes, in reference to a story from the closely related Clackamas Chinook, "The social function of the myth appears to be to reinforce in audience members their ideology of, acceptance of, and symbiotic ties with animistic supernaturals. For no greater security could be had in a precarious Chinook world than the certainties which people acquired when individual nonmaterial helpers came and stayed through a lifetime." It is the negative of this security of spirit guardianship that is at stake in the Wasco story, and Jacobs's concluding remark points to the possibility of spiritual calamity as well as of spiritual success: "Tragedy befell when such helpers departed." [13]

Now let's consider "The Hunter Who Had an Elk for a Guardian Spirit," not just as an ethnological vehicle but as the structured and textured script of a story—as an imaginatively unified narrative. Curtin and his editor Sapir do not offer a Wasco-language text (although there is evidence that Curtin transcribed from performances in Wasco [14]); hence it is impossible to examine and reconstruct the text according to Dell Hymes's monumental discovery that Chinookan narratives (as presented, for instance, prose-fashion in Sapir's dual-language *Wishram Texts*) are in reality elaborately "measured," that is, structured in terms of units of ascending scope: lines, verses, stanzas, scenes, and acts, as if in poetic drama. In fact, as numerous writers have suggested, poetic drama is the most serviceable analogy in Western literature to traditional Indian narrative, given the tacit, inherently "dramatic," performable, and (it now seems more and more clear) poetically measured qualities of the latter as well as the former.[15]

Lacking the Chinookan-language text of the story, we can only approach it on the macrostructural level of "scenes" and "acts." I would hazard the guess that its five-paragraph translated form bears closely upon a "five-act" structure in the original. Certainly Curtin's paragraph divisions correspond exactly to and mark off the chief movements of the narrative, as the following outline will show:

Act I. The Father and the Son
   A. the boy's birth
   B. the father's injury
   C. the son's early success at hunting
   D. the father's lie about his scar

Act II. The Son and the Elk Spirit
Act III. The Son as a Hunter
   A. the son's success
   B. the father's censure
   C. the slaughter of elks
   D. descent into the lake
Act IV. The Elk's Revelations to the Son
   A. assembly of game animals
   B. censures, and revelation of father's lie
 Act V. The Son's Revelations to His People
   A. return to village
   B. preparation to die
   C. revelation to the people of his guardian spirit and of his father's lie

If this structure does correspond to the articulations of the original text (and according to Hymes's theory there would be verbal evidence, in the form of stock "marking" words and phrases), then the five-part format would presumably manifest to a Chinookan audience the sacramental power of the number 5—warranting the story's hieratic significance. For us, adventitiously of course, such a five-part articulation may suggest tragic drama—and it is to an examination of the tragic elements of the narrative that I want now to turn.

From his boyhood on, the nameless young hero is caught up in a cruel conflict of allegiances, between his natural father and the Elk, his guardian spirit. One of the persistent impulses of traditional Western Indian narrative is to dramatize and imaginatively mediate such polar oppositions between values or attitudes that in and of themselves are "good" but that may, in combination, lead a protagonist to evil consequences. In the much-discussed Clackamas story, "Seal and Her Younger Brother Lived There," for example, Seal's brother is murdered by a trickster disguised as his wife because Seal's instinct for social propriety overcomes her little daughter's acute perception and warning that there is something suspicious about her brother's "wife." [16] In the Wasco story, of course, the father's attitudes and actions are not merely inappropriate, as Seal's are, but reprehensible. He is greedy, deceitful, exploitative, hypocritical, boastful, status-proud—yet he is the hunter's father, to whom the young man owes, as he poignantly recognizes throughout, filial obedience, even though obeying his father's demands for bigger and bigger kills means disobeying his guardian spirit's precepts.

The first act tersely reveals the father's shabby character. The fact that he received his scar while carrying wood during the period of his son's birth seems to be the fatal germ of the whole story: wood gathering was generally women's work, analogous to men's hunting,[17] but whereas for normal husbands it would be nothing to be ashamed of, under the circumstances, this husband is compelled later, in the face of his son's initial success as a juvenile hunter, to memorialize his unheroic scar with an elaborate and evidently defensive lie about a heroic encounter with an elk. As the story unfolds, of course, the father's vicarious designs on his son's career are manifested all too clearly: it is to be assumed that he is benefiting both circumstantially (status, wealth) and psychologically from his deceitful exploitation of his son's ability, the spiritual basis of which he neither recognizes nor even considers as a possibility.

Over against the bad father, as if in compensation, comes the spirit-elk, with its noble and generous offer of hunting prowess apparently in response to the boy's own virtue ("he was a good shot"). The terms of the offer amount to a kind of shorthand paradigm, a code for hunters according to widespread Indian belief—to kill only what is needed, to practice humility in success, both before the animals one kills and before the human community that honors the killing, and above all to maintain grateful reverence toward the spiritual source of one's capabilities as a hunter ("serve me and hear what I say").

At first the hunter (now, significantly, the "young man") prospers according to these terms, but in the complication of Act Three his father recalls for him the lie of his much greater success at an equivalent age, and by scolding his son and urging him to kill more and more wantonly, he initiates the swift and continuous tragic actions of the last two acts.

Melville Jacobs has observed in his psychoanalytically oriented studies of Clackamas and related Chinookan narratives that they reveal, to a striking degree, "an intensity of feelings about older persons, that is, about persons who possess control over others,"[18] especially Oedipal tensions between parents and maturing children. In particular, as Jacobs points out, there are numerous stories about "heavy," tyrannical fathers, whose attempts to control and/or exploit their children, especially sons, are sometimes motivated by a kind of defensive and vicarious ambitiousness for their offspring. Apropos the ambitious father in our story, for example, there is the Coyote in the Clackamas "Badger and Coyote Were Neighbors," who urges his children (four sons and a daughter) to take the lead in stealing a wonderful ball, with the result that they are all killed.[19] Another story, known to all Chinookans along the Columbia, is a veritable paradigm of the Oedipal conflict. A giant chief, with especially large feet, keeps many wives and raises only daughters, killing all male offspring at birth. Finally some of his wives rebel and save a boy-child by disguising it as a girl and eventually sending it away with its mother. The boy grows up, learns about his father, and after acquiring great spirit powers, goes to the paternal "mansion" and matches his father's sexual prowess by sleeping with all of his wives in one night. The son then attacks his father on the Columbia River and (depending on the version in question) either slays him and succeeds him as chief, or spares him but seizes all his property and power. In either case the son "becomes" his father in approved Oedipal fashion.[20]

In still another tale bearing on the one under discussion, when a young man falls into a trance during a spirit-dancing episode, his father refuses to acknowledge that his son may be in communion with a guardian spirit and, to prove his point, places a glowing coal on the unconscious boy's hand—with the result that a hole is burnt right through the hand! In terms of the focusing of our sympathies in a story like this one, or in "The Hunter Who Had an Elk for a Guardian Spirit," Jacobs's general remarks seem apt: "Paternal hostility to sons appears frequently in northwestern states myths," and "the fact of paternal initiation of Oedipal feelings seems to have been taken for granted."[21]

Another of Jacobs's ethnographic observations (specifically on a story from the Clackamas titled "Stick Drum Gambler and His Older Brother") serves to point out a particularly reprehensible aspect of the hunter's father. In that story, two boys receive hunting power (with eventual unhappy consequences) from their uncle, Stick Drum Gambler, who happens to be an incarnated spirit. Jacobs notes that "a person often received the supernatural of an older relative with whom he had been comparatively intimate. The psychological mechanism of identification with a parent homologue is expressed as a kind of inheritance or acquisition of that homologue's spirit-power."[22] Later in the story, the two boys also manifest their father's power by turning into deer. If spirit-power can then be communicated from older to younger kin, as from uncle to nephew or from father to son, or if at least the latter's acquisition of power can be facilitated by the former, then the Wasco father's lie appears as a cruel mockery of such kinship advantage, the implication in the lie being that the young hunter's prowess derives spiritually from his father's own, but does not measure up to it. And the peculiar detail in the lake-bottom revelation scene in Act Four, whereby the Elk engages the "plot" of the father's lie, in acknowledging that indeed he too had a father Elk who might have met the hunter's father under spirit-power circumstances—this detail now can be seen to suggest "what might have been," according to Chinookan belief, that is, authentic transmission of spirit potency (or at least receptivity) from father to son in the human as well as the spirit world, a most auspicious interlocking of kinship relationships. Instead, the younger Elk discloses not only the father's deceit, but also his perversion of a rich spiritual possibility. "Your father lied to you. He never saw my father."

In these terms, the tragic interaction of familial and spiritual ties in the story, the terrible "double bind" of the hunter's predicament, is illuminated by and in turn extends one of Jacobs's observations on the Clackamas Chinook view of "fate": "It is my impression that myths support the formulation that human life is not affected by some ill-defined destiny; rather it is swayed concretely and decisively by family and more remote kin, and almost equally by spirit-powers, that is, by kinlike supernaturals with all their sharply defined attributes."[23]

Is it not reasonable to assume that real-life conflicts occurred for young Chinookan men and their fathers and other elders upon the advent of spirit-powers: conflicts which realized the potential antagonism between duty and obedience to elder kin, and the secret and imperative duties of a young man to his spirit guardian? Jacobs is right; in no way does our story suggest "some ill-defined destiny"; on the contrary it is axiomatically tragic in the way it mediates for the poor hunter between human kin and spirit kin. One wishes that Jacobs, with his unique and now irreplaceable wealth of ethnographic and literary knowledge about Northwest Indians, had followed up the implications of his remarks here about "destiny."

What with his help we have found out about the hunter's fate is full of significance for the ecological understanding of the story, but before turning back, in conclusion, to that, I want to adduce two direct analogues to "The Hunter Who Had an Elk for a Guardian Spirit," from neighboring tribes, so as to set up what Dell Hymes, following Lévi-Strauss, calls a "semantic field," or "typology." [24]

First, there is in Sapir's *Wishram Texts* a rare, rather garbled Clackamas text collected by Franz Boas, titled "The Boy That Lied about His Scar."

She gave birth to a male (child), her son. Now he [the son] went to get wood, sticks he gathered. Then a stick ran into him right here [on the head]. Now his son became older. Then (his father) louses him on the head and finds his scar on his head. After they had given birth to him, a stick had run into him on his head (whence his scar). Then (his father) said to him: "How did you come to get this scar of yours?" Then he whipped his son. Then he said to him: "Where did you get to be so?"—"Once a deer struck me with its horns."— "Then bathe!" he said to his son. Then the boy bathed. Now he, the boy, became older, but elks never appeared to him (when he hunted, for he had falsely accused them of inflicting the scar upon him). Now then it is finished; he got to be old. Story, story.[25]

Clearly, for undetermined reasons, cultural priorities or simple garbling, our Wasco story is radically transformed in its Clackamas form. There is no conflict of obedience between elder kin and spirit guardian; the moral positions of the human actors have been reversed. Now it is the son who is a liar, and it is the father who, ignorant of his son's lie, appears to be scrupulous about spiritual observances and about truth-telling. The father does not urge impossible hunting exploits on his son, and the story offers neither a dramatic revelation in the spirit world nor one in the human realm. The ecological justice enacted is simple and private compared to what happens in the Wasco tale—for the Clackamas boy it is a lifetime of failure at hunting, dramatized by the laconic statement "He got to be old," so different from the stark finality of the Wasco narrative.

The other text, too long to quote in full, is from the Sahaptin-speaking Klikitats of south-central Washington and called "The Hunter Obtains a Deer-Hunting Power." [26] In content it is much closer to the Wasco narrative, but there are some illuminating differences. A one-legged man tells his son that he was once a great hunter until an elk tore off his leg. "You may also encounter elk," he warns the son, "and it may do to you as it did to me." The son does not know that this is a lie, nor do we, until in the course of a hunt he encounters an "old man," who is really a Spirit Elk and who tells the young man, "Your father (when out hunting) awakened, with only one leg. I did not do it, not I. He falsely deceived you. He was gathering wood, and there at that place he was hurt by a log. The log fell on him, and because of that his leg became that way."

The old man-elk goes on beyond this revelation (which seems to take place, as in the Wasco story, by or in a lake) with instructions that the son return to his father, expose him, and in effect supplant him—"When you return, speak to him in this manner. 'Here I am.' [Say] you saw me. 'You were no hunter of deer. I will be ruling. I see you, when you travel about, that you are a poor hunter. You should not just hunt and shoot deer. I will give it (game) to you.'" The son then returns, catches his father in his persistent lie, exposes and upbraids him ("Then the old man was ashamed"), but instead of taking over his father's authority and duties, he opts to return to the Spirit Elk at the lake, where he "dies" (whether literally or through some sort of spiritual transformation—into an elk?—is not clear). The text ends, "That is how the old man no longer had a child."

What is important about the place this story occupies in our typological field is that the son does not act upon the father's compensatory lie about his injury until the Elk's disclosure about it; then, in terms of the conflict of parental and spirit-guide obedience, he acts out of his new knowledge without hesitation in favor of the latter, and indeed eventually chooses to leave his father altogether and go back to the Elk. The fact that we as audience do not know about the father's lie until the son learns about it, in itself structures a simplification of the son's predicament: contrast the Wasco narrative's declaration to us in Act One of the real origins of the father's scar, with its effect on us of an ironic foreshadowing that dramatically intensifies the father's villainy.

In terms of Lévi-Strauss's system of entabling and analyzing the permutations of bipolar oppositions in a "field" of cognate myths (see essay 6 for further applications of this procedure), we end up with the following set (in which "+" represents allegiance and "−" represents rejection in terms of the protagonist's relationship to father and spirit guardian):

	Father	Spirit-Guardian
Wasco	+	−
Klikitat	−	+
Clackamas	−	−

(The Clackamas entry is conjectural—the lie the boy tells his father presumably expresses insensitivity to the possibility of spirit acquisition, and of course it costs him all hope of gaining hunting power.)

We are left, then, with an incomplete set—missing a "++" story, in which a young hunter would somehow maintain a proper measure of allegiance and obedience both to father and to spirit guardian. It would be, clearly, a "hero-story," with an idealized protagonist; in structural terms, something like Faulkner's novella *The Bear,* in which Ike McCaslin is in his fashion faithful to several sets of "fathers." Such narratives do exist in the Western Native literatures,[27] but as in our own narrative tradition, Indian stories tend to dwell upon the *difficulties* of mediating a way between two conflicting goods, rather than upon the rewards of doing so.

Now, perhaps, this brief excursion in structuralist comparisons will allow us to see the Wasco text for the triumph of dramatic clarity it is, even in its transcribed and translated state. The narrative is so shaped from the outset that, in Acts Four and Five, the full tragic enormity of the son's predicament between two masters is dramatized in just a few details. The Elk's crushing disclosure of fatherly perfidy in Act Four does not offer the son any hope of extenuation of his offense through ignorance of his father's lies, or because of filial obedience to what a Native audience would recognize as immoral demands. More than human justice is involved here, and the act of the crime, not the motive, will be decisive. Our sympathies notwithstanding, has not the young man in fact killed wastefully, and thus gone beyond what the Elk commanded?

If we ask, "Why does the Elk allow the hunter as his protégé to abuse his spirit gift?" we miss the crucial point about that gift; namely, that it is given freely and absolutely. Once he accepts it the young man is free to use it properly, as he is instructed to do, or to abuse it, with calamitous results when at last he "goes too far." The limit for "going too far" is left vague, intentionally I think; in demanding that it be specified or in denying that the story affirms a salient, if severe, moral order, one might as well also complain that "Nature" doesn't play fair with us today when she "gives" us *without warning* the ecological horrors of Love Canal or sudden outbreaks of Minamata's disease, in return for our technological abuses of natural science.

As the hunter returns home to tell his secrets and die, we meet the father once more; in a marvelous stroke of irony, he is "talking, feeling well." Perhaps nothing in the story reveals more vividly how steady and whole is its imaginative view of what might seem, to Anglo readers at least, a relatively simple "ecological" issue, or just a matter of concern between the hunter and his guardian spirit. The son's "crime," instead, is projected tragically across the whole spectrum of human life in all of its major categories—personal and psychological, familial (the father, the two wives), social ("call my friends"), economic (the hunter's evident wealth), spiritual. And, subsuming all these, in terms of what he has lost, there is what we in our mostly unimaginative way call "ecological"—but here meaning the imaginative perception, underscored by calamity, that our personal, familial, socioeconomic, spiritual, and environmental obligations are precariously, that is to say organically, interrelated.

If I were a storyteller, and I were to try to appropriate "The Hunter Who Had an Elk for a Guardian Spirit" specifically for modern American purposes—in other words, make it out however reductively as "a fable for these times"—my attempt would hinge, I think, on the conflict of generations in the story as in life. The Wasco father hides his inadequacies and failure behind a lie and recklessly exploits his son's great gift and his very future by demanding more and more wasteful hunting, as if his kills were a kind of gross national product that had to grow. Is not our present environmental predicament (to say nothing of what is to come) premised on some such false and ruinous relationship between the "elder" members of our culture, and the "younger"? (Let World War Two be the generational dividing line.) "Produce, produce; consume, consume; grow exponentially; do as we have done in our heroic careers, only bigger and better if you are worthy of us!" the elders of American capitalism seem to say, still, in actions if no longer so blatantly in words. And if I see this, resentfully, as a "son" of the elders of my culture, when I look in turn at my children, I find, helplessly it seems, that I am instilling some such ecological rapacity in them. The irreducible moral of the Wasco story in these terms—the bitter truth it might help us to imagine—is that in the ravaging of the natural order, it is always the young who will suffer most.

  "He wanted me to kill more than was needed. He lied. The spirit has left me, and I die."

6 / The Wife Who Goes Out like a Man, Comes Back as a Hero: The Art of Two Oregon Indian Narratives

ONE OF THE FEW STORIES IN A NORTH AMERICAN Indian repertory to receive genuine analysis from more than one writer is a brief, starkly horrifying text in Melville Jacobs's collection of Clackamas Chinook literature from Oregon titled "Seal and Her Younger Brother Dwelt There." [1] With full and penetrating commentaries on it by Jacobs himself and by Dell Hymes, and illustrative references to it in an important essay on the nature of fiction by Frank Kermode and several other commentaries, "Seal and Her Younger Brother" might be said to have "arrived," critically. [2] My intention here is not so much to add to its understanding and fame (it is still a long way, I imagine, from inclusion in a freshman literature anthology) as to draw on the attention given it by Jacobs and Hymes in order to introduce another, closely related, Northwest myth-narrative, and, in discussing it, to raise some issues about our long overdue reclamation of Native American literature.

About that literature, the reader is reminded here at the outset that in general terms it is an oral, formulaic, traditional, and anonymous art form; that ultimately its engagement with reality is mythic and sacred; that what survives of it comes to us at two removes, translated from an oral-traditional mode into print and from a native language into English; that it flourished through public performance (generally during winter religious festivals) by skilled recitalists whose audiences already knew the individual stories and prized not plot invention but rather the recitalists' ability to exploit their material dramatically and to weave stories into sequences and cycles. Indian myth-narrative, being dramatic in conception and performance, inevitably strikes us as a highly tacit expression; motivation and emotional states are generally implied rather than directly specified. And Indian literature is likely to seem all the more terse, even cryptic, to us for being the verbal art of highly ethnocentric, tribal people, whose infinitely diverse cultures we still don't know much about. An elderly Papago singer said to Ruth Underhill by way of commenting on this difficulty: "The song is very short because we understand so much."[3]

Our two Oregon narratives are indeed short and concentrated, and yet, with some ethnographic help, we can hope to understand and appreciate them as instances of Native American literature. First the text of "Seal and Her Younger Brother," as narrated by Mrs. Victoria Howard in Oregon City, Oregon, in 1929 and transcribed and translated by Jacobs, and in the present form retranslated by Hymes as a *poetically* structured text.

Seal and Her Younger Brother Lived There

[i. The "wife" comes]
They lived there, Seal, her daughter, her younger brother.
After some time, now a woman got to Seal's younger brother.
They lived there.
    They would 'go out' outside in the evening.
The girl would say,
    she would tell her mother:
    "Mother! Something is different about my uncle's wife.
    "It sounds just like a man when she 'goes out.'"
"Shush! Your uncle's wife!"
A long long time they lived there like that.
    In the evening they would each 'go out.'
Now she would tell her.
    "Mother! Something is different about my uncle's wife.
    "When she goes out it sounds just like a man.
"Shush!"

[ii. The uncle dies]
Her uncle, his wife, would 'lie down' up above on the bed.
Pretty soon the other two would lie down close to the fire,
    they would lie down beside each other.
Some time during the night, something comes on her face.
She shook her mother,
    she told her:
    "Mother! Something comes on to my face."
    "Mmmmm. Shush. Your uncle, they are 'going.'"
Pretty soon now again, she heard something escaping.
She told her:
    "Mother! Something is going t'uq t'uq.
    "I hear something."
"Shush. Your uncle, they are 'going.'"
The girl got up,
    she fixed the fire,
        she lit pitch,
            she looked where the two were:
                Ah! Ah! Blood!
She raised her light to it, thus:
    her uncle is on his bed,
        his neck is cut,
            he is dead.
                She screamed.

[iii. The women lament]
She told her mother:
    "I told you,
    'Something is dripping.'
"You told me,
    'Shush, they are 'going,'"
"I had told you,
    "Something is different about my uncle's wife.
    "She would 'go out'
        with a sound just like a man she would urinate"
"You would tell me,
    'Shush!'"
She wept.
Seal said:
    "Younger brother! My young brother!

9 8

"They are valuable standing there [house posts].
"My younger brother!"
She kept saying that.
As for that girl, she wept.
She said:
"In vain I tried to tell you,
'Not like a woman,
'With a sound just like a man she would urinate, my
uncle's wife.'"
"You told me,
'Shush!'
"Oh oh my uncle!"
"Oh my uncle!"
She wept, that girl.

* * *

Now I remember only that far.[4]

Despite the raw imaginative power of this story—its sinister convergence of aberrant sexuality and apparently motiveless homicide, the vivid evocation of darkness, liquids dripping, and screams, the sense of horror obliquely rendered and thereby intensified—one might in rereading it conclude that it is manifestly only a fragment of something longer and draw back from full appreciation of its art on the grounds that, however engaging they may be, fragments and oddments ought not to be interpreted into occult masterpieces. To do so is of course a familiar form of literary sentimentality—what is lacking or incomprehensible in a work, especially if it comes from a remote culture, becomes in such a reading a covert virtue of the work.

But although they acknowledge the possibility of fuller, more explicit versions, both Jacobs and Hymes emphatically argue that the story has its own effective unity of parts and can be understood and appreciated as it stands. Summary and paraphrase cannot do justice to their interpretations, and the reader is urged to turn to them as models of two very different ways of proceeding with Native literary texts. It will have to suffice here to say, on the one hand, that Jacobs's interpretation proceeds along characteristic psychosocial lines: he concludes that "the myth is . . . a drama whose nightmarish horror theme, murder of one's own kin by a sexually aberrant person who is an in-law, causes profound fear and revulsion as well as deep sympathy. The tension around in-laws [which Jacobs finds to be a feature of Clackamas literature generally] is basic to the plot." In the case of this story, the trouble begins when "a woman [gets] to" Seal's wealthy younger brother, the master of the household, and he brings her home as wife apparently without the formalities that should attend such an important transaction. In Jacobs's view this sinister "wife" is a homosexual who, as the main actor, murders her husband so as to "avenge herself on a family the daughter of which casts aspersions upon her manner of urinating, that is upon her sexuality."[5] In effect, however unwittingly, the daughter occasions the murder.

On the other hand, Hymes, employing a highly modified form of the structural analysis of Claude Lévi-Strauss, engages the verbal text of the story in the context of related Chinookan narratives and finds a unity in it very different from that of Jacobs. In simple terms, the story belongs not to Seal's brother and his homicidal "wife," but rather to Seal herself and especially to her young daughter, whose perspective on the action we most attend to and who is in fact the "heroine." Following Lévi-Strauss's method, Hymes sets up a systematic analysis of the way the story's structure unfolds; in the process he discovers that it effects a complex mediation between preservation of Social Norm, at one pole, and awareness of Empirical Situation, at the opposite pole.

In summary, the analysis, which goes beyond Lévi-Strauss's practice into consideration of imagistic and verbal elements, reveals that "the leading theme of the myth is the conduct of Seal. The behavior of the girl is not a device to express the horror of an ambiguously sexed and hateful 'female' in-law, but rather an ambiguous 'female' is a device to express the failure of a proper woman to relate to a danger threatening one she should protect. The myth uses a stock villain [Hymes means a trickster in disguise, common in Northwest Indian stories] to dramatize a relationship subtler than villainy."[6]

The two readings, then, are mutually exclusive, differing on the fundamental interpretive point as to what and whom the story is about. In my view, at least, Hymes's reading opens "Seal and Her Younger Brother" to a literary understanding much more fully; in its careful attention to structure and texture and in the effort it makes to relate this one Clackamas story to general patterns in Native literature from the region, it points to a viable way of engaging such work as literature, and indeed it suggests possibilities for interpreting Indian verbal art and ours together, as dissimilar as they are in mode, subjects, and artistic conventions.

For example, Hymes's emphasis on the stylized conflict in the story between two goods, preservation of social propriety versus alertness and openness to the situation immediately at hand, might remind us that, although our literature is not 'tribal,' it often dramatizes such conflicts, too—"The Emperor's New Clothes" being just one obvious comic example, and Dylan Thomas's immortal "Aunt Prothero" in "A Child's Christmas in Wales," who politely offers the firemen "something to read" when they arrive to put out a Christmas Day fire, being another.[7] In fact, most of our fiction dealing with children and youthful initiations into experience centers on such a conflict between the formal, received "way" of society and the tentative and untutored ego-way of the young protagonist.

By way of illustration, it would be interesting to consider Hemingway's Nick Adams story, "Indian Camp," alongside "Seal and Her Younger Brother." Beyond the strange resemblances, centering on the mysterious cutting of an Indian husband's throat, there is Nick's predicament: he is caught (like Seal's daughter) between a set of adult norms and stock responses, as embodied in his father and uncle, and his own raw, immediate registering of experience. Happily, no one's life depends on how Nick's conflict is resolved. Whereas Seal's daughter ends her story in bitter lamentation, a sort of tragically valid "I told you so" to her mother, Hemingway allows Nick to conclude with a child's naive joy—he has made it through a terrible, "grown-up" experience involving violent birth and death; his faith in his father's powers remains unshaken; with his hand in the lake water he is so richly alive in the moment that he feels he "will live forever."[8] It is tempting to ask which represents a higher literary realism: the dramatization by writers like Hemingway of such romantic illusions, with heavy irony, or their simple exclusion from Indian myth-narratives like the one under discussion?

Now we have seen how Hymes devalues Jacobs's emphasis on the "wife" as a principal actor, identifying "her" instead as merely the catalyst of the crucial action between Seal and her daughter. Arguing that it is beside the point of the story to seek for psychosocial motives for the murder, Hymes supposes that the sinister "wife" is in origin not a murderous homosexual or transvestite, but a trickster.[9] That is, a conventionalized being like Coyote or Raven (or Loki in Nordic myth) who "travels around" and who, by acting habitually without restraint or any motives beyond those of greed and appetite, and short-term cleverness, creates *possibility* (mainly disorder, confusion, imbalance, crisis) in the plots of myth-narratives.[10] As Radin, Jung, Roheim, and others have pointed out, the Indian trickster figures seem to serve a wide variety of psychological and social purposes at once: Hymes reminds us that, in addition, the Trickster may simply be an indispensable plot agent: he makes things happen for the narrator. With this in mind, Hymes glances at some analogous stories about mysterious domestic murders from various Northwest Coast tribes and concludes that as a disguised trickster (Raven) is responsible for those killings, so too with the slaying of Seal's younger brother. According to the conventions of the Northwest trickster, no special purpose or provocation for killing is necessary; it follows that Seal's daughter does not trigger or provoke her uncle's murder.

This seems to be indisputable, and, once it is granted, it is hard not to admire the narrative artistry by which means the ostensible primary action (the deception and killing of the husband by his "wife") is muted and left obscure so as to bring the apparent secondary action (the interplay between Seal and her daughter) into the foreground. Yeats speaks of Shakespeare's similar practice of leaving the rational motives and purposes of some of his protagonists unclear (as with Richard, Leontes, Hamlet himself) so as to rivet our attention on the play of tragic emotions themselves.[11]

So here, against the sinister enigma of the "wife's" actions, the little heroine and her mother play out their immediate and unresolvable conflict of consciousness. At the end, Seal's lament for her dead brother is characteristically decorous and conventional, not expressive of what has actually happened; her daughter, having been painfully open to experience throughout the story, is transfixed by feelings of helplessness, frustration, horror, and grief—

> Seal said:
> "Younger brother! My younger brother!
> "They are valuable standing there.
> "My younger brother!"
> She kept saying that.

As for that girl, she wept.
She said:
    "In vain I tried to tell you,
        'Not like a woman,
        'With a sound just like a man she would urinate,
                    my uncle's wife.'
    "You told me,
           Shush!
    "Oh oh my uncle!
    "Oh my uncle!"
She wept, that girl.

But now I want to turn to another Northwest Indian myth—from the Coos people, who lived along the southern Oregon coast about two hundred miles from the Clackamas and spoke a different language. The story, titled "The Revenge against the Sky People" (narrated by Jim Buchanan to Harry Hull St. Clair in 1903 and translated by Leo J. Frachtenberg),[12] is at first sight much more accessible than "Seal and Her Younger Brother" because it is more detailed, especially in terms of character and motivation, and because it conforms more closely to our conventional expectations of fictional art. What is immediately striking about it is that it contains within its hero-tale structure a version of "Seal and Her Younger Brother"!

A man lived in Kiweet. He had an elder brother, who was always building canoes. Once he was working on a canoe, when a man came there to him. "What do you do with your canoe after you finish it?"—"I always sell my canoes." He kept on working, with his head bent down, while the man was talking to him. Alongside the man who was building lay his dog. All at once he [the stranger] hit the neck of the man who was building, and cut off his head. He took his head home.

The man who was building did not come home, and they went out looking for him. They found him lying in the canoe, dead, without a head. The little dog was barking alongside the canoe. The dog would look upwards every time it barked. Straight up it would look. So they began to think, "Someone from above must have killed him!" Then the next day the man's younger brother looked for him. The young man shot an arrow upwards, and then he would shoot another one. He was shooting the arrows upwards. Every time he shot, his arrow would stick in the one above, and as he kept on shooting that way, the arrows soon reached him.

Then he climbed up there. He went up on the arrows. He saw people when he climbed up, and he asked, "From where do you come?" They were taking home a man's head. "We danced for it," they said. They were taking home his elder brother's head. They said to the young man, "At a little place [nearby] the wife of the murderer is digging fern-roots. Every forenoon she digs fern-roots there." So he went there. He did not go very far. Suddenly, indeed, [he saw] a woman digging fern-roots. There was a big river.

So he asked the woman, "Do you have your own canoe?"—"Not so."—"Who ferries you across the river?"—"My husband ferries me across."—"What do you do when he ferries you across?"—"He does not land the canoe. I usually jump ashore."—"What does he do afterward?"—"He usually turns back. Then, when it is almost evening, I go home. Again, he comes after me. A little ways off he stops the canoe, I jump in with that pack. I get in there all right."—"What do you do with your fern-roots?"—"I usually dry them."—"What do you do with your fern-roots after they are dry?"—"I usually give some of them to all the people who live here. A little ways off in the next house, there lives an old man and an old woman. I never give them any fern-roots."—"What do you usually do?"—"Then I cook them in a big pot."—"What do you do then?"—"I stir them with my hands."—"Doesn't your hand get burned?"—"Not so, it does not hurt me."—"What does your husband do when you lie down?"—"I lie a little ways off from my husband."—"Does your husband usually fall asleep quickly?"—"He usually falls asleep quickly."

Now he asked her all [these] questions, and then he killed her. He skinned the woman, and put on her hide. Indeed, he looked just like the woman. Then he took her load and packed it. He saw the husband there as he arrived. The husband was crossing back and forth. A little ways off in the river he stopped his canoe. Thus [the young man] was thinking, "I wonder whether I shall get there if I jump! I will try it from this distance." He packed the load and jumped. One leg touched the water. He pretty nearly did not get there. Thus spoke the man, "Is that you, my wife?" Then he spoke: "I am tired, this is the reason why I almost did not get there. My pack is heavy." [The husband] did not think any more about it.

Whatever the woman had told him, indeed, the young man did it that way. He made only one mistake. He gave fern-roots to those old people. He opened the door. The two old people saw him when he entered. They did not take the fern-roots that he held in his hands. [They] shouted, "Someone from below gives us two something!" They did not hear it [in] the next house.

When the thing he was cooking began to boil, he stirred it with his hands. "Ouch! It burned my hands!" The husband heard it. "What happened to you?"—" My finger is sore, this is the reason why I said so." And he was looking at the head that was fastened to the ceiling. It was his brother's head.

He cried there when he saw his elder brother's head. Thus spoke the husband: "You seem to be crying."—"There is so much smoke, my eyes are sore." [The husband] no longer paid any attention to it.

Now it got to be evening. The woman was going upstairs. Thus spoke the little brother-in-law, "My sister-in-law looks like a man!" Thus his grand-mother said to him, "The women from there look just like men! You must keep quiet!" Nobody thought about it. From everywhere people came there to the murderer to help him. They were dancing for the head. For it they were dancing. Blood was dripping from the head that was hanging there.

Then it got to be evening, and they all went to bed. When they went to bed she had a big knife under the pillow. The husband went to bed first. The woman was walking outside. So she bored holes in all the canoes in the village. Only in the one in which she intended to cross she did not bore a hole. As soon as she got through, she went inside. Then she went to bed a little away from her husband. At midnight the husband was asleep. She got up on the sly. She cut off the head of the husband, and seized her eldest brother's head. Then she ran away, and crossed alone in the canoe.

[The husband's] mother was lying under the bed. The blood dripped down on her, and the old woman lighted a torch. "Blood! Blood! What have you done? You must have killed your wife!" She heard nothing. So everybody woke up. They saw the man lying under the bed, without a head. His wife had disappeared, and the head that was hanging from the ceiling was gone. "The woman must have killed her husband."—"It was not a woman."

Then they followed him. Other people shoved the canoes into the water, but they kept sinking, and they could not follow him.

Then [the young man] went down on his arrows, on which he had climbed up. Then he returned there. He brought back his elder brother's head. He assembled all his folks. Now, it is said, they were going to join his elder brother's head. Now they commenced to work. A small spruce tree was stand-ing there. Alongside of that small spruce tree, they were joining his head. Then they danced for it. His head climbed up a little bit and fell down. Four times it happened that way. His head would go up a little bit, and then fall down again. The fifth time, however, his head stuck on. Then thus [the young man] said to his elder brother, "Now you are all right." Then he came down from the spruce tree.

None of those people from above could come down, and none could take his revenge.

These are the Woodpecker people; this is the reason why their heads are red today. The blood on the neck, that's what makes the head red. Thus one said to them, "You shall be nothing. You shall be a woodpecker. The last people shall see you."

Now one might very well get the impression on reading this rousing story that it "explains" everything that is obscure in "Seal and Her Younger Brother" and go on to conclude that that story is in fact no more than an interesting fragment now that the "true" version has been found. But both the impression and the conclusion would be wrong. Indian mythology, like all oral literature, relies on narrative motifs and situations that may be current in different combinations over a wide area, through intensive borrowing. The story analogues and parallels produced by dissemination are certainly worth studying, but (as Lévi-Strauss points out) such study should aim at gaining knowledge of relationships between myths, not at somehow discovering "the true version" behind them all.[13] As Hymes has demonstrated, the story of Seal and her younger brother has its own artistically sophisticated unity of parts; and keeping that particular unity in mind as we take up a different narrative unity involving the same parts—in the Coos text—should help us to understand both stories better.

"The Revenge against the Sky People" is a genuine hero story, a fast-paced thriller in which the younger brother's fidelity to a code of vengeance on behalf of his slain brother propels him through a series of desperate adventures—of tests, really—his triumphant passing of which reveals him to be not only faithful but also remarkably courageous, quick witted and alert, and self-controlled. Whereas the slayer in the Clackamas story is, as Hymes observes, mainly a means to an end, the younger brother is unambiguously the protagonist here; from his ascent of the arrow-ladder (a very widespread Indian narrative motif), his perspective is ours, and, although what Melville Jacobs says about the tacit/dramatic nature of most Native American storytelling—"the feelings of the actors remain wholly the task of the audience to project and devise"[14]—is true here also, the clues as to our hero's feelings are so vividly dramatized throughout that our empathy with him is, I think, unusually rich.

In his analysis of "Seal and Her Younger Brother," Hymes concludes that the story is of a tragic type, in which social norms are upheld, but at the expense of failing to reckon with an empirical situation: Type Two $(+-)$ in the Lévi-Straussian code of bipolar permutations in myths. He then observes that Type One $(++)$, in which social norms are upheld and the empirical situation successfully reckoned with, is not common in the Clackamas collection: "I suspect that myths told aboriginally by males might have had more examples of male heroes to whom the type would apply."[15] ("Seal and Her Younger Brother" was told by a woman, who in turn had her repertory from three generations of female raconteurs; there seems to have been special male and female subrepertories among Western tribes.)

Now, discounting the fact that "The Revenge against the Sky People" is from a different tribal literature, we can claim it as the missing but predicted Type One (++) story par excellence. That is, the young avenger is able to uphold his people's social norm of loyalty-in-revenge precisely because he is so successfully in command of the empirical situation, so alert and nervily resourceful as an improviser in his disguise. That perspicacity will be important in the story is established very early, in fact: negatively, when the canoe builder carelessly converses with the stranger "with his head bent down," and positively, when even before the hero appears the victim's people quickly interpret the eldritch clue of his little dog barking "straight up"—at the sky. And the placement within the Coos story structure of an analogue to the Clackamas story—the child who observes something sinister about his "sister-in-law" but is shushed by his grandmother out of an adult's regard for propriety and ethnocentric wisdom ("The women from there look just like men," declares the grandmother)—is, surely, a brilliant stroke of counterpointing, perfectly setting off the hero's keen-eyed and canny exploits at the expense of his unwitting hosts. (I am not suggesting, of course, that the Coos storyteller or his audience necessarily knew the Clackamas story as a separate item, only that our knowing it helps us to understand how its analogue functions in the Coos narrative.)

The central conflict of "The Revenge against the Sky People" is "located" with unusual dramatic intensity (as already noted) in the mind of the hero.[16] Will he make it? Can he possibly be resourceful and composed enough to maintain his desperate disguise, or will he slip up, or break down, and be found out? The creation of a high degree of psychological tension in a narrative is never a casual happenstance, as devotees of the thriller know; by turning now to the text of the Coos story, perhaps we can see the narrative art of the story for what it is and look beyond it to some features of Indian narrative art generally.

From the direct opening sentence, the translated verbal style of the piece is simple, unobtrusive, "linear," and in general highly serviceable for oral narration of a "thriller": in the original Coos-language text, sentences very frequently begin with *Tso*—"Then . . ."—leading the action on its way. Though unadorned, the style is not as sparse or paratactic as that of the Chinook narrative, and although there seem to be fewer verbal cues for mimicry, gesture, and "sound effects" on the part of the narrator than in other Coos stories (especially those with humorous content), there are some cues—as in the hero's conversations in disguise with his various Sky Country hosts and in the final ritual to restore the brother's head to his body. In general, like the best of his contemporaries, Frachtenberg seems to have aimed in his translation at a literal, readable accuracy, and probably not much more. As so often with American Indian texts, it is hard to say much more than this: without fluency in the native language, of the all-too-rare sort that informs Jacobs's and Hymes's commentary on "Seal and Her Younger Brother" and indeed their translation of it, we are obliged to bypass matters of diction, wordplay, and other elements of verbal texture in favor of larger stylistic elements that constitute the story's narrative artistry per se, the cunning of its telling.

The teller opens his tale, then, with a small but effective bit of *foreshadowing*—of all storytelling devices the most frequently used in Native literature, in part I suppose because narrators could count on audiences knowing their stories in outline and thus being able to respond to narrative anticipations. The murderer from Above interrogates the elder brother at his work before decapitating him—just as eventually the younger brother interrogates the murderer's wife while she is digging fern-roots, at greater length and for more obviously practical reasons. In turn, of course, this second interrogation serves, as it often does in Native stories, to outline roughly and foreshadow the ideal course of events from this point on in the story: each of the younger brother's questions to the unsuspecting woman reveals habitual actions on her and her husband's part that, we guess, the young hero will have to imitate in the course of his most unhabitual mission in disguise. The overall effect of such foreshadowing, I imagine, is to deepen the tense imaginative bond between the hero and the listeners (or readers): we come to share a detailed secret knowledge that will be for the hero the basis of highly risky actions and for us the basis of highly dramatic expectations.

In these terms, the younger brother's momentary lapses of attention are heart-stopping, and his improvised excuses are all the more impressive because of what we know. When he forgets what he has learned about local customs and offers the two old pariahs some fern-roots, we are reminded forcibly that he is after all in a strange, alien country in the sky, where such a norm as kindness to the aged is apparently not honored (Sky and Under-Sea are frequently separate "worlds" in coastal stories, culturally as well as physically set apart from earthly life). Here our hero's adherence to a point of Coos etiquette is dangerously at odds with his adherence to the empirical situation. But although the old couple recognize and point him out with apparent vindictive glee, the danger passes, and he moves on into the scene of greatest risk, the house of his brother's murderer, where he must play the part of "wife."

Here a second major foreshadowing occurs, in the gruesome dancing of the Sky People around the elder brother's bleeding head. Presumably, the dance is intended to help the killer obtain its spirit power, as in the practice of most Western Indian groups: according to the Coos custom concerning killings, for example, "the inhabitants of the village in which the murderer lived danced for a number of nights (usually five) in a dance called *saat*—the murderer dance." [17] In our story, the Sky People's *saat* is ultimately interrupted; the measure of their defeat and the younger brother's triumph is taken at the end of his successful dance with his people to revive the elder brother and restore his head to him.

The crises now come pell-mell. First the younger brother cries out against the physical pain of the boiling water on his hand, and then, as if one level of torment has prepared for a deeper one, he cries out in implied grief and outrage as he recognizes his brother's gory head hanging from the ceiling and yet must improvise an excuse for his tears. The scene is starkly effective, like a piece of highly economical stagecraft; and we may recall Jacobs's view that the art of Indian myth-narrative is in general best considered and appreciated as a dramatic art. [18] Especially so in the present scene, of course, with the hero's very survival dependent on his skill as a self-conscious "actor."

Now comes the story's convergence on the incidents in "Seal and Her Younger Brother"—and what a difference! Despite the earlier assurances of the murderer's wife that her husband "usually falls asleep quickly," there is clearly the possibility of a violent sexual encounter and unmasking of the younger brother (in the Alsea form of the story, the husband, already in bed, actually calls out for intercourse: "Come up here: make war upon me!" [19]). The first thought of the mother after the murder (empirically wrong, predictably), that her son "must have killed his wife," underscores this implicit threat of sexual violence against the false "wife," our hero. As for the little boy who warns that "My sister-in-law looks like a man," the story seems to allow him a distant sympathy; he is given the last word on the matter, at any rate—" It is not a woman." Following Hymes's idea that "Seal and Her Younger Brother" is profoundly a Chinookan woman's story, told by women, with a sensitive young girl as its heroine, we might say that "The Revenge against the Sky People" is complementarily a man's story in these respects, as in others, that it was told by a man, that the unheeded discoverer of the killer is a sharp-eyed *boy* (a faint counterpart of the hero himself), and that it is his grandmother, one of the heedless female adults, and not the boy himself, who is made to feel the drops of blood and actually discover the murder.

But we have gotten a little ahead of the narrator's strategy, which takes a surprising turn just at the outset of the murder scene. "Now it got to be evening. The *woman* was going upstairs. . . . When they went to bed *she* had a big knife under the pillow. The husband went to bed first. The *woman* was walking outside" (emphasis mine). Whatever Percy Lubbock and James himself might say about such a drastic shift of pronominal point of view, clearly it works here. We have been brought into so full an engagement with the younger brother's predicament and the secret trial of his attention and composure that now the narrator can afford to reverse the perspective, calling the hero "the woman," just as he is known to his victim and his household, and thereby preparing to render the hero's grisly revenge from the standpoint of those who discover and suffer it. So complete is the reversal, in fact, that the victim's brother is referred to by the narrator as "the little brother-in-law."

The effect is to deepen the horror through a kind of double vision of the climactic action—we know the actor now called "the woman" for what he is, but at the same time that we are (presumably) wishing him well, we perforce find ourselves in a world of nocturnal household terror and helplessness that is much like the world that the heroine of "Seal and Her Younger Brother" herself inhabits. It is a notable and sophisticated strategy; Shakespeare does something like it in *Macbeth,* after all, in dramatizing Duncan's murder and the events leading to its discovery from an "inside" and then an "outside" perspective. Even after he has given us back the hero's perspective, as he returns safely to his home and successfully revives his brother, the narrator returns once more to the victims' point of view—

"None of those people from above could come down, and none could take his revenge."

According to our own narrative conventions, the story ought to end at this point, with an unusually perfect revenge heroically concluded (the initial victim is even living again) and with the possibility of counter-revenge precluded. Part of the power of "Seal and Her Younger Brother," of course, derives from the utter finality of *its* ending. Here, instead, the narrator goes on to translate the entire action into simple mythic terms— the hero and his folks constitute the Woodpecker people: "The blood on the neck, that's what makes the head red. Thus one said to them, 'You shall be nothing. You shall be a woodpecker. The last people shall see you.'" After the tensely dramatic action of the younger brother's mission, this seems regrettably anticlimactic, especially the promised reduction of the hero— "You shall be nothing"; students with whom I have discussed the story have generally responded, "Shucks, is *that* all it means?" Even admitting a certain logic in the creation of woodpeckers out of a man who at the first of the story is a canoe maker, a worker in cedarwood, and, beyond that, noting that like other Western Indians the Coos prized woodpecker feathers as tokens of sexual prowess and social status,[20] it is hard not to agree with the students' dissatisfaction.

Still, it is possible to assert the functional integrity of this conclusion, I think, although not necessarily according to the rules of our fiction, especially those dictating strong, programmatic endings. In both the Clackamas Chinook and Coos repertories, and others in the West, mythic explanatory endings like this one are common, often sounding similarly "tacked-on."[21] Specifically, the Alsea and Tillamook versions of "The Revenge against the Sky People" also end with the woodpecker motif. What is involved, perhaps, is a Native generic convention, a set of formal storytelling options. Although we might not have guessed it from the relatively realistic quality of much of the action, the story of the younger brother's revenge is implicitly set, like the great majority of Northwest Indian narratives, in the "Myth Age," a time before Time when the world was unfinished and ungoverned by precedent, and inhabited by freaks and monsters as well as beings with human form. Ultimately, the Myth Age gives way to an era of Transformation, in which the *lusus naturae* are cleared away, usually by an itinerant transformer (often a trickster), and the Myth Age beings are transformed one by one into the various natural creatures, according to their personalities and conduct—all of this in preparation for the coming of the *real* people, i.e., the Clackamas or the Chinook, if you belonged to one tribe or the other.

Now such a "historical" context or matrix would surely exert heavy pressure on the formation of individual stories and, during their recitation in cycles, lead at their conclusions away from localized events in the Myth Age to the transformations and precedents, great and minor, that produced the "real world" as it is today. In the preface to his collection of Coos myths, Melville Jacobs observes that when finishing his narration of a folk-tale or myth involving a Myth Age being, "the raconteur would usually close with a conventional phrasing something as follows, 'When the people next to come (the Indians not yet here in the land but soon to arrive and make their home here) see you, you will run, whenever you see a person.' "[22] Likewise, to take a somewhat farfetched modern example, there is clearly a strong tendency in the historical novel to shift at the end of its narrative of a historical continuum into the reader's own time reality—"And here's how it turns out ultimately." Indeed, as T. T. Waterman argued long ago in a classic essay on the instability of etiological elements in Indian stories, what appears to be mythic explanations of the "Just So" variety may actually constitute a narrative device whereby the story asserts its cogency and "truth" to the audience—as if the Coos narrator were to say on behalf of his completed story, in effect, "Now then, if you don't believe it, just look at the woodpeckers' heads!"[23]

The fact that "Seal and Her Younger Brother" does not end with an explanatory mythic foretelling, unlike a number of other stories in the Clackamas Chinook literature, suggests to me that the Indian raconteurs worked with options, not ironclad generic rules; and in this case, and others like it, the exclusion of all mythic consequences from the narrative probably indicates some sort of special strategy, perhaps aimed at intensifying the story's immediacy. In terms of cultural purposes, perhaps we can suppose (following a footnoted hint from Hymes[24]) that the bare drama of "Seal and Her Younger Brother" was especially recast by Mrs. Howard or one of her recent female predecessors so as to dramatize, in the era of white contact and Native deculturation, the insufficiency of traditional social norms and the corresponding importance of keeping your eyes and ears open and your tongue at the ready, as the little heroine tries to do. In

Edgar's formula at the end of *King Lear,* with the elders dead and the old way crumbling: "Speak what we feel, not what we ought to say."

As for "The Revenge against the Sky People," as anticlimactic as the etiological "coda" may seem to us, still, it does accomplish a certain graceful distancing of the main action. Not only is it promised that the heroes of this horrendous story will become the familiar woodpeckers of today (source of socially valuable feathers), but the listeners themselves are drawn explicitly into the action, as myth gives way to here-and-now "reality." The actors are told: "The last people [meaning us, the present knowers of such inherited stories] shall see you." So we do, and remember our mythic legacy as a consequence. And such distancing, which might very well have had special value for an audience including small children—allowing for the dissipation of their awakened fears—is prepared for, before the end. The younger brother's ritual dancing, with its magic-formulaic five repetitions leading to his brother's revival, points beyond the "improvised," that is, dramatic, action of the main story; as does, more subtly, the narrator's one self-conscious comment just as he turns his tale to ritual and transformation for posterity—"Now, *it is said,* they were going to join his elder brother's head" [25] (emphasis mine). So, having framed his gripping and well-made story as a traditional Coos "saying," the narrator concludes his performance of it.

In the mid-1830s a Protestant missionary named Samuel Parker surveyed the Clackamas Chinook homelands along the Willamette River in Oregon for possible converts and, regarding Native mythology, reported: "I am far from believing the many long and strange traditions with which we are often entertained. It is more than probable, that they are in most instances the gratuitous offerings of designing and artful traders and hunters to that curiosity which is ever awake and attentive to subjects of this description. The Indians themselves would often be as much surprised at the rehearsal of their traditions, as those are, for whose amusement they are fabricated." [26]

Fortified with hindsight, one winces at the opportunities for studying Indian literature firsthand thus wasted on an educated observer who could not bring himself to accept the fact that the Indians had a genuine oral literature and that "the many long and strange traditions" (he offers no examples) represented authentic Native art, not the idle coinage of white visitors. One ought to wince all the more, then, in realizing that although our libraries contain a wealth of carefully transcribed and translated Indian texts from all over western America, collected by men like Melville Jacobs and other students and followers of Franz Boas, the literary significance of this wealth is still, years later, virtually unknown. Such opportunities as we have we have so far mostly ignored.

There are serious obstacles to our study of America's first literatures, to be sure—ignorance of original languages, incomplete ethnographic information, difficulties with the oral basis of the material, academic biases, and so on. But as the work of Jacobs and Hymes demonstrates, and as I hope this essay has at least suggested, the art of Native storytelling is worth trying to elucidate, both for itself and for the light it may shed on the literature we call our own.[27]

7 / Uncursing the Misbegotten
in a Tillamook Incest Story

IN 1898, FRANZ BOAS PUBLISHED A SMALL COLLEC‑
tion of narratives, the first ever to appear from the Salish-speaking Tillamook Indians of the northern Oregon coast, including an arresting story
entitled *"xi'lgo,"* which can be abstracted as follows:

Xi'lgo, an ogress, kidnaps a brother and sister and brings them to her
home up the Nestucca River. Unable to feed them properly, she tells the
children to visit an old man who lives farther up the river. The old man
feeds them salmon, and tells them a story. When they report this to Xi'lgo,
she becomes angry and goes off, she tells them, to kill the old man. In reality she goes to have sex with him. The sequence of visit / meal and story /
report to Xi'lgo / her anger and vow of murder / her visit for sex is repeated
four times, until at last the children follow her and spy on her and the old
man in bed. Xi'lgo becomes aware of their spying, and they run away in
fright, but she finds a "husband doll" and a "wife doll" they leave behind,
and uses the dolls to lay a curse of incest upon them. The children run to
Clatsop, where they build a house, and the girl initiates incestuous sex with
her brother, per Xi'lgo's curse.

They have a baby boy. Eventually Xi'lgo comes and kills the brother. The sister sets their house afire and leaps in, but first gives the baby to a neighbor to adopt. The baby grows up playing with a ball made of his mother's wrist-bone and a bat of his father's rib; one day another child tells him that he is playing with his parents' bones. His adoptive mother tells him about the deaths of his real parents because of Xi'lgo's evil. The boy vows revenge and sets off in the guise of an eagle, with a girl in the shape of a mole as comrade. She is to burrow under villages and steal valuables while he is looking for Xi'lgo. He finds the ogress, snatches her up, and dismantles her over the ocean—but four times she returns to life, until Blue Jay tells him that Xi'lgo's heart is in her hat. The boy finds Xi'lgo one more time and succeeds in killing her by destroying her hat. He and the girl divide the valuables and go home.[1]

In the early 1930s, two young ethnographers visited what remained of the Tillamook community at Nehalem, and each transcribed stories from one of the last surviving speakers of that language, Mrs. Clara Pearson. First, May Edel recorded stories in Tillamook Salish; then, a few years later, Mrs. Melville Jacobs (Bess Langdon) recorded a much fuller repertory as narrated in English.[2] In 1944 Edel published a study based on a comparison of Boas's texts, hers, and Mrs. Jacobs's, demonstrating that the Tillamook repertory was remarkably stable and resistant to variation.[3] And in 1959 Mrs. Jacobs published with her husband's editorial assistance an edition of sixty texts in English, *Nehalem Tillamook Tales*.[4]

In 1805, Lewis and Clark estimated the Tillamook tribe at several thousand, and until decimated by disease a generation later they were the most powerful and feared group on the central West Coast. It is likely that nobody fluent enough in the Tillamook language and culture to tell the stories is now living.[5] What survives from our century, albeit in neglect despite Edel's important study and Mrs. Jacobs's fine edition, are the texts of Mrs. Pearson's stories. But how do they live in a reading? Do they have literary and imaginative value beyond what they can show us as verbal relics? The question of literary reclamation is especially interesting here because of the existence of two overlapping sets of texts from different narrators spanning over forty years, permitting a kind of interpretive double vision. Let's consider the text of Mrs. Pearson's much-expanded version of Boas's "Xi'lgo" story: "Wild Woman and the Brother and Sister Who Marry," as transcribed by Mrs. Jacobs.[6]

Wild Woman was living alone. Her husband, High Class Crane, lived upriver in his own place. Every day she would go to the beach for children. She wanted to raise some grandchildren.

There on the beach at Nehalem, many children went swimming every day. One boy had no father, no mother; his grandmother took care of him. His name was Stcheelgeelun, but the boys had given him a nickname, Sore Back. They named him that because they threw mud on him and urinated on his back until his back was all sore. The other boys were awfully mean to him. They did not treat him well because he had no father and no mother. He was some kind of a blackfish that could squirt water from the top of his head. He had a sharp fin along his back. His grandmother would tell him, "I want you to quit running with those mean boys." He would not mind, no, he liked it. They would call him, "Come on, let's go swimming." All ready! He would run. He could not be taught anything.

When the boys got through swimming, they would go lie down on the hot sand and go to sleep. Sore Back went to sleep too. He always slept on the end. Wild Woman would come along with her big soft spruce-root basket and look at those boys. "I will steal them." Then she would pick up Sore Back first, because he slept on the end, and put him in the bottom of her basket. She would continue picking them up till her basket was full. Then she would put some dry rotten wood on the top so no one could see the boys, and walk home. When she got home she would put her basket down. "Wake up! grand-children!" She removed the rotten wood; there were never any children there. Sore Back wriggled back and forth until that fin on his back wore a hole in the bottom of the basket. Everything had fallen out except the rotten wood. There would always be just that rotten wood in the basket. Then she would feel sorry, "Oh, I lost my boys." She never found out how it happened that those boys fell out. Day after day it happened that way.

Then one day it happened that a boy and his sister lay on the end and Sore Back was the third one in the row of children. That day Wild Woman put the brother and sister in the bottom of the basket and Sore Back was on top of them. Then she filled her basket with children. She put rotten wood on top, she covered them. She arrived at home, she put her basket down. "Wake up! grandchildren!" She took out the rotten wood; there she had a girl and a boy. Sore Back had made a hole in the side of the basket and he himself and all those children on top of him had dropped out. Just those two remained in the bottom of the basket. Oh! She was pleased. She had a boy and a girl now. They awoke, they saw, "Goodness, a strange woman." She said to them, "You are my grandchildren." Then she told them, "You go and see grandpa. Grandpa will feed you; he has quantities of little fish." They went to Crane. "Grandmother

told us to come and see if grandpa would give us something to eat." "Yes,"
he said, "I have a lot of trout already cooked." He fed them. They ate, they
returned. Ah, Wild Woman liked those children. Every morning she got ready,
she took her basket, away she went traveling in the mountains. She pretended
that she was going to dig roots. But she really went to get poison lizards, water
dogs, and such things, and she brought a basket full of them in the afternoon.
That was the time she did not want the children around. The children kept
her fire for her while she was away. She would tell the children. "Do not look
at me. Go to grandpa and tell him to feed you." Then she would dig in the hot
ashes and she would roast those lizards there. She would say, "Up at Tillamook
Mountain, I dug one. At Nestucca, I dug one." In that manner she would name
all the rivers and mountains, and in each place she had dug but one. She could
travel all over in an hour; she went in a different way from the way an ordi-
nary person travels. She would tell the children, "Do not look at me. You go
to grandpa and tell him to feed you." She did not want the children watching
her and seeing her eating those animals. Every day she did like that.

Those children grew very rapidly. She spent a great deal of time amusing them. She gathered sea shells for the little girl to play with as dolls; and she
told her husband, "You make that boy a little canoe to play with." Indeed she
liked those children, but she had nothing for them to eat. She always had to
tell them, "You go to grandpa. He will feed you."

At times she neglected to go for those animals. And sometimes she
would get peculiar. Then she would tell those children, "Go tell grandpa to
tell you a story." Those children would go, usually evenings, though maybe in
the afternoon once in a while. They would arrive there. "Grandmother, she
said you should tell us a story." "Oh," grandpa would say, "you do not want to
pay any attention to her. She talks funny sometimes. There is no story to tell."
Then after a while grandpa would start in and tell a story to the children, and
of course they did not understand what it was or why he always told the same
one. He would finish and say, "There! That's all. That's a short story." They
would run home then. There Wild Woman would be poking in the fire with
her face turned away. "Well, did grandpa tell you a story?" "Yes, he told us a
story." Then the old woman would rub her eyes and say, "Oh, that smoke got
in my eyes. It is making me cry. That smoke went in my eyes. What did grandpa
say?" The little girl would not tell, but the boy would, he would repeat it word
for word. "Grandpa said, 'I looked down the river, and there was a small canoe
down there and there was a person paddling. He does not sit up straight, that
one who paddles, he is kind of stooped over. And that canoe is not perfect, it
is somewhat lopsided, that canoe!'" (She would get a little angry because he
[Crane] was really talking about her.) "And grandpa said, 'After a while I looked

up in the sky, and oh, that sky was all clouds, and I saw a bunch of grass growing up on that sky.'" Then Wild Woman would seem very angry. "He is always
talking about my dead people!" She called it talking about a dead person so the
children would think he was talking straight. Then she would get ready, put on
her best shawl, and take her double-bladed knife. "I'm not going to hurt him
very much," she would say, "because you children get your meals there. I'm
not going to hurt him very much." When Wild Woman returned she always
had scratches on her arms. She dug them with her own fingernails to make it
appear to the children that she had been fighting. After she had gone, the little
girl would always say, "Oh, what did you want to tell her for? Every word that
grandpa said? That always makes her angry. Maybe she will go kill grandpa."

So it kept up. Sometimes she would go get her lizards and water dogs
and then she would tell the children, "Go get your meal at grandpa's." But
whenever she wanted it [coitus], then she wanted that story business. After a
while the children were grown up. They had become smarter. They liked Wild
Woman, but they liked the old man better because that was where they ate.
Again she sent them for a story. After she had gone with her double-bladed
knife, the girl said, "Oh, maybe she will kill him this time. Let us go and watch.
What does she do to grandpa all the time?" They went, they hurried, they
sneaked around where they could see through a crack. Wild Woman arrived,
she said, "Mmmmm, you are always talking bad about my dead people." Crane
said, "Aw! Do not be always talking, just keep still." Then Wild Woman received what she wanted. The children watched. "Oh, they are doing something
that does not look good." Somehow they knew what it was. "Ah! She cannot
be killing him since grandpa is on top." Suddenly Wild Woman realized that
someone was looking at her. She said, "Let me up. Eyes are looking at me."
She called outside, "I will fix you when I get hold of you." Crane would not let
her up because he knew it must be his grandchildren watching, and he feared
she would kill them. The children were frightened. "Let us go. She said if she
got hold of us she would fix us."

They went, the girl gathered up her dolls, the boy took his bow and
arrow, and they ran as they went away. The girl overlooked two of her dolls,
a boy doll and a girl doll. She had not picked them all up. Their grandfather
held Wild Woman as long as he was able. Finally she pulled herself away from
him. She went home, she looked around. No children anywhere. After a while
she went and looked in the corner where the little girl played with her dolls.
She found those two that were left. "Oh, they have run away," she realized. She
picked up those two dolls, the boy and the girl, she talked to those dolls. She
said, "You are my grandson, and you are my granddaughter. I will cause them
to do the same thing they watched me do. They are to do it before the night is

past. They were looking at me, they watched me." Then she started out to follow them. Her husband followed her. That husband, Crane, he himself had [spirit] power. He made hills. "Oh, I wish everything may become a big hill, so she will be unable to get around quickly." After a while night came, Wild Woman gave it up. She went back home.

That brother and sister crossed a creek. Then they made it [magically] into a big river so it could no longer be waded. The boy got some slivers from a tree, he made a tiny house, like a real one. He put beds inside, fixed a place for the fire to be built, he put shelves in the corners, made a door, everything exactly as in a real house. When he finished he sat down by the little door of his tiny house. He put his hands together, he blew through them right into the door. Lo! He blew into that tiny house until it became a large house. He had a strong power. Then he said to his sister, "Well, we will go in and try to build a fire." He took a drill, he built a fire. Since he was the bigger, he made decisions. He told her, "That is your bed on the other side of the fire, you will stay there. I will stay on this side." After a while they went to bed. The girl got the full effect of Wild Woman's wish. She had left her two dolls. But the boy did not get any effect because he had not forgotten any of his belongings. Presently the girl said, "Oh, it is leaking on me. This roof, it leaks." Her brother said, "Isn't that strange? There is no leak here by my bed." She kept on, kept on talking about the leak. He got tired of listening to her. He had made very long beds. "Well," he said, "you may come and lie at the foot of my bed." She did that. Still she was not satisfied. She was not close enough to him, you see. She began to complain again. "It leaks, it leaks!" He wondered, "Why? Why should it be leaking?" He did not believe it. After a while he got up. He went outdoors and looked. "There is no rain! Lots of stars, and clear!" And he thought, "What is wrong with her anyway?" He said to her, "Why, there is no rain. It is quite clear outside." Nevertheless she kept on crying out. After a while he told her, "Lie down at the back of my bed, next to the wall." She did that. Pretty soon she cried out again, "Oh, this is leaking over here." Then he knew, "Oh, she must want something." She cried out again and he told her, "Well, you may cover with my own cover." Now they were to sleep under the same blanket. She did that. She shut up then. She did not cry out. They went bad then. And right away she became pregnant.

After a while their baby was born. It was a boy. Every day the father would take his baby boy and they would go and sit on top of the roof of the house. He would sit there with that baby, so the baby would not cry. The mother heard somebody yelling on the other side of the river, daily. She looked across, "Oh, my! That is grandmother." Every day grandmother would call out, "Come across and get me." But they were afraid of her. No one knows what that grandmother might have done if they had gone across for her. It is possible that she would have made up with them. On the other hand she may have come just to kill them. Anyhow that brother just sat on the roof with his son, and the sister just stayed indoors out of sight. Wild Woman would call nicely, "Come and get me, dear grandchildren! I am [have been] searching for you. Come and get me!" He would not go across for her. Perhaps he should have gone in the house. Finally she knew they would never come for her. She had her walking cane with her. She said, "All right, you do not want to get me." She took her walking cane, she pointed it at the man on the roof. She said, "You drop dead!" He dropped dead. But the baby was not killed. The mother in the house would not show her face outside. She was afraid of Wild Woman. The baby cried and cried. The mother called out, "Bring the baby in the house." No answer. Wild Woman went away.

Finally the mother saw, "Grandmother is gone." She went outdoors then. Ah! Her husband was lying dead. She wept and wept. She took that baby and fastened him on her back. She left her husband lying; she set the house on fire. There was no neighbor near her, she was just by herself. Ah! It just broke her heart. She wanted to jump into that fire with her husband; but she did not like to take her baby with her into the fire.

Now there was a man who liked to go along the beach and watch to see what might be washed ashore. This very day he was going along the beach. This man was Bald Eagle. He looked, "Well! There is a house burning, I am going there. I wonder if the people are burned up, or what has happened?" He got there, he saw a woman with a baby on her back. "My goodness! That woman acts strangely; she acts as if she wants to jump into that fire. My goodness! I want to grab that baby if I can." He listened to that woman crying. She said, "Oh, my brother-husband! Upper half, brother! Lower half, husband!" He listened. He thought, "Oh! Does that not sound queer? One-half brother, one-half husband? I wonder who she is?" He did not get to talk to her at all. She became somewhat crazy. He got there just in time to seize that baby, and away! She jumped into the fire! He wanted to save her also, but he was unable to do it.

"Oh, I am not going down to the beach again. I am going to turn around and go right back home and bring this baby to my wife." Bald Eagle started home then. That baby cried and cried. He jiggled him, he still cried. He put him inside his shirt. Still he cried. He tried everything, but no, he could not make that baby become quiet. That little boy just cried and cried. "Oh goodness! Whatever can I do with him?" Bald Eagle worried. Bald Eagle and his wife had one child, a daughter. She was small yet, but she was a talker! She was a cranky little devil, that little girl. Bald Eagle kept thinking, "Oh, how am

I going to keep that bad girl of ours from knowing I have gotten this baby?" At last he had an idea. He put that baby boy between his legs. Right up close to his testicles he placed the baby. Then that baby kept still; he stopped crying because no one could see him then; he was hidden.

Bald Eagle arrived at home. He called his wife aside and told her what had happened. He said, "I saved a little boy; I want you to [pretend to] become ill, and lie down as if you are going to have a baby." When night came, they told their little girl, "You must go to bed, early." She had a separate room. She went to bed. She did not like it a bit. After a while Bald Eagle took the baby out from between his legs and handed him to his wife. Pretty soon that baby squawked. The little girl had her covers open, she was peeping. She thought, "Huh! That is no new just-born baby. That is a big strong kind of baby." Next morning the mother acted as if she were ill. She remained in bed and Bald Eagle waited on her. But the little girl, she knew all the time!

The little boy grew very rapidly. In what seemed like no time at all, he could walk already. They told the little girl, "He is your little brother. You do not want to fight with him. Do not hit him."

After some time Bald Eagle went to that place where the house had been burned up. He went there and looked around. He found a rib of the man which had not been all burned up. He picked that up. He looked some more, he found the ankle bone of the baby's mother. He picked them up. He came home, he said, "These are for the baby. He can play ball with them. This round bone will be his ball, and he can strike it with this long bone." That little girl, she had a playhouse outdoors. Whenever the little boy hit his ball, the girl would run and get in the way of the ball so it would hit her. Then she would bawl. She would say, "Oh! He hit me! He is playing with his mother's ankle and his father's rib, and he hit me!" The little baby boy would hear that. It just broke his heart. He was getting bigger and of course he was getting smarter, because he was to become very smart indeed. He would run in the house. "Mother! Sister said I was playing with my mother's ankle bone, and I was playing with my father's rib bone." Oh, they went after that girl, they abused her dreadfully. They gave her a beating. As the boy grew bigger he began to abuse his sister also. He became so he himself would hit her purposely with that ball. She would put her hands up in front of her face like this [palms outward at the sides of her cheeks]. She would say, "Do not hit me! Do not hit me!" And she would cry and cry and wipe her nose. Her nose grew long and sharp from that continual wiping. Her eyes grew smaller and smaller from constant weeping. Her parents would abuse her just to treat the boy better. They thought the world of that baby boy. Finally the little girl's hands grew up at the sides of her face and she could not take them down any more. Her eyes almost disappeared, and her nose was even longer and sharper. She became Mole.

When the boy became a young man his [foster] parents sent him to the woods [to obtain a spirit power]. They said, "You go into the woods. Go and learn something." He did that. He became most powerful. He learned many things [acquired guardian spirits]. He obtained Thunder Bird as a guardian. That gave him power to fly around just like Thunder Bird. He came home and told his father and mother; he did not know he was not supposed to tell anyone about his power. That Mole felt terribly jealous of him. They treated him better than her, though she was their own child. He told his people, "Well, Mother! Father! I am going to leave you. I have learned many things [acquired many spirit powers]. I can even go and fly in the sky." They became very proud of him. They decided to tell him about himself. They told him, "Your mother jumped in the fire. Your father died. That Wild Woman, she is the one who killed your father. Your mother grieved so, just as soon as I grabbed you from your mother's back she jumped in the fire then." The boy's feelings were not hurt by this news; he thought this way, "I have a good father and mother in these people. They have treated me so well, I have never known any difference from having my own father and mother." They told him that Wild Woman was living in a certain town. He said, "I am going to kill her. I will take my sister along with me." Then he tried to teach his sister to fly, but she could not do it. She would fly just a short distance, and then she would drop down. She could not fly. He said to her, "Well, I would like to take you along; you could be my comrade and do some different sort of damage for me." She wanted to do that, but she could not fly, so they had to stop and study. Then her brother asked, "Can you go under the ground? Let's see you try." He sent her, she started out. She went under the ground, indeed she went swiftly. He could see the ground moving where she went along underneath, he saw that she went fast. He called, "Stop! Now you can come out." She came out. The father and mother were watching their children. Her brother said, "Do you think you can do that all the time?"

Mole replied, "Yes, that does not trouble me at all." "All right! That is the way you will go!" Then he explained to Mole where they were going, and he told her, "If I am seen, those people will get excited and they will all come out to look at me while I fly around close to that town. You will go under the ground and come up inside the houses and take all those people's valuables, such as their money beads [large and valuable dentalia]."

So they started off. Mole had a soft rush basket with her in which to put whatever she might take. Oh, the old folks hated to see them both leaving; both of their children would be gone. The brother flew, he arrived at the town. Ice lived there. Ice was the first one to come outside. He looked up. Oh, he yelled, "Hey! Come out all you people. Everybody, come out! The strangest thing I ever saw, it is a bird with person's feet." Everyone ran outside to look. Presently

Wild Woman came out. She was the same old woman but she was disguised as a young girl. She was wearing a basket cap. He recognized her in that basket cap, nevertheless. Blue Jay had told him about her. Wild Woman was aware of all that. She came outside, she looked up. "Oh, that is Placed-Next-to-Testicles," she said. That made the young man angry, he did not like it that she named him that, and he did not like it that she knew him already. After a while he flew down and grabbed Wild Woman by the hair and away he took her. After a while her cap dropped down, but he paid no attention to that. He thought, "Everything is all right as long as I have her herself." He flew far, far out over the ocean; he tore her all to pieces and dropped the pieces in the water. He flew back home. He found his sister, she was back also, she arrived at the same time. She had many things which she had stolen. He said, "Maybe I killed her, Wild Woman. I seized her, I took her out over the ocean, I tore her to bits." His father and mother advised him, "You had better try looking every day. You had better go all over to different towns and places and see if you did kill her for good [forever]."

He said to Mole, his sister, "Well, we must go again." Mole emptied her basket. She gave all those things to her mother. Then they went. They arrived at a different place. Again Ice came out first. He called out again in the same manner for everyone to come out and look. Everyone came out. Lo! Wild Woman came out! She was alive! There she was in her basket cap. She said, "Oh, that is Placed-Next-to-Testicles." Then he flew down and grabbed her. As he flew off with her, her cap dropped down again. He did not know there was any meaning to that cap always dropping down. He took her out over the ocean, he tore her to pieces. He went home. He got there, his little sister arrived at the same time. She had gotten her soft rush basket half full of valuables. He said, "Maybe I killed her, Wild Woman. She was alive, I found her." His people advised him, "You cannot be sure. You see she is a different sort from a real person."

Next day he had to go again to see if Wild Woman had come back to life. The same thing that day, and the next day. The fifth day he went. His sister went underground again. As he flew along Blue Jay came. She said, "Nephew! You are on your way to kill Wild Woman?" "Yes, Auntie." "Ah, she is fooling you all the time. If you really want to kill her, you must watch that basket cap. That is where her heart is, in that basket cap. You watch it. If you get it, you mash it up. Mash the crown up. That is her heart: her whole life lies there." "Yes, Auntie. Is that all?" "That is all. You will surely get her if you do that." He went, Ice saw him. He yelled for everybody to come out. "A funny bird! He has a person's feet!" Presently Wild Woman came out. She was alive. She had her cap on. She said, "Oh, that is Placed-Next-to-Testicles." He flew down, grabbed her, and he took that basket cap away from her so it could not drop down any more. (Wild Woman must have been surprised. That Blue Jay tells all the time. Whenever you are in trouble of any kind she will tell you what to do.) He took Wild Woman out over the ocean, he tore her to pieces, he threw her in the water. He took that basket cap, he tore it, he mashed it up, he threw it in the water. Now he came away, he got home. He told, "I met old auntie Blue Jay; she told me what to do. I did that. Maybe Wild Woman is dead now." His sister was home too. Next day, he said, "I had better go look for her again, to see if she has come back to life this time." His sister started also. He stopped at the first town. Ice saw him, he came out. Everyone came out. There was no Wild Woman in that town. He left, going on to the next town. Ice, he was there already! He saw the young man flying, called everybody to come out. Wild Woman was not there. In this manner he went on to those towns. He went on to the last town. Ice saw him again, everybody came out. She was not there either. She was dead. He had killed her. He came home. He said, "Maybe I killed her this time. She was not anywhere."

Then he talked to his father and mother. "Well, my people! I must leave you. I am going to leave this place. I cannot take my sister. I like her, but since she is unable to fly I cannot take her." Oh, those old people did not like it. His mother felt badly. She wept. He told her, "I cannot stay around here. I do not like it around here." He said, "Just the same, I think a great deal of you, my people." He left. Mole had to remain with the old folks.

(In the story's sequel the boy Placed-Next-to-Testicles ventures into the sky and comes to the house of Old Man Thunder, where he meets and falls in love with Thunder's daughter. The old man imposes a series of murderous "bride-trials" on him, which he heroically overcomes, and so marries Thunder's daughter. Eventually he comes to exceed even Thunder in power.)

Stories about incest are numerous in the repertories of Western Indians, and the relative insistence upon the theme ought to remind us that myth-recitals served specific pedagogical purposes within Native culture, in this case "bringing into the open" for children the theme of incestuous conduct and dramatizing it as a primary evil to guard against. As D. Demetracopolou demonstrated long ago in her study of "Loon Woman" motifs, sibling-incest stories in the Far West are strikingly formulaic and conventionalized, duplicating one another as between tribes and languages and persisting in the recombination of a distinctive inventory of story elements.[7] Perhaps no Western "story-set" is more uniformly conventionalized, over a wider area of distribution, in fact, and one may speculate that (1) the "set" is very old, and (2) its elements have over the ages come to constitute a sort of authoritative "objective correlative" for feelings about incest, so that to think of incest without conjuring up the basic story would have been, as with the Oedipus story for us, virtually impossible.

The conventional elements of the sibling incest story, of which our Wild Woman narrative is an example, include the following:

– emphasis on the *family* in which the incest occurs, so that it is a family calamity;
– the sister's initiation of sexual contact with her brother;
– incest committed formalistically, "by stages," generally as the sister moves closer and closer to her brother's bed;
– a symbolic fire which generally consumes the sister, and sometimes the brother, and often other members of the family;
– survival of their offspring, a boy; his adoption by another family;
– recovery of bones of his parents, to serve as toys or ornaments for the child;
– his emergence as a hero with unusual powers.[8]

Now in the great majority of such narratives, the sister's initiation of sex with her brother is essentially unprovoked; perhaps she is wayward to begin with, and/or the brother is "too beautiful" and too much made over by his parents. But in Mrs. Pearson's story (and in Boas's earlier version), the evil is, we see, initiated externally by a stock character named "Wild Woman" (in Tillamook, *xi'lgo*), who has already kidnapped the children and established herself as an unnatural grandmother to them. Before we turn to the distinctive features of this story, it is worth noting that in the Tillamook repertory Wild Woman appears in numerous stories (she has her own "set," in fact) as a fearsome older female creature in whom the impulses of lust, mothering, envy, and anger are monstrously exaggerated and coexist in a state of utter volatility.

As a bugaboo to careless children, she is revealed as a habitual kidnapper, in a few instances cooking and eating her young captives, more frequently forcing sex on the boys and young men she has claimed as "grandson"—hence a specialist, if you will, at incest. In one story, disguised as a girl in order to seduce one of her grandsons, she even gives birth to a baby (who becomes a sea creature, a source of spirit-power), but otherwise Wild Woman is, however promiscuous, barren. At the apparent end of her turbulent career as a Myth Age being, she turns herself, fittingly enough, into Surf![9]

As a traditional Indian narrative, "Wild Woman and the Brother and Sister Who Marry" strikes me as being unusually rich in expressive detail; its texture is more explicitly rendered, more descriptive, than what we have found, say, in the highly tacit and understated Wasco "The Hunter Who Had an Elk for a Guardian Spirit" or the Clackamas Chinook "Seal and Her Younger Brother Lived There" and its Coos analogue. So, to a degree unusual in the Native literature, we are often informed as to what participants in scenes are thinking, what their reactions are, and so forth, as in the crucial episode where the Brother and Sister spy on Wild Woman and High Class Crane in bed, and we are told, interpretively, "'Oh, they are doing something that does not look good!' Somehow they knew what it was."

Indeed, Mrs. Pearson's narration of the story to Mrs. Jacobs is much more detailed than either Boas's 1890 version of it (which in fact reads like a summary) or her own earlier recitation of it in Tillamook to May Edel.[10] Mrs. Pearson's general penchant for description and interpretation may in fact reflect the influence of Caucasian modes of narrative, especially given the fact that in the case of our text, she was narrating directly into English for Mrs. Jacobs. And in the story under consideration—perhaps the most full featured of all the items in *Nehalem Tillamook Tales* and the most preoccupied with sexual matters—a special factor seems to be working: a condition of sexual candor as between women that Mrs. Pearson made amused note of herself in comparing Mrs. Jacobs, as a listener and transcriber, and Miss Edel. "You're a married woman, but she was only a young girl and I couldn't." [11]

Along with relative richness of texture, the story seems to me to reveal an unusual tightness of narrative structure. The plot is not especially complicated—there are no functional disguises in the main episodes or mythic anticipations or narrative frames, and it is certainly not notably concentrated, running as it does over considerable time and space—but as

I hope to show, the evidence of artistic design controlling the parts of the whole is unmistakable. It is, surely, for all its wild and repugnant subject, a well-made story; it holds together, as we say.

What is "Wild Woman and the Brother and Sister Who Marry" about? Not only about the terrible sin of sibling incest. Mrs. Pearson's interpretive impulse carries through past the end of the story and its sequel: in a postscript that is rare in Native texts, she suggests that "This story shows how a young person who is born in disgraceful circumstances through no fault of his own will obtain a very strong [spirit] power."[12] As a "moral," this is accurate enough; it reminds us that, taken as a whole, the story narrates a transformation of appalling evil and calamity into something good and auspicious—that is, the heroic power of the boy whose parents were brother and sister. Out of helplessness, shame, fear, and death in the one generation come strength, confidence, and status in the next; the potency of Wild Woman's curse on the Brother and Sister becomes in their offspring a rare gift.

How this radical "redemption" takes place emerges, I think, as the organizing concern of the story. It is structured in two parts of about equal length and strikingly parallel to one another (as if the left and right halves of a diptych). Part One runs up to the twelfth paragraph, at which point the Brother is dead, and the Sister is about to join him in their burning house, but holds back because of their baby. But in effect Part Two has already begun with the casual arrival on the scene of Bald Eagle, a good-hearted fellow, who knows nothing about the tragedy being consummated, but is ready and able to snatch the baby to safety as its mother leaps into the flames.

The most obvious analogue in our classical literature to this dramatic Janus-like moment, the very fulcrum of the whole story, is, of course, Act III, Scene iii of *The Winter's Tale*, where the shepherd who is to become the foster-father of Perdita comments to the clown on the teleological confusions at hand; "Now bless thyself: thou mettest with things dying, I with things new-born." As in the Tillamook story, so the two parts of *The Winter's Tale* are point-by-point structural reflections of one another. And the odd similarity between Indian narrative and Shakespearean romance involves more than just features of structure: indeed these features are means whereby, in their different ways, the two stories effect a transformation over two generations of powers of evil into powers of good. The comparison becomes even more strangely suggestive when we remember that in Shakespeare's source, Greene's *Pandosto,* incest is an explicit part of the plot! But lest we run the risk of "considering too curiously," in the name of comparison, let's take up the Tillamook story in earnest.

We can best do so, I think, by "reading" it diachronically, as it were, from left to right, but with our attention conditioned by the fact that we *know* the story as readers (even as Tillamook listeners would have known it), so that we can attend synchronically to the unusually formal elaborations of the structure.[13] For, as we will see, this is a narrative replete — almost redundant — with foreshadowing and "echoes" between Parts One and Two, with parallelism and balance of detail and episode, with repetition-with-variation, and the like. And in the course of narrating the transformation of Wild Woman's evil power into the admirable power of the emerging hero, the story seems especially intent on maintaining a kind of counterpoint between the mentality of adulthood and the mentality of childhood, with sexuality the common denominator. Innocence is always in peril here; play seems to correlate with copulation; a pair of dolls serve as the magical vehicles for inducing incest. We see the husband-and-wife dolls Sister leaves behind: and soon thereafter we see Brother and Sister in bed. The effect of this kind of counterpointing I find impossible to characterize in full, but it certainly evokes a constant sense of dismay and apprehension on behalf of the juvenile characters through Part One and well into Part Two; and the story's impact on Tillamook children must have been considerable.

Perhaps what is being "said" is that incest is the ultimate adult corruption of the condition of childhood. But, if so, the curse dies within its own generation, surviving only in our knowledge as audience, and the narrative labors to preserve and magnify the unfortunate child which is its issue — in Antigonus's words on infant Perdita: "To save the innocent: anything possible" (2.3.167).

The story begins, in a way, off-center, dwelling on a juvenile character, "Sore Back," who literally "drops out" (of Wild Woman's basket), as Brother and Sister come to the foreground. But before he disappears, Sore Back does serve a structural purpose: with "no father, no mother," he is the subject of general abuse and scorn, and as such he figures as the antitype of the orphan boy who is to become the hero of the story; more immediately, of course, he prefigures the fate of Brother and Sister, soon to be "orphaned" by Wild Woman in her role as kidnapper.

Our initial encounter with Wild Woman swiftly puts her "in character" in terms of her typological identity in "Wild Woman" stories, and prepares her for the particular role she will take in this story (a similar double characterization can be observed at the beginning of many stories about Coyote).[14] She and her quondam husband, High Class Crane, live apart and do not constitute a family unit; hence, her mothering instinct is suspect from the start and appears all the more stupidly unnatural when we learn that she maintains a witch's diet of reptiles and cannot feed the children, leaving that duty to Crane. Wild Woman's gathering basket is emblematic in context of her unnatural and indiscriminant cravings for sex and for children. It is like a kind of nightmarish externalized uterus (it is described as "her big soft spruce-root basket"), and in the logic of the story, the Brother and Sister are unnaturally reborn from it into the ogress's household after the kidnapping.[15]

The equation of childhood pursuits and adult sexuality mentioned above first appears when Wild Woman instructs the Brother and Sister to ask Crane to tell them a story, and then interrogates them about it, and reacts with apparent anger—all, it seems, as an elaborate sexual self-arousal and foreplay. The whole episode is hanky-panky of a kind to interest Krafft-Ebbing, and what is important about it is the way Wild Woman reprehensibly involves the children in the course of her lust. Crane's little story about the stooped-over person in the lopsided canoe seems oddly innocuous, even after we realize that it serves as a sexual signal. It is a measure of Mrs. Jacobs's sensitivity as a transcriber that, puzzled herself, she asked Mrs. Pearson why the story should anger Wild Woman so much. The answer is an interpretive revelation and a reminder of how much we have lost in the understanding of Native literature because transcribers haven't asked their informants such questions.

Oh, that old woman was only pretending to be mad. She was just excited (sexually). That story was a description of her genitals. The canoe was her vagina and the one paddling was her clitoris. The grass on the sky, that meant her (pubic) hair and her belly. Oh, she did not like it when he said the canoe was lop-sided. That was making fun of her, a little.[16]

(Later, when Wild Woman complains to Crane that "you are always talking bad about my dead people," her coy euphemism assumes a thoroughly unpleasant significance: ostensibly in chiding Crane, she refers to the widespread Native taboo against talking about the dead, but given the nature and the consequences of her sexuality, the euphemism has a literal appropriateness as well. It is possible that a wordplay in the Tillamook language is involved.)

So, in a bawdy jest conveyed by as-yet-unheeding children, the trouble begins. And it is characteristic of the structural artistry of the whole narrative that the trouble begins with two prophetic details. First, when the children return from Crane after he has told them the canoe story, Wild Woman, we are told, "would be poking in the fire with her face turned away"—precisely foreshadowing shameful events to ensue, and in particular the Sister's last agonized moments by her burning house. Second, in the detail of the Sister's refusal to tell the Wild Woman the story, there is a deft hint, I think, of her special susceptibility to the ogress's sexual curse. Her brother blithely reports verbatim what Crane has said: is there not a suggestion here, in his sister's reticence, that already she intuitively understands more than she should? At the least, she is much more sensitive than her brother to the emotional effect the story invariably has on their "grandmother"; she worries lest, in her apparent anger, Wild Woman "will kill grandpa."

Again, Wild Woman's strategy of disguising her sexual excitement as violent anger has a peculiarly infantile quality to it; anger is what a child might well think is at stake in observing uninhibited adult lovemaking, and of course this misperception colors the Brother's and Sister's eventual observation of Wild Woman and Crane in flagrante delicto—"Oh, she cannot be killing him since grandpa is on top." But if they are relieved on that score, it is made very clear that they *do* come to understand, precociously, the grown-up significance of what they are observing. "The children watched. 'Oh, they are doing something that does not look good.' Somehow they knew what it was."

Freudians would identify this as a variation on the primal scene. No doubt, given the crowded and unprivate living conditions prevalent among coastal Indian groups like the Tillamooks, such juvenile discoveries of adult sex in action were not infrequent[17]—but it is important to remember that this is a very special and unnatural case. The children are in effect orphans, isolated from elders and even peers who might interpret what they have seen and minimize its shock; they are, on the contrary, in the custody of an oversexed and irresponsible "wild woman."

A comparison with a similar scene in the Clackamas "Seal and Her Younger Brother Lived There" is instructive.[18] The situation is interestingly reversed: whereas the Tillamook Brother and Sister expect to see physical violence and instead discover copulation, Seal's little daughter, hearing something dripping at night, is told that her uncle and his "wife" are copulating overhead, but instead discovers that her uncle has been bloodily murdered. In either case, the association of sex and violence is remarkable, and richly expressive, I think, of a child's mentality; but whereas the little Clackamas girl has her mother, Seal, to mediate the trauma for her (albeit rather obtusely and ineffectually), the Tillamook children have only one another. Wild Woman's magical curse is thus prepared for circumstantially and psychologically; its victims are made ready on a realistic basis.

Indeed, the detailed realism of the entire scene is striking: how many accounts of the "primal scene" render the perspective of both observed adults and spying children with such plausibility? As we have seen, the children's responses are wholly in character and would even be amusing if the context were benign; and the steamy intimacies of Wild Woman and Crane, likewise: "'Mmmmm, you are always talking bad about my dead people.' Crane said, 'Aw! do not be always talking, just keep still.' Then Wild Woman received what she wanted. The children watched." And their remarks counterpoint the adults' exactly—the story's deft if unpleasant balancing of such elements continues.

Now, knowing what they know and having heard Wild Woman's threat, Brother and Sister run away, but—a Freudian slip if there ever was one, but also merely "childish"—the girl leaves two of her dolls behind, "a boy doll and a girl doll."[19] Hence Wild Woman is able, voodoo-wise, to project her curse to the children—evil, according to the story's pattern, being conveyed by childish toys: "You [the dolls] are my grandson, and you are my granddaughter. I will cause them to do the same thing they watched me do." But of course it will not be the same thing in a psychological and moral sense; it will be, as Wild Woman knows, incest.

With Crane's help (in many Western stories, he figures as a plot device whereby fleeing children escape over rivers from monsters) Brother and Sister escape over a creek which, beginning to assert magical powers themselves, they transform into an uncrossable river. Then Brother constructs for them "a tiny house, like a real one"—a childish toy, in other words, with doll-sized furnishings. The house, in keeping with the other items of childhood in the story, indeed, like the children themselves, is then unnaturally "blown up" to adult proportions and put prematurely and wrongly to adult uses. The stage for their incest is set with an uncomfortable appropriateness: Brother and Sister are "playing house."

It is likewise appropriate, symbolically, that the domestic act that seems to initiate the incestuous event is Brother's kindling a fire. His sense of household order leads him to position them on opposite sides of the fire; but his sister, having gotten, as the narrator tells us, "the full effect of Wild Woman's wish," is driven to "cross over" this barrier. As noted earlier, the suspenseful step-by-step narration of this climactic episode is conventional in Native incest stories, but in context it acquires a complex symbolic coloring peculiar to *this* story. The boy has built the fire and placed the two of them suitably by it, but apart; the girl, "inflamed" by Wild Woman's curse, or "wish" as the text has it, maneuvers closer and closer to her brother's bed by claiming, falsely, that rainwater is leaking on her wherever she lies. (Perhaps a sexual pun is involved.) Fire and water, real homes and false homes, hot and cold, male and female, restraint and abandon, innocence and experience, childhood and adulthood: the episode brilliantly focuses such linked opposites in terms that are at once conventional and realistic, and richly symbolic. It is another instance of traditional Indian narrative artistry at its best, a wonderful example of a conventional element being reinvented, "restoried" in a particular context—and an illustration therefore of the limitations of structuralist interpretation, which would ignore such features of texture in favor of an exclusive preoccupation with structure.[20] The expressive power of the scene is underscored by the terseness that comes into Mrs. Pearson's language as the boy realizes what his sister is up to—and accepts it as a fate he will now share with her. The sense of a skilled narrative performer "bearing down" is unmistakable: "Pretty soon she cried out again. 'Oh, this is leaking over here.' Then he knew. 'Oh, she must want something.' Now they were to sleep under the same blanket. She did that. She shut up then. She did not cry out. They went bad then. And right away she became pregnant."

Safe in their own playhouse, free for the time being from conventional sanctions and from shame, Brother and Sister and their infant son live through a brief idyllic period together—until Wild Woman finds them out, and, rebuffed by Brother, kills him from across the river with her magical cane. That she does not kill the baby, perhaps is unable to do so, prefigures, of course, his emergence in Part Two as a hero in whom the curse of his misbegetting is not only forgotten but transfigured as power.

The Sister, however, must kill herself, and in emotional agony, in keeping, presumably, with the fact that it was she who reprehensibly left the dolls behind in the first place, and she who initiated the act of incest. Her final helpless isolation is underscored: "There was no neighbor near her, she was just by herself": what has happened to her and her brother might not have happened had there been "neighbors," a family, and so on. She is torn between joining her brother-lover in the symbolic pyre and saving their baby; and her final cry sums up the contradictions of their tragic relationship with grotesque exactitude: "Oh my brother-husband! Upper half, brother! Lower half, husband!"

Enter, casually, Bald Eagle (who represents both family and neighborhood), to "things dying, things new-born." What is newborn is rescued from its parents' consuming funeral pyre, and Bald Eagle's humane act fittingly inaugurates the second half of the story, the premise of which will be altogether different. In effect he rescues the story, and we can outline the conditions under which it continues more briefly than with Part One, because Part Two is largely a happy transformation of what we have already found in Part One. In these terms the two parts together seem to exemplify what John Bierhorst has identified as the form of "double myth"—a myth "divisable into two more or less equal parts, rehealing the same plot twice, the second time with a quite different set of images and connotations."[21]

First of all, auspiciously for the rescued infant, Bald Eagle does not seem to understand its shameful incestuous origins: he cannot construe Sister's outcry over her "brother-husband." Therefore, one overwhelming burden for the infant is stripped away immediately; no one henceforth is to know of the boy's unnatural begetting, including the boy himself—no one, that is, except for the villainess, and the narrator and audience, who must judge what happens according to their uneasy fictive "secret."

But if the infant will be spared the opprobrium of incestuous parentage, we encounter circumstances in Bald Eagle's household that ominously seem to resemble, in a twisted way, the circumstances under which his parents suffered. Bald Eagle and his wife already have a child, a little daughter, precocious, a "cranky little devil." And as Brother and Sister were in a sense unnaturally reborn out of Wild Woman's basket at the start of Part One, so here their infant son is most strangely "reborn" from his adoptive father's thighs into a simulated delivery on the part of his adoptive mother! But this well-meaning subterfuge whereby the boy enters Bald Eagle's household is found out by the little girl; for her to be "peeping" here is a most uncomfortable parallel to that scene in Part One where the boy's mother and father initiated their tragedy by "peeping" at two grown-ups in a bed-chamber. We are to react, I think, "Uh-oh," but for the time being nothing untoward happens to the boy, except for the little girl's growing hostility toward him.

The eldritch detail of the bones of Brother and Sister becoming the bat and ball of their unwitting son is conventional, but as with other such details it is given a special meaning beyond conventionality in the context of this story. We have noticed how in Part One items properly associated with childhood—dolls, playhouses, and so forth—tend to acquire malign adult significance for Brother and Sister; here, as part of the overall redemption of evil influences to which their son might be subject, their bones are transformed into toys for their son! However grotesque Bald Eagle's gift may be, his motives for it appear to be irreproachable, and although the envious foster sister again brings matters to a crisis by telling the boy what the toys really are, the crisis passes—in large part it seems because of the benevolent attention of Bald Eagle and his wife.

There is no blinking at the fact that this attention seems to be obtained at the expense of maltreatment of the little daughter—but the story belongs to the boy, and as "a cranky little devil," perhaps the daughter deserves what she gets. Indeed, it is as if the unfortunate girl draws to herself the misery, abuse, and rejection that might well be the lot of the incest-boy, under less favorable circumstances. As it is, her fortunes complementarily fall as his rise; as he acquires the heroic power of flight, she is transformed into Mole, burrowing underground, her hands held tight to her face.[22]

Now the benign order of Bald Eagle's household (at least so far as the boy is concerned) and therefore the redemption of Wild Woman's malign disorder is emphasized in the fact that Bald Eagle and his wife wait until the boy has acquired spirit-power in adolescence, that is, a spiritual identity of his own, before officially telling him what they know about his real past. (Again, they do not know that he is a child of incest.) Earlier Mole's naughty remarks about the ball and bat troubled him, but lacking parental confirmation, they passed by. Now he is mature enough to accept the news with equanimity, and even with something like generosity: vowing revenge on Wild Woman, he offers to take unfortunate Mole along as a companion. In the Boas text of the story, the hero is told by his foster mother (there is no father), "A girl must go with you," and some girl is found, not his foster sister.[23] Looking at the two versions together, it appears that the boy must have a girl companion for the mission of revenge to be authentic; that is, it must be carried out by a pair corresponding to the objects of the revenge—Brother and Sister. The superior unity of Mrs. Pearson's version is manifested in the way her hero chooses his "sister" Mole for comrade-in-arms: a new kind of sibling relationship is effected, positive where his parents' relationship was illicit and destructive.

The two set out in search of Wild Woman, the boy flying and the girl burrowing, and when they find her she is disguised, with ironic appropriateness, as a young girl wearing a basket cap! The cap would mark her in Salish culture as being no more than a year beyond the onset of puberty, and thus about the boy's own age (and perhaps about the age of his mother when her trouble came?); as an expressive detail it intersects with Wild Woman's original insignia, her "big soft spruce-root" gathering basket. The fact that in this disguise her heart is in the basket-cum-basket cap,[24] and that she is invulnerable to the boy's attacks until he learns this secret from Blue Jay, in effect symbolically structures the heroic outcome of the whole story.[25] For in destroying the basket cap after four failed attempts to kill her by more conventional mayhem, the boy attains a perfect revenge, more perfect than he knows. That is, he succeeds in "gathering" and killing the ogress who once gathered his parents and is responsible for their deaths, and he does so by destroying the symbol of Wild Woman's malevolent and perverted womanhood, her basket—now represented, unpleasantly enough, by a maiden's cap.

Despite her masquerade, Wild Woman hails the boy on his first arrival and thereafter as "Placed-Next-to-Testicles," mocking his remarkable rescue and rebirth as the adopted son of Bald Eagle. As a genital innuendo, it echoes Crane's slur on Wild Woman's pudendum in Part One; but with the boy in the ascendancy, the name testifies to his special powers—the bearer of such a sobriquet must be a real *mensch,* a manly hero indeed.[26] And we need not push such details to a hyperfreudian extreme to see a pattern in them. All through the story a sexual polarization favorable to maleness seems to attend the boy's emergence as a hero, centering on the facts that the villain of the piece is female, that the incest is initiated by the Sister, that Bald Eagle's daughter is mean, and abused, and becomes a mole as the boy acquires powers of flight, with the implication of sexual ascendancy, and it culminates here, as "Placed-Next-to-Testicles" sets out to kill a witch who wears her heart, as it were, in her sexual basket. Wild Woman has met her match in the young hero; she is "gathered" and "unbasketed."

Mrs. Pearson's narrative carries on at some length with "Placed-Next-to-Testicles's" heroic adventures up in the sky, where he eventually bests even Old Man Thunder and marries his daughter; clearly, the evil that destroyed his parents has been redeemed in him, in accord with Mrs. Pearson's interpretive postscript as to what the story reveals. But these episodes constitute a sequel to the story per se, which really reaches its proper closure with the killing of Wild Woman and the triumphant return of the boy and his sister Mole to Bald Eagle's house. Knowing what we alone know about the hero's shameful begetting, we can appreciate his ignorance of it as a source of strength in itself, and interpret, as no one in the story can, what is as against what has been. *What has been* and indeed *what might still be* are deftly invoked in the hero's farewell to his adoptive family. Turning to Mole, he says, "I cannot take my sister. I like her, but since she is unable to fly I cannot take her." The simple, normal generosity of this statement derives much of its force, of course, from its echoes of the career of the boy's wretched parents—a brother and sister who "liked" each other entirely too much, who could not separate, who were helplessly "taken away" from their family by an ogress, and then fled together to disaster.

And, although like any young hero the boy is impatient to leave home for the world at large—"I cannot stay around here," he says, "I do not like it around here"—his last words to his adoptive family constitute a very touching tribute to the human order, not perfect but essentially benign, of Bald Eagle's household, an order that has rescued and redeemed this misbegotten son of the brother and sister who came to grief in Wild Woman's malign and disordered household. "He said, 'Just the same, I think a great deal of you, my people.' He left."

What the boy doesn't know about his real origins literally won't hurt him now. It is as if in the structuring of the story, we, the audience, who as usual know everything, must carry that terrible secret right out of the story, for such living edification as we can find in it. Meanwhile, the grateful hero sets out for new adventures, unburdened by the past.

8 / Genderic and Racial Appropriation in Victoria Howard's "The Honorable Milt"

ONE OF THE MAJOR LIMITATIONS OF THE SYSTEM of structural analysis of oral narrative formulated by Claude Lévi-Strauss and developed by Edmund Leach and others is that it resolutely ignores the bearing on the stories being examined of individual performances and performers working within literary conventions. Structuralism seeks, instead, to understand the generation and evolution of myth-narratives as being, in Dell Hymes's trenchant phrase, "an imperturbable self-transmogrification."[1]

The perception that, on the contrary, oral narratives (mythic and otherwise) are significantly localized, textured, and sometimes highly personalized entities is one of the chief contributions of the ethnopoetic movement, as it has emerged in recent years in the translative and interpretive work, chiefly on Native American oral literature, of Hymes, Dennis Tedlock, J. Barre Toelken, Joel Sherzer, and others. Looked at "emically," that is, scrupulously "from inside" the originating culture, beginning if possible with the Native language itself, and drawing on ethnographic data, many Native American texts turn out to be not "imperturbable" artifacts of a classical and fixed tribal tradition, but rather literary expressions of particular and identifiable viewpoints between and within tribal communities on matters of gender, morality, social class, race, aesthetic preference, and so on.

On the basic issue of literary modality, for example, whereas structural analysis does not challenge the long-standing Western assumption that traditional oral narrative is a kind of *prose* (so far as it worries about such issues at all), recent ethnopoetic analysis of several Native oral repertories indicates that, on the contrary, they constitute a *poetic* art, involving measure according to line-units, expressive repetition, and other elements of versification. Hence to translate, present, and read such material in text-form as prose may well be a fundamental misappropriation of modes.

And in some instances—fewer, alas, than would be the case if only more Anglo fieldworkers had seen fit to identify and interrogate their "informants" as more than just linguistic or ethnological sources—it is possible to delineate and appreciate the individual literary skills, the distinctive *styles,* of Native recitalists. This is true, for example, in the texts recorded in the Pacific Northwest between the 1890s and the 1930s from the tellings of three gifted individuals who happened to be the last bearers of their tribes' repertories: Charles Cultee (Kathlamet Chinook), Clara Pearson (Nehalem Tillamook), and Victoria Howard (Clackamas Chinook).

In his ethnopoetic study of Cultee's performance of "The Sun's Myth" (as recorded by Franz Boas in the 1890s in Bay Center, Washington), Dell Hymes has found compelling evidence of Cultee's reshaping of traditional Kathlamet material so as to formulate a personal view of his people's apocalyptic predicament under Anglo encroachment at the end of the nineteenth century.[2] And in my own recent work on Clara Pearson's Tillamook stories, as told in English to Elizabeth Jacobs in the 1930s, I have been able to identify what appear to be Mrs. Pearson's distinctive narrative adaptations of her tribal repertory (which she learned in the Tillamook language) for Anglo understanding—specifically for reading rather than hearing.[3]

Further, close study of the transcribed repertories of Mrs. Pearson and Mrs. Howard reminds us that one of the crucial "local" variables capable of operating in oral tradition is *gender*—especially so where the line of story-transmission is known to have run through only one sex over several generations. Mrs. Howard told Melville Jacobs that her knowledge of Clackamas oral literature had come from her mother-in-law, wa'susgani, and her maternal grandmother, waga'yuh, with some indication that this female lineage may have extended even further back in time.[4]

Hymes and I have both explored en passant what appear to be female appropriations and reconfigurations of a traditionally male-centered hero-story type in Mrs. Howard's "Seal and Her Younger Brother Lived There" (see essay 6 in this volume).[5] The hero-story, widely distributed throughout the Northwest and typified by "The Revenge against the Sky People" narrative of the coastal Coos tribe, recounts the exploits of a young man in revenging the murder and decapitation of his elder brother by the "Sky People." By means of a ladder of arrows, he ascends into the Sky Country, locates and interrogates the murderer's wife and then kills her and puts on her skin, and then after several near-disasters (notably when a child in the murderer's household observes that "she" looks like a man), succeeds in killing his brother's slayer. He returns to earth with the missing head, which is then reattached to the brother's reanimated body.

This rousing story dramatizes the young hero's ability to be both "smart" and "proper"—indeed, he is heroically successful in his proper moral mission of revenge and recovery of kin precisely because he is so "smart," so self-controlled and resourceful in carrying out his mission. Mrs. Howard's "Seal and Her Younger Brother" in effect turns this narrative inside out, for what appear to be special women's purposes. The young male hero is replaced by a young girl, who lives with her mother Seal and her brother, the girl's uncle, who is head of the household. When the uncle takes a "wife," the girl notices that the "wife" sounds like a man when urinating at night, but she is repeatedly chided for making this observation by her decorous mother: "Shush, your uncle's wife!" When the girl is awakened one night by something dripping down on her from her uncle's bed, she finds that it is blood and that her uncle's throat has been cut, apparently by the ambiguous "wife," who has vanished. In this compelling story, as Dell Hymes was the first to point out, being "smart" and being "proper" are tragically in conflict. As the story ends, while Seal is conventionally mourning the death of the head of their household, her daughter bitterly denounces her for not paying attention: "In vain I tried to tell you!"[6]

Although it is difficult to generalize about Mrs. Howard's narratives in terms of her culture, because we have so few instances of Clackamas literature from other recitalists, there is warrant, I believe, to claim that one of the persistent cultural themes reflected in *Clackamas Chinook Texts* is the predicament of women in a time of rapid and chaotic change.[7] How should the old ways of keeping a home and dealing with members of the opposite sex be adjusted to the new realities of Anglo life? What should older women be telling young girls about the traditional Native values of hospitality and deference to strangers, for example; and how much of the traditions of social propriety should the young girls credit, given the disruptive pressures of acculturation? No wonder that the perplexities and anguish of older women and young girls figure so prominently in Mrs. Howard's stories, and no wonder that she (or one of her female story-telling predecessors among the Clackamas) turned the "Revenge against the Sky People" story quite inside out, replacing its point of view of the heroic disguised invader with the point of view of the "invaded" household, and specifically replacing the "smart and proper" male protagonist with the terribly conflicted young female protagonist, caught between her mother's traditional sense of propriety (which the story does not denigrate in principle) and what she comes to know experientially about the threat to her household from the sinister "wife."[8]

Another one of Mrs. Howard's Clackamas narratives, "The Honorable Milt! I Supposed Him for Myself," can provide us with a purer and in some ways more revealing instance of the process of appropriation in Native oral literature, and it also offers a welcome glimpse of the possibilities of humor in such appropriations. Before giving the text of the story, I should explain that its original title, as derived by Melville Jacobs from the protagonist's magical song, was "She Deceived Herself with Milt," but recent work on the text by Hymes makes it clear that the words of the Widow's song and hence of the title are more accurately rendered as given above.[9] Words and phrases in brackets are Jacobs's editorial interpolations for the purpose of clarification, as in cases of pronoun ambiguity, which would not be problematic in oral performance in the original language.[10]

People were living there. They were continuously smoke-drying salmon and various things. There was one widow. They [fishermen] would come, they would come ashore there. Now she would be going about at that place. Right after they threw them [their catch of fish] ashore, she would get one or two to take with her. She smoke-dried them. [In consequence] her house was full of food. In the winter they [other villagers] would get hungry, and they would buy various things from her. That is how she had many valuables.

I do not know how long a time, and then she got one [large and fat] salmon, she butchered it well, she took out its milt. She thought, "Dear oh dear. It is nice. I shall not eat it." She wished, "Oh that you become a person." I do not know where she put it.

I do not know how long a time afterward, and then some person was sleeping beside her. She thought, "Oh my! I wonder where the person came from to me." She lay there for a while. Then she thought, "Perhaps he is not from here. Perhaps the person got to here from a long distance away." Presently as she was thinking about it, he then said to her, "What is your heart making you know [what are you thinking about]? You yourself said to me, I wish that you would become a person." She reflected. "Oh yes," she thought. "It just has to be that milt." She looked at him in the morning. "Goodness. A fine-looking man, he is light of skin." Now they remained there, I do not know how long a time they lived there.

Then some other woman began to steal him away from her. After quite some time then she [the other woman] took him away from her. She continued to live there. When she [the other woman] saw her, she would say, she would tell him, "Oh dear me. Your poor poor [former] wife! Look at her!" He would reply to her, "Leave her alone!" After quite some time then she laughed at her all the more. They [villagers] said to her [the deserted wife], "Dear oh dear. Why does your co-wife laugh and mock you all the time?" She said, "Oh let it be!"

Now time after time when they [the married couple] were sitting there, she [the deserted wife] passed by them [two], she [the second wife] nudged her husband, she said to him, "Look at your [former] wife! Oh dear! The poor poor woman!" He replied to her, "Leave her alone!" She laughed at her all the more. She [the deserted first wife] went along, she went back to them [the married couple], and now she danced in front of them. She said [in the words of her song]:

> The honorable Milt!
> I supposed him for myself.
> The honorable Milt!
> I supposed him for myself.

She [the second wife] nudged him again [and again mocked his first wife by saying], "Oh dear oh dear! That poor poor wife of yours." He continued to say, "Do leave her alone." The fifth time [when she had sung the song five times], she extended her spirit-power regalia [toward the couple]. The woman [the second wife] turned and looked, only milt lay beside her. She [the second wife] arose, she went away. That first woman took the milt, she threw it at her, [saying] "This thing here is your husband!" She [the second wife] went back home, she reached her house, and there she remained, she stayed there. And that is what she continued to do.

Now I recall only that much of it.

This funny and revealing story, although unique in its details in the surviving Clackamas repertory and in the literatures of neighboring tribes, *is* relatable to several narrative patterns in Native American oral tradition.[11] Many tribes, for example, have had stories about girls who "wish upon a star" for husbands—and wake up finding, often to their distress, that the star has come down to take up housekeeping with the wisher! Such stories, classified in Stith Thompson's *Motif Index of Folk-Literature* under the heading "C15, Tabu: Wish for star husband realized," generally convey a Native conviction that wishing is no idle imaginative indulgence, but rather a powerful and potentially risky mental activity for both sexes—the psychological implication of this belief being that even if wishes do not come true, they are important as training for real-life volitions.[12]

So it seems to be in Mrs. Howard's own Clackamas Star-husband offering, titled "The Two Stars Came to the Two Girls." One of the girls, the elder, is rewarded with a young man, but the younger finds herself encumbered with an old man for a husband.[13] Mrs. Howard's rich widow in "The Honorable Milt" is no green girl, of course, and the object of her wishing is not a celestial object but the sexual fluid of a male salmon; but her story of wishing leading to complications can be seen as part of a general transtribal "set" or field. Presumably Mrs. Howard and her Clackamas listeners would have recognized the relationship—just as, in our own literary/cultural competence, we recognize fictional or movie "extensions" of the Cinderella story when we see them, or an analogue of *Othello*.

Another set of Clackamas stories premised on wish-fulfillment involves not heavenly bodies as objects of wishing and transformation but—coming closer to "The Honorable Milt"—earthly items, tools, foodstuffs, and so on. Mrs. Howard offers several such narratives from Clackamas tradition—involving, interestingly enough, mostly male wishers. For example, in "Stick Drum Gambler and His Older Brother," a solitary hunter, having cut a limber hazel branch to tie some deer meat to a tree, later says to the branch, "I wish you would become a person and keep me company." Voilà—the hunter soon discovers that a male being, "Hazel Drumstick Gambler," has come to live with him as the result of his wish, taking the role of a helpful and spiritually potent younger brother.[14]

A less auspicious story of wish-fulfillment in a tool or useful article is "Awl and Her Son's Son." A hunter breaks his awl while at home repairing his moccasins, and throws it under his bed, saying as he does, "I wish you would turn into a person." Returning home later from a hunting trip, he finds a fire burning, and his bachelor household all spruced up. Eventually he discovers that his mysterious housekeeper is none other than "Awl," transformed into an older woman, who claims and dotes on him as her grandson. At length five sisters notice how well the hunter is living, and one by one (eldest to youngest) they visit his house—only to be murdered by the homicidally jealous Awl, until at last she is killed by the youngest sister, who then marries the hunter.[15]

For a wishing story specifically involving milt, we must go outside the Clackamas culture, to their Sahaptin-speaking neighbors the Cowlitz, across the Columbia River in what is now Washington State. The Cowlitz have a story, "Coyote Loses His Milt Daughters" (collected by Melville Jacobs from Joe Hunt), in which Coyote, the Trickster, finds white milt in a salmon and wishes for it to become "something nice." The sexual inclinations of his wish are soon manifested: two "very pretty girls" appear, and before long Coyote has them rowing him in a canoe like dutiful daughters; but true to his tricksterish nature, he commits a Freudian slip and addresses them lecherously as "my nice little girl wives," whereupon the Milt girls, offended, run away.[16]

I have taken this much time to contextualize "The Honorable Milt" in Clackamas/Chinookan literary terms in order to set off its own distinctive features within a thematic "field," in particular its patterning as a woman's story. If most Chinook wish-fulfillment narratives focusing on objects seem to involve male wishers, "The Honorable Milt" involves a *female*, whose wish brings her a husband-of-sorts—and with a story like "Coyote Loses His Milt Daughters" in mind, it therefore appears that "The Honorable Milt" represents a generic appropriation, equivalent to the transformation of "Seal and Her Younger Brother Lived There." But to understand the whys and wherefores of this appropriation and its full scope, we must now turn to the details of Mrs. Howard's text.

First, unlike her analogues in the "Star-husband" stories, our protagonist is presented as a mature, sexually experienced, canny woman, a widow whose affluence is the result of astute trading in salmon. Further, she possesses the advantage of spirit-power, as expressed in the story's climax, when she is able to ritually transform her errant "husband" back to milt. So her wishing on the seminal fluid of a male salmon is not idle or "innocent"; rather than eat it, or offer it for sale (both interesting alternatives!), she chooses to "wish" on it for herself, with an expectation that her wishing will be "profitable." Although Mrs. Howard's Clackamas phrasing for her actual wish, *ánixcwa emgwetilx mxátxax* ("Oh that you become a person") is apparently an oral formula, appearing verbatim in every one of her stories when someone wishes for something to be humanly transformed, here the neutral "person" clearly means "male person," and so, when the Milt-man makes his appearance, it is in the posture of a husband, obligingly sleeping beside her.[17]

What should we make of his attractive whiteness, which seems to draw the widow's attention initially when he is just milt, and after his metamorphosis elicits her satisfied admiration, "Goodness. A fine-looking man, he is light of skin"? Salmon-milt is in fact a pure milk-white, but clearly the Milt-man's coloring figures more expressively in the story than just as a piece of ichthyological realism. For once, we can refer an interpretive question directly, emically, to a Native critical source—specifically, to an ethnographic note Mrs. Howard herself gave to Jacobs, which implicates this story. (I use a new translation of the note by Hymes.[18])

> Our house (was) near the road.
>> Someone will pass by us.
>> She will look at them.
> Now she will laugh and laugh,
>> she will say:
>> "Dear oh dear . . .
>> "A light one!
>> "Maybe it's Milt!"

Now she will sing,
    this is what she will say:
    "The Honorable Milt
    "I supposed him for myself."

Mrs. Howard's amusing note serves to remind us that a Native oral literature served, even as ours does, the social purposes of allusion, quotation, and embellishment of occasions, for those competent in it: in fact such competency amounts to a better illustration of the workings of what Stanley Fish has called "interpretive communities" than anything he provides in *Is There a Text in This Class? The Authority of Interpretive Communities* (1980). But for our story about the Widow, Mrs. Howard's note indicates that Milt's whiteness is to be understood in a *racial* context, and that the story therefore involves not only a generic appropriation, but a kind of racial appropriation as well, one reflecting with wicked humor a particular set of contact-era tensions between Indian women and Anglo men. Jacobs notes that when Mrs. Howard got to the Widow's exultant remark about her husband's whiteness, she "bubbled with mirth," and wondered in an aside if maybe he was a "half breed."[19] It looks as if our Widow has gotten herself, then, one of those white husbands by wishing, instead of through the troublesome and in fact often tragic cross-racial/cross-cultural alliances common in the Far West of Mrs. Howard's own early life. But her new husband's true colors (so to speak) appear as soon as he is noticed by "some other woman." If he has great sexual attractiveness to both women, in his actions between them he is revealed to be a wimp, a will-less and passive embodiment of male sexuality, the potency without the affect—a "milt-man" indeed. He allows himself to be taken away from the Widow, and when the Other Woman obnoxiously mocks her for losing him, he merely protests the insults, telling his new wife to "stop it" but doing nothing.

With Mrs. Howard's anecdote of her mother-in-law's joke in mind, it is irresistible to see Milt-man in his story as a mischievous depiction, from a Clackamas woman's perspective, of the white male as sexual object . . . attractive, but unstable, not to be depended upon and likely to be the source of much trouble, and in some ultimate cultural sense, not real. The fact that Milt-man is such a colorless actor in the story's romantic triangle—no more than a pawn, really—serves to emphasize how completely the story has appropriated its traditional male elements to become a woman's narrative. In an odd sense, in fact, it is a very grown-up and ironical version of the cautionary "Star-husband" tales. What is "cautionary" here, as the plot unfolds, is that women's sexual wish-fulfillment and romantic predation are seen to be equally risky, especially when the object of either or both is a male "white-eyes" (to use a very old but still current Indian racial epithet).

"Equally risky" and likely to be profitless—but at least the Widow, with her command of spirit-power, has the advantage over her odious rival. Apparently at first willing to give up her new husband (that she is willing perhaps indicates her knowledge of his unreality), she is at length provoked to take a most peculiar but fitting revenge. Having "wished" Milt into a kind of manhood, now she ritually un-wishes him (perhaps his disapproving remarks to his new wife earlier express not so much feckless sympathy for the Widow as fear over what she will do if provoked?), in the form of a magical song and dance in public view, repeated the requisite five times, with appropriate gestures involving spirit-power regalia—until only a pile of fish-semen remains, where there had been an attractive man.

The Widow's deployment of her magical song represents yet another line of appropriation in the story, involving a generic switching from narrative to lyric; but such switching is a conventional feature of Clackamas and other Native literary art, typically brought into play, as it is here, at some especially dramatic moment in the story, where formal lyrical expression of emotion can briefly refract and focus action and dialogue, very much as Shakespeare's lyrics do in the romantic comedies. In Hymes's retranslation, the words of the song bristle with sarcasm in context—an impression that is heightened if one listens, as I have, to Jacobs's Ediphone recording of Mrs. Howard singing the song in a separate performance.[20] Her voice seems to descend, as she vocalizes the Clackamas words, in a kind of sarcastic sing-song suggestive of schoolyard mockery and abuse.

But of course the mockery here is "adult" and complex, beginning with the Widow's socially conscious sneer at her quondam husband's status as head of two households: "The Honorable Milt!" The complexity is compounded in the second line—"I supposed him for myself—in that "suppose" seems to have a double force: (1) meaning "making-up" or conjuring into a kind of suppositious existence, mere milt into Milt-husband;

and (2) meaning, with a certain rueful admission of lack of knowledge about outcomes, "I thought he was mine," applying directly to the Widow, because she is speaking, but also of course applying to the Other Woman, who foolishly did her own "supposing," and now stands publicly humiliated, indeed bespattered with gobbets of milt because of her "supposes."

In an extended commentary on Mrs. Howard's rendition of *wa'susgani*'s literary joke about white men being Milt-figures, Hymes identifies in it and in several other short texts a pattern of Chinookan humor: a two-step exchange involving a joshing insult or insinuation, and then a second statement that tops or outdoes the first by echoing it ironically. So, in the anecdote from *wa'susgani,* she first mentions the possibility that the white passerby is just milt ("Maybe it's milt!"), and then she caps her own sly insinuation by identifying the uncomprehending victim of her humor for all Clackamas speakers listening by quoting the myth and actually performing "The Honorable Milt! / I supposed him for myself."

What Hymes goes on to say about the effect of *wa'susgani*'s "two-step invention" seems to me to identify the complex irony of the myth itself, lacking only the specifically *female* emphasis I have been laboring to illuminate here:

The first echoic mention ["Possibly it is Milt"] demeans the white; the second entertains the possibility that the white is but a figment of Indian imagination, existing on Indian sufferance. . . . Probably there is a sense of satisfaction in being able to name the situation of the presence of a white as one encompassed by Indian tradition stretching back before whites came. Certainly there is satisfaction in being able to entertain the proposition, through quotation of myth, that whites are shameful and that a widow could both conjure them up for sexual satisfaction and dismiss them.[21]

In applying this comment on *wa'susgani*'s literary joke to her daughter-in-law's narrative itself, I would add only two related points: (a) that throughout the narrative, as in the anecdote alluding to it, a Clackamas woman's perspective seems to be all-pervasive and self-consciously "appropriative," and (b) that the Widow's song in effect "out-tops" her sarcasm at the expense of Milt and the Other Woman, by including *herself* within the range of her irony: "I supposed him for myself" (as if to say, "How could I have been so dumb!").

At the outset, I argued that a serious inadequacy of Lévi-Strauss's procedure for structural analysis of oral narratives (at least for literary purposes) is its disregard of mode, texture, verbal and narrative style, and indeed the possibilities of local, "authorial" inventions and appropriations of traditional elements. But, as Hymes and others have shown, a modified form of structural analysis—using the procedure as a supplement to close reading of verbal patternings—can be profitable. It can usefully identify a given narrative's structural and thematic affiliations with other stories comprising its "set" within a tribal literature, or between tribal groups; and it can, in the very abstractness of its attention to synchronic rather than diachronic or narrative form, help to illuminate the way a given story is organized.

The latter advantage seems pertinent to "The Honorable Milt." In what follows, I will assume that the reader is familiar with Lévi-Strauss's brilliant, sometimes exasperating "demonstrations" of his method in the celebrated essay, "The Structural Study of Myth." [22] Beginning with the reduction of the story to its basic narrative elements (Lévi-Strauss calls them "sentences"), we arrive at the following diachronic outline:

1. Widow notices and wishes on milt.
2. Milt-man appears.
3. Other Woman notices and desires Milt-man.
4. Other Woman steals Milt-man.
5. Other Woman mocks and harasses Widow.
6. Widow sings her magical song.
7. Milt-man is transformed back into milt.
8. Widow mocks and harasses Other Woman.

The next step is to break this diachronic listing up into vertical columns of related sentences, so as to "discover" the true synchronic structure of the story—whose elements the story's narrative repetitions are, according to Lévi-Strauss, accentuating. Typically, following his conception of the *mediative* function of myth, this step should reveal a pattern of bipolar oppositions, which the story serves to mediate (to use his own examples, "Nature" vs. "Culture," "Raw vs. Cooked," the autochthonous account of human origins vs. the sexual account, and so on). What emerges with "The Honorable Milt" after this step seems odd: a diachronic list with *three* columns (note that, as Lévi-Strauss would have it, the story can still be "read" from left to right as well as vertically):

1	2	3
Widow notices/ wishes on milt.	Milt-man appears.	Other Woman mocks/harasses Widow.
Other woman notices/desires Milt-man.	Other woman steals Milt-man.	Widow mocks/ harasses Other Woman
Widow sings her magical song.	Milt-man transformed back into milt.	

The "sentences" in column 1 pertain to *wishing;* those in 2, *transformations;* those in 3, *mocking and harassment,* so that in its ultimate structuralist reduction the story can be seen to embody the formula Wishing:Transformation:Mockery, with the first and third terms in the position of bipolar opposites, and the second standing as a mediating term. But what would this formula mean? Wishing and mockery are not prima facie opposites, in the abstract; and yet in the generic narrative patterning of this story perhaps they are.

Wishing for a husband is to posit sexual and social gratifications for which mockery and ridicule *are* exact emotional opposites; such wishing, then, even for someone with the Widow's special powers, involves a certain vulnerability, a wearing of the heart on the sleeve. As for transformation as a middle or mediating term: as the modality whereby wishing leads to consequences, it seems to express both the potency of wishing, and the instability of what it leads to. There is something of this pattern in the Native "Star husband" stories mentioned earlier as distant cognates to "The Honorable Milt"—for the unlucky girl-wishers, the ones who obtain elderly star-husbands, mockery and ridicule are often at least implied. But of course, as we have seen, "The Honorable Milt" is very much an adult story, involving both sexual wishing or supposing and sexual predation by women—and although our structural-analytic procedure shows its interpretive limits by failing to register the *racial* overtones in the story, those overtones are crucial to the understanding Mrs. Howard and her mother-in-law (and presumably other Clackamas women) had of the Rich Widow's romantic adventure.

The tonality of that understanding is difficult to verbalize, but surely it involves sympathy for the Widow throughout, along with reservations about the "raw material" of her wishing; concomitant disapproval of the Other Woman's predation and her outrageous harassment of the Widow; and finally, satisfaction both righteous and hilarious in the exposure of Milt for what he really is, and the truly devastating exposure of the Other Woman for her choice of a husband. As the story closes, the Other Woman is keeping indoors, in shame, while the Widow is at large again, unencumbered, freed from the consequences of her "supposing." Perhaps she is wiser, but I do not imagine her forlorn: given the literary, sexual, and racial appropriations at work in the story, perhaps her condition at the end constitutes an ultimate contact-era Clackamas woman's wish-fulfillment!

Finally, having endeavored to contextualize "The Honorable Milt" in Native literary and cultural terms, I want to sketch out a place for it in a wider context of women's appropriative storytelling. In the domain of Native autobiography, Maria Chona's telling of her life story, as edited by Ruth Underhill in *Papago Woman,* emphasizes her "official" acceptance of and fulfillment within the restrictions of the traditional Papago concept of womanhood, but all through her narrative, she seems to resent and subvert this limiting concept, sniping at men's privileges and asserting her equality with men in knowledge and spirit-power. Her feminist bias is nowhere more tellingly expressed than in her conspicuous appropriation of the Papago myth of the origin of Corn. Whereas standard versions of the myth relate that the Corn God simply bestowed the plant and its ceremonial mystique upon the Papagos after taking up with one of their women,[23] in Chona's version (unique to her, so far as I know), full mythic credit is given to the woman:

The corn was once a man and he lured a woman away to sleep with him. She stayed a long time, and when she came home, she knew the songs that made the corn grow. So when the men all went to their meetings, this man [her husband] did not go but he stayed home hearing his wife sing. The men from the meeting came to speak to him. "Why are you absent?" "Because I am listening to my wife." "How can it be that a man can learn more from a woman than from talking with us? Let us hear her, too."

So she came to the men's meeting and she sat between the chief and her husband. "Sing." And she sang the corn songs.

At the first song those men began to sing. At the second, they danced. At the third, the women came out of the houses, creeping to the council house to listen to the singing. At the fourth, they were all dancing, inside the council house and outside, to that woman's singing.[24]

I have no doubt that close inspection of mythic and personal texts from other Native American cultures will turn up similar *pro femina* appropriations of traditional material—and something of the same impulse seems to operate in modern literary terms in Ursula Le Guin's remarkable 1985 novel, *Always Coming Home*. Le Guin's novel concerns a people, the Kesh, who "might be going to have lived a long, long time from now in Northern California," after some unspecified catastrophe. The Kesh have taken on many of the folkways of California's original Indian cultures, including a rich and complicated oral-literary tradition of stories and songs. Le Guin's invented Kesh myths sound like their Indian prototypes except that her Coyote stories invariably feature a *female* trickster! The manner of Le Guin's slyly feminist/subversive appropriation of the mystique of "Old Man Coyote" can be illustrated by the beginning of a Kesh myth about a war between bears and humans:

Well, Coyote was going along inside the world, you know, and she met old man Bear.

"I'll come with you," Coyote said.

Bear said, "No, please don't come with me. I don't want you. I'm going to get all the bears together and make a war on the human beings. I don't want you along."

Coyote said, "Oh, that's terrible, a terrible thing to do. You'll all destroy each other. You'll be killed, they'll be killed! Don't make war, please don't make war! We should all live in peace and love each other!" All the while she was talking, Coyote was stealing Bear's balls, cutting them off with an obsidian knife she had stolen from the Doctors Lodge, a knife so sharp he never felt it cutting.

When she was done she ran away with Bear's balls in a pouch. She went to where the human people were. . . .

[Coyote hopes to sabotage the war by getting the bears and the men to use each others' testicles as ammunition, but her plan fails, and after a one-sided battle the humans drive the bears into the wilderness, where they live to this day.[25]]

An equally remarkable imaginative appropriation of gender has appeared in our popular culture in the crypto-feminist rewritings and reinventions of *Star Trek* narratives. Produced so far mainly in the specialized realm of "Trekkers" and "fanzines," such stories take as their premise that the heroes of the original *Star Trek* series, the earthling Capt. Kirk and his half-Vulcan associate Spock, are homosexual lovers, with a wholesale sexual and political revision of the *Star Trek* mythology proceeding from this discovery. According to Constance Penley, the authors and readers of such "slash" fiction (after "Kirk/Spock") are nearly all women, and most of them—despite the gay-pornographic coloring of their work—are probably heterosexual.

Penley has argued that much can be learned from slash fiction "about how women, and people, resist, negotiate, and adapt to their own desires the overwhelming media environment that we all inhabit."[26] In her view, the "slash" authors and their fans are co-opting the *Star Trek* stories and gay pornography to each other not just for the rebellious, subversive, naughty pleasure of it, but also in order to imagine for themselves a utopian condition of free equality in love for which the Kirk/Spock alliance is, however startling, a satisfying projection out of popular culture—satisfying because outré, far out, requiring (or rather licensing) the making up of new rules for self-determination and romance.

Penley's analysis of slash fiction usefully invokes the work of the French ethnomethodologist Michel de Certeau, and although his fascinating study of the everyday tactics whereby we subvert or co-opt mass culture is literally worlds removed from the culture and oral literature of the Clackamas Chinookans, he has I think identified an art of appropriation humanly common to contexts as radically different as French factory-employees "working" the System; American women "Trekkers" co-opting a popular commercial TV series to make it functionally their own; and contact-era Clackamas Indian women appropriating a male-oriented story-tradition to "say" something mischievous and useful about the sexual and racial inequalities in their lives:

A way of using imposed systems constitutes the resistance to the historical law of a state of affairs and its dogmatic legitimations. A practice of the order constructed by others redistributes its space: it creates at least a certain play in that order, a space for maneuvers of unequal forces and for utopian points of reference. That is where the opacity of "popular culture" could be said to manifest itself—a dark rock that resists all assimilation. . . . Innumerable ways of playing and foiling the other's game, that is, the space instituted by others, characterize the stubborn, resistant activity of groups which, since they lack their own space, have to get along in a network of already established forces and representations. People have to make do with what they have.[27]

PART THREE

9 / Simon Fraser's Canoe;
or, Capsizing into Myth

HOW DO MYTHS ORIGINATE? HOW, THAT IS, BEFORE
the self-transmogrifying process through which, according to structuralist
theory, motives, episodes, and characters combine and recombine and
evolve with an almost geometrical thoroughness? What must happen for
the growth of what formalists call "motifemes" (stock patterns of complication, like "taboo/violation") into a complex myth-narrative? For that
matter, how do "motifs" (stock incidents) grow into motifemes? [1]

The question of myth-origin is only slightly less quixotic than John
Donne's "who cleft the devil's foot," and I do not propose to "ride ten thousand days and nights" in pursuit of it, leaving that endless journey to the
solar-myth theorists, the ritualists, the literal euhemerists, and other speculative travelers. I am convinced, let me say, that the really memorable
myth texts from Western Indian cultures have gotten much of their imaginative power and resonance from individuals, men and women (and no
doubt children) whose dreams and inventions were too remarkable and
apt, too expressively verbalized, to be forgotten. But if this is so, and if there
is in fact a significant element of conscious individual artistry in myth, then

it must be admitted that such artistry may have figured late in the history of a given myth, in terms of idiosyncratic tellings, rather than at the beginning, and that whether it comes into play early or late, the energy of such creative imaginations would presumably work within the conventions of the tribal mythology. For a traditional Chinookan or Sahaptin storymaker, say, to undertake to invent *ab ovum* a *female* trickster called "Magpie" who goes downriver rather than up, and then attach this figure and its stories to the myth, would be most unlikely, I think: such an invention would not "compute."[2] The only identifiably individualized imaginings we have from the traditional cultures are autobiographical accounts of what spiritualism calls "out-of-body travel" during comas and trances; and, although interesting and worthy of study, most of these texts are strikingly conventional both in content and in form.[3]

That certain myth "sets" in the West are very old, possibly thousands of years old, is not to be doubted, given their wide distribution; and in the case of a special category of narratives, one wonders if *they* did not originate as oral records of prehistoric natural events. It is known, for example, that Indians were living in the Oregon High Desert at the time of the cataclysmic eruption of Mount Mazama seven thousand years ago, leading to the formation of Crater Lake—and there is a theme in Northern Paiute mythology of eruptions, world conflagrations, and the like that might derive from the blowup of Mount Mazama, or from other eruptions in the area before or after it. Certainly the widespread story among Northwest tribes about how several heroes fought over one beautiful girl and were eventually transformed into active volcanoes in the Cascade Range (with the girl as Mount St. Helens) points to the translation of the "news" of eruptions into narrative well before the coming of the whites, a topic I will discuss more fully in essay 10. And the presence in several Paiute stories of odd details about impassable "walls of ice" even raises the possibility, admittedly pretty remote, that such details refer back to the last period of heavy glaciation in the Northwest some seven to ten thousand years ago![4]

What is certain is that in historic times, Western Indian mythologies have been augmented by adaptive contact with whites, their stories and their doings; such augmentation is, of course, only like a creative eddy against the general flood of Anglo influence that inundated the traditional Indian way in the nineteenth century. But by studying the process of this "eddy" we may be able to catch some glimpses of how myths are originally engendered; and certainly we can come to a better understanding of how mythology "works" for those whose apprehension of reality depends on it as, in Malinowski's phrase, "a hard-working active force."[5]

Myth is, I believe, an essentially *conservative* way of grasping and ordering reality, for all of its apparent imaginative wildness. Once it acquires (through processes yet to be fully understood[6]) a system, a "grammar" of characters, motives, and events, it seems to want to assimilate all new "real events"—what we might call "News"—according to this grammar, extending and confirming its elements thereby, but not changing or contradicting or canceling them. Which is only to say that so long as they are viable to their adherents' way of life, chartering their collective identity as peoples and serving to mediate between this collectivity and individual life, mythologies are *dynamic* entities, growing by accretion, adaptation, assimilation, and synthesis. In the nineteenth century, all the Western tribes were sooner or later confronted by the "News" of Anglo expeditions and arrivals, in most cases not without some advance notice, but in a few instances, it appears, without rumor or warning—as shocking as an interplanetary arrival would be to us. In such confrontations, it must have been in Native American terms essentially Mythology versus News, and while News eventually wins out, so to speak, in the historical sense, Myth can be seen as triumphing in an imaginative and literary sense, making accountable Native meaning, that is, of intrusive and unaccountable happenings.

Several Salish-speaking Indian tribes of interior British Columbia have oral-historical records of their apparently unanticipated encounters with Simon Fraser's canoe expedition as it struggled down the rugged Fraser River toward its Pacific mouth in the summer of 1808. (Fraser, an official of the North West Company, was in the company of John Stuart, Jules Quesnel, nineteen voyageurs, including one named D'Alaire, and an uncertain number of Native guides and canoes.) One of these stories, from the Lillooet tribe, gives a quite detailed and literal account of "the drifters," as the Lillooets nicknamed the visitors who suddenly appeared on their stretch of the river, literal, that is, except for one gnomic detail. The expedition's headman, presumably Fraser, is said to have had "a tattoo of the sun on his forehead and a tattoo of the moon on his chest."[7]

Now there is no reason to suppose that Fraser was so ornamented (the Lillooets did practice tattooing themselves), yet he is vividly identified with the sun and the moon in the oral tradition of another group, the Thompson River Indians (or Nlaka'pamux). When the party reached the Thompsons' country immediately above the Lillooets, they suffered a spectacular canoe-capsizing some miles below the present-day town of Lytton, and when James Teit transcribed the Thompsons' oral literature for Franz Boas a full century later, he recorded the three accounts of the accident given below. Taken together with Simon Fraser's own journal narrative of the event, they offer a rare illustration, a paradigm in fact, of the working process of adaptive myth-making.

A. Simon Fraser's Account of the Accident, Wednesday, June 21, 1808

Early in the morning the men made a trip with two of the canoes and part of the things which they carried more than a mile and returned for the rest. I sent Mr. Quesnel to take charge of the baggage in the absence of the men. About this time Indians appeared on the opposite bank. Our guides harangued them from our side, and all were singing and dancing.

After breakfast the men renewed their work, and Mr. Stuart and I remained in the tent writing. Soon after we were alarmed by the loud bawling of our guides, whom upon looking out we observed running full speed towards where we were, making signs that our people were lost in the rapids. As we could not account for this misfortune we immediately ran over to the baggages where we found Mr. Quesnel all alone. We inquired of him about the men, and at the same time we discovered that three of the canoes were missing, but he had seen none of them nor did he know where they were. On casting our view across the river, we remarked one of the canoes and some of the men ashore there. From this incident we had reason to believe that the others were either ahead or perished, and with increased anxiety we directed our speed to the lower end of the rapids.

At the distance of 4 miles or so, we found one of our men, La Chapelle, who had carried two loads of his own share [of the baggage] that far; he could give us no account of the others, but supposed they were following him with their proportions. We still continued; at last growing fatigued and seeing no appearance of the canoes of which we were in search, we considered it advisable to return and keep along the bank of the river.

We had not proceeded far when we observed one of our men, D'Alaire, walking slowly with a stick in his hand from the bank, and on coming up to him we discovered that he was so wet, so weak, and so exhausted that he could scarcely speak. However after leaning a little while upon his stick and drawing breath, he informed us that unfortunately he and the others finding the carrying place too long and the canoes too heavy, took it upon themselves to venture down by water—that the canoe in which he was happened to be the last in setting out.

"In the first cascade," continued he, "our canoe filled and upset. The foreman and steersman got on the outside, but I, who was in the centre, remained a long while underneath the boards [thwarts]. The canoe, still drifting, was thrown into smooth current, and the other two men, finding an opportunity, sprang from their situation into the water and swam ashore. The impulse occasioned by their fall in leaping off raised one side of the canoe above the surface, and I having still my recollection, though I had swallowed a quantity of water, seized the critical moment to disentangle myself, and I gained but not without struggle the top of the canoe. By this time I found myself again in the middle of the stream. Here I continued astride [the canoe], humouring the tide as well as I could with my body to preserve my balance, and although I scarcely had time to look about me, I had the satisfaction to observe the other two canoes ashore near an eddy, and their crews safe among the rocks. In the second or third cascade (for I cannot remember which) the canoe from a great height plunged into the deep eddy at the foot, and striking with violence against the bottom splitted in two. Here I lost my recollection, which, however, I soon recovered, and was surprised to find myself on a smooth easy current with only one half of the canoe in my arms. In this condition I continued through several cascades, until the stream fortunately conducted me into an eddy at the foot of a high and steep rock. Here my strength being exhausted I lost my hold, a large wave washed me off from the wreck among the rocks, and another still larger hoisted me clear on shore, where I remained, as you will readily believe, some time motionless; at length recovering a little of my strength I crawled up among the rocks, but still in danger, and found myself once more on firm ground, just as you see."

Here he finished his melancholy tale, and pointed to the place of his landing, which we went to see, and we were lost in astonishment not only at his escape from the waves, but also at his courage and perseverance in effecting a passage up through a place which appeared to us to be a precipice. Continuing our course along the bank we found that he had drifted 3 miles among rapids, cascades, whirlpools, &c., all inconceivably dangerous.

Mr. Quesnel being extremely anxious and concerned left his charge and joined us. Two men only remained on shore carrying the baggage, and these were equally ignorant with ourselves of the fate of the others. Some time after, upon advancing towards the camp, we picked up all the men on our side of the river. The men that had landed on the other side, joined us in the evening. They informed us that the Indians assisted to extricate them from their difficulties. Indeed the natives shewed us every possible attention in the midst of our misfortune in this trying occasion.[8]

Summarizing Fraser's narrative, then, it appears that the accident happened in the morning and involved three canoes and an unspecified number of men in a foolhardy attempt to run a course of rapids instead of portaging around them. The first two canoes to set out upset early and were brought ashore by their occupants, but the third canoe, with D'Alaire and two companions, swamped in the first cascade and turned over, and although the other two men were able to swim ashore, D'Alaire was carried along down through a series of cataracts and cascades for three miles, losing the canoe, and finally being washed to safety among some rocks. Fraser's last lines indicate that the whole event was watched closely by the Indians. (His favorable impression of the Indians' part in the accident contrasts amusingly with a Lillooet account of Fraser's visit with them a day or two after this: "There were some Indians there who wanted to go after these white men and steal all their possessions, but their leader told them, 'Don't bother them; they might be able to help us one day.'"[9])

Now, of Teit's three Native texts (the ordering "B," "C," "D," is mine), the second and third manifest, in what looks like evolutionary degrees, the *conservatism* I referred to above; that is, the tendency of myth, when it is still an active mediating force in peoples' lives, to imaginatively transform "real events," no matter how strange, according to its system, so that the people can assimilate such events, and "believe" in them. I will give these two texts in a moment, but first let's consider Teit's first text, as narrated around 1900 by an elderly Thompson lady named Semalitsa:

B. *Semalitsa's Account*

My grandmother told me that when she was a young girl she was playing one day in the summertime (about the time the service berries get ripe) near the river-beach at the village of Strain, when she saw two canoes, with red flags hoisted, come downstream. She ran and told her mother, and the people gathered to see the strange sight. Seeing so many people gathered, the canoes put ashore and several men came ashore. Each canoe carried a number of men (perhaps six or seven in each), and many of them wore strange dresses, and everything about them was strange. . . The Spences Bridge chief was presented with some kind of metal or brass badge, and a hat worn by the leader of the strangers whom the Indians called "the Sun." He was called this because of some kind of shining emblem he wore on his hat or cap, which resembled the symbol of the Sun. The Indians applied names to most of the strangers, all taken from some feature of their appearance or from certain marks or emblems on their clothing. After leaving Lytton, at some place close to Si'ska, one of their canoes was swamped in a rapid, and some of the men were saved with difficulty, after having been some time in the water. . . . . Some Indians thought they were just people from a far country and of a different race, for they had heard vague rumours of the strange people with guns, who, it was expected, might find their way to this country some time; but very many people thought they were beings spoken of in tales of the mythological period, who had taken a notion to travel again over the earth; and they often wondered what object they had in view, and what results would follow. They believed their appearance foreboded some great change or events of prime importance to the Indians, but in what way they did not know.[10]

Now Semalitsa's account, as detailed and literal as a newsmagazine article, reminds us that there have always been Native skeptics, dissenting individuals who would resist all or part of the prevailing mythological interpretation of the world and its events.[11] Whether it is the grandmother's skepticism that is involved, or Semalitsa's own, working "historically," or both, the details of her narrative correspond closely to Fraser's own account of his visit to the Thompsons and the canoe adventure, and the mystery of the sun-and-moon tattoos is dryly explained away as deriving from a shiny badge or medal of some sort worn by the explorer; other members of the party were similarly nicknamed, Semalitsa tells us, according to their appearances. I have not found any references in Fraser's *Journal* to such medallions or badges, but in fact the practice of wearing them and bestowing them on Indian leaders was standard in the early expeditions to the American and Canadian West, as witness the famous "Peace and Friendship" medals Lewis and Clark distributed in 1804–5, several of which have actually survived, testifying to the Indians' high valuation of them.[12]

Thus the factuality of the event: but the fact that Fraser and his men—nameless and uncanny strangers to the Thompsons—were *nicknamed* as to appearances may suggest in itself that the mythologizing process began on the spot, or very soon after, as "Sun" and the others began to figure in Native reports and stories about the episode. "What's in a name?"—probably not, as Max Müller claimed long ago, the power to generate mythology through a "disease of language," but rather in this instance the power to hasten the assimilation of Fraser and his company into the Thompson myth-system.

The genuinely mythological accounts of the capsizing are effectively prefaced by Semalitsa's remark that, although there were skeptics, many Thompson people viewed Fraser and his men with wonder as "beings spoken of in tales of the mythological period, who had taken a notion to travel again over the earth." Clearly Versions C and D are expressive of this response to the event; the appearance of the white men among the Indians was here and elsewhere ipso facto a mythic happening, an unprecedented but possibly precedent-setting "first time," and the Thompsons seem to have come to terms with it collectively by interpreting it according to their mythological system. Let us see how.

C. First Mythological Account

Many years ago, but at a time long after Coyote had finished arranging things on earth, he appeared on the Fraser River in company with Sun, Moon, Morning-Star, Kokwela, the Diver, and the Arrow-Armed Person. These seven came in a bark canoe, and came down from the Shuswap country above. They landed at Lytton, where my people saw them. Continuing their journey, and when in the middle of the river, a short distance below Lytton, the Moon, who was steersman of the canoe, disappeared with it under the water. The others came out of the water and sat down on a rock close above the river. Then the Arrow-Armed Person fired many lightning-arrows, and the Diver dived many times into the river. The Sun sat still and smoked; while Coyote, Kokwela, and Morning-Star danced. Coyote said, "Moon will never come up again with the canoe"; but Sun said, "Yes, in the evening he will appear." Just after sunset, Moon appeared, holding the canoe, and came ashore. All of them embarked and, going down the river, were never seen again. This is the only time Coyote has appeared since the end of the mythological age.[13]

Now the traditional mythologies of the Thompsons and other Interior Salish peoples contain no less than four distinct "transformer" story-cycles, one involving a primal creator, possibly of Christian extraction, known as "Old One"; another featuring a team of three brothers, the Qwo'qtqwal; a third centering on Coyote in his usual Western upriver transforming capacity; and a fourth set of stories involving a heroic local figure known as Kokwela. This redundancy of stories is probably to be explained by dissemination and incorporation: the Thompsons and their neighbors, being centrally located between the coastal and the plateau cultures, must have taken on some features of both.[14]

What is important for the mythifying of the Simon Fraser story is that as the Thompson mythology narrates how these personages once variously traveled upriver transforming the world to its present status at the end of the Myth Age, so it is logical that they might eventually reappear in the Historical Age, headed *downstream*, with various mythic companions. Narrative C appears to synthesize these traditions: now at least two of the Thompson transformers appear to be conveniently "in the same boat," headed downriver, revisiting the world they "fixed up" so long before.[15]

Coyote in this narrative is not to be identified with Simon Fraser per se, who figures here and in all other accounts as Sun—rather, Coyote seems to be the mythic patron or "headman" of the whole amazing episode, just as he is the dominant Transformer in Thompson mythology. Of his companions in the canoe and on the rock, Kokwela ("hog-fennel" in the Thompson language, a local plant with an edible root, formerly important in the Thompsons' diet) figures as the local hero of a number of Thompson and Lillooet stories, including one in which Kokwela wins a great transforming contest with the brothers Qwo'qtqwal on the Fraser below Lytton, somewhere near the site of the capsizing, in fact. He then goes on down the river a certain distance, before returning—accounting for the growth of hog-fennel in Thompson country. The general parallel with Coyote's and the Qwo'qtqwals' river travels is obvious.[16]

It is not clear whether Coyote's other companions in the canoe include the qwo'qtqwals and "Old Man," corresponding to the third and fourth Thompson transformer cycles. It is certainly not improbable that "the Diver," who "dived many times into the river," actually represents, submythologically, one of Fraser's unfortunate men, mythically simplified forever, as it were, in terms of one of his observed actions during the emergency. And the "Arrow-Armed Person," who "fired many lightning-arrows," may likewise correspond to someone who fired signal shots. Semalitsa's remarks about how "the Indians applied names to most of the strangers" based on their appearance strengthens this conjecture, but it is also possible that both epithets may represent novel applications for names that once figured in Thompson mythology; if so, I have not been able to identify them, mythologically speaking, in Teit's texts.

As for Sun and Moon, although Fraser's journal makes it clear that he was not actually involved in the capsizing, it is mythologically inevitable, according to the conserving and simplifying process we are exploring, that Fraser (the headman who wore a sun badge) should come to figure as "Sun." And it is equally "logical," according to this process as it seems to have operated within the Thompson myth-system, for poor D'Alaire, the voyageur, to be identified as "Moon," who disappeared with the canoe into the river. Teit notes that the Thompsons had a proverb that when the faint disk of the old moon appears in the evening within the crescent of the new, "it is the moon holding the canoe"—in our narrative, bringing it back to Sun and his companions.[17]

Almost certainly it was not the historical episode that gave rise to the proverb, but rather the ready-to-hand proverb that contributed to the mythologizing of the episode. As we have noted in earlier essays, it was once widely held that the world's mythologies were created in order to humanly "explain" the appearance and motion of the heavenly bodies: but here, clearly, a piece of lunar lore, a metaphor really, has been adduced to explain, or rather to record and translate into traditional order, an earthly event.

In the third Thompson account of the capsizing, briefly summarized by Teit (D), this ad hoc ordering and stylizing process is even more obvious and would seem to have gone about as far as possible. Now the only passengers in the canoe are the three heavenly bodies from C—Morning-Star, Sun, and Moon—and they reappear after the accident in perfect diurnal order, with Moon predictably bringing back the canoe! Mythology has, as it were, succeeded in redeeming News utterly.

D. Second Mythological Account

The canoe was of birch-bark and disappeared under the water with all hands. The first to appear very early in the morning was Morning-Star, who rose to the surface and came ashore. At noon, Sun rose and came ashore; and in the evening, Moon rose holding the canoe, and came ashore. During the night, the canoe and all disappeared.[18]

We are a far cry in these two mythic accounts from what must have been the sweaty, grumbling, and often desperate realities of Fraser's expedition on the one hand, and the surprise and consternation that it must have provoked among the Indians, on the other. Perhaps a clue as to the Indians' feelings is given by Semalitsa. In observing how the arrival of Fraser and party was seen by many as a fulfillment, indeed a culmination of myth (and we have been examining the details of this culmination), Semalitsa goes on to remark that the people "believed their appearance foreboded some great change or event of prime importance to the Indians, but in what way they did not know." [19] Certainly by Semalitsa's time this sense of foreboding in the event could be interpreted ex post facto in the light of history: the sudden appearance of the Fraser party foretelling, that is, the appearance fifty years later of white miners and settlers, whose manifold arrival—*not* by mythical canoe—changed the Thompsons' way of life utterly. Perhaps—we can only speculate—such apprehensions attending the original event may have spurred the Thompsons, at least the orthodox among them, to transform the details of the event as rapidly and as completely as possible into the familiar lineaments of myth.

As we turn to our newspapers and to Tom Brokaw and Dan Rather and their associates, all this may sound very foreign, remote from our objective usages, "primitive." In Pound's sarcastic epigram, "We have the press for wafer," [20] and we think, not without self-congratulation, that ours is not any such mythological mentality. Yet a little reflection tells us, I think, that in our own response to "Hard News"—the assassinations of presidents, for example, with their retinue of prophetic dreams, numerological and calendrical formulae, and so on; or Hiroshima and Nagasaki, in response to which Japanese writers and filmmakers turned back to "primitive" Native myths of retributive monsters; or the Jonestown suicides; or even the moon landings—we too must invoke what remains of our a priori mythological systems, lest the unmediated news, "bloody with reality," prove unassimilable to the listening imagination—that is, unreal.

10 / Fish=Hawk and Other Heroes

THE APPETITE OF WESTERN INDIANS FOR HEROES and heroic actions exemplifying courage, physical prowess, self-control, resourcefulness, and gallantry manifests itself abundantly in their myth-repertories, in narratives dramatizing the emergence and exploits of bona fide heroes like the Tillamook "Placed-Next-to-Testicles," the Chinookan Eagle, and the Coos "Younger Brother"; and also, indirectly, in many of the trickster stories, whose protagonists seem to embody comically all that is a denial of the heroic.

But apart from mythology, the Native interest in heroes and exemplary action is also vividly illustrated in another kind of traditional literature: the "hero-story," or geste. It is clear from the ethnographic commentary on most western tribes that these stories have always been important to the Indians, and it therefore says something about the working biases of Anglo scholarship that such narratives have been neglected by transcribers (who often chose to collect only "classical" myths) and all but ignored by commentators.[1]

Some hero-stories at least do exist as texts, and in many tribes they are still in fact being told as part of the surviving oral tradition, even as the myth-repertory part of it fades away. As a genre, their variations and apparent literary evolution from "real-life" adventures offer, I think, a fascinating and invaluable view of Native imaginative and literary processes at work outside the systems of mythology. And because most of these gestes derive from contact-era happenings, and often appear to be conditioned by Native attitudes toward the whites, they offer an excellent opportunity to study some of the imaginative ways Indian cultures have attempted to accommodate themselves to a new historical reality—ways that still have validity in Indian communities today.

Although Indian hero-stories clearly share conceptions of the heroic with myth-narratives, their literary evolution from historical event to verbal tradition does not seem to proceed along mythic lines. Where myth can and does forcibly incorporate "real events" into its highly conservative and stylized system, utterly transforming them (as we saw in essay 7), in hero-tales the evolutionary changes are more modest, more the result of "art," more a matter of narrative exaggeration and stylization of details with respect to the "real event" than of transformation. To put it most simply, a Native hero-story seems to "become more so" as it goes. There seems to be no evidence of a euhemeristic connection between the heroes of these stories and their counterparts in the tribal myths. Figures like Fish-Hawk of the Cayuse and Chiloquin of the Klamath are certainly "larger than life," but they are far from having mythic status in their stories, and I conclude from this and other reasons that euhemeristic theories do not apply to the Indian myth-literature of the West.[2]

Unquestionably the best-known Native gestes are those from the great equestrian cultures of the western Plains—stirring tales of horseback raids and escapes and glorious feats of unpragmatic derring-do according to strict rules among the Sioux, the Cheyenne, the Crow, and others; tales that suggest in fact a close analogy with chivalry and its pursuit of danger for honor's sake.[3]

Apparently such narratives originated in the regular practice on the Plains of recountings by braves of their exploits, especially on the occasion of intertribal meetings, or meetings with whites, where not just personal reputation but tribal honor was at stake. Needless to say, modesty Anglo-style was irrelevant to such tellings, but universally the tellers were required to claim no more for themselves than could be verified—and there are numerous accounts of braggarts and liars being exposed and discredited on the spot.[4] What a warrior's story of his exploits became when others in the tribe began to tell it is, of course, a different matter: but still, if Native hero-stories show signs of "heroic license" and considerable artistic reshaping, they rarely amount to tall tales or whoppers. As a genre, their heroic purpose is clearly too serious to those who told and celebrated them to allow for exaggeration to the point of implausibility and self-mockery.

Not that such stories and their codes of heroism aren't burlesqued in Native tradition. Although Black Elk's celebrated narrative centers chiefly on his tragic life as a prophet and visionary, occasionally he recounts traditional heroic feats among the Lakotas (he was, after all, Crazy Horse's cousin), and one memorable story, "High Horse's Courting," amounts to a genial parody of the typical Plains hero-tale. It is a story that Sir Philip Sidney and Shakespeare, those connoisseurs of heroism tending to foolishness, would have relished, and worthy in theme and tone of the *Arcadia* or *As You Like It*. A young and untested warrior, High Horse, falls horribly in love with a girl whose wealthy parents keep her under close guard, even to the point of tying her in her bed each night. Poor High Horse is reduced to ignominious and hilariously unsuccessful tipi-creeping and skulking in pursuit of the girl—until he and his faithful friend Red Deer reject love as a theme for action and mount an authentic horse-stealing raid against the Crows. The raid is successful; High Horse returns to his village a wealthy hero, and then

they drove the whole herd right into the village and up in front of the girl's tepee. The old man was there, and High Horse called out to him and asked if he thought maybe that would be enough horses for his girl. The old man did not wave him away that time. It was not the horses he wanted. What he wanted was a son who was a real man and good for something.[5]

Beyond the Plains culture and its celebration of equestrian bravery and coup-counting skills, Far Western Indian hero-stories predictably take different forms, reflecting other, often less familiar ideals. It has to be supposed, given the relative scarcity of transcribed hero-narratives from the Far West, that transcribers didn't bother to ask for them, or didn't recognize their cultural and literary value and so ignored them. But, if not often embodied in epical accounts of night raids and pitched battles, the heroic values of these tribes have been celebrated and kept alive in stories, too, as the following Klamath tradition about one of their heroes (a historical figure, and member of an important family) will illustrate.

Chiloquin the Hero

Chiloquin was a short man, deep chested, powerful, and exceptionally hardy. It is related that he overtook a party camped in the deep snows atop the Cascades. Not being properly equipped, he lay beside a fire covered only with a single blanket. In the morning he was covered with frost, but apparently had not suffered.

Somewhere in the north, possibly Warm Springs, was a man who owned a big slave who was very much a bully. While the slave was absent Chiloquin traded three horses for the master's best horse. When the slave returned, he inquired for the horse and sent a man to demand it. That man went twice but each time Chiloquin sat quietly sewing and did not reply. Then the slave himself went out and demanded its return but Chiloquin paid no attention. When the slave went to untie the horse, Chiloquin tripped him. The slave struck at him with his hatchet but missed. Then Chiloquin wounded him and he retreated.

Chauchau, a northerner, wanting Chiloquin's daughter, offered horses and other valuables. The latter refused. He came to Chiloquin at night and fought with him till daybreak. Chiloquin clung to Chauchau's hair despite the beating he was receiving. Chauchau came again the next night and again they fought. This performance kept up through the whole winter. When spring came, Chauchau acknowledged his defeat: "Yes, Chiloquin, you are fierce," and they were again friends.

Again in the north some northern shamans went into a sweat-lodge. They wanted a shaman among their Klamath visitors to accompany him. None was present so the Klamaths insisted on Chiloquin joining them. One after the other each northern shaman sprinkled water on the hot rocks as he sang his song, hoping to force the others out. Some, overcome by heat and steam, had to be dragged out. Once outside they wondered what had become of Chiloquin; he was nowhere to be seen. They thought he must have died. After a long time he began to talk, throwing water on the rocks. When he was quite ready, he came out and walked to his own people. He had bested the shamans.[6]

The contrast between "heroic mobility" in the Plains stories, and Chiloquin's quiet, rocklike hardihood—values especially prized by the Klamaths—is striking. Another set of heroic ideals emerges in a long, richly detailed personal narrative by Louis Simpson of his participation with other Wishram and Wasco Chinookans in the military campaign of 1866–68 in central Oregon against their traditional enemies, the Northern Paiutes, under the leadership of Paulina and Weawea, a campaign that descendants of both sides now refer to wryly as "sort of our Civil War."

That the venture was aimed at achieving something like extermination of the Paiutes is gruesomely clear in the diary kept by one of its officers Dr. William C. McKay (himself part-Indian[7]); Simpson's account dramatizes the heroic significance of the action for him and his comrades, with references to prophetic dreams, formal speeches and vaunts, ritual desecrations of the enemy victims, and so on. There is not a single notice of McKay or the other Anglo officers and troops with whom the Chinookans traveled and fought; instead, Simpson emphasizes the valor of both his comrades and Paiutes, at the expense of the whites: "Thus the Indians have strong hearts; not thus are white people. Indians could pass five days and eat nothing, nor would they drink any water. So strong are the Wascos, they are not cowards. So also they too, the Paiutes, are not cowards."[8]

A similar nineteenth-century recognition that, even as Indians were "heroically" fighting Indians, their ultimate common enemy was the white man, emerges in an unpublished Cayuse account by Gilbert Minthorne (in Nez Perce) of a climactic event in the brief "Sheepeaters War" in Idaho against the Bannocks in 1878. Led by "Capt. Sumkins," a Cayuse soldier, a detachment of Indians surrounds a band of Bannocks and calls for the surrender of their leader, Tamanmo, on behalf of General O. O. Howard. When Howard arrives, the following interesting scene ensues:

Capt. Sumkins told General Howard, "Now we've captured them"—he
pointed—"this many are the Snakes; this is the bunch that was whipping
you whites. Here they are, the Snakes; Indians captured Indians." Silent was
General Howard, he walked back and forth; he used to do that; he turned back
and forth, and walked around back and forth, until he said, "Pretty good, you
have taken them all."[9]

Perhaps needless to say, this episode is not given in any of Howard's memoirs; Minthorne's emphasis throughout is not only on how dependent Howard and his troops were on Sumkins and his braves, but more than that, as in this scene, on how much more able and stalwart they were, as warriors. After Howard recovered from his silent pique, Minthorne reports that he paid his Native allies this much tribute: "It is true you people have captured them now. Indians are brave. You are brave Indians, many times in war; an Indian man has a brave heart." [10]

The perspective of this story is consistent with the special efforts of the Cayuses, especially in the years immediately following the Whitman Massacre in 1847, to persuade other Far Western tribes to unite against the whites and drive them out. Because of the Massacre (Capt. Sumkin's father, in fact, was one of the participants) and because of this desperate campaign, conducted as if with nothing to lose, to stir up a pan-tribal uprising, the Cayuses have received more than their share of infamy in the West. Even before the Whitman episode, the Cayuses, who spoke a language neither Sahaptin nor Chinookan,[11] had begun to merge culturally and linguistically with the Sahaptian-speaking Nez Perces—but their loss of language and political identity was certainly hastened by the repercussions of the Massacre, most of the tribe being forcibly resettled and "pacified" on the Umatilla Reservation in Northeast Oregon. The Cayuses have always suffered in Western popular opinion by comparison with their kinsmen, the Nez Perces, and it is a sad commentary on Anglo culture in the region that, apart from their reputation for skill in breeding tough horses ("cayuses"), almost nothing is known about their ways except for their belligerence in the mid-nineteenth century—no language records, little ethnographic commentary, virtually no trustworthy historical or literary traditions exist in print.[12]

Yet when Morris Swadesh (later to become a distinguished linguist) came to the Umatilla Agency in 1930 to do field work, he was able to transcribe from performances by an able raconteur, Gilbert Minthorne, a number of historical narratives that are distinctively, "heroically" Cayuse— celebrations (even though given in Nez Perce) of a sense of continuing heroic pride in being Cayuse, and of a set of virtues that ought to force us to reconsider the ugly stereotype that the nineteenth century stamped upon these people.

Central to these narratives is a marvelous geste, as epical in its way as the Night Raid against the Trojans by Odysseus and Diomedes in Book Ten of *The Iliad,* about the horse-stealing raid into buffalo country of a Cayuse warrior named Fish-Hawk and five friends. Publications of it in *Alcheringa* in 1977 marked the first time any distinctively Cayuse material had ever appeared in print,[13] and what I have discovered since then is the existence of a number of stories about the raid, shared by the Cayuses and the Nez Perces, but clearly differentiated as to tribe, and showing to a greater or lesser degree the signs of literary (not mythical) transformation. A happening becoming through artful retellings, that is, a memorable story, a geste.

Morris Swadesh's interlinear translation of Minthorne's performance in Nez Perce is literal, and follows his transcription phrase-by-phrase and in some passages word-by-word. Without departing extensively from his choice of words in the following free reworking, I have tried to bring the lines into some readable degree of conformity with English syntax. For example, here is the beginning of the third paragraph, in Swadesh's literal rendering—"they discovered them and they yelled Sioux and he told them brothers good think go slow lo they are going to take us and now horses they swept along Sioux and they took not far little ways they drove along horses and there they turned now." In my verse reworking, the passage runs:

> Then the Sioux discovered them
>   and yelled in Sioux!
>
> Fish-Hawk said,
>   "Brothers, think good, and take it easy—
>   look! they are going to try and take us."
>
> And now they swept the Sioux horses along with them;
>   they drove them along a little way,
>   and then they all turned.

It is very likely that Fish-Hawk's story is poetically structured, perhaps according to some variation of the order Dell Hymes has discovered in Chinookan narratives, but if so I have not been able to find the grammatical or syntactical keys to it, and so have reworked the text according to an experimental system of lineation that, unlike prose, emphasizes the verb-intensive, incremental, paratactic narrative progression of the original, and highlights its poetic elements of style, as in the epic epithets, magnifying Fish-Hawk as "the pipe leader," "the thinker in travels," and so on. What has emerged in this reworking is a simple stanza form made up of indented lines: each stanza generally including one complete sentence in the original; a new line, progressively indented, for each additional verb phrase, until the sentence is completed. Stanzas are separated by line spacing, and what turned out to be the ten main narrative segments of the story are indicated by numerals.

I can't claim that the following re-working of Gilbert Minthorne's story is based on new linguistic evidence of poetic measure in the Nez Perce/Cayuse oral tradition; and I certainly don't want to assert that my experimental scheme for recasting Fish-Hawk's adventure in measured lines necessarily breaks new ground for the translation of other Native American oral material. But the scheme, simple and arbitrary though it may be, does seem to me to realize much more of the wonderful narrative sweep and acumen that I sensed in Minthorne's telling than my original prose adaptation of Swadesh's interlineal wording did. But of course what Fish-Hawk and Minthorne and the Cayuse heritage really deserve is a systematic translation of the story according to ethnopoetic principles by someone fluent in Nez Perce Sahaptian. [14]

How Fish-Hawk Raided the Sioux

1

A long time ago,
    when many Nez Perce and Cayuse lived to the east,
        they used to go buffalo hunting.

Once a man dreamed of the Sioux;
    he saw them in his sleep,
        and he told the young men,
            "Now I am going on the warpath day after tomorrow,
            and I shall travel to the Sioux."

He was a tough man;
    many times he had fought and come out all right.
        His name was Fish-Hawk.

Four Cayuse men and two Nez Perce men were going,
    the one named Fish-Hawk
        and one named Come-with-the-Dawn
            and one named All-Alighted-on-the-Ground

and one named Charging Coyote
and two Nez Perce men.

Fish-Hawk took the lead;
   he held the pipe;
     he was the thinker in travels.
2
They all had red jackets;
   they were on the warpath, all six of them.

They traveled, and it snowed;
   it snowed like winter on the prairie.

They traveled on horseback,
   and they came upon the prairie
     and went down into a canyon.

Many Sioux lived close by there.
   Fish-Hawk stopped, and he turned around toward his friends.
     "We've come right into camp;
     see, here are the tents,
     and they don't know we're here."

Tents were all around,
   maybe two hundred or more;
     they saw the tents.

Then the Sioux discovered them
   and yelled in Sioux!

Fish-Hawk said,
   "Brothers, think good, and take it easy—
     look! they are going to try and take us."

And now they swept the Sioux horses along with them;
   they drove them along a little way,
     and then they all turned.

"Look! they are catching up with us,"
   he told the others,

the pipe leader told them.

"Younger brothers, move on from here;
   don't shoot yet;
   from now on they will try and take us.
   Look, there is brushy ground ahead;
   there will we dismount,
   and soon they will try and get us.
We shall not desert each other;
   look to your guns—"
     and the Sioux chased them along.

And the people's chief in battle turned his horse,
   and he waved at the Sioux;
   he told them,
     "I am Cayuse. we all are!
     We are only six,
     and you are three hundred or more!
     Come on! You are only Sioux,
     And you are just like old women;
     you will never kill us, for we are Cayuse!"
   3
So they yelled at the Sioux during the chase,
   and shot at them;
     they killed them as they went.

He told his brothers, the pipe leader,
   "Now turn your horses loose,"
     and they got off,
       and they took off the bridles
        and took off their jackets
         and left it all behind
           and took only the guns and bullets into the brush
            among the cottonwoods.

He told them, the pipe leader,
   he told them,
     "Younger brothers, look:
     we can dig trenches
     and fight well from there."

They dug out the ground
    and crossed cottonwoods over the trenches
       and got under it all.

They yelled at the Sioux;
    the Sioux yelled back at them and hurled insults,
      they yelled back again.
        They were killing Sioux.

    4

Now then one of the Sioux used up his bullets,
    and he came up to them,
      one Sioux, a tough man, dog-disguised;
       he came up singing.

Fish-Hawk said, their chief,
    "Little brothers, now he comes;
      take good aim!"
      and they hit him close by the trench.

He came on
    and now he shot at Fish-Hawk with a bow and arrows.

Fish-Hawk cried,
    "Little brothers, he shot me!"

He got mad, the one the people call Fish-Hawk.
    He told them,
      "Look, friends, watch your leader, now!
      He shot one of us;
      now know me;
      now I am going after him,
      and I am going to drag him right into the trench!"

And he stood up suddenly
    and threw himself out of the trench,
      and they yelled, the Sioux,
        they shot at him,
          and he hopped;
            he grabbed the Sioux warrior by the legs
            and dragged him along;

he threw him into the trench,
   and he hit him.

They took his bullets and gun
   and scalped him.
      5
Fish-Hawk told them,
   "Little brothers, maybe I am dying;
      now pull out the arrow—"
         and they pulled it out,
            and the pipe leader, chief in war, breathed good again,
               but he was bleeding and getting weak,
                  and they tied up the wound.

He started shooting again;
   he told them,
      "Little brothers, think carefully,
      look, they are many,
      and they are trying to get us.
      Try to shoot straighter—"
         and they yelled.
      6
He saw now that there was fire all around them,
   below and up above,
      and he told them,
         "Now, look, it's burning;
         they are trying to kill us by burning.
         Dig deeper now;
         we are going to be burned.
         See! they're scared and that is why
         they are trying to burn us to death.
         But we will never die of fire;
         we are younger brothers, tough ones with guns;
         they can't get us killed,
         and they will never kill us with fire."

So he told them,
   and when night came,
      he gathered them in the mouth of the thicket;
      he told them,

"We killed many Sioux;
    now we're going;
    we're going out.
    We're in the midst of them,
    but with my knowledge soon we will get through anyway."

And he told them,
    "A little wind will come up presently;
    now get ready, little brothers;
    let's travel!"

And it came, the whirlwind,
    and they got out of the trench.

When the fire flared up, they went down;
        they passed the Sioux all huddled up in a ditch;
            they passed by unseen;
                they traveled on.
    7
Dawn came.
    The Sioux said,
        "Now, look, they're all burned up—"
        and they went up to the trench.

When they got there, they found nobody.
    The Sioux were surprised.
        "Where are they?
        How could they live?
        On which side of us did they pass?"

They were greatly surprised;
    and as they went home, they cried on their way;
        they took many bodies home.
    8
The Cayuse got out from the trench all right,
    and from there they traveled without pants,
        shirtless,
            pantsless,
                shoeless—

All they had were guns,
    and he told them, their chief, the pipe leader, he told them,
        "Younger brothers, now we have traveled far,
        and one of us is getting cold,
        and can travel no farther."

It was Charging Coyote;
    he told them,
        "Friends, now leave me;
        I will be too much bother;
        I'll stay, I'll stay right here.
        My forefathers died too;
        I'll just rest my body."

Then the others told him,
    "No, friend, it's the same with all of us:
        without shoes,
        without pants,
        without shirts,
        somehow we will all get back.
        This is what we went looking for,
        and now we are coming back together."
      9
Then they came upon a buffalo bull,
    and Fish-Hawk told them,
        "We have traveled far without eating;
        now kill it."

And they killed two buffalo;
    from them they made shoes and pants and shirts,
        and they ate buffalo meat,
            and they went on traveling.

But they had no tents;
    they got black from freezing
        and were awful to look at;
            thus they came back to the tents of their own people.
      10
This is all of the story about the raid on the Sioux:
    now they told it at the big war dance at celebration time,
        how this man,

Fish-Hawk, the pipe leader,
   went on the warpath;
      he was the man!

"Only six of us, and you couldn't get us killed,
   only six, and maybe you were three hundred and maybe more!"

Thus they told the story,
   and now all the people know it.

This is a true story;
   now there, we have made it,
      and it will always be the same story.

One thing that is special about the provenience of the story is that its hero is a certifiable historical figure, in later life (after the turn of the century) a subchief on the Umatilla Reservation, and the subject of a famous photograph by Colonel Lee Morehouse (a Northwest rival of Edward Curtis).[15] Gilbert Minthorne told Morris Swadesh that he had actually heard the story from Fish-Hawk himself around 1920, as well as from others.

Both in content and form, Fish-Hawk's adventure illustrates the special affinities of the Cayuses and Nez Perces for the Plains cultures beyond the Rockies. In the 1860s and 1870s, the two tribes repeatedly mounted expeditions into buffalo country in central Montana and even further east, making a heroic name for themselves among the Cheyennes, Sioux, Crows, and Blackfeet. Merrill Beal observes of the Nez Perces:

The expeditions required able leadership and large numbers, because access to the hunting areas involved inter-tribal contentions, and the hunters were subject to attack by the Blackfeet and the Crows. However, this prospect did not intimidate the Nez Perces; indeed, the danger inherent in the situation was an impelling factor. They made enemies and allies depending on the circumstances. In any case, the experience of the long hunts had a mighty impact upon the tribe. Young men made big medicine; great reputations were acquired for skill and bravery.[16]

Clearly, it is "big medicine" and reputation, and not buffalo meat, or even horses, that Fish-Hawk and his mates ride off to seek, and the general

Plains culture orientation of their escapade is further clarified in this description of the "mystique" of similar raiding parties among the Blackfeet:

A war party usually, or often, had its origins in a dream. Some man has a dream, after he awakes he tells of it. Perhaps he may say, "I dreamed that on a certain stream is a herd of horses that have been given to me, and that I am going away to get, I am going to war. I shall go to that place and get my band of horses." Then the men who know him, who believe that his medicine is strong and that he will have good luck, make up their minds to follow him.[17]

The Blackfeet and their Plains neighbors would have understood Fish-Hawk's motives very well. In fact, the sort of courage he exhibits would probably have earned him membership in the legendary Dog Societies of these tribes, consisting of the fiercest, most accomplished warriors—as represented by the "dog-disguised" Sioux in Minthorne's respectful reference, who wounds our hero and is eventually killed by him.[18]

Now there is nothing in the story that is inherently implausible, or fantastic, and in turning to its literary dimensions I do not mean to suggest that Fish-Hawk's tale as we have it is not quite possibly founded on historical facts consistent with those mentioned above. But the plot does seem to share particular motifs with other Nez Perce–Cayuse exploit stories, to a striking degree, and one wonders if some sort of heroic literary archetype isn't involved. For example, though translation makes it impossible to be sure, the special epithets applied to Fish-Hawk seem to be echoed in this formal description of the Nez Perce warrior Red Grizzly Bear by his grandson, "He knew and took part in all the wars of his day. Always a leader, when foraging he went ahead of his band; no one ever traveled in front of him."[19] The numbers of raiders in these stories is invariably no more than six, ensuring that they will be vastly and grandly outnumbered. Discovered and pursued by the enemy, they usually take refuge in a canyon, gully, thicket, or some other "tight place," and manage to escape under cover of darkness, through some ruse and /or the intervention of spirit-aid, returning to their tribal camp under extreme hardship to tell their illustrious tale.[20]

Having noticed this conventional quality in Fish-Hawk's narrative, I began to wonder if in fact other versions of it, not just analogues, had survived and somehow been transcribed. As with myth-narratives, it seemed possible that if I could find variant texts and establish a "set," I could identify the literary qualities of Minthorne's telling more certainly through comparative analysis within the set. Perhaps, in addition, the versions might arrange themselves in a clear evolutionary order, shedding light (so I hoped) on the complex fictive process whereby the Native oral imagination creates such stories out of happenings.

What I found, in fact, were two distinctively Nez Perce versions, similar in motive and circumstance and yet illuminatingly different in details and emphasis, and thus capable of throwing the Cayuse narrative into a clarifying relief. Such comparison reveals in particular (1) that Fish-Hawk's story is even more pointedly and self-consciously a Cayuse artifact than appears to be the case, and (2) that it seems to represent a much more advanced degree of fictive transformation than do the Nez Perce texts. I hope that reading these two variants, good stories in their own right, will help suggest how and why Gilbert Minthorne's version is especially compelling, even in cold print.

The first variant was narrated to L. V. McWhorter by an elderly Nez Perce tribal historian, Wottolen, in his own language, presumably in the 1930s.

The early seventies saw our last fight with any of the distant buffalo-hunting tribes. It was summertime. Kilkiltom, also called Koolkooltami (far back ancestral name) with five select men, went to the buffalo country somewhere on the Little Missouri River. The names of these five warriors were Ipsuspa Owyeen [Shot in Hand], a great warrior known to the whites as John Hill, who lived at [now] Shalway on the Clearwater; Ealaotkeh Kaunis (Flying Birds Lighting on Earth], who was from [now] Stites on Clearwater and known to whites as Dick Brown; Atpallatkitsith Kilkiltom [Moses Monteith, later a Presbyterian minister at Kamiah]; and the other two, Kaaupoo [known also as Morning Eagle], and Sahsoch [Fish-Hawk], both Cayuses from Oregon. But speaking the same language they were counted as Nez Perces. The other warriors were all of the Clearwater band. All now dead.

From their camp they traveled several suns into the Sioux country. It was about mid-sun when they stopped. Soon they saw a moving object, three, maybe five miles, away. It is a horse! Might be a man on horseback. They watch close. After a short time they see about ten mounted men coming towards them. Eh! More! Still more horsemen join with the company! Riding swiftly, they head for the Nez Perce camp. It is now seen that they are a great body of Sioux warriors.

Koolkooltami gave order to mount and be gone. It is a race. Sioux pressing hard are in pursuit. The chase is long and Koolkooltami's horse gives out. He jumps to the ground and runs afoot some distance. Ipsuspa Owyeen was not best mounted. He called to the others, "Some of you have good horses. You might double-ride one!"

Kaaupoo stopped his horse and the chief mounted behind him. They ride, whip-driving their horses. They ride, but the enemy is overtaking them. The fighting is no easy feeling during the retreat. But the larger enemy force is strongly matched by Koolkooltami's smaller band. Fighting hard, guarding both flanks, the pursuers are held to the rear.

When the sun is far down the evening sky, the Nez Perce chief, seeing their horses tired down, unable to continue the retreat, directed all to continue fighting off the enemy, and make slowly for a creek now appearing on their front. This place they had seen the sun before, and knew the lay of the country [southeast of Lodgegrass, Montana].

Reaching the creek they quickly dismount. Leaving horses, blankets, everything but arms and ammunition, the Nez Perces hurried across the stream. They found a hollow place and some rosebushes. These rosebushes were dry, and soon the enemy set fire on the windward side. The flames drew nearer, growing as they came. Back of the smoke the enemies came creeping on. It grew bad for Koolkooltami and his few warriors. Besieged by far greater numbers and scorched by fire heat, they must expect the rush to come soon.

But it was to be different. As night drew on, one of the bravest of the enemies, a fine-looking young man, was killed. This discouraged the others, and having all of the Nez Perce horses, the chief called his warriors and quit the fight. Koolkooltami's band was left afoot and without blankets. When night settled they slipped away in the hiding darkness.

This was the last battle that the Nez Perce ever had with any of the tribes. But it was not Sioux that they had fought. These Indians were Cheyennes. [Wottolen's Nez Perce interpreter, Camille Williams, added a final note, linking the episode most oddly with the defeat of Chief Joseph and the Nez Perces a few years later:]

No peace was ever made between the two tribes after that fight, from the simple fact that they had no tribal meetings. Never met until at the Bear's Paw Mountain battle. Thirty Cheyennes enlisted to fight the Nez Perces, as their chief told them they could do so, enlist with the whites, because it was his son that the Nez Perces killed previously.[21]

The second Nez Perce variant was told in English to Dell Skeels by Owen Gould in the 1940s.

Six men kind of grouped themselves together so that they could start out and look for the enemy camp to secure themselves what horses they might find. These six men were *kul kultsálm*, Dick Brown, and John Hill, Moses Monteith and *kau pul* and Fish-Hawk. They were the six. They decided that they would start out any time after midnight, and they all agreed that they would, and they provided themselves with saddle horses and enough provisions for several days, and they started out to look for the enemy camp. Their intention was to find a Sioux camp.

They traveled one day and part of a night. They camped that night to rest and early before dawn they started out again. The leader, I think, was kul kultsálm. He carried a peace pipe, a great big red pipe, and the one who was leader was required to carry it. And when they came near to a high hill, there they stopped, and they saw a man riding through on horseback. Some one of them said to the leader, "Let's get after him and kill him and get our scalps." The leader cautioned them not to "because we are not looking for scalps. We are looking for good horses that we might find to take."

So they listened to him because he was their leader, and they watched this man on horseback, they rode on in the direction he went. They learned that the enemy camp was near some place there. While they were discussing among themselves what action they would take they heard a sound of horses tramping, and when they came into sight there were numbers of warriors. They were going to attack them. So they decided to retreat to the bushes which were near. This particular place was kind of round, pool-like, with plenty of brush and undergrowth for their protection, and they started toward that particular place.

They had quite a time crossing the little creek. The beavers had dammed the little creek, and it had backed water and made a kind of slue. Finally, they found a place where they could cross. Their enemy was almost on their heels with their war whoops and howls and war chants. They finally found a little knoll, and they got on the opposite side, and they started to dig and made a trench, a protection where they could shelter themselves from the fire which was coming pretty heavy.

In the meantime while they were digging, their leader, kul kultsálm, was shot with an arrow which went in from the back. He could not pull the arrow out. The only way they could get the arrow out was to push the arrow clear on through his chest because the arrowhead was wrapped with sinew and the blood would soften it and the arrowhead would remain. One of them pushed it clear on through and broke the end off on the side of the feathers and he got it out. And they gave him first aid the best they could from bleeding too heavily.

They were exchanging fire, shooting. These six men were not shooting in vain but they were hitting the target every time they made a shot. There was one from the Cheyennes, they had a man, translated in our language, "dog." In other words, he was a suicide man. So they sent him to drive them out. He made a couple of shots at these six men but he happened to miss each shot. When he turned back Dick Brown raised and shot him and he never returned again, and he thought he might have killed him.

So they started a fire when they couldn't drive them out of the brush. The Cheyennes started a grass fire from the direction the wind was blowing. It was night when the fire started. These six men knew they would be burned if they stayed there. They asked their leader, kul kultsálm, if he could stand to travel. He answered them that he was able to travel, that he was not very seriously wounded. They asked among themselves if they had any nature spirit such as an animal, fowl, or beast of any kind, that had ever (before) directed them what to do in a case like this. They all, each one of them, told what they could do as they had learned when they were young boys from their nature spirits.

So they started out, trusting they would go through without anyone seeing them. Four started out with their wounded leader, kul kultsálm. Dick Brown and Moses Monteith stayed for a while until they thought they were far enough away before they started out themselves. While they were staying there they were exchanging shots now and then and making the enemy think they were still there because they were surrounded by the enemy, and the enemy thought they were still there, and they were going to wait until morning before they made the attack on these six men. The fire was bright in the brush all around them and Dick Brown said to Monteith, "Let's go out too. The fire is getting awful close to us."

And they started out in the direction they said they would go, and they made it through the enemy guard and followed the other four men who were ahead of them to a particular place. When they caught up with them they asked, "How is the leader kul kultsálm coming?" They answered them that he was doing all right. "He is able to ride." And they came to a little creek which had been washed out deep and they followed that up towards the head of it. It led towards the mountains. Before morning they reached timber line and they were up in the safe (country), and when it was daylight from the high peak they watched their enemies. They could see them scatter all over the prairie so they could find some track. But they seemed to give up because they couldn't find their tracks, and they went on back to their own camp safely, taking their wounded leader back.[22]

The three stories together provide an object lesson in the possibilities of variation in oral transmissions. Which is most faithful to "the way it was"? On the evidence, that would be Wottolen's account—not only because of his age and official status as Nez Perce historian, but because of the factual interest his story manifests.[23] As if clearing up a tribal misconception, for example, he insists at the end that the enemy were not Sioux, but Cheyennes "in Sioux country," and he locates with some precision the date ("summertime," "early seventies") and the sites of both the Nez Perce main camp and the encounter with the enemy. Further, he and his interpreter, Camille Williams, frame the narrative with references to its historical importance—it was "our last fight" in the buffalo country, and as a consequence of the killing of the Cheyenne chief's son, thirty Cheyenne warriors fought against the Nez Perces at their defeat at Bear's Paw a few years later in 1878. By comparison, Minthorne's and Owen Gould's narratives are unspecific as to time, place, and overall historical significance.

The most striking difference, of course, is over the six-man membership of the party, and especially over the identity of its peerless leader. Clearly a tribal bias is at work. The two Nez Perce accounts agree that the Nez Perce warrior Koolkooltami (or kul kultsálm in Gould) was leader, and they name the same comrades, in almost the same order—each list concluding with Kaaupoo (or kau pul) and Fish-Hawk, as Cayuses. Unmistakably, Minthorne's account reverses this bias, with Fish-Hawk given as leader, plus three Cayuse companions (including "All-alighted-on-the-ground," or Ealaotkeh Kaunis, who is listed as a Nez Perce in Wottolen and Gould!), and concluding with two unnamed "Nez Perce men" (presumably Koolkooltami and Ipsuspa Owyeen). Whose story is it? One wonders what would have happened if Koolkooltami and Fish-Hawk had told their versions to one audience. Certainly, by the time these transcriptions were made, the Cayuses were thoroughly (and officially) dispersed among the Nez Perces and the Umatillas, and intermarried therein: but in Fish-Hawk's geste the old tribal pride clearly runs unabated—not anti-Nez Perce, but strongly pro-Cayuse.

Now neither of the Nez Perce texts mentions the fact, but in Nez Perce tribal tradition some of these braves figure together romantically as "The Brothers," or us-ka-ma-tone, a heroic team of variously five or six young warriors who "made frequent visits into the buffalo country"[24] and distinguished themselves in several exploits, not just this one, against the Cheyennes, the Sioux, and others. Actual texts of other stories about "The

Brothers" have not survived, to my knowledge, and so it is impossible to know whether one leader figures in all of them, and to what extent their adventures as retold adhere to a heroic archetype. But it is clear that within the broad context of "hero-exploit" traditions which the Cayuses–Nez Perces shared with their Plains rivals, there was a subset of traditions about "The Brothers," of which the present story in its versions was the most popular, or at least the most enduring. Do these texts owe something—details, episodes—by loan from other "Brothers" stories?[25] Impossible to tell, but likely, especially in terms of the differences between the Nez Perce and Cayuse versions.

I will return to this crucial tribal difference in a moment, but let's carry on with other kinds of variations, and what they can reveal about Minthorne's Cayuse narrative. Behind the striking "pipe-leader" epithet which Minthorne applies to Fish-Hawk, for example, stands Gould's remark that the leader carried "a peace pipe, a great big red pipe, and the one who was leader was supposed to carry it." In neither of the Nez Perce versions does the party actually succeed in driving off horses before being discovered, as happens in Minthorne; indeed, in Gould there is a debate over whether they are after horses or scalps! Only the Cayuse story gives formal vaunts and insults during the chase that follows the discovery, and in general this text relies most heavily on actual dialogue throughout.

As for the heroic stand-off: in Wottolen a "fine-looking" enemy (later identified as the son of the Cheyenne chief) is killed anonymously, in effect ending the fight; in Gould, kul kultsálm's disabling chest wound is answered by Dick Brown's shooting of the "dog-soldier." Only in Minthorne is the blood-shedding exactly reciprocal: Fish-Hawk, wounded in the chest by the dog-soldier, leaps out of hiding and wrestles his adversary back to the trench, and kills and scalps him, after which his wound is treated and he recovers somewhat, ready to face the next challenge.

Fish-Hawk's scheme for escape via whirlwind derives, he says, from "my knowledge" (whirlwinds do often accompany brush fires); but there is a possible implication, underscored by the Gould narrative, that the escape has a spiritual basis, too. Gould has it that the men invoke their spirit-guides, or wey-ya-kin, together, and accordingly succeed against all odds in getting away. In another widely known Nez Perce hero-story, a leader named "Cloud-Gatherer" saves his mates (again the enemy are the

Cheyennes) by calling on his special wey-ya-kin to bring up a snowstorm, which hides their escape and covers their tracks in retreat.[26] Something of the sort may well be suggested by Fish-Hawk's prophetic reference to his "knowledge."

Finally, Minthorne's version of the homeward retreat is, of the three, by far the most detailed and evocative. He prepares for it, first of all, by briefly and adroitly shifting to the point of view of the enemy, as they discover our heroes' miraculous escape, and their triumph turns to grief over their "many bodies." Like Wottolen, Minthorne stresses the hardships of the barefoot return home, but of course for the latter the season is winter! And Minthorne's story is crucially unique in dramatizing both the gallantry of poor Charging Coyote, who asks to be left behind lest he impede the others, and the spirit of solidarity and loyalty in the others, who refuse his offer—"No, friend, it's the same with all of us." Small wonder that when they do get home, they are "black from freezing and awful to look at"—and that once their story is told, "all the people know it."[27]

Gilbert Minthorne concludes his performance with a proud boast about the story's value and his skill in narrating it to Morris Swadesh. Perhaps he is also expressing, in an era of rapid cultural loss, a sense of satisfaction in getting it transcribed, and in his version. "This is a true story," he asserts; "now then, we have made it, and it will always be the same story."

Whatever the factuality of this narrative—and clearly there have been some rearrangings of emphasis and details!—the teller's assertions are no mere boast, I think, on literary grounds. What is rendered "true" by virtue of considerable narrative art is the exemplary bravery, acuteness, and leadership of Fish-Hawk, the Cayuse hero. It is a highly unified story, and Fish-Hawk's virtu is the premise of its unity. From the opening apostrophe to him as "the thinker in travels" (inescapably one recalls another epic traveler who is "never at a loss," "the man of many ways") through his rousing exhortations to his brave comrades as "little brothers" and his stratagems and deeds on their behalf, to the final apotheosis—"he was the man!"— the storyteller misses no opportunity, so it seems, to bring alive the greatness of his hero. Comparison with the Nez Perce versions reveals, I hope I have shown, how persistently and effectively Minthorne's account magnifies its protagonist.

Why does it do this for him so much more emphatically and artfully than its Nez Perce equivalents do for their heroes? I imagine that in the face of his people's loss of language and official tribal identity and their historical notoriety, Gilbert Minthorne the storyteller would simply reply, "Because Fish-Hawk was Cayuse!" And the story he told would heroically bear him out.

11 / Retroactive Prophecy
in Western Indian Narrative

THE CULTURAL FALLOUT OF THE CATACLYSMIC
eruption of Mount St. Helens in May 1980 included a popular rediscovery
of the fact that the mountain had erupted violently several times in the
nineteenth century, and also the publication in the Northwest and elsewhere of Indian lore (much of it pretty badly garbled) about the mountain.
Thus, editors widely recalled the Chinookan story about how Wy-East
(Mount Hood) and Klickitat (Mount Adams) went to war over the beautiful maiden and guardian of fire, Loo-wit (Mount St. Helens), angering the
Great Spirit, who eventually destroyed the Bridge of the Gods, and turned
them all into mountains. And a Cowlitz tribal leader was quoted in newspapers and magazines to the effect that Mount St. Helens was simply giving stern notice that it would no longer tolerate Anglo desecration of its sacred lands and waters.[1]

Perhaps predictably, the most interesting and expressive Indian text
concerning the mountain and its eruptions went unnoticed. It was recorded in 1841 from an elder of the Spokane tribe, whose Christian name
was Cornelius, by the naval officer and explorer Charles Wilkes, and pub-

lished by Wilkes during a period of intermittent volcanic activity in the 1850s. Cornelius recalled an eruption from his boyhood; that is, long before the coming of the whites (probably in the 1790s):

Cornelius, when about ten years of age, was sleeping in a lodge with a great many people, and was suddenly awakened by his mother, who called out to him that the world was falling to pieces. He then heard a great noise of thunder overhead, and all the people crying out in great terror. Something was falling very thick, which they at first took for snow, but on going out they found it to be dirt: it proved to be ashes, which fell to the depth of six inches, and increased their fears, by causing them to suppose that the end of the world was actually at hand. The medicine-man arose, and told them to stop their fear and crying, for the world was not about to fall to pieces. "Soon," said he, "there will come from the rising sun a different kind of men from any you have yet seen, who will bring with them a book, and will teach you everything, and after that the world will fall to pieces." [2]

So the eruption was interpreted as an omen of the coming of the whites to the West, armed with a book (presumably the Bible), out of which the Indians would be taught new ways, and as a consequence the world, at least the aboriginal world of Cornelius's boyhood, would "fall to pieces." It is a fascinating and resonant text, expressive of the strains of living through the first period of Anglo-Indian contact in the West and illustrative, I think, of the kind of imaginative accommodations the Indians made to their trial-by-change.

In effect, Cornelius's story is an example of what I'd like to call "retroactive prophecy." That is, it is one of a numerous set of Native texts, some mythological and others historical or personal, in which an event or deed in pre-contact times is dramatized as being prophetic of some consequence of the coming of the whites. "Retroactive" because, without denying the possibility of authentic prophecy (by which most Indian groups set great store), I think that these texts poignantly suggest that during the contact era, Western Indians tried to assert the traditional continuity of their disrupted and disordered lives by retroactively fixing upon or inventing prophecies, set in past times, of present calamities. In the case of Cornelius's memoir, the reference to "the book" suggests in itself a dimension of interpretive hindsight from a time subsequent to the prophetic event itself—from a time, that is, when the Indians would have known what a "book" is.

Sometimes the prophetic anecdotes involve human errors and misdeeds, the consequences of which are now seen with painfully resigned retrospection, but more commonly the omens are just that, proleptic events that now come into focus as clues to an inevitable future. We should ask, why generate such stories; what was their value to those who knew them? We must get more examples in hand to do justice to these questions—but a provisional answer has already emerged, I think: that for people suffering experiences that in traditional terms were literally "unthinkable," there was some consolation and reassurance in believing that at least it had all been anticipated in traditional Native terms long before. One thinks of the Melanesian cargo cults and the "revisionist" attitudes toward myth they seem to have entailed.[3] It would seem that when a people's history becomes discontinuous, they are moved to "restory" the past so as to make it all seem at least continuous again, even if the trend is ultimately dismal. That there is a considerable satisfaction in making such adjustments of the past in terms of the present, few serious students of history and the writing of it will deny. But let's postpone further consideration of the rationale of "retroactive prophecy" until we've looked at some additional examples of it.

In the context of a series of brief ethnographic notes about "the good old days" among the Santiam Kalapuyas of Oregon, Melville Jacobs recorded the following text of a shaman's dream:

Long ago the people used to say that one great shaman in his dream had seen all the land black in his dream. That is what he told the people. "This earth was all black (in my dream)." He saw it in a dream at night. Just what that was likely to be he did not know. And then (later on) the rest of the people saw the whites plow up the ground. Now then they said, "That must have been what it was that the shaman saw long ago in his sleep."[4]

Here, of course, unlike his Spokane counterpart, the shaman is represented as only providing the enigmatic details of the prophecy, not the actual interpretation; not until later, when the dispossessed Kalapuyas were watching the whites clear their lands and plow up the black Willamette Valley loam, were the remembered details properly interpreted. Scant consolation, but worth something as a way of keeping the present connected with the past.

A rather more auspicious prophetic dream (although not without its ironies) was recorded among the Columbia River Wishram Chinookans for Edward Sapir by his half-blood interpreter, Peter McGuff. McGuff's informant, Sophia Klickitat, remembered an old man dreaming that

he saw strange people, they spoke to him, and showed him everything; and he heard something like three or four Indian songs. In the morning he spoke to all the people. And then everybody gathered to hear him—women, men, children, old men—everybody. . . . He told the people what he had seen in his sleep at night. And then they gathered together to hear him; they danced every day and every night. They were made glad because of his story.

He said: "Soon all sorts of strange things will come. No longer (will things) be as before; no longer, as will soon happen, shall we use these things of ours. They will bring to us everything strange; they will bring to us (something which) you just have to point at anything moving way yonder, and it will fall right down and die." As it turned out, it was a gun of which he spoke. "There will be brought to us a bucket for boiling purposes; no longer will you use your old-fashioned buckets made of stone." As it turned out, they really brought to us what he told the people of. "No longer will you make fire by drilling with sticks as before." Still more were they glad, they danced with energy. "Certain small pieces of wood will be brought to us with which you will make a fire." As it turned out, it was matches whereof he spoke.

For days and nights they danced. They were not at all hungry, truly they did their best (in dancing). Everything they saw—axe, hatchet, knife, stove. "Strange people will bring us such things. White people with moustaches on their faces will come from the east. Do you people be careful!" Then indeed they would again jump up and down; they did their best strongly.[5]

The old Wishram dreamer's final admonition, "Do you people be careful!" points, of course, to the ironic significance built into the tale, in terms of the cultural cost of all these wondrous innovations ("everything strange"). In context, it is as if the old man dramatically foresees, in his listeners' uncritical jubilation over his prophecy, the dangers inherent in such irresistible gifts. To put it more exactly, it is as if the narrator of the text is looking back from a time when such dangers had been amply realized for the Wishrams, and is offering a stern criticism of her people's recklessness and greed in the form of a prophetic warning. As an ironic statement, in fact, this is not far removed from the Fool's bitter "prophecy of the present" in King Lear (3.2), the so-called "Merlin's prophecy"—"When priests are more in word than matter; / When brewers mar their malt with water . . . / Then shall the realm of Albion / Come to great confusion."

A prophecy that projects the evolution of Anglo culture to an apocalyptic finale close at hand for whites and Indians alike has been published recently by the Zuni Indians, in *The Zunis: Self-portrayals*. The form of this jeremiad (which is attributed by the editors to "our grandfathers") is traditional; the content is, I think, unmistakably modern, invented for the admonition of our age.

Cities will progress and then decay to the ways of the lowest beings. Drinkers of dark liquids will come upon the land, speaking nonsense and filth. Then the end shall be nearer. Population will increase until the land can hold no more. The tribes of men will mix. The dark liquids they drink will cause the people to fight among themselves. Families will break up; fathers against children and the children against one another. Maybe when the people have outdone themselves, then maybe the stars will fall upon the land, or drops of hot water will rain upon the earth. Or the land will turn under. Or our father, the sun, will not rise to start the day. Then our possessions will turn into beasts and devour us whole.[6]

Sometimes a more lighthearted prophetic impulse is involved, whereby the dubious wonders of Anglo high technology are revealed to be nothing more than belated rediscoveries or imitations of Indian inventions or achievements of long ago! For example, when the first canal around the Willamette Falls at Oregon City was excavated in the 1870s, the Clackamas Indians noted with amusement that the whites were merely exposing a channel which, according to Clackamas mythology, Coyote once dug to bury the two-mile-long tongue of a terrible skookum which had been afflicting the Indians.[7] More up-to-date yet, the Thompson Indians of British Columbia have a marvelous yarn about a member of the tribe who long ago flew to the moon in a basket, learned the arts of fishing, hunting, firemaking, and cooking while there, and then returned home, a la Eric van Däniken, to teach them to his people! The text ends with a genial nod to Neil Armstrong and the Apollo Project: "One day, the young man gazed up at the moon, and someone spoke to him, 'There is no one up there now,' said the voice, 'but some day, people will again go up there. They won't find it the same, for everything is gone.'"[8]

The same motive, and the fundamental conservatism of mythological systems, can be seen in an Arapaho text which finds the origin of railroad trains in the "Rolling Head" stories, now seen as prophetic, and in a Tlingit story which similarly looks back from steamboats to traditional narratives about "magic canoes." [9]

But most Native prophecies of the Anglo era are deadly serious, reflecting all too clearly the historical circumstances they imaginatively engage. More than one Western American tribe reported to early ethnographers that they possessed a myth of primeval human dispersal and reconciliation, wherein the long-dispersed brothers with white skins were expected to eventually return "home" to become part of the People again. The celebrated Sarah Winnemucca, granddaughter of the Northern Paiute chief Truckee, tells in her memoirs how, rather like the Aztecs greeting Cortez and his men as foretold mythic beings, Truckee insisted on actively welcoming the whites to Nevada in the 1840s, because he was sure that their arrival auspiciously confirmed a long-standing mythological prophecy of this kind.

In the beginning of the world there were only four, two girls and two boys. Our forefather and mother were only two, and we are their children. You all know that a great while ago there was a happy family. One girl and one boy were dark, and the others were white. For a time they got along together without quarreling, but soon they disagreed, and there was trouble. They were cross to one another and fought, and our parents were very much grieved. They prayed that their children might learn better, but it did not do any good; and afterwards the whole household was made so unhappy that the father and mother saw that they must separate their children; and then our father took the dark boy and girl, and the white boy and girl, and asked them, "Why are you so cruel to each other?" They hung down their heads, and would not speak. They were ashamed. He said to them, "Have I not been kind to you all, and given you Everything your hearts wish for? You do not have to hunt and kill your own game to live upon. You see, my dear children, I have power to call whatsoever kind of game we want to eat; and I also have power to separate my dear children if they are not good to each other." So he separated his children by a word. He said, "Depart from each other, you cruel children; go across the mighty ocean, and do not seek each other's lives."

So the light girl and boy disappeared by that one word, and their parents saw them no more, and they were grieved, although they knew their children were happy. And by and by, the dark children grew into a large nation; and we believe it is the one we belong to, and that the nation that sprang from the white children will some time send someone to meet us and heal all the old trouble.[10]

Perhaps the term "retroactive" is less applicable here than elsewhere, in that Truckee's "open-door policy" was by all accounts really founded on this myth—even though other Paiutes, including his son Winnemucca, doubted the chief's interpretation of the prophecy in the light of the whites' behavior. After the Paiutes' precious winter food caches had been wantonly burned, Winnemucca is reported by his daughter Sarah to have said: "I fear we will suffer greatly by their coming to this country; they come for no good to us, although my father said they were our brothers. But they do not seem to think we are like them."[11]

A more subtle instance of imaginative prophecy as an interpretation of Native history is recorded in a well-known oral-historical text of the Clatsop Chinookans. The text narrates in authentic-sounding detail the first Caucasian shipwreck in Clatsop country and the survival of two white castaways, perhaps Russians; what is striking in our terms is the dramatic circumstances of personal tragedy and grief under which the shipwreck is said to have been discovered. It begins:

The son of an old woman had died. She wailed for him for a whole year and then she stopped. Now one day she went to Seaside. There she used to stay, and she returned. She returned walking along the beach. She nearly reached Clatsop; now she saw something. She thought it was a whale.
    When she came near it she saw two spruce trees standing upright on it. She thought, "Behold! It is no whale. It is a monster!" She reached the thing [*qix e'kta*] that lay there. Now she saw that its outer side was all covered with copper. Ropes were tied to those spruce trees, and it was full of iron. Then a bear came out of it. He stood on the thing that lay there. He looked just like a bear, but his face was that of a human being. Then she went home. She thought of her son, and cried, saying, "Oh, my son is dead and the thing about which we have heard in tales is on shore!"[12]

(Ultimately the ship is plundered, and then burned; the Clatsops and other Chinookan groups quarrel over the plunder, and accept copper, brass, and iron as a new inflationary currency ["a piece of brass two fingers wide was exchanged for one slave"] and the two surviving sailors become the slaves of two Clatsop chiefs.)

Now unlike most of the other texts I have been adducing, this one is not given as a formal prophecy—but unmistakably the narrative is structured for prophetic emphasis ex post facto. By the time the story was transcribed, of course, the Clatsops would have understood the shipwreck, so strange and unaccountable to its witnesses, to be an omen of all the white sea landings to come, and all that trouble. And, historical coincidence or not, the fact that the shipwreck is first seen by an old woman who has been mourning the death of her son, and reported by her as the confirmation of something heretofore only foretold in tales, and that her report centers on seeing a bearlike and therefore (to Chinookans) dangerous being on the vessel—all this sets the uncanny and ominous tone of dreadful things to come. The narrative shaping here is unmistakable, and inasmuch as the story was told to Franz Boas by Charles Cultee, whose genius as a recitalist of myth-narratives we are only now beginning to appreciate, it seems proper to conclude that literary art has had a lot to do with such shaping. "Oh, my son is dead and the thing about which we have heard in tales is on shore!"—so it all begins, prophetically, with a convergence of personal death and revived grief, and the eerie realization of fiction as fact; and the story ends, remember, with another manifestation of that glittering and irresistible metallic "wealth" that is a recurrent motif in these prophecies, and for good reason.

The combination of elements that this story shares with the Clackamas Chinook "Seal and Her Younger Brother"—dead younger man (head of household?), mourning older female kin, dangerous and mysterious intruder, objects of great value at hand—reminds us that the Clackamas story itself, while not a "prophecy," is probably expressive of deep apprehensions about contacts with whites. In recognizing such recurrent patterns we begin, perhaps, to understand something of the literary system within which—even in disrupted times—the Native imagination worked.[13]

One of Charles Cultee's formal myth-narratives, "The Sun's Myth," has been retranslated and elucidated by Dell Hymes.[14] In it, a headman becomes obsessed with the Sun, and at last leaves his family and town and journeys to visit Sun's house. When he arrives there, he finds all sorts of valuable Native weapons and ornaments, but what captivates him is a wonderful "shining thing" that Sun hangs on the wall each night. This is what he wants, and after Sun has, like a good Chinookan hostess, offered him all her other traditional valuables, she at last reluctantly gives him "the shining thing" to take home, warning him as she does so about its powers. He goes home—and discovers that, as he approaches each of his people's towns, "the shining thing" comes alive in his arms and kills everybody. He cannot get rid of it; it destroys his own hometown and his immediate family, and, at length, the old woman comes, denounces him ("It is you who chose"), and retrieves the lethal thing, leaving the poor man apparently alone in a desolate land.

Hymes interprets "The Sun's Myth" as an instance of contact-era mythopoetic invention. It is, from the evidence he offers, literally Charles Cultee's story, a new symbolical rendering in traditional style of Indian reality in the late nineteenth century, when the Indians' heedless preference for the "shining things" of Anglo material culture and their susceptibility to Anglo diseases had all but destroyed many Native groups like Charles Cultee's. The historical terms of the catastrophe—epidemics, liquor, money, armies, laws, missionaries, schools, reservations—are scrupulously omitted in the story; the only "outsider" in it is the Native chief himself, first in recklessly going beyond his own country to visit Sun's house, and then in coming back with the terrible outlandish trophy. The effect of such a strict focus, in Hymes's view, is to emphasize how the catastrophe is not the result of an invasion, and is not something to be understood and judged, even excused, according to new, external standards; rather it happens within the traditional order of the Native world, whose moral validity is upheld, albeit negatively, in the crushing words of the old woman to the chief: "It is you who chose." As if Charles Cultee were saying in 1894: "What has happened to us, we have chosen, in the last analysis; the order of things remains, though it no longer favors us."

Charles Cultee's "The Sun's Myth" is, in Hymes's sensitive restoration, a powerful and haunting narrative, and it might well lead us to consider the possibility that mythopoetic invention and individual "authorship" by storytellers was more important in Indian literatures, at least in the last decades of the nineteenth century, than we have thought. For our purposes now, we can observe again the working of the Native imaginative impulse to find or create "prophetic" stories, wherein the apparent loss of the traditional order, or in this instance its cataclysmic operations, could at least seem to be foretold, and thus appear to be intelligible and continuous with the past.

Such an impulse is, of course, universal and manifests itself in individual as well as collective experience. As Kierkegaard puts it, "Though life must be lived forward, it can only be understood backwards."[15] We all know, I take it, the rueful and helpless but real consolation of hindsight in unhappy circumstances. For example: after someone has died suddenly, there is the common discovery, even among the nonsuperstitious, of "omens" and "prophecies" of the event—"prophecies" that most often turn out, under scrutiny (at least in my own experience), to be invented, either out of whole cloth or through an arbitrary transfer of meaning. Why? Because, apparently, we abhor the experience of discontinuity, and although most of us wouldn't know an omen before-the-fact if it stood on its hands before us, afterwards, ex post facto, experiencing the discomfort of a broken order, we would like to believe that the break was in fact imminent in the programmatic order of things, and thus imaginable in terms of portents.

I wonder if part of the very real pleasure most of us feel in the experience of "dramatic irony" in, say, Oedipus the King, comes from a vicarious gratification of this impulse? That is, for once we know the "whole story" as prophecy, and can follow its fulfillment for Oedipus through all the appalling exactitudes of Sophocles's dramatization. In doing so, as numerous writers have argued, we seem to be affirming a moral order; we do the same, of course, in attending to episodes in the Old Testament as typological anticipations of the story of Christ.[16]

I wonder, too (if a little more extracurricular speculation can be allowed), whether we haven't brought into view from our Native American perspective a conspicuous and puzzling feature of contemporary poetry. Namely, its preoccupation with the experience of déjà vu, the uncanny feeling of having been in a present situation sometime before—in W. S. Merwin's phrase, "familiarity without memory."[17] Wallace Stevens once observed that the imagination always seems to find itself at the end of an era.[18] Certainly it seems to be for poets like Merwin and Ted Hughes, as they foresee the prospect of a nuclear-and/or-environmental apocalypse, an End to all continuities. And yet the sharp sense they often render in extremis of having been there before at the apocalyptic edge might be, in our terms, a kind of therapeutic imaginative short-circuiting of time, whereby dejâ vu is both fulfillment and prophecy—"fulfillment" of some earlier apocalyptic moment and also therefore prophetic of future such moments. A way, that is, of imagining oneself on into an otherwise largely unimaginable future. With Indian texts and modern poems in mind, one might revise Stevens's dictum, then: "The imagination is always trying to avoid finding itself at the (unforeseen) end of an era."

In these terms I have up to now neglected one important traditional condition of the Indian prophecies. That is, the mythologies of most Western tribes are alike in dividing their story of the world into two broad and to some extent overlapping ages. First comes the great "Myth Age" per se, when the great primal beginnings take place; there are no human beings yet (that is, "the People" are as yet far off); the world is inhabited by animal-spirits in more or less human form; monsters, freaks, and confusions of nature are abroad, threatening general disorder. The circumstances of the Myth Age intermittently converge on what might be called "intervals" of transformation, in which Coyote or some other transformer (most commonly a trickster enacting his other mythic role) sets about ordering and fixing up some aspect of the world (not necessarily "perfecting" it—is it perfect now?), transforming animal-people into animals per se on the basis of their inclinations and deeds, and turning certain beings into natural landmarks, and setting precedents for human life to come. A high percentage of classical Indian texts are set, not surprisingly, in such dramatic intervals of transformation, and many of them end with some variation on the Chinookan formula, "The People [that is, the real Indians, those who are hearing the story] are coming soon." [19]

The second age, then, it follows, is the age of Real Happenings—when reality has more or less taken on its present form, and the People have indeed arrived and accommodated themselves to the finished world, through the system of myths, ceremonies, and animistic conceptions known to anthropologists as "participatory maintenance." [20] Presumably, as the epoch of the perfected Native "Way," this second age runs on into perpetuity. So it must have seemed to the Clatsop Chinookans, let's say—until that outré ship washed up on the beach, and was rapidly followed by others laden with metal objects, whiskey, Bibles, and unknown infections.

What I am getting at is that in their formulation of "retroactive prophecies" in response to contact with Anglo culture, the Western Indians were only being formally consistent with their mythological view of what we call history. The myths of such Native groups, it is clear, had always served to uphold the people's world view as a continuum, by accommodating real and imagined changes in their world. In some cases, the changes were real, or "historical" as we would say. For example, the Kiowas evidently did migrate in the seventeenth century from confined origins in the rugged Yellowstone country into the freedom of the Great Plains, and their cycle of origin-myths follows the migration closely; but my point is that these narratives of change must have served to underscore the Kiowas' sense of continuity. Through the cycle, they knew they were the same people.[21] Likewise, in terms of purely mythic "history," the Clackamas Chinookans and others seem to have understood that all the large and small transformational events narrated in stories of the Myth Age collectively amounted to a manifold prophecy that, in the words of the Chinookan ending formula, "the People are coming soon." Knowing themselves to be the People, the Clackamas and their kind must have felt in such proleptic references a profound sense of continuity; in a sense, they represent the ultimate mythic retroactive prophecy, through which each generation could feel itself securely predicted and indeed prepared for in the fabulous past.

Now as they entered in the nineteenth century a historical age no less convulsed with transformations of the world than they believed the Myth Age to have been, the Indian people of the West must have felt that the imaginative continuity of their way could be, indeed had to be, affirmed through myth-based prophecy—even if only retroactively, the disordered present looking for unbroken links with the traditional past; even if "The People are coming soon" had to be revalued bitterly to mean the race of white settlers already entering and occupying their homelands. Malinowski's functionalist description of myth as not an idle tale but "a hardworking active force" takes on special point and poignancy when we observe the Indian mythologies endeavoring to preserve the continuums of the old ways in the face of their apparent utter disruption.[22]

Percy Cohen has argued along somewhat similar lines in proposing that in general, prophecy flourishes as a cultural form when a people's myth-system weakens.

When the different functions of myth become detached from one another . . . myth loses some of its power and is either replaced or complemented by other systems of belief. One such form is prophecy. If myth anchors the present in the past, then prophecy anchors it in the future. Prophecy is a sort of myth in reverse. So prophecy should emerge in those social conditions where the basis of tradition and legitimation is weak and where there has been, in any case, a weakening of other bonds of traditional, multiplex structures of relationship.[23]

Cohen could be talking here, obviously, about the precipitous break-down of the traditional Indian culture in the nineteenth century, and up to a point the special prophetic strain we have been examining illustrates his thesis. But it appears that his conception of the relationship between myth and prophecy is too narrow. First, his use of "emerge" is misleading to the extent that it seems to mean "appear on the scene." On the contrary there is every reason to believe that Indian systems of belief have always included prophetic elements; there seem to have been "prophet cults," for example, before the nineteenth century. Then, too, contrary to Cohen's observation, prophecy is not necessarily distinct as an entity from myth ("prophetic myths"?), nor does it necessarily serve as a substitute or compensation for myth. And on the contrary, as we have seen, the prophetic impulse may serve paradoxically to do what Cohen rightly says myth does—"anchor the present in the past." Perhaps it reveals something important about the bent of the Native imagination to observe that where Christian chiliasts have al-ways prophesied the Second Coming to earth of Christ, bringing with Him a new order, a comparable desperation among the Western Indians in the late nineteenth century produced (chiefly out of aboriginal elements it seems) the Ghost Dance movement, with its fervent prophecies of the coming back of an idealized, traditionally mythic past.[24]

What Dell Hymes has said about Charles Cultee's prophetic myth of the Sun might be said as well about these more modest but no less poignant texts we have been considering: "That the narrative has such power shows that in assimilating the disaster to his people through the genre of myth, in creatively interpreting that situation within his tradition, Charles Cultee created a work of art whose performance, even in another century and an-other language, can speak for mankind."[25]

To revert to our first example: in narrating his boyhood memory of an erupting volcano in prophetic terms, Cornelius of the Spokanes was not consciously engaged in the creation of a work of art. But perhaps in telling his story as he did, he too could feel that he was assimilating and construing his time of disorder the best way he knew—through the imaginative traditions of his culture. As long as those traditions survived, and went on fulfilling themselves in being put to such uses, the world would not fall to pieces.

12 / The Bible
in Western
Indian Mythology

READING THROUGH THE LETTERS AND REPORTS OF the first generation of missionaries among the Indians of the Far West, one looks nearly in vain for transcriptions of or even sympathetic allusions to the Indians' own mythological repertories. Indeed, several evangelists expressed open doubt that the stories they heard from western Natives in the 1830s and 1840s were anything more than the tangled yarns of white traders and explorers.[1] However exasperating to us now, such indifference on the part of the missionaries to the sacred mythology of the tribal people they were striving to convert is hardly surprising; it is to be doubted that Augustine of Canterbury and his coworkers in the wilds of late sixth-century England were especially interested in the traditional stories of the Britons, Angles, and Saxons either. (They were, however, directed by their sponsor, Pope Gregory, to study the aboriginal ceremonies closely and if possible adapt them to Christian uses—a syncretic policy that would have horrified their nineteenth-century American and Canadian successors in the faith.[2])

If not texts of Native literature courtesy of the early missionaries, what we do have is vivid evidence of the impact of Catholic and Protestant evangelism and preaching on the mythologies of the Indians of the West. The evidence at hand does not support recurrent speculation that most Indian texts bear the signs of missionary influence; but it is clear that the Indians did accept stories from the Christian Bible into their oral repertories, with or without accepting the doctrines that the stories embody for Christians. Apart from a scattering of general commentaries by Stith Thompson, Horace Beck, Richard M. Dorson, and Francis Lee Utley,[3] the topic is a neglected one. But it is well worth pursuing for the light it sheds on the historical circumstances of early white-Indian contacts in the West and on the mythic and oral workings of the Indian imagination.

The fact that the topic has been neglected is worth considering itself. From the beginning, North American anthropologists and folklorists have in the main followed a classicist line in their endeavors as transcribers and commentators, positing the ideal of a classical precontact Native literature and relegating everything else—assimilated Bible stories, Indianized European folktales, and so on—to the status of impure curiosities. One can understand why a hard-pressed fieldworker, dealing with a last surviving storyteller, would concentrate on transcribing only the texts native to that language—and yet there is a kind of incipient racism in such a focus, and it ought to be recognized as such. By classicizing Indian traditional literature, we are, in effect, denying its historical continuities. Are we not saying to today's Indians, "We decree that your mythology, indeed your mythopoetic powers as a people, ended with the white settlement of the West?" So, even when we get beyond the missionaries' indifference and attempt to take up Indian literature and religion seriously, there is a danger that we will impose a sort of false-classicist purity on these endeavors.

The issue deserves a fuller discussion than I can give it here, but perhaps an anecdote from the folklore of anthropology will help keep it in mind. Somewhere in the Southwest a few years back, so the story goes, a young ethnographer was lucky enough to find an elderly storyteller who had never been transcribed before. He plied her with attentions and favors, and all one winter she responded with superb recitations, which he taped. The old lady enjoyed the ethnographer's company very much, and when, unknown to him, she reached the end of her repertory of stories, she went right on in the traditional style, but now inventing her content, or borrowing it from Anglo secular or Biblical sources. When (back in his study) the ethnographer realized what his informant had done, he erased the nontraditional tapes in a scholarly fury and denounced her in an open letter to his colleagues. I would argue that it was precisely at the moment when the old lady began to invent and borrow stories and adapt them to her narrative tradition (proving its vitality and no doubt revealing its formal "rules") that the ethnographer should have been most alert—and most grateful. He could have been studying mythology-in-progress.

In these terms, then, I think that we can be grateful for such assimilated Bible stories as have actually been recorded in the West and elsewhere; the wonder is that they were ever taken down at all. The same can be said, of course, for the somewhat more numerous Native texts derived from French folklore, apparently related to the Indians by French Canadian voyageurs.[4] But there is a special fascination, I think, in what the Western Indians did with Scripture. This is a cultural and literary convergence that can tell us some interesting things about the importance of mythology to the Indians and about how it felt in the 1830s and 1840s to encounter the Gospel as astonishing, but not necessarily good, news.

There are Bible-derived texts in print from the following western tribes: in Oregon, the Klamaths, the Clackamas Chinooks, and the Northern Paiutes; in Baja California, the Dieguñas; in Washington, the Klikitats and Cowlitz; in British Columbia, the Thompson Indians, Lillooet, and Flathead tribes; and there are, no doubt, other instances. Of the tribal groups mentioned, by far the fullest representation is from the last-named, Salish-speaking Indians of interior British Columbia, especially the Thompsons, thanks mainly to the tireless and open-minded transcribing of James Teit for Franz Boas at the turn of the century.

How these tribes first met the stories of the Bible can be briefly described as follows. When Protestant missionaries like Marcus Whitman, Asa Bowen Smith, Elkanah Walker, and Cushing Eells, and Jesuit and Oblate padres like Father F. N. Blanchet, Father Peter De Smet, and Father J. B. Z. Bolduc first came to the Northwest in the late 1830s, they all reported that most of the tribes they visited had at least heard of the Christian faith some ten or fifteen years before, apparently from North West Company and Hudson's Bay Company engagés.[5] But it remained for the first generation of missionaries to introduce the Scriptures per se, and it is my assumption that these initial contacts with Bible stories were the mythologically seminal ones.

The evangelical system developed by both factions depended heavily on what we might call Sunday School methods. In 1840, for example, Rev. Eells reported from Nez Perce country in Idaho that,

for want of a thorough acquaintance with the language, much of the instruction communicated has related to Scripture history. . . . It is strictly true that they must have "line upon line," every new idea must be repeated many times. The nearer our teaching approaches to Sabbath-school instruction, appropriate for small children, the better it is understood.[6]

As for the Catholic fathers of the so-called "Quebec Mission" based on the Willamette River, they too relied on simplified versions of the great Biblical narratives, ingeniously supplemented after 1838 with a sort of chronological chart, nicknamed the "Catholic Ladder," on which the major events of the world according to Catholic doctrine were depicted symbolically in linear order for all to see—including the Protestant Reformation, symbolized by a leafless branch projecting awkwardly from the main line of history! Father Blanchet exulted in a letter on his work among Salish-speaking peoples in Puget Sound that,

it was a sweet satisfaction to each of them to comprehend the origin of created things, and how the world is now getting along; the point where Adam died; that of the Deluge; when God gave His Ten Commandments; when Jesus was incarnated, died and rose to Heaven. "Well, Father," a native said to me, "make a mark at the year 1838, when the Great Master sent you to the Columbia to teach the poor natives."[7]

And, never ones to ignore hints from their subjects, the enterprising fathers soon brought out a new edition of the ladder, in which, sure enough, the names of converted Northwest tribes and chiefs were recorded at the near end of Christian history.[8]

The embattled Protestants soon devised their own storytelling chart, and at least once, in 1841 in a Clackamas Chinook village near Oregon City, the whole issue of faith came down to a critical comparison of Catholic versus Presbyterian charts. Father Blanchet reports the outcome with glee: "Chief Katemus goes to get the evangelical ladder of his minister and spreads it out beside mine. The natives see with their eyes that the religion of the poor Mr. Waller does not begin with Jesus Christ."[9]

How freely the Bible stories were retold and adapted for such exotic purposes is unclear, but as part of his continuing quarrel with his colleague Henry Spalding of the "Oregon Mission," Asa Smith complained to eastern patrons of the mission that Spalding "was in the habit of mingling his instructions from the Bible with a good deal of fiction," narrating the Creation and the Fall of Man in the manner of Paradise Lost, embellishing the story of Abraham and Isaac with dramatic dialogues between the main characters, and so on.[10] Perhaps the independent Spalding did go to extremes, but, given the circumstances, it is hard to imagine that any of the early missionaries were able to avoid taking some liberties with their texts, drawing either from what Francis Utley has called "the Bible of the folk" or from their own imaginations. As Utley points out in discussing the importance of Biblical folkways, casual exegesis of the Bible, following noncanonical traditions, may influence what Native peoples make of missionaries' teaching as much as the Gospel stories themselves, or the peoples' own mythology.[11]

And of course there was the problem of translation itself; one has to marvel at the vitality of stories that, having passed from Hebrew to Greek to Latin to English or French, could suffer translation into the five-hundred-word Chinook Jargon and thence into Native languages, and then, years after the Native assimilation, be redacted into English again, and still sound like Biblical narratives! It is a transformation that would tax Claude Lévi-Strauss and his followers. Father Blanchet notes in January 1841 that he and his comrades in Oregon Territory and "New Caledonia" were often forced to work through three translators, and on occasion four. And even the super-critical Asa Smith admitted, when he began to learn Nez Perce and use it in his own preaching, that because of the concrete and verb-centered nature of the language and its lack of general terms, "we are obliged often to say more than we want to, and more than the Bible itself says."[12]

Still, allowing for all this, it was clearly in the minds of the Indians that the stories underwent their most striking changes. Protestants and Catholics alike soon learned that, although their Native listeners seemed to find the Bible episodes in themselves absorbing, they were generally puzzled or even repelled by certain moral interpretations insisted upon by the Christian narrators. Smith observes sourly that "as long as they listened to the interesting historical parts of the Bible, they were pleased, but the great truth that all are under condemnation to the penalty of the law while in their present situation is very offensive to them."[13] The redemptive value of the Crucifixion did not easily "take" among people lacking any traditional yearning for redemption. Smith notes that the Nez Perces had "no just idea of the object of Christ's death."[14] And, most telling, A. B. Meacham reports the following response of an Indian named Push-wash to a sermon on the Siletz Reservation in Oregon as late as the 1860s: "What for he say Jesus Christ so many times? All the time he talk the same. . . . What for a good man die for me? I am not a bad man. I did not tell him to die."[15] By the same token, the Catholic evangelists reported that they found it hard, except in the case of deathbed conversions, to shift the Indians' attention away from this life, to the promise of heavenly joy.[16]

Small wonder, of course, that the Western Indians hearkened to the narrative medium of the Bible but not necessarily to the spiritual message. Theirs was a shame-culture morality, by and large, enforced mainly by fear of public shame for wrongdoing rather than private guilt in the sight of a god; their view of the afterlife of the soul was in most groups a sort of teleological afterthought—irrespective of the moral tone of one's earthly career, the souls of the dead journeyed to a sort of shadow-land, where life was a pleasant-but-attenuated version of this life. Even the Northwest Ghost Dance teaching of Smohalla, with its overtones of a Christian millennialism, is aimed squarely at the restoration of an avid, full-bodied earthly life such as the Indians had once known.

Nonetheless, the stories were taken in by the Native oral imagination; as Stith Thompson has remarked, the Biblical bread cast upon these tribal waters by the missionaries did return, but "as a much changed article."[17] Not surprisingly, the range of recorded Indian Bible stories corresponds very closely to the range of stories the early missionaries say they emphasized: the Creation and its immediate aftermath, especially the creation of Adam and Eve and their temptation and fall; the Flood and Noah's survival; the Tower of Babel and the Confusion of Tongues; the Dispersal of the Tribes; Jonah and the Whale; the Red Sea Crossing; and, in the New Testament, the main episodes of Christ's birth, life, and ministry, and His Crucifixion and Resurrection. The appeal to the Indians of the Old Testament narratives, with their evocation of nomadic tribal life, is obvious (although the Holy Land settings are usually localized, owing to the Indians' intense ethnocentricity and sense of place). The apparent appeal of the more exotic story of Christ owes much, I think, simply to the missionaries' insistence upon it, and also, as we will see, to some odd parallels between it and certain Native myths.[18]

In general, looking from Scripture to the Native texts, I propose that there are three main kinds of assimilation—really, three broad and no doubt overlapping degrees of Bible-story derivations. First, there is simple incorporation: a story is taken in and recited with simple alterations, generally centering on details of setting. Second is adaptation: a story is adapted more or less drastically, often so as to fit into a preexisting Native cycle or scheme, and often with dislocation of narrative order and alteration of motives and meanings. Third, we see a kind of mythopoesis, in which, through what looks like a genuine free play of imagination over the convergence of Native and Christian traditions, "something new" is created. A similar scheme might be imposed on dissemination of stories between Indian cultures, but what is special about our topic, of course, is that the Bible originals are so well known to us, and that the time and circumstance of the dissemination are unusually documentable.[19]

Under the heading of incorporation, then, we can include many Old Testament stories which the Indians may have accepted because they resembled some of their own traditions.[20] It is not necessary to rehearse once again the endless battle of archetypist versus diffusionist to notice that most Western mythologies did contain aboriginal "Adam and Eve" and "deluge" stories, for example, the latter often in connection with myths about the dispersal of tribes and languages. Apparently, then, when a Bible story seemed congenial to begin with, it was taken in and retold without much change, except for environmental and cultural details. Among the Thompson Indians of British Columbia, for example, the Tower of Babel episode, following a Native dispersal myth, goes as follows:

After God has made the flood, he went up to the sky again, but, feeling lonely, he thought he would let some of the people come up and live with him. He gave the chief of the people a dream in which he told him to build a pole ladder on which they could ascend to the sky. The chief told the people God wanted them up above, so they commenced to build as directed. Each day they added a pole, and at last one night the ladder told them, "Tomorrow by noon we are going to reach the sky." Now God changed his mind, and said to himself, "If people come up here and see what a beautiful country it is, they will all wish to remain here and the earth will be deserted." Therefore that night, while the people slept, he took a language out of his mouth, and threw it into the mouth of the chief. Then he took another language, and threw it in his brother's mouth, and thus he threw a different language into each man's mouth. When the people awoke in the morning, each spoke a different language, and they could not understand one another. Wives spoke the tongues of their husbands, and children, that of their father. The chief talked Shuswap, and his brothers spoke Okanagan and Thompson respectively. Thus people began to speak different languages, such as Yakima, Cree, Kootenai, Chilcotin, Carrier. As the men could not understand one another, they were unable to add the last pole, which would have taken them up to the sky. The people got angry with one another, and the pole ladder at last rotted away.[21]

The fact that the tower is begun because of God's ill-considered invitation and not Nimrod's pride, by the way, follows a theme in aboriginal Thompson mythology, and is characteristic of a Native indifference to pride as a story motive, least of all as a cardinal vice. Interestingly enough, the use of the ladder motif bypasses a widespread Indian motif whereby ascent to the sky takes place on a magic chain of arrows; and perhaps that is just the point here: the ascent on such a contraption as a ladder is doomed from the start. (Indeed, one wonders what the Indians really thought about the symbolism of the missionaries' "Heavenly Ladder" charts.)

In the case of stories that represent what I call "adaptation," there are signs of radical reinterpretation and revaluation of the texts (sometimes hostile), and an often dramatic sense of the Native imagination trying to cope with Scriptural challenges to the traditional way, trying to keep new and old kinds of mythic knowledge separate and yet continuous.[22] For example, like virtually all other Western tribes, the Salish-speaking Thompson Indians celebrated a trickster-transformer figure in their mythology—Coyote—who, at the end of the myth-age of initial creations, went round the Thompsons' world fixing things up, molding reality to more or less its present shape, and doing all this not out of obedience to a divine plan but rather out of very mixed, recognizably human motives, often simple greed and mischief. In Lévi-Strauss's terms, he is a bricoleur or handyman, a mediator between the creator and the human race to come.

Now, enter Jesus Christ, on the insistent tongues of the missionaries. Certainly the two story lines could not be merged, as in the case of simple incorporation like that already mentioned; but the Thompson recitalists clearly recognized certain functional similarities between Coyote the Transformer and Jesus the Redeemer, and so—with God knows what uneasiness or irony—at least one of them made a place for Christ in the traditional mythological scheme, as follows. The aboriginal creator, "Old One," made the animals and then the first people, to whom he gave a garden, but they soon proved unworthy of it. After the Fall,

the people were much oppressed and preyed upon, and so much evil prevailed in the world, that the Chief sent his son Jesus to set things right. After traveling through the world as a transformer, Jesus was killed by the bad people, who crucified him, and he resumed to the sky. After he had resumed, the Chief looked over the world, and saw that things had not changed much for the better. Jesus had only set right a very few things. He had done more talking than anything else. . . . Jesus worked only for the people's spiritual benefit. . . . He had tried to induce them to be good, and taught them how to pray to the Chief. He taught them no arts, nor wisdom about how to do things, nor did he help to make life easier for them. Neither did he transform or destroy the evil monsters which killed them, nor did he change or arrange the features of the earth in any way. . . . Now, the Chief said, "If matters are not improved, there will soon be no people." Then he sent Coyote to earth to destroy all the monsters and evil beings, to make life easier and better for the people, and to teach them the best way to do things.

As if to say, "Nice try, Jesus." The narrative goes on from here to pick up the traditional exploits of Coyote, who is certainly no saint or savior, though he does get things done: "Coyote did a great deal of good, but he did not finish everything properly. Sometimes he made mistakes; and although he was wise and powerful, he did many foolish things." [23]

Another Thompson adaptation of the life of Christ is somewhat more orthodox, in that the invidious succession of Coyote is omitted. But now Christ's birth (to a maiden named "Patliam" [Bethlehem?]) and His maturation are clearly adapted to conform with Native hero-tale conventions (remarkable birth, rapid growth, and so on); in mature life He becomes a shape-changer, like Coyote. And, in keeping with Salish and Sahaptin stories about prophet-heroes who get their powers from ritual death and spirit-travel to the afterworld, this Thompson Christ (whose name, Sú sakre, indicates a French connection) is crucified at Salit Lake near Osoyoos, B.C., goes to the land of souls, and then comes back, bringing with him a selection of ghosts to serve as priests: He then commences His ministry in earnest, including the miracle of the loaves and fishes. The missionaries' complaint that the Indians could not or would not grasp the sacrificial and redemptive meaning of Christ's life and death seems well founded: God, we are merely told at the beginning of the story, was lonely in heaven (as in the Babel myth just given), and so, "he made a trail for the dead which led up to his abode, and sent his son down to show the good people where to branch off to the new trail."[24] The son's death in pursuit of this purpose seems to give him, not eternal moral significance, but simply more power, in the Native sense.

One detects a degree of antimissionary irony in these attempts to adapt the Christ story to Native tradition, and in some instances of adaptation a Bible story becomes the vehicle of a direct attack on Anglo culture. Consider the following bitter twisting of the Adam and Eve story, from a Northern Paiute narrator named "Piudy," a member of the so-called "Snake" tribe. Now it is the whites who are identified as "snakes":

Almost everything was Coyote's way. The Indian planted the apple. When he planted it, he said for all the Indians to come and eat. When he told them that, all the people came. The white man was a rattlesnake then, and he was on the tree. The white people have eyes just like the rattlesnake. When the Indians tried to eat the apples, that snake tried to bite them. That's why the white people took everything away from the Indian; because they were snakes. If that snake hadn't been on that tree, everything would have belonged to the Indians. Just because they were snakes and came here, the white people took everything away. They asked the Indians where they had come from. That's why they took everything and told the Indians to go way out in the mountains and live.[25]

The bitterness implied in the statement that white intruders "asked the Indians where they came from" is especially keen; it is as if to say, "You took away this land without ever recognizing our mythological claim to be its people, and you even tried to force your origin myth on us. Here, we give it back to you, as adapted to recent history."

Finally, I know of a few Northwest Indian Bible stories in which the interplay of Scriptural and Native details is so intricate, so imaginatively speculative, that the label of mythopoesis seems warranted. One of these is a Thompson Indian text taken down by James Teit and titled by him, "The Orphans Who Ascended to Heaven":

Somewhere in the White Man's country there was a populous village. Two brothers belonging to this place strayed away playing, and did not return until late in the evening. Meanwhile a thunderstorm destroyed the village and killed the people. When the boys returned, they found nothing but smoking ruins. They said to each other, "Our parents and relatives have been killed. There is nobody left here. Let us go away!" After some days they arrived in a starving condition at a town situated in a hollow. The people of that place were all adult men; there were neither women nor children. The boys saw the high house of the chief, and his kitchen nearby. In a pen were several pigs, and the chief's cook was feeding them with bread and meat. The elder brother descended and stole some of the bread and meat from the hogs, and carried it to his brother. They ate it. On the next morning the cook saw a child's tracks around the pig-pen, and reported to the chief what he had seen. The chief told him to watch and capture the child. Soon after this, he saw both boys gathering food at the pig-pen. After chasing and catching them, he brought them before the chief, who questioned them. They told him their story. Then the chief told his cook to look well after the boys, and to feed them on the best, for he would adopt them as his sons. He said, "I have no children, and there are none in this country. I want to have children." The boys grew fast. They stayed there, and helped in the housework. They swept floors, carried wood and water.

One day the chief let loose his eight cows. Then he called the elder boy, took his eight bay horses out of the stable, and asked him to choose one for a saddle horse. They were all exactly alike. The boy chose the best one—one that could run around the edge of the earth in two hours. Then he brought out eight saddles and eight bridles, and the boy chose correctly the saddle and bridle belonging to his mount. Now, the chief knew that the boy was gifted with magic. He said to him, "Mount your horse and look after my cattle. I want them grazed on that far hillside, where there is much grass. Herd them and bring them home every evening." The boy followed the tracks of the cattle until they entered a rough piece of country, hilly and full of rocks and timber. He followed them through it; on the other side he came to a grassy country with steep open slopes, and a wide road leading up between them. The road was [as] if lately mown with a mowing-machine or like a wide smooth swath cut out of the grass. The smell of grass and flowers on it was very sweet.

He turned back from here; and when he reached home, the cook scolded him for not bringing back the cows. The chief heard the cook scolding him, and asked him what had happened. Then the boy told how he had followed the tracks of the cattle all the way, and how he had discovered the road. The chief said, "Very well, go there again in the morning, and try to find the cattle." Early in the morning the boy started off. Soon he reached the road, and followed along. At last he found himself on the top of a hill, and in another country. It was beautiful, like the mountain-tops; in some places open, and covered with grass and flowers. Here, on the edge of the hill, he saw great piles of clothes and other things. This was the place where the dead people left their earthly belongings. Here, or a little farther on, just over the top of the hill, he saw a golden staff stuck into the ground.

The boy halted here, and was wondering about these things, when a man appeared suddenly and addressed him. He was the chief who meets the dead, and admits them to their respective places in the spirit land. He asked the boy who he was, and the latter told him his story. He said, "You are a living being and cannot stay here. Only people who have died can stay here. You must go back." Then, bethinking himself, he said, "However, seeing that you have come here, I will show you some things, so that on your return to earth you may tell the people what you have seen and enlighten those who are bad as to the terrible fate awaiting them." He said, "Tie your horse to the Golden Staff, and come with me."

The boy did as directed. On turning around, he saw two houses. The man said, "Open the door of that one to the left." The boy answered, "I have no key." The man smiled, pulled out a key, and unlocked the door. Then he asked the boy to look in. As soon as he did so, the people tried to spear and knife him, but they could not reach him. They were all quarreling and fighting, and many reptiles of different kinds crawled around among them. They lived on raw reptile flesh. Their chief (the Devil) sat there with a huge frog in front of him. He was cutting up pieces of the flesh with a large knife, in the manner of butchers. The boy said that he had seen enough.

Then his guide asked him to open the door of the other house. The boy said that he had no key, so the man opened the door for him. He saw many people inside, ranging as far as the eye could see, and the country looked very pleasant and beautiful and clean. The people paid no attention to him. They were all singing and praying. Some were on their knees praising God. All of them had hair of the same length, reaching down to the shoulders. The boy said he had seen enough and would go home. Later on he would return again and join the good people. His guide said to him, "No one can enter there unless he is pure in body and mind. A person must have no sins, and must have no thoughts of earth and earthly things." The boy mounted his horse, and soon reached the chief's house.

He told the chief everything; and the latter called his people together, and told them they would go in a body to the new land that the boy had discovered. The boy said to him, "You are wealthy and well provided for here, and it is hard to go there. You have to forget everything here on earth, and think only of good and heaven." The people formed a procession, all the soldiers marching ahead. The chief and the two boys drove behind in the chief's buggy. The soldiers and others cut a wide path through the bad tract of country. At last they reached the wide road. After marching a long time, the people, one by one, would think of what they had left behind, and at once they became transformed into crows or snakes, which flew or crawled away. They became dissatisfied, and could not fix their minds on the place to which they were going. They thought of the earth and the things they had left behind them. Thus one by one they became transformed into birds, animals, reptiles and insects, and at last none was left to reach the end of the road, except the chief and the two boys. These three reached the other land and remained there. They are the only people with mortal bodies who live in heaven.[26]

One is immediately struck by the weird syncretic texture of the story, and by its mood, something like that of a medieval romance. (Would that we could be sure of its style in actual performance!) Certain Christian and Anglo elements stand out: the all-male city the orphans come to seems to be a military camp (or possibly a priestly community); the "wide road" to Heaven is familiar from gospel phrasing; the chief by the golden staff who unlocks doors is clearly a derivation of St. Peter; the chief in the left-hand house of reptile-eaters is the Devil; the price of admission to Heaven seems to be Christian asceticism; the Elijah theme of bodily translation is present, and so on. Yet such motifs are for the most part in suspension with traditional Thompson Indian elements. The Thompsons did believe aboriginally in a pastoral afterworld, reached by a long trail to the West; en route the dead were supposed to throw off their clothes in piles. They were met at the borders by three spiritual elders; traditionally there was just one lodge for all souls, full of grass and flowers and berry-bushes, and naked souls singing and dancing.[27] Teit's note on the text is apt: "The story shows strong missionary influence. It also shows a fusion of Indian and Christian ideas. It has some analogy to Indian stories of visits to the ghost country."[28]

Yet, if the interplay of details is, as I am suggesting, mythopoetic and syncretic, it does seem to lean toward a Christian allegorical vision, overall. The Devil's lodge is added to the original Thompson afterworld (although, following Indian logic, "Hell" is located on the same plane as "Heaven"), and indeed only three of the pilgrims—the two orphan brothers and the chief—escape the Devil's household and are transplanted into the lodge of happy souls, apparently as a reward for their spiritual purity and concentration, and as a stern, possibly Protestant reminder that true Christians should build up their treasures in Heaven by renouncing earthly pelf. Yet again—lest we Christianize the story too much and too easily on behalf of the Indians—we should note the subtle underscoring, clearly from a Native point of view, of the sterility of the all-male community to which the boys come; and the initial "testing" of the boy-hero on the matter of horses and gear, although it does have its Caucasian equivalents in Grail literature and elsewhere, seems mainly to derive from the ubiquitous "test-theme" in Western Indian literature. And above all we should remember that the narrator sets his story explicitly "somewhere in the white man's country"; the actors are presumably not Indians but whites. If the narrative embodies, then, a sincere nineteenth-century Thompson-Salish grasp of Christian teachings, it does so only at a strange and subtle distance. I find myself unable, finally, to sort out adequately the Christian and the Native strains in its unity as a story. That it possesses imaginative unity is, I hope, beyond question.[29]

Perhaps it is exactly this kind of unstable mythopoeic playing with parallel elements of two cultures that has led to the formation of such new syncretic faiths as the Indian Shaker Church of the Pacific Northwest and the Native American (peyote) Church, both of which, interestingly, are emphatic in their rejection of the limiting text of the Christian Bible. But, as the Indians say about Coyote's adventures, that is another story. What I want to end with is a reminder that, as these Indian Bible stories represent a small but vivid chapter in the joint history of Indians and whites in the American and Canadian West, so the crucial Preface of that ongoing history itself begins in comparative mythology. On the one hand, many explorers and missionaries and their patrons from the seventeenth century on wanted to believe that the Indians represented the Lost Tribes of Israel, now found at last in the New World. On the other hand, many North American Indian tribes—the Northern Paiutes for example—believed that the oncoming whites represented a tribe of brothers that according to myth had been lost to the view of the Indians since the original dispersal of the first human family.[30] These are auspicious myths of convergence, and yet, when they met in the West, they somehow turned into our sad interracial history.

13 / Ti=Jean and the Seven=headed Dragon: Instances of Native American Assimilation of European Folklore

A NEGLECTED TOPIC IN THE LITERARY STUDY OF American Indian history and culture is the assimilation of European folktales into Native oral traditions. Important early work in this area by James Teit and other ethnographers (mainly working in Canada), and the pioneering bibliographic studies of Stith Thompson, have not been followed up, and, as a result, we still know very little about an intercultural literary process which, if properly documented and understood, could tell us much about the imaginative circumstances of Indian acculturation and about the internal rules and dynamics of traditional oral literatures.[1] As Dell Hymes has remarked,

Folklorists have commonly identified their object of study, traditional material, as a matter of texts, not of underlying rules. The frequent consequence has been that the very material which would decisively test a structural analysis has been disregarded. The occurrence of a reworked European tale in an Indian pueblo (say, *Beowulf*) might evoke amusement, or embarrassment, if one thinks of one's goal as autochthonous texts. If one thinks of one's goal as natively valid rules, such a case may be an invaluable opportunity to verify the principles of the native genre through an instance of their productivity.[2]

Two main lines of European literary influence have manifested themselves in the Native repertories: biblical stories, as disseminated in the middle decades of the last century by Catholic and Protestant missionaries; and continental folk-tales, mainly from Provençal traditions by way of Canada and eventually spread by French Canadian voyageurs, bushrunners, and squaw-men. Of the European traditions assimilated by the Indians, by far the most popular and widespread are the stories about the Provençal folk-hero Le Petit Jean, "Ti-Jean" as he is still called in Quebec or "Little Jack" in English. Within the Ti-Jean cycle, the story most widely adopted by Native tradition was the tale about Ti-Jean's heroic victory over the Seven-headed Dragon. Versions of this rousing story appear in the collections of almost every collector or transcriber who was open to collecting "impure" as well as classical narratives from Native sources, and the geographical and cultural range of texts is extraordinary—from the Tlingit, Thompson River, Shuswap, Okanagan, and Kalapuya of the Far Northwest; to the Zuñi in the Southwest; to the Nez Perce, Kutenai, Cree, and Blackfeet on the Great Plateau and Rockies; to the Osage, Ponka, and Omaha in the Midwest; to the Biloxi of southwest Louisiana; to the Ojibwa and Mohawk of the northeast woodlands.[3] Clearly, Ti-Jean enjoyed popularity among the Indians, especially in his role as a slayer of monsters. The sheer extent of his distribution reflects, of course, the almost ubiquitous operations of the French among the Indians in North America, and it also suggests that, once in the Native imagination, the Ti-Jean stories traveled on their own between tribes, with Indian tellers as vehicles.

Presumably Ti-Jean was attractive to Native storytellers and audiences first of all because he seemed familiar to them, conforming in general character and role to the "heroic-boy" protagonists featured in so many Native repertories. In general, these figures emerge into fame and fortune from obscure or even ignominious origins. The Nez Perce, for example, have a number of stories about orphan-boys who end up accomplishing great things despite their obscure and deprived beginnings; the Blackfeet have a cycle of tales featuring "Blood-clot Boy," who originates in a clot of blood picked up by an old man along the trail.[4] In the repertories of other Rocky Mountain tribes, the hero of equivalent stories begins his career as "Snot-boy." Likewise, Ti-Jean is, at the outset of his adventure, the youngest and weakest of a poor family, and, as an example of the "youngest/smartest" motif, he thrives (like his Indian equivalents) because he is alert, intelligent, fearless, and tricky, and comes to have good magical connections.

The fact that he is, on occasion, capable of deception and trickery probably made his stories all the more congenial to the Native imagination, suggesting elements of the great Indian trickster sequences that feature Coyote, Raven, Nanabush, and so on. Like these wily Native protagonists, Ti-Jean is given to "traveling around" in picaresque fashion, causing mischief and confusion as well as performing heroic deeds. He lacks, of course, the outrageous quality of mischief-as-an-end-in-itself that motivates Coyote and his kind, and in none of his adventures does he perform the mythic transformations of reality that distinguish the careers of the Native tricksters. But, as a tricky protagonist if not a full-fledged trickster, Ti-Jean would, I think, have appealed to audiences who knew and loved stories about Coyote et al.

Ti-Jean's immediate appeal and accessibility in Native terms meant that he and his stories were open to adaptive changes, including alterations of details, additions, and deletions. When Ti-Jean enters Indian narrative tradition, he becomes, as we will see, subject to Native spirit power instead of European magic, he does things according to Native cult numerology (four or five times rather than the European three times), his powers and indeed his very motives are Indianized, and so on.

Yet perhaps most revealing of Native attitudes is the evidence in many of these stories of a functional *limit* to such assimilation through adaptation. As pleased as Native raconteurs appear to have been with Ti-Jean as one white-culture imaginative figure with whom they could comfortably identify, nonetheless they seem in general to have resisted assimilating him utterly. Even incorporated within a Native language by the name Laptissan (among the Nez Perce), he remains something of an exotic figure. Perhaps this limit is simply the mechanical result of the very short time (short at least in terms of folklore dynamics) between the introduction of the stories to the tribes and their transcription by collectors—only two to four generations in most cases, perhaps simply not long enough for Ti-Jean to become wholly domesticated in the Native mind. A typical case would be Melville Jacobs's Kalapuya text: it was recorded in the Willamette Valley of Oregon in the 1910s, and it could not have entered the Kalapuya repertory (from French-speaking employees of the Hudson's Bay Company, probably) much before the 1830s.[5] No doubt time is a factor, then, in limiting Ti-Jean's assimilation, but I think another factor is cultural self-consciousness: if he was congenial to Indian performers and audiences, they nonetheless seem to have persisted in viewing him as "other"—a welcome import, but an import still.

In order to sort out such matters in detail and bring the adaptive processes themselves into focus, at least for the story of Ti-Jean and the Seven-headed Dragon, we need to inquire as to what the probable form of that story was at the point of its entry into the Indian repertories and as to what the circumstances of that entry were. If we were considering Indian adaptations of Bible stories (see essay 12), questions of *ur*-texts and provenience would be relatively easy to engage. The biblical narratives are, ultimately, *fixed* as texts. That is, we can point to the canonical texts in Holy Writ as the points of origin for all biblical adaptations and derivations. As for provience, the Catholic and Protestant missionaries and preachers who first introduced the Indians of the American and Canadian frontiers to Christianity did so under fairly set circumstances and left extensive notes on their methods. I have discussed such matters in detail elsewhere; what the Reverend Cushing Eells reported in 1840 about his work with the Nez Perce seems to typify how western evangelists, both Protestant and Catholic, undertook to introduce their Indian listeners to the Bible. Clearly, the emphasis was on biblical storytelling, a la Sunday school:

For want of a thorough acquaintance with the language, much of the instruction communicated has related to Scripture history. . . . It is strictly true that they must have "line upon line"; every new idea must be repeated many times. The nearer our teaching approaches to Sabbath-school instruction, appropriate for small children, the better it is understood.[6]

In trying, then, to sort out the changes that the Bible narratives underwent in entering Indian oral tradition, we can at least begin with the sacred texts and be reasonably confident that contact-era missionaries did not, as a rule, take drastic liberties in adapting these texts for presentation to Native audiences.[7] But—returning to European secular folklore—who knows when, how, why, and by whom our story of Ti-Jean made its way into the minds of, say, the Shuswap of British Columbia, and in what version out of its many Provençal and Quebecois forms? Lacking a canonical text or "primary version" of the European story, can we, in fact, hope to learn anything about the process of folkloristic assimilation between European and Indian culture, if the initial stages of that process are so undocumented and obscure?

I think that we can do better than guesswork, on some points anyway. We can legitimately assume that the story was typically told and audited in Native settings simply as a secular telling between two intersecting cultures, not as part of the expounding of a new faith, to which the Native listeners were being constrained. Indian Bible-story texts are sometimes vividly expressive of bitter resentment against the missionaries and their teachings; the twistings and distortions of biblical details in them often appear to be deliberate, a kind of imaginative sabotage against the imperious new order. In a Northern Paiute version of Genesis 1–2, for example, it was Coyote who gave the apple tree to the Paiute, but a snake with the eyes of a white man crawled into the tree and drove the Indians away. The story ends: "Just because they were snakes and came here, the white people took everything away. They asked these Indians where they had come from."[8]

The bitterness of such alterations of Holy Writ is eloquent—but no such animus pervades the Native adaptations of the Ti-Jean story, even the most drastically altered. We can hypothesize that it (and stories like it) came into the tribes under circumstances that were, for the contact era, unusually happy and easy—drawing together people of two cultures, perhaps as hosts and guests, for the shared enjoyment of good stories. Not infrequently, of course, stories of the Ti-Jean kind must have appeared in Native communities in the context of French Indian families. In the Willamette Valley in Oregon, for example, a whole racially mixed community—"French Prairie"—grew up in the 1830s as a settlement of Hudson's Bay pensioners and their families. One such household was that of Louis Labonte, a Montrealer who married a Chinookan chief's daughter and raised a large family at French Prairie. His dictated reminiscences are full of somewhat Frenchified versions of Chinookan tales, and it is clear that, in the Labonte family circle French folklore and Native traditions coexisted with equal honor and influenced one another.[9] Further indication of such easy commerce between French and Indian oral traditions comes from the Colville Indians of Washington State, who differentiate between three kinds of stories: *kumaixìts,* narrative of a recent event; *captĭkwl,* myth; and *insim'a'pEluks,* "'French' fairy tale."[10]

Lacking a canonical French text for the story, how should we proceed in our investigation of its transformations among the Indians? Specifically, what should we take as a narrative norm whereby to measure adaptive alterations? In his tabulation of Native instances of the tale in *European Tales among the North American Indians,* Stith Thompson sets forth five "types" of the French original, each type differing from the others in inclusiveness and ordering of details, plus a sixth category reserved for "Mixed Types." Under each heading, Thompson lists, by way of illustration, one or more Indian versions. *European Tales among the North American Indians* is still indispensable, the necessary starting point for any serious examination of our subject, but Thompson's predilection for drastically *abstracting* oral narratives (which becomes, somewhat later in his career, both the governing method and the functional limitation of his great *Motif Index*) here severely limits the usefulness of his system of tabulating and typing European stories and their Indian versions, at least for the purposes of literary analysis. For example, his "Type II" is characterized by the following formulation of motifs: (a) Heroes' magic animals, (b) Life-token, (c) Dragon rescue, (d) Impostor, (e) Tongues used as proof.[11] It is not at all clear on what basis this particular formulation constitutes one of five main types, nor is it clear why this particular type should have inspired versions (to use Thompson's own examples) among Indian groups as widely dispersed and culturally unlike as the Biloxi of Mississippi and the Tlingit of the North Pacific Coast. Are we to proceed from the assumption that, somehow, the Biloxi and Tlingit stories fitting the Type II formulation came about because these two groups happened to hear only this one variation on the Ti-Jean theme? Surely other factors must have come into play in determining the passage of a European tale into a Native oral repertory—preeminently, one would think, the conventions and typologies of that repertory.

With these considerations in mind, it seems necessary to reject Thompson's motif-based categories and, instead, begin by devising a hypothetical version of Ti-Jean and the Seven-headed Dragon, a sort of composite or "averaged" version based on selected formulations of it in French and English. This procedure is familiar to folklorists as a way to facilitate analytic study of variability and dissemination in a "set" of closely related stories; a form of it is also the starting-point of Claude Lévi-Strauss's celebrated structural analysis of the Oedipus mythos, and it is consistent with his dictum that, instead of searching for the original formulation of a myth-narrative, analysts should consider many versions, in an attempt to discover what constitutes the shaping "rules" or grammar of that particular myth.[12]

In attempting to set up such a model, I have taken into special account a French-language version of Ti-Jean's story that probably represents the nearest thing to textual authenticity that we will find, "authenticity" meaning, again, what the story was like when it was first transmitted to Indian audiences. This text was recorded by Marius Barbeau in Quebec before World War One, among rural French Canadians. As Barbeau himself notes, it was from precisely such people, only two to four generations before, that the great cadres of voyageurs, trappers, and *coureurs de bois* went forth to travel all over the western frontiers, trade, and intermarry with the Indians—and tell stories about Ti-Jean. Barbeau's text may well approximate more closely than anything else what the Quebecois trappers and woodsmen actually told their Native audiences.

Here is the composite story, then, in outline form, drawn from Barbeau's French text and checked against and supplemented as to details from texts of the story in collections edited by Cosquin, Massignon, and Delarue.[13] (Where there are major variations between the composite text and these versions, I have noted them.)

1. The youngest and smallest of three brothers in a poor family, Ti-Jean sets out, last of the three, into the world.[14]
2. Either just as he sets out, or along the way, he comes into possession of some magical properties—in varying combinations, a multicolored shirt, a sash, a talking stick, a trio of horses, a dog.[15]
3. Ti-Jean arrives in a country terrorized by a seven-headed dragon, whose special appetite is for maidens. Now, Ti-Jean learns, it is the King's own daughter who is to be sacrificed.
4. Ti-Jean takes a menial job.
5. He intercepts the Princess on her way to be sacrificed and, with the aid of his magical helpers, succeeds in cutting off the dragon's heads in the course of three battles in as many days, until the monster is slain. After each battle, he wraps up the dragon's tongues in a handkerchief given him by the Prin-

cess. He sends her back to the King but maintains his own
anonymity.[16]

6. Upon hearing that his daughter is safe and that his realm is
   free from the dragon, the King announces that he will give
   the Princess in marriage to her rescuer, if his identity can
   be learned.
7. An impostor, usually a charcoal-maker, finds the dragon's
   heads and presents them as evidence that *he* is the dragon-
   slayer.[17]
8. At the last moment, usually at the wedding-feast, Ti-Jean appears at Court, challenges the impostor's story, and identifies
   himself by exhibiting the dragon's tongues, wrapped in the
   Princess's handkerchief.[18]
9. Ti-Jean and the Princess are joyfully married.
10. The impostor is punished.[19]

Native adaptive variations on this "standardized" story take several
forms. First, on a superficial level, there are what might be called "ethnocentric adjustments," alterations or substitutions in the case of textual details in the French original that would not be readily understood in Native
cultures. An example of such adjustments in the case of Indian assimilation of Bible stories would be the Thompson River account of the Tower
of Babel episode in Genesis: in place of the Judeo-Christian *tower,* the
Thompson people imagined an enormous, extendable *pole-ladder,* com-
prehensible in terms of the pole-ladders used in Thompson households.[20]
In terms of our Provençal story and *its* Native legacy, whereas, in the French
versions, Ti-Jean's future father-in-law is a king, living in a palace, in the Indian versions he invariably becomes a great chief or headman, living in a
fine lodge. The grief of the people over the impending death of the Princess
as Ti-Jean arrives on the scene is charmingly translated into Native terms
in the Kalapuya version: "They all had black feathers."[21] On the level of
narrative numerology, the invariable formulaic threes of European folklore
and the biblical tradition give way to standard Indian cult numbers—five,
for northern versions, four, for the Pueblo Zuñi. Where Ti-Jean's serial decapitation of the dragon takes three battles in the original, for example, in
the Kalapuya text it takes five. Indeed, in this text, as if *really* to assert a Native grip on the story, Ti-Jean leaves his grandmother five houses full of

venison before setting out, there are five impostors, and so on. The fact that in nearly all Native versions the distinctly European seven-headedness of the dragon is retained simply follows an aboriginal story-telling tradition of incorporating unusual creatures and beings verbatim without changing the descriptions or the cult numbers, thereby emphasizing both the freakishness of the creature itself and the story's foreign origins. Seven must have been associated in Native minds early on with European culture through gambling and other usages, so "seven heads" would have seemed like an especially *outré* detail.[22]

One of the oddest and most revealing ethnocentric adjustments involves the figure of the impostor, who tries to claim the royal rewards for Ti-Jean's heroic deeds. In some Native texts (as with the Kalapuya story noted above) there are multiple impostors working as a team, but, in a majority of these narratives, Ti-Jean is said to have a single rival, someone identified, rather puzzlingly, as a "black man." He is so depicted, for example, in the Omaha/Ponka, Osage, Cree, and Ojibwa versions.[23] European racist color-symbolism is doubtless not at issue here. In Barbeau's Quebec text, the impostor is identified (as he is in other French texts) as a *charbonnier* or charcoal-maker. How else to represent such a figure to an audience ignorant of the charcoal trade than by suppressing his professional function, which would not be understood, and by emphasizing, instead, his sooty, grimy appearance? Thus, I think, we get "black man"—dirty, undesirable in appearance as in motives, but not originally Negroid.[24] It is precisely the kind of casual accommodation of the details of a narrative to the experience of an alien audience that any good storyteller would make in the interest of intelligibility. In this instance, of course, the change from *charbonnier* to "black man" actually gives the impostor a strangeness and prominence in the Indian versions that he lacks in the French.

More substantive kinds of adjustments are expressive of Native conventions of characterization and narrative form. I asserted earlier that Ti-Jean must have seemed immediately congenial to Indian audiences in many tribal groups because he and his stories corresponded to Native traditions about boy-heroes who rise with magical rapidity from utter weakness and obscurity to heroic fame and power. Bruno Bettelheim has emphasized the orthogenic value for children of such narratives in western folklore, notably in the kindermärchen of the Brothers Grimm:

Fairy tales . . . direct the child to discover his identity and calling, and they also suggest what experiences are needed to develop his character further. Fairy tales intimate that a rewarding, good life is within one's reach despite adversity—but only if one does not shy away from the hazardous struggles without which one can never achieve true identity. These stories promise that if a child dares to engage in this fearsome and taxing search, benevolent powers will come to his aid, and he will succeed.[25]

For all the differences between Northern European cultures and the Indian cultures of North America, what Bettelheim says here about the functional value of the Grimms' "young-hero" stories seems equally pertinent to their Native equivalents—to the Ti-Jean adaptive stories—as well. In a number of these latter texts, in fact, as if to emphasize the hero's lowly origins in Native social terms, and thus magnify his climb to high status, he is identified simply as "Orphan." In a Kutenai version, the story begins with the orphaning of the hero, so that the narrative order follows his rise to prosperity from a condition of helpless misery. Similarly, the Osage variant opens with the boy incurring his father's wrath and being thrown out of the household.[26]

On the question of Ti-Jean's *virtue*—his natural fitness to grow into a hero—there is considerable diversity among the Indian texts. In the French originals, his first adventures after leaving home show him to be both stout-hearted and good-hearted. Thus he seems to deserve the magical weapons or assistants with which he will eventually slay the dragon and make his fortune. Likewise, in the Kalapuya version, the boy's innate virtue is established early but in expressively Native terms: he is a good hunter, even as a child; he dutifully swims every morning; a stick he has always used to whip his hair dry in the approved Native manner identifies itself to him as his guardian spirit, saying, "Now you and I are one. Nothing will be too difficult for you"; he thoughtfully provides his grandmother with venison in abundance before leaving on his adventure, and so on.[27] But, in other Indian versions, such characterizing details are lacking, and Ti-Jean becomes merely a protagonist who is lucky and successful in his story. Typical in this regard is an Ojibwa story collected by Alanson Skinner, in which the protagonist is simply given, as he sets out into the world, a magical horse and dog (each with "silver ears"), a sword that will rust only if he gets into trouble and so is left at home, and so on. At the time of his setting out, he is, as a character, a cipher.[28]

Such diversity in heroic characterization is observable in traditional Native hero stories in general. Magical weapons and helpers figure in many tribal repertories, corresponding to those which come to Ti-Jean—but traditions differ greatly as to whether the hero-to-be acquires them *because* of his virtue or simply acquires them and, then, with such advantages, becomes heroic. On the whole, the Kalapuya story notwithstanding, I surmise that, in general, the conventions of Indian storytelling would have resisted our assumption that a young hero like Ti-Jean should be properly characterized as heroic material before his adventures begin. What counts in Native terms, rather, seems to be the story itself; it is action that is heroic, not so much the quality of one's character. Thus, whereas, in the French story and others like it, Ti-Jean's insistence on his anonymity until the end may strike us as expressive of a rather winning modesty, or at least an admirable prudence, in most of the Indian analogues, it seems to figure simply as a plot device, whereby the hero's last-minute recognition becomes that much more dramatic. Even in the Kalapuya text, which does establish the hero's merit before sending him out on his career, there seems to be neither innate modesty nor cunning in his refusal to come forth to be identified until the last possible moment. Instead, he is merely following the advice of one of his magical helpers, a talking stick.[29]

It would be all too easy, given the uncertainties we face in dealing with transcribed and translated Indian stories, to overdraw such contrasts between their conventions of characterization and motivation and the conventions that operate in our own literary tradition. For one thing, it is never a simple task to determine whether a given Native text renders the full scope and texture of the story—as it would in the ideal case of a transcribed performance—or whether it represents only a summary, omitting textual features of the sort that flesh out character. Still, looking at the Native Ti-Jean adaptations in general, I would assert that their tendency to emphasize what the young hero *does* more than what he *is,* is typical of Native traditional storytelling. The story is always what counts; character attends upon action.[30]

Then there is the dragon itself. As with the basic figure of Ti-Jean, this staple of European folklore would have registered plausibly, if exotically, in most Native American systems, for the simple reason that they had their own traditional equivalents—great, vile, autochthonous monsters, generally given to sucking in their victims indiscriminately, until slain by some transient hero, most commonly a trickster/transformer who works from inside, as it were, after he has been himself swallowed. In the Nez Perce repertory, for example, the monster depopulates an entire region, inhaling whole villages at a time, until Coyote lets himself be ingested and rescues all the people still alive in the monster's belly by cutting its heart off with five knives. Like others of its kind, the story then becomes a kind of origin myth, as Coyote cuts the monster up and distributes its parts all over the West, "by that act destining and forenaming the various peoples." Having forgotten about the Nez Perce themselves in this distribution, Coyote corrects himself and blesses them with the monster's blood, promising that, although "you will be little people because I have deprived you, nevertheless you will be very, very, manly."[31] Perhaps it is no accident, given their possession of such an auspicious *Native* monster story, that the Nez Perce accepted only a very much diminished version of Ti-Jean's dragon: the dragon retains its seven heads but is first seen running with the cows of a Nez Perce chief. Eventually, it acquires a taste for beef and then for people— before Laptissan arrives, hypnotizes it by riding round and round it on a mule, and then whacks off its heads with just one stroke. Clearly, both monster and hero are only poor distant cousins of their authentic Nez Perce equivalents, iltsewitsix (the monster) and itsayaya (Coyote).[32]

This Nez Perce dragon is, like its French original, a dry-land monster, but, in many of the Indian versions, Seven Heads is clearly aquatic. This alteration is, I think, a further indication of how Native narrative conventions and typologies have shaped the assimilation of foreign stories: that is, the presence of water-monsters in a tribe's repertory meant that Ti-Jean's dragon has to be one, too, for typological reasons. In the Omaha/Ponka text, for example, it lives in a lake and is called Wakandagi or "water-monster," conforming precisely to Native monster-lore in the Omaha/Ponka tradition. The Kalapuya "Seven Heads" also lives in a lake, and, in this detail, it is in conformity with an aboriginal monster known as Amhuluk, said to live in a certain lake in the woods and prey on children.[33] Again, in the face of such a Native tradition, a land-based bogy would not have seemed imaginatively plausible.

The Indian versions of the Ti-Jean narrative discussed thus far represent degrees of simple adaptive assimilation, wherein the French story is adjusted to conform to the facts of Native life and Native literary conventions but retains its mythemic identity and, perhaps, to Native listeners, something of its foreignness. An unusual text, that seems to represent a more radical and complex degree of assimilation, was recorded among the Osage by George Dorsey at the turn of this century. The story, "The Boy and Big Nest," can be summarized as follows:

A monster called Big Nest lives by a creek and eats people, until it is caught and put in a little house. A boy playing shinny nearby rolls his ball into the house, and Big Nest persuades the boy to let it escape. The boy confesses to his father; the father expels him from home. The boy finds Big Nest by the creek; Big Nest gives him four magical clay balls for hunting. The boy goes on and meets a man with two dogs. The boy reveals that he has turned Big Nest loose; the man says that the chief has announced that the one who kills Big Nest will win the chief's daughter. The man finds Big Nest and, with the aid of his dogs, kills it. The boy goes on, sees some deer and throws one of his clay balls at them; the ball becomes a mountain lion which kills the deer. The boy eats well and, in succession, the other balls, when thrown, bring him fish, wild turkey, and buffalo. The boy moves in with an old man and hunts for him. At length, the boy is sent for by the man who killed Big Nest to confirm the deed. The boy arrives back at camp to find the people washing a black man in hot water, trying to make him white. The black man has claimed that *he* killed Big Nest. The boy confirms the real killer's claim; the people cut off the black man's ears and throw him in the creek. The boy is reunited with his father. The killer of Big Nest marries the chief's daughter and holds a wedding-feast; the boy and his father refuse to attend because the boy wants the chief's daughter for himself.[34]

Clearly, by comparison with the relatively straightforward alterations we have been considering, something very strange has happened to the Ti-Jean story here. The Big Nest story is like an Osage anagram of the standard elements of Ti-Jean's career. The boy, setting out, receives magical properties according to the familiar pattern—but he gets them from the monster itself and uses them for hunting only. The monster is unmagically slain by someone else, a second hero, who prosaically depends on the boy to confirm his story and refute the "black" impostor's claim. The chief's daughter has not been a candidate for sacrifice; the dramatic detail of the monster's tongues (one of the essential hallmarks of the French original) is omitted. At the end, instead of marrying the girl and giving a feast, the boy is left sulking at home, imagining for himself, too late, the heroic role taken by his counterparts in the French story and in all the Indian versions we have considered up to now.

In a note on the text, in his *European Tales among the North American Indians,* Stith Thompson remarks that, although it differs markedly from the typical story of Ti-Jean and the monster, incorporating "much purely Indian matter" and indeed showing signs of internal confusion (the doubling of heroes, for example), nonetheless, "there can be no doubt that we have here the European tale." Thompson characterizes the story's peculiar transformation of details as an "amalgamation." [35] It is a useful term, in that it *is* virtually impossible to be sure any longer where French folklore leaves off and Osage takes over. But the term is also somewhat misleading, in that *amalgamation* suggests an equality of things being merged, whereas what has happened in the Osage story, it seems to me, is more of a submerging of European parts in a medium that is distinctively, if somewhat peculiarly, Indian. There are some Native renderings of Bible stories on record that really do seem to embody a mythopoetic impulse whereby Native and European narrative elements have become fused, amalgamated if you will, into new unities, neither obviously Indian nor European, but partaking equally of both and exhibiting, interestingly, something of the spirit and form of romance (see essay 12).[36] But here we see, I think, something less creative, literarily speaking, but no less interesting for what it may reveal about the dynamics of intercultural folklore. That is, the story, garbled as it is by either European or Native standards of coherence, may represent a sort of terminal phase of adaptive assimilation. Perhaps it comes from a fourth- or fifth-hand knowledge of the French original, either passing between tribes, or developing over several generations in the Osage repertory, or perhaps evolving in the mind of Dorsey's unnamed narrator. At any rate, we seem to see a narrative losing its foreign mystique (note that the monster's seven-headedness is gone) and its original order and unity of parts, breaking up beyond adaptive change and, in effect, disappearing into what the late Nez Perce scholar Archie Phinney aptly called the Native "mythbody." [37]

In wondering how often this was, in fact, the ultimate fate of European stories, and how much exotic narrative debris of this sort may be floating in Native texts, I am *not* trying to revive that old, many-headed monster of folklorists, the notion that the Native literary traditions of

North America are everywhere infected with hidden European borrowings and influences. That notion is an insult both to the astuteness of the transcribers of the Boas era—all of whom were professionally familiar with Continental folklore and were quick to point out what appeared to them to be foreign elements in the Native texts—and to the imaginative and cultural acumen working in the traditional literatures themselves, their ability to keep things straight between the authentic elements of their own repertories and what the whites offered from their folklore.[38] But those Native literatures cannot be viewed as hermetically closed, classically fixed imaginative systems, either, as I hope this brief survey of one segment of Ti-Jean's career in "Indian captivity" has indicated.

Given the way such assimilations and adaptations implicate and thus throw into prominence the formal dynamics of tribal narrative repertories, it is regrettable that stories in the Ti-Jean line were not more actively pursued and collected during the heroic era of ethnographic and linguistic field work. But given what *does* exist in textualized form—Native appropriations of "John the Bear," "The King of the Golden River," "The Golden Birds," and so on, as well as other Ti-Jean adventures—and given the likelihood that in some tribal groups such stories are still being told today, it is doubly regrettable that the subject has drawn so little scholarly attention since Stith Thompson first emphasized its importance nearly eighty years ago.[39]

14 / Francis La Flesche's
"The Song of Flying Crow" and the Limits of Ethnography

Long ago her mother
had to sing this song and so
she had to grind along with it
the corn people have a song too
it is very good
I refuse to tell it

—Armand Schwerner,
"What the Informant Said to Franz Boas in 1920,"
in Rothenberg, *Shaking the Pumpkin*

THE UNPUBLISHED WRITINGS OF "THE FIRST PRO-
fessional American Indian anthropologist,"[1] Francis La Flesche (1857–
1932) of the Omaha tribe, include a folder of handwritten and typed
manuscripts in the National Anthropological Archives of the Smithsonian
Institution in Washington, D.C.[2] The bulk of these manuscripts reflect
La Flesche's literary inclinations; more specifically, they seem to represent

his ongoing interest in finding new ways of "doing" ethnography, beyond the standard forms of discourse established in the Boas era of American anthropology and followed by La Flesche himself in his monumental collaboration with Alice Fletcher on the culture of his own people, *The Omaha Tribe,* and other scholarly writings.[3]

Thus, the "La Flesche File" includes a fascinating range of pieces, all centered on Omaha culture and history but written in a variety of forms, from the personal essay to the short story to what appears to be the beginnings of a novel to the outline of a grand opera, *Da-o-ma* (eventually completed by La Flesche and Nellie Eberhart in 1912, with music by Charles Wakefield Cadman, but apparently never performed) to poetry. Clearly, La Flesche had literary aspirations (on the occasion of receiving an Honorary Doctorate of Letters from the University of Nebraska in 1926, he remarked that "as a lad he had planned to be a great buffalo hunter, but the white people came and ate up the buffalo, so he turned to writing"[4]), and he did publish two short stories in his lifetime,[5] but the manuscript material in the Smithsonian file indicates that he was also interested in adapting literary forms and strategies to the task of "writing culture."

In this, of course, he was in league with a persistent "literary" impulse in American ethnographic and anthropological writing, aimed at supplementing the social science methodology of Boasian anthropology with the techniques of the personal essay, the autobiography, and the novel. Adolf Bandelier's ethnographic novel of Pueblo life, *The Delight Makers* (1890), is a memorable early expression of this impulse, which, late in La Flesche's own career, produced a remarkable collection of ethnographic short stories written by distinguished scholars of Indian culture, most of whom were trained by Boas: *American Indian Life (by Several of Its Students),* edited by Elsie Clews Parsons (1922). The avowedly fictive cast of these narratives can be appreciated in the title and opening lines of one of them, T. T. Waterman's "All Is Trouble along the Klamath (a Yurok Idyll)": "(Mrs. Oregon Jim, from the house Erkiger'i or 'Hair Ties,' in the town of Pe'kwan, speaking): 'You want to know why old Louisa and I never notice each other? Well, I'll tell you why. I wouldn't speak to that old woman to save her life. There is a quarrel between her and me, and between her people and mine.'"[6]

In his introduction to the volume, A. L. Kroeber observes approvingly that "[the] fictional form of presentation devised by the editor has definite merit. It allows freedom in depicting or suggesting the thoughts and feelings of the Indians, such as is not possible in a formal, scientific report. In fact, it incites to active psychological treatment, else the tale would lag. . . . The method is that of the historical novel, with emphasis on the history rather than the romance."[7]

Putting aside judgment of its strictly literary merits, *American Indian Life* is a fascinating, adventuresome, but oddly neglected experiment. As Kroeber's comments suggest, the central aim of its contributors' dalliance with the art of fiction seems to have been to transcend some of the felt limits of scientific ethnography—to try to register the individual subjectivities (Kroeber speaks of "psychological treatment") of Native subjects. Against the too often faceless, lifeless generalizations of conventional ethnography, individual subjects' diverse and conflicted lives reduced to static formulae of collective cultural identity, Parsons and her contributors (who included Kroeber and Boas himself) were seeking to evoke their sense of their subjects' lives as ongoing "stories" unfolding within the vague but pervasive "plot" of a given culture. If they persisted here, as in their conventional scholarship, in neglecting questions about their own subjectivities as social scientists, at least they were attempting to find ways to bring "character" and "conflict" and "narrative" into play in the arenas of cultural study. Their experiments point at least symbolically toward the modern "ethnographic novel," of which Chinua Achebe's *Things Fall Apart,* Laura Bohannon's *Return to Laughter,* Jorge Amado's *Tent of Miracles,* James Welch's *Fools Crow,* and Ursula LeGuin's *Always Coming Home* are notable specimens.

Apparently Francis La Flesche was not invited to contribute something to *American Indian Life* (a pity all around), but early on in his career he followed his literary inclinations in seeking for more sensitive and evocative ways of writing about the phenomena of culture than what current scientific modes allowed. In particular, as a Native American scholar, a staff member of the Indian Office and later of the Bureau of American Ethnology, and the son of an Omaha chief, Iron Eye (Joseph La Flesche), as someone who had participated as a boy in the last of the great Central Plains buffalo hunts, he clearly felt a strong need to legitimatize in writing his own subjective, *imaginative* identification with Omaha culture and, concomitantly, his awareness of belonging to two worlds, Indian and Anglo, even of existing uncertainly between them. His first nonscholarly publication of note, *The Middle Five*,[8] is a richly textured memoir of his boyhood years in a Presbyterian mission school at home on the reservation in Nebraska. Most of the unpublished pieces in the Smithsonian Archives are literarily self-conscious explorations in forms of autobiographical discourse, with persistent emphasis on figures such as the author himself, moving equivocally between Native and Anglo cultures.

One of the shorter compositions in the file, a brief memoir of a summertime return to the Omaha reservation entitled "The Song of Flying Crow," especially stands out. I don't know of a more subtle and resonant evocation of the intercultural predicament than this eight-paragraph sketch, which seems to me to be a small gem of its kind, a kind of poem of ethnographic experience, if you will. In what follows after the text itself, I try to contextualize "The Song of Flying Crow" and then to explicate its form and content, whose unifying principle seems to be the author's deeply felt need to mediate between his new life as a government-sponsored ethnologist and his old, but persisting, life as a member of the Omaha tribe.

The manuscript of "The Song of Flying Crow" is undated, but an educated guess as to date would be 1898. La Flesche is known to have used a "graphophone" (an Edison-type recording cylinder phonograph) as early as summer 1898; by then he had already collaborated with Alice Fletcher and the musicologist J. C. Fillmore on *A Study of Omaha Indian Music* (1893), and was carrying on his own efforts to record and preserve Omaha music, leading to his contributions to that subject in *The Omaha Tribe*.[9] Eighteen ninety-eight seems like a likely date for the composition of the essay because in that year, although he had not yet begun to compose *The Middle Five,* he was no doubt preparing for that task by reflecting on the friends and events of his childhood.

The exact date of the singing of Flying Crow's song is not crucial: what *is* important to notice at the outset is the writer's indication that, once again, he has journeyed home from Washington, D.C., to take up residence on the reservation, indeed in a tipi![10] But what Norma Kidd Green has written about such vacations, that "Frank entered fully into the life of the family and of the reservation, leaving the other half of his life far away,"[11] must have been true only for outward appearances—a much more complex and problematic mental occupation must have been the rule for La Flesche, judging from this text.

"The Song of Flying Crow"

At the risk of being accused of "going back to the tent," as many Indian students returned from eastern schools have been accused of "going back to the blanket," I had erected near my brother's cottage, when at home on my vacation, last summer, a real Indian tent for my comfort and pleasure during my stay. The last days of my real tent life came to an end years ago when I with other Indians traveled one whole winter through western Kansas in search of buffalo. At that time my proud possessions were a saddle, a bridle, a lariat, and a gun. In singular contrast to those things, I had with me in my temporary "return to the tent" a number of books, magazines, a leather case, and a graphophone. The great herds that my people and I followed over the plains in the days of my youth have gone the same way that my forefathers have gone, never to return. The songs that expressed the emotions of my people, the songs of war, of peace, and of love that used to ring through the wooded hills of my birth were also passing away, and it was to catch as much as possible the dying echoes that I made my visit home armed with a speech and song catching instrument. The tent was a bit of sentiment, the indulgence of which the civilized people will forgive.

It was late in the afternoon when I took possession of my tent. A gentle rain drummed on the heavy canvas and my thoughts traveled back to the days which my life among the white people has since taught me to look upon as wild. The sound of approaching footsteps brought me back to the present and a familiar voice commenting on the weather warned me of a coming visitor. We exchanged the usual greetings and then began to talk of the various things in which we had a common interest. Then other friends came one by one until the tent was full of people all eager to learn and to teach. My well starched collar and cuffs and polished shoes made not the slightest difference in the intimate friendship that we enjoyed before I left the reservation years ago to dwell in the city of the Nation's Capital.

When we had all enjoyed the supper that my brother and I had provided and were feeling very good, we filled a huge pipe which we passed around and smoked. A fire was lighted so that we could see each other's faces, and being in a reminiscent mood we began tales of our own adventures and those of other men in other days. Then when the stories of adventures and misadventures, of pathos and of humor began to flag and somebody yawned I said, "Uncle, start for us a song and we will sing, just as we used to do before I went away," addressing a little old man. "Yes," said a friend who sat near me, "let's sing some of the old songs that used to stir the warlike feelings of the men who lived and died long ago."

In a clear and musical voice the little old man gave the first bar of a song familiar to us all and we took it up and made the hills around echo with the sounds of song. Of the thousands of songs in the tribe I knew a few, some five or six hundred, so I did my part of the singing and enjoyed the thrill of the rhythm. Many other songs were sung and the story of each repeated just as I had heard it years ago. The little old man complimented my memory for songs, then said, "Let us see if you know this one." He started it and all sang with a precision that denoted thorough knowledge of the song. I knew the class to which it belonged, from the vocables used and the terminating notes, but I could not follow, for the song was new to me. "It must be an old one just re-called by some old man." "It is a new song," said the little old man, "made and given to us by your friend Flying Crow just before he died not very long ago."

"How did he come to make the song?" I asked. "He knew he was near death," replied the little old man, "and before he died he wanted to say to his friends some words that would not be forgotten the moment he spoke them, so he made the song to hold the words. He lay in his tent one day, all silent, but thinking of the many, many people who came into this life, endured its hard-ships, and enjoyed its pleasures for a little space of time then passed to the land of mystery, the land of spirits. Then he thought of the countless numbers that are to open their eyes to the light of the sun and pass on in the same way. He thought of the lives of the birds, the animals, and the little creatures that crawl and burrow in the earth, how their time, as well as that of men, was measured out long before they were brought to the earth. He had no fear of death but he thought of these things as being full of mystery. Struck with the realization that the duration of life at the longest was but brief he desired his friends to strive to make each other happy so that they may enter the next world without fear and with a joyous spirit. Although the words in the song are few they at once bring to our minds all these thoughts—and the memory of our friend."

"Let's sing it again," I said. "I like it and I must learn it."

We sang it again and again and now it is so fixed in my memory that I shall never forget it even if I should live to be a hundred years old.

It was past the hour of midnight when my friends took leave of me to go to their homes among the hills. I could hear their voices in the still night until they gradually died away in the distance, then I took to thinking of the song I had just learned and its maker, Flying Crow. We were boys together and went to the same school that was maintained by the missionaries on our reser-vation for the education of Indian youth. I remember he used to run away quite often and finally he stayed away altogether. He inherited the beliefs of his fathers who for generations had been the keepers of the sacred rites of the tribe. He learned very little of the instructions given in the schoolroom and much less of those given in the chapel which meant nothing to his untutored mind. Born a pagan he died a pagan, with the song of a pagan upon his lips.

From the first sentence on, the author's predicament and something of his sensitivity to it are manifested. He has "come home" again, but can he really claim to be home, given his present affiliations and the loss of the Omaha ways of his boyhood: the use of tipis and the great buffalo hunts? To be sure, he has set himself up in a tipi (apparently on his younger brother Carey's farm [12]), but if the tent is "real" (albeit canvas), he knows that his occupation of it is not, and at the very outset of the sketch he wonders jokingly if his Anglo readers will accuse him of atavistic behavior in his whim of going back to the tent, if not, as the saying has it, "to the blanket." The defensive self-mockery of the circumstances of his return in effect brackets and conditions his identification of its *purpose*—to record, against inevitable loss, the traditional songs of the Omaha. Can this purpose itself be just as sentimental and self-indulgent as "going back to the tent"? And is his own position as both returned native son and government researcher tenable?

Already, La Flesche has situated his discourse in a cluster of interlocking bipolar oppositions: not just Omaha Indian versus Anglo but, more broadly, "civilized" versus "wild" ("the days which my life among the white people has since taught me to look upon as wild"), past versus present (specifically *his* past and present but also that of his people), cultural loss versus the possibility of recovery and preservation. Thus, he reflects on the material possessions of his buffalo hunting days, "a saddle, a bridle, a lariat, and a gun" in contrast to what he brought with him for his scholarly work: books, magazines, a briefcase, and a graphophone. His juxtapositioning of vanished buffalo and vanishing songs, and the instruments for "catching" them—guns and graphophone, respectively—is especially expressive of his predicament: there is nothing much heroic about recording songs with a spring-loaded contraption, he seems to be saying to himself, and if the way of the buffalo is truly gone for the Omaha, "never to return," then is there really any vital value in transcribing some surviving songs from that lost world?

As an ethnologist and cultural historian of his own tribe, La Flesche had had to struggle in his work with the bleakly pragmatic philosophy of many tribal elders, who, when they recognized that the buffalo were gone, decided that the ceremonies and songs sacred to the buffalo cult should die with them and not be uselessly left to posterity. As Norma Kidd Green puts it, the elders "would not teach the sacred words to any young man; these things could never be a part of the young men's lives."[13] Against such opposition, La Flesche seems to have felt, in Margot Liberty's words, "a sense of almost unbearable urgency" to record the Omaha legacy;[14] but at what point does one's ethnological advantage of being a tribal member become the basis of exploitation? At what point does the effort to "translate" Omaha culture into ethnographical discourse become a kind of betrayal— *traddutore, tradditore?*

In a few sentences, by way of setting the scene, even before beginning to narrate the events attending the singing of Flying Crow's song, the author establishes a distinctive pattern of emotional and imaginative movement between the polarities of his experience: a kind of dialectic, whose overall purpose seems to be the mediation of these polarities of race, culture, identity, and temporality. I am using "mediation" here as Lévi-Strauss uses it in discussing myth and, in particular, the function of Trickster-figures—to mean a sort of mental dance between opposites, not effecting their resolution or even reduction but rather providing a useful way of holding conflicted and conflicting experience all in mind, rather as Yeats claimed that his ad hoc all-mediating cosmology allowed him to "hold in a single thought reality and justice."[15]

In these terms, La Flesche's sketch really does have the density and unity (and the pervasive irony!) of a baroque or modernist poem: Nearly every sentence unit makes its own nervous move between opposites and thereby contributes to what seems to me to be the overall effect of the text, one of a bitter and knowing balancing, as if the author were making in words an image of himself not *en abyme* but *en equilibre,* constantly shifting and adjusting to the conflicting claims on his identity as they come to mind, and in the process endeavoring to register a center of gravity for himself.

In the second paragraph, the author's attention fixes on the immediate social concerns of a native son who has returned home to meet his old friends: will they accept him? Will they let him "come home" without ironic difference, despite all that now divides him from them? Far from "going back to the blanket," La Flesche notes that he is ostentatiously dressed to meet his friends in "well starched collar and cuffs and polished shoes," as if forcing the issue of Anglo acculturation, as if deliberately seeking to put off his Omaha guests. But for a wonder, nothing, he claims, seems to interfere with the cordiality of his homecoming. At least for now, all differences between now and then, here and there, *him* and *them*, seem to fade away, or so the author gratefully believes.

He and his brother have, in effect, prepared an old-style Omaha social, presumably conducted in the Omaha language, with a meal, followed by a campfire, the passing of a pipe (the most sacred of all Omaha ritual articles),[16] and then the traditional mutual entertainment of storytelling and singing. All goes well, and, at length, after the storytelling has begun to slow (apparently the stories are not *hi'gon*, myths, which would require a more formal setting, but rather personal tales), La Flesche hearkens to his professional business on the reservation and proposes a session of singing, personalizing the request a little self-consciously: "just as we used to do before I went away." The fact that his guest list happens to include an elderly singing-master further indicates that La Flesche is aiming to combine scholarly business and nostalgic pleasure here—although there is no mention of the graphophone being brought into action.

What ensues in the singing appears to be doubly affirmative and reassuring, although typically he is reticent about his feelings. First, against La Flesche's earlier assertions that his people's music is "passing away" (as the buffalo did), he finds that this particular group of Omaha men— presumably of his own generation for the most part—are able to perform the old songs with confidence and pleasure and to recover "the story of each," meaning, apparently, their origins and local meanings. For the moment, at least, the hills are made to resound with something more substantial and vital than the "dying echoes" of a fading culture.

Second, he proves to himself and to his tribal friends that he is still authoritatively conversant with the Omaha repertory of traditional songs, and not just as a scholar armed with a graphophone but as a performer: "I did my part of the singing," he reports with no small self-satisfaction, the personal implication being that if he knows only a "few" Omaha songs (some five or six hundred out of thousands!), he has confirmed that he knows them both *etically* and *emically*, both as a scholarly outsider and as a functioning insider.

At this emotional high point in the narrative, with the author indicating that he is feeling quite at home, maybe even a little smug, he deftly introduces the first of two dramatic reversals in his story. No sooner has the old singing-master complimented La Flesche for his "memory of songs" than he pointedly challenges that knowledge by introducing yet another song. It is a tense moment, with poignant consequences. I conjecture that the old man has a point to make to his host, one that sharply qualifies the author's earlier assurance that his urban costume and Anglo big-city life and career are inconsequential back on the reservation and that there is not "the slightest difference" between him and his old friends. The old man deliberately chooses a song that everybody in the tipi knows, except for the visitor from Washington; for the first time in this Omaha sing-along, La Flesche is left incapable of performing—with all eyes on him, no doubt.

Without yet knowing *whose* song it is, La Flesche somewhat defensively succeeds in classifying it according to "the vocables used and the terminating notes," thinking now like the scholarly informant who has been collaborating with Alice Fletcher and the musicologist Fillmore in a systematic study of Omaha music. In the schema of that study, what he has heard would fall under the general heading of "Individual Songs"—sung either as solos or by companies of persons who are about to engage in a common action—and, more specifically, under the subheading of "Mystery Songs" ("songs of mystery which directly appeal to the unseen forces that surround man"), but, under the circumstances, such taxonomic knowledge is a painfully inadequate substitute for the simple *emic* knowing of the song, as manifested in his friends' performance of it.[17] No wonder that the author responds with some asperity to the singing-master's challenge to his musical competency: "It must be an old one just recalled by some old man." The reply—as if the final element of a stern lesson—is, in context, unlooked for and devastating: "It is a new song . . . made and given to us by your friend Flying Crow just before he died not very long ago."

What has happened? Characteristically, La Flesche does not directly reveal his emotions here, but given the circumstances as reported, he must be experiencing a pang of conflicting feelings. In the embarrassment and irritation of not knowing a tribal song well known to everyone else, he learns that it was, in fact, recently composed by his boyhood friend and schoolmate Flying Crow, just before his death, about which, presumably, La Flesche has not heard until now! Further evidence, then, that, in truth, he is deeply out of touch, "other" to his people—and the old man's phrasing of the facts seems to be notably disjunctive: "made and given to *us* by *your friend*" (my emphasis).

On the other hand, to the extent that the author is still thinking about the survival of Omaha culture and, failing that, the scholarly preservation of its remaining traditions and artifacts by workers such as himself, there must be something heartening in the recognition that one of his contemporaries has knowledgeably used one of those traditional forms in composing an authentic Omaha mystery song for himself and his friends, thus demonstrating the continuing vitality of the form.[18] But would not La Flesche also ask himself, reacting further and more personally to what he has just learned, "If Flying Crow was capable of composing such work, what could I, La Flesche, compose in my turn?" What he has been brought to—more exactly, what he has brought to us, by means of some very skillful writing—is a moment of dramatized ethnological truth, the personal and the tribal, the experiential and the scholarly, the emic and the etic, all interpenetrating one another.

Who was Flying Crow historically? Although La Flesche explicitly identifies him as one of his schoolmates at the Presbyterian mission school on the Omaha reservation in the 1860s, he does not, in fact, figure in the author's memoir of those schooldays, *The Middle Five* (probably written not long after this sketch, and in a sense narrating early deculturative causes whose adult effects "The Song of Flying Crow" describes), nor is Flying Crow listed in the extensive allotment rolls of the Omaha tribe, as prepared in 1883–1884 by La Flesche's mentor and collaborator Alice Fletcher.[19] Nor does the name appear in the Omaha scholarly literature, from James Dorsey's work in the 1880s on, with one tantalizing exception: In their exhaustive inventory in *The Omaha Tribe* of personal names in relation to clans, Fletcher and La Flesche note under the Hon'gan clan the name Kaxe'giun, "Flying Crow"—adding, gnomically, "two of this name"![20] That one of these two may have been La Flesche's friend is suggested in an unpublished Omaha genealogical record which lists *Kaxe'giun,* "Flying Crow," the son of *Shi'kanon'thin,* born about 1853. His American name was Benjamin Morris.[21]

But could it be that Flying Crow is, in fact, invented, a fictive composite of tribesmen that La Flesche knew and left behind as his career led him out of Omaha life and into the world of those he calls in the first paragraph "civilized people"? Certainly there are plentiful ethnographic and anthropological instances of such inventions: Most of the protagonists in the tribal fictions in *American Indian Life,* for example, are, in one way or another, composite figures. Raising such a question about the historicity of Flying Crow inevitably raises a larger question: Can it be that the whole sketch is, however realistic, fictional, made-up, not an ethnographic personal sketch but a tale in earnest?

I know of no way, short of finding autobiographical evidence from the author himself, to settle either question definitively. But does it really matter, much, as a leading question? As I hope I have already demonstrated, it suffices to recognize that "The Song of Flying Crow" is very much, self-consciously point-for-point, *about* the life and circumstances and intercultural predicaments of Francis La Flesche. And whatever we can document about the real Flying Crow, the author's presentation of him here is expressly, personally symbolic. Rediscovered too late for actual resumption of friendship, he emerges in words and indirectly in music as a haunting symbol of the traditional Omaha life that La Flesche has long since departed from, an alter ego figuring what the author has given up or put aside in the course of his career off the reservation.

Indeed, in his resolutely *pagan* condition (to use the author's own heavily emphasized term), un-Christianized, unschooled (at least in Anglo ways), and unnamed in Anglo terms, Flying Crow may well represent in the author's imagination the programmatic opposite of acculturative processes going back at least two generations in Omaha history, to the years in the middle of the nineteenth century when Francis's half-French father, Joseph/Iron Eye, was seeking controversial accommodations with the Anglo way, and, in particular, was founding his "progressive" Anglo-oriented community on the reservation, which his traditionalist opponents in the tribe scornfully labeled "The Village of the Make-believe White Men." [22] Against such longstanding acculturative processes, there is clearly nothing make-believe about Flying Crow's Indianness.

First and last, however, his significance is personal and immediate to La Flesche. To a scholarly recorder of tribal music and an aspiring writer, Flying Crow appears abruptly, out of the forgotten past, *as a song,* as a work of literary and musical creation, distinctively personal in content, traditional in form. Just as all of the preceding pieces in the songfest were given their "stories" of origin and personal meaning, so the little old man reveals—specifically to La Flesche—why and how Flying Crow composed his mystery song. His motives were, it appears, universal; a kind of Omaha *ars poetica,* in fact. In the face of death, apprehending with the acuity of the dying the mysteries of life, in particular its mysterious combinations of experiential richness and preordained brevity, and the mortal commonality of humans with all living creatures generation after generation, and wanting to express his affirmative feelings about life to his friends in a form that would give them permanence after his death ("the song to hold the words"), he composed the song now bearing his name.[23]

La Flesche's response to this account is expressively terse: "Let's sing it again. I like it and I must learn it." If we have an explicit account of Flying Crow's motives for composing his song, we are left to infer what the author's reasons are for wanting so urgently to possess it. What seems to happen is that the dialectic movement of the sketch, its incessant nervous dance between the polarities of the author's self-awareness, now stops; an unexpected balance point has been reached. For the author to say "I like it and I must learn it" is to assert in one breath two heretofore conflicting kinds of claims on his friend's composition: as yet another Omaha song, a late survival of tradition; and as the final artistic testament of his lost boyhood friend and tribal alter ego. He perforce likes it and must learn it for equally compelling and (for the moment, at least) nonconflicting reasons.

Perhaps it is not considering the moment too curiously to find in La Flesche's dramatization of it an auspicious analogy of purpose linking him and his "pagan" tribesman together, despite their radical differences. That is, as Flying Crow's motive has been to preserve in traditional song, against oblivion, something of his identity and his understanding of life's mystery, so, as he tells us at the outset, La Flesche has aimed at preserving, against cultural oblivion, a record of Omaha culture. The latter effort, in effect, is validated, analogically, by the former.

If, however, Flying Crow's lyrical record was composed for his Omaha friends (now, at last, including La Flesche), for whom does our author perform his conserving work of transcription and interpretation? For Alice Fletcher back in Washington, D.C.? For the Indian Office and the Bureau of American Ethnology? For the academic or institutional people who have loaned him his graphophone? For all the "civilized people" who have shaped his career? *Yes, of course*—although those allegiances are attended with ironies and complications, as we have seen. In the reader's eternal pause at the end of the text, as La Flesche's words run out quietly in renewed rapport with his dead friend, he makes, in effect, a very different answer to the question, "for whom." It is, simply, that *he does not give us the song of Flying Crow*. Not here, in this unpublished manuscript, despite the promise of its title; not in any of his subsequent publications over a long and prolific ethnographic career. "Now," he tells us, "it is so fixed in my memory that I shall never forget it even if I should live to be a hundred years old." In this fashion, then, it is recorded in memory, preserved alive, carried on in the old oral way, cherished but not published, not offered to us as an artifact.

So, the story reaches the second of its two reversals. In the first, the song the author does not know turns out to be by a deceased boyhood friend—in tribal terms, his adult opposite; now, in this second reversal, having learned the song, he deliberately and without comment withholds it from this writing and, in fact, from all subsequent publications! If it is a tacit denial of our expectation as readers to learn something else about the Omaha, it is also an act of self-fashioning refusal, and it stands as a deeply moving affirmation, I want to suggest, of the wholeness of what La Flesche knows about himself.[24] Flying Crow's "pagan" song has, against all the intercultural odds, come home to the author, there to stay. Ethnography has stopped short of betrayal.

Searching in vain through the extensive Omaha literature for the text of Flying Crow's song (and more and more hoping, I must admit, that I would not find it, thereby tending to prove that what appears to be the author's deliberate withholding of it is just that), I came upon the following text in Dorothy Clarke Wilson's biography of La Flesche's celebrated half-sister, Susette. Wilson gives it as an "Omaha Death Song," as heard by Susette's mother, Mary Gale, in her girlhood in the 1840s; hence, it cannot be attributed to Flying Crow. Regrettably, Wilson does not give her source for the song, but it appears to be authentic, a fine specimen of Native American traditional lyric in translation; and whatever its provenience, it seems to catch better than I can the poignantly self-reflexive burden of Francis La Flesche's homage to Flying Crow and his mysterious song:

Where can I go
That I might live forever?
The old fathers have gone to the spirit-land.
Where can I go
That we might live together?[25]

15 / Tradition and Individual Talents
in Modern Indian Writing

SINCE 1971, I HAVE OFFERED UNDERGRADUATE AND graduate courses, in a variety of formats, in Native American literatures. Perhaps I should say, "traditional American Indian literatures," for my main bent has been to explore the art and wisdom of traditional oral narratives and songs, in so far as this is possible given the inherent problems of loss or distortion in transcription and translation, and misunderstanding through our ethnological ignorances. But in all my Indian courses, I do try to devote the last several weeks to the study of poems by a range of modern Indian poets and several modern Indian novels, so as to examine the continuities of the Native literary impulse and the forms it is taking. In the quarter-century or so in which I have been offering such courses myself, a new field of American literary scholarship has grown up, devoted to the study, teaching, and promotion of works by American Indian writers.

The kind of teaching and writing that I do, and what I see my colleagues pursuing, suggests to me that there is an inherent conflict of interests in what we undertake as academic partisans of the work of living Native American writers. It is, in fact, a version of that conflict every student of literature confronts in the first of graduate school—whether to set up as a scholar or as a critic and theorist. In terms of our kind of work with Native writers, it amounts to an ethnically conditioned choice between perspectives: on the one hand, looking at a poem by a Klallam or Acoma poet as an expression of the author's grasp of his or her people's traditions and, in a real sense, as an extension of those traditions; and, on the other hand, looking at the poem as the work of a contemporary American writer, certifiably an Indian, but who probably reads *Newsweek*, Russell Baker, and an indifferent newspaper like the rest of us, and must likewise make poems out of the available words and the interplay of imagination and tradition.

I call it a conflict of interests, notice, not a dilemma—it *can* be resolved, and I will assume that everyone would agree that the resolution should come through some sort of integration, involving a balance of the scholarly perspective and the critical. But what kind of balance? That is the question: and at the risk of dissecting the obvious, I want to consider what can go wrong when, as teachers and well-wishers of Native writing, we lose our balance, or fail to strike it at the outset. Again, it is a very old and familiar issue—but what is important to remember as we encounter it in Indian studies is that our field is still new, and uncertain, and what we are doing now as teachers, critics, reviewers, and editors will have a significant effect on what Indian writers will be able to do in the near future, or at least what they will be given credit for.

Consider the scholar's temptation first. It is very tempting, if a work is as ethnically rich as Leslie Silko's or N. Scott Momaday's fiction, and if one knows something about the relevant ethnography, to try to account for everything in the work according to a postulated mythic and cultural matrix—so that a particular episode is seen to derive from one origin narrative or another, or perhaps a tribal ceremony, and major characters are found to have their prototypes in the mythology. We need our ethnographies, as I will try to demonstrate in a moment; but the danger lies in the way ethnographic literary study tacitly tends to deny the imaginative freedom of the individual writer. The problem is compounded, of course, by the current political expectations of most American readers (college students, for example), that if you are an Indian you write perforce as a spokesperson for your people and their interests. African American writers have chafed for several generations under such expectations; my conversations with younger Indian writers suggest a growing impatience on their part with the role being defined for them by ethnographically slanted teaching and criticism. To quote one of them: "I think of my people's traditions as my most sacred possession as a writer—but dammit, if I want to write a novel about Henry Ford or Mick Jagger, I'll do it! Without such freedom I'm dead as a writer, Indian or otherwise." So it must be, surely, for all our writers, red, black, Asian, Latino, WASP, whatever—in our teaching and commentary, we must be prepared to grant them an artistic range and identity beyond ethnography.

I first identified the abuse under discussion when I was preparing a critical anthology of traditional verbal art from the Oregon Country.[1] I had hoped to find some texts of stories in which European literary materials— French folktales, for example, and Bible narratives—were assimilated by the Native oral imagination, thereby demonstrating, I thought, the vitality and adaptability of the traditional literatures. I found a few such texts, and they are fascinating and significant—but what I came to realize was that most collectors and transcribers to this day impose a kind of *classicism* on Indian literary materials and relegate everything else (assimilations, adaptations, and so on) to the status of impure curiosities, unworthy of serious attention.[2]

It is, I think, only one or two steps from this false classicism with regard to traditional Indian verbal art, to the kind of scholarly abuse that would draw a tight ethnic circle around the meaning and value of an Indian writer's work. In either case, we are in effect telling Indians what they can do with their imaginations—and that is an old and especially shabby "white-eyes" trick.[3] To take an extreme example, would anybody seriously want to "explain" James Welch's unforgettable horse in *Winter in the Blood,* the old gelding Bird, as basically an expression of Blackfeet cultural values, or Plains Indian horse lore? I hope not, but the temptation to construct such scholarly explanations is real.

And in the case of work by Indian writers that does not seem to lend itself to ethnographic interpretation and classification, should we doubt its "Indianness"? A controversy arose over Welch's harrowing second novel, *The Death of Jim Loney,* whose protagonist is a Gros Ventre half-blood in whom Indian and Anglo elements have apparently cancelled each other out; Loney seems to be, in cultural terms, a tragically "unaccommodated" man. Should such a work be classified as an "Indian novel" at all, some have asked—both Anglo critics intent on authenticity and Indians who apparently feel that Welch has an obligation to do better at representing his cultural heritage. Alongside the extraordinary *realist* power of Welch's portrait of Jim Loney, for whom all Native and indeed all human ties inexorably fail, such controversy seems beside the point altogether—but it does illustrate the dangers inherent in our critical designs on Native American writers.[4]

Equally problematic is the now-notorious review of Louise Erdrich's *The Beet Queen* by Leslie Silko. Silko disparages Erdrich's work as an artifact of post-modernism, full of "self-referential writing" and culpably deficient in Indian "consciousness" (Silko's term). One wants to ask the reviewer, "Well, how much 'Indian consciousness' would be *enough?*"[5]

On the other hand, there is what might be called the critic's temptation—most common among reviewers but also prevalent, I suspect, with teachers today, especially those who have chosen to teach an Indian writer's work chiefly for the political correctness of it. This temptation, or rather the abuse it leads to, rarely occurs any more in its purest form, as in a review of a Native writer's book in which little or no recognition is made of his or her background, when such recognition would be in order. Instead, what we get most commonly nowadays is a payment of effusive lip service to the writer's heroic Indian qualities, and to the "Indian heritage" somehow behind the work—as if there were a single homogeneous body of beliefs and traditions common to all American Indians, or a warrantable pan-Indian vision shared by modern Blackfeet, Kiowa, and Spokane writers alike. Such pseudocritical effusions mainly serve a rhetorical purpose: they invest the subject matter with a useful dimension of ethnic mystery, and in effect they preclude the asking of difficult interpretive questions about what in the work may be a bona fide reflection of Blackfeet, Kiowa, or Spokane experience. (There is a tale about a nineteenth-century European tourist on the Great Plains who habitually asked the Crow, Sioux, and other tribesmen he met "to please talk real Indian, not all this gibberish.")

Critics and teachers who are content to engage Native American writing on the level of an all-inclusive "Indianness" are only too well served by books like Hyemeyohst Storm's *Seven Arrows* and Jamake Highwater's *Anpao*, in which an unlocalized Indian mystique is fashioned out of a wide, loose, and sometimes contradictory assortment of Native tribal materials.

Perhaps a centralized American Indian racial identity and aesthetic *is* beginning to emerge in this country, encouraged by travel and education and by archaeological and philological investigations into what the Native cultures have had in common as to origins, folkways, and languages and mythologies, and urged along by political assessments of what they share now, surrounded by, implicated in, and resisting Anglo culture. The Acoma poet Simon Ortiz has argued forcefully that the best Indian writing already embodies "a theme, national in character and scope, common to all American Native peoples and to all peoples indigenous to lands which have suffered imperialism and colonialism"—namely, the theme of *resistance*.[6]

Likewise, political writers like Vine Deloria Jr. are pointing this way, in addressing themselves to the common denominators of modern Indian experience, above and beyond tribal distinctions. Yet Deloria (member of a distinguished Yankton/Standing Rock Sioux family) never loses sight of those traditional distinctions in his appeals for Indian unity and action; he seems to be concerned that the headlong pursuit of a pan-Indian racial, spiritual, and aesthetic consciousness could lead to a grotesque Native re-invention for Indians of that discredited Anglo utensil, the Melting Pot. For Native Americans to stamp themselves with "national" stereotypes, as writers like Highwater seem to do with their sweeping pronouncements on "being Indian," at the expense of the diversity of Indian experience, would be the bitterest historical irony of all.[7]

Sooner or later, of course, the relationship of Native American writing to that sprawling and increasingly pluralistic domain known as American literature will have to be worked out, academic politics and all—in conjunction, let us hope, with the resolution of two related issues: the American literary status of the oral/traditional Native literatures, and the status, too, of Native materials old and new from Canada and Mexico. Will Native American writers come to be seen as constituting a kind of special colony, a valued but distant part of the American Empire, rather as New Zealand poets figure in London? Again, will the works of the likes of James Welch never be seriously addressed in the future by Americanists, except as "Indian novels"? Heaven forbid such colonizing—but those who run to the opposite extreme (as some Indians and their apologists are now doing, in the name of a wholly separate and exclusivist Indian literary aesthetic) are wishfully ignoring, among other things, how much Native writing continues to owe, in the best sense, to Anglo writers like Faulkner and Hemingway, and how deeply the use of the American language involves writers of whatever ethnic identity in its traditions and associations, its inherent forms and pressures. Until such issues become officially important in our study of an expanded American literature, there will continue to be a costly neglect of both the "literary" and the "Americanist" significance of the Native heritage, I think—and a certain regrettable blindness in the purview of American literary scholarship will be perpetuated.[8]

Earlier (to return now to interpretation of contemporary Native writing per se) I warned against the interpretive pursuit of ethnographic significance as an end in itself, as if Native poets and novelists were writing chiefly to validate the conclusions of cultural anthropologists. But, if that extreme line of scholarship is unfruitful and, finally, demeaning to Indian writers, so is critical commentary and teaching that is indifferent to, or ignorant of, ethnography. As Anglo readers, my students and I need to be constantly puzzling over what look like ethnic allusions and turns of style and narrative in their work, even in so austerely unmythic a book as Welch's *Winter in the Blood*. What *is* the Native etymology for the name "Earth Boy" in that novel; why *would* the hero's grandmother hate the Crees with such ancestral passion?

Before Maria Chona sang one of her father's songs to Ruth Underhill, who later included it in *Papago Woman,* she defined with memorable precision the task of interpreting the art of one culture to another. "The song is very short," Chona explained, "because we understand so much."[9] Well, to the extent that today's Indians still think of themselves as members of "we" groups, writing for and some extent *to* such communities, it behooves us to take pains to understand what is implied, hinted at, left out, taken for granted. And—for all its defects and limitations—we need ethnography to do so.[10]

In a general sense, obviously, a knowledge of the history and culture in which works by Native Americans are and have been written can help us to understand their character. For example, one distinctive characteristic of the printed texts of the traditional Indian literatures is their tacit, economical texture, even allowing for losses in transcription and translation; typically, more is suggested in the withholding of narrative and descriptive details than in the outright rendering of them. This is especially true in respect to details of emotion, motivation, and the like. To use Maria Chona's term, by our standards of compression and selection these are generally short songs and stories indeed, with so much tacitly understood. Hence the closest Anglo literary experience to reading myth narratives is (as many writers have pointed out) reading dramatic texts; in either case one is compelled to participate in the story, eking it out of what the characters say and what they do. The succinctness of traditional narrative and song is not just an artistic consequence of cultural homogeneity, either, as Chona's remark about "we" might suggest; it is rather, I think, a deeply ingrained habit of the Native imagination, with enormous implications for what modern Indians do with the stories they tell.

This habit of mind bears on our experience with mainstream American literature. It may be said that whereas in Anglo literature we expect and take pleasure in *redundancy,* in a writer's inventive proliferation of related but differing details (in Renaissance rhetorical terms, *copia*), in Native literature, both traditional and modern, the corresponding emphasis is on *repetition*—ritualized repetition of actions and events in stories, of refrains and other elements in song lyrics, and so on. Traditional performers of a Pueblo emergence-myth or of the Navajo *Night Chant* would no more think of omitting or abridging the stately formulaic repetitions in their material than would a Melville enthusiast tolerate cutting the "redundancies" about whales and whaling in *Moby Dick.* That there is a ceremonial and magical basis for this habit of thought in Indian experience, and also a basis in *orality,* seems obvious.[11]

More specific kinds of ethnographic information are more patently useful and necessary, in regard to particular writers and their special affiliations. In that shadowy region where ethnography blends into biography, for example, we need to know more than we can get from dust-jacket blurbs and publishers' releases about how and where Indian writers have come by their sense of heritage, and about their education as writers. Surely it matters, critically, that N. Scott Momaday does not speak Kiowa (at least did not when he wrote *The Way to Rainy Mountain*), and that he studied intensively at Stanford with Yvor Winters; and it may matter a great deal that one writer grew up on a reservation while another grew up, say, in the Indian community of Minneapolis, and a third was reared in a nuclear family in Boston.

A more obvious task is to elucidate the *geography* of modern Indian fiction and poetry. The sense of place inherent in the Indian cultures is not like the vaguely guilty and nostalgic sense of place and feeling for "land-scape" that we inherit from Romanticism: it is altogether sterner, more pragmatic as to ecological necessities, and more caught up in narrative. But one can do a lot worse for the spatial orientations in Welch's or Silko's novels, or Ortiz's poetry, than to begin with a good highway map and try to lay out the field of action. We all know that there is no limit to the geographical ignorance of Americans, especially easterners—but it does give one pause to hear, as I have, a critic referring to "the priest from Harlem" in *Winter in the Blood* as "a Catholic fugitive from the ghetto." (Harlem, Montana, is east of Chinook.) By the same token, we miss a lot if we fail to locate "Mt. Taylor" as the sacred mountain in *Ceremony* in relation to Silko's other locations—and of course our knowledge of the location sharpens our understanding of the irony of her use of the flat presumptuous Anglo name instead of the Keresan name for the mountain *(Kaweshtima).*

On the score of ceremonies and tribal customs as they figure in modern work—as in the great Pueblo chicken-snatching race in Momaday's *House Made of Dawn* or the citations in the same novel of the Navajo *Night Chant,* or the ritual whipping of Archilde's mother, Catharine, in McNickle's *The Surrounded*—I need say little on behalf of conventional ethnographic research. Most readers can see the need and look the information up. But less obvious cultural allusions by Indian writers may be ignored altogether unless there is a general disposition to survey the culture involved. For example, in *Ceremony,* the hero Tayo frequently responds to moments of stress in the first half of the novel by vomiting. As a detail it graphically adds to our sense of his physical and mental wretchedness, but there is good reason to believe that the vomiting also derives from and alludes to the practice of induced vomiting in Laguna and Acoma healing rituals.[12] Once the connection is made, then what may strike the casual reader as only a realistic symptom of the hero's illness can also be seen more generally as part of Silko's foreshadowing of his cure, according to the implications of the book's title.

Without meaning to slight the monumental tribal cultural studies of scholars like Benedict, Kluckhohn, Parsons, Kroeber, Spier, and Underhill, I would propose that in some cases the most valuable ethnographic resources we can turn to on behalf of modern Indian writing are the transcribed oral-traditional literatures of the tribes or groups in question. This is true not only in terms of the codification of rituals and folkways in myths, but also in terms of less obvious, more personal matters regarding a writer's intentions. For example, to know something about Kiowa folklore is to recognize that N. Scott Momaday has omitted from his personal memoir, *The Way to Rainy Mountain,* all reference to the beloved Kiowa trickster-hero Saynday, a human figure much given, like other Native tricksters, to outrageous and often hilarious scheming for status, power, and physical gratification, sexual and otherwise. Clearly, the Saynday part of the Kiowa mythic heritage was not compatible with what Momaday was trying to do in his book—and this is an exclusion worth knowing about.[13]

But, beyond their ethnographic value, the traditional oral literatures can have direct literary-critical value in helping us to understand what the best of today's writers are up to. Momaday's brilliantly selective use of Kiowa myth-narratives as a subtext for his own highly personal imaginative quest for selfhood in *The Way to Rainy Mountain* is a kind of paradigm of the achievements of these writers as artistic mediators between the old ways and the uncertain present. T. S. Eliot thought he was announcing a new literary mode in 1923 when he praised Joyce's *Ulysses* for following "the mythic method"—which Eliot saw as "a way of manipulating a continuous parallel between contemporaneity and antiquity"[14]—but in fact, traditional American Indian storytellers have always had such a continuous mythic parallel to manipulate, and now their fiction-, play-, and poetry-writing descendants are bringing the Native "mythic method" (the phrase is too simplistic to bear much weight) to bear on Anglo literary forms and contemporary experience, with remarkable results. What they are affirming in doing so is truly auspicious for American culture—a line of literary continuity extending unbroken from the first human occupation of the Americas up to the present.

Among poets, there is Simon Ortiz's wry re-creations of Pueblo Coyote stories, and his eerie gift for introducing into the stuff and nonsense of modern reality the ancient Pueblo talismen—myths, songs, prayers. A toothless, drunken whore under a Gallup bridge begins to sing a rain song:

> She sings then,
> the water in her eye
> is clear as a child
> of rain.

It shall.
It shall.
It shall.
It shall
be
these gifts
to return
again.

It will happen again, cleansing.
The People will rise.[15]

And here is the poet in a jetliner bound for San Diego, craning his neck and mind to keep the known earth in view according to the traditional Pueblo orientation:

I recite the cardinal points of my Acoma life,
the mountains, the radiance coming
from those sacred points, gathering
into the center.
I wonder: what is the movement
of this journey of this jet above the earth?[16]

And there are Duane Niatum's elegant invocations and reconstructions of the Klallam Raven cycle—through many fine books of poetry he has (beyond any other Native poet) established a rich personal relationship with the tribal traditions, amounting to a coherent "grammar" of allusions, so that the naming of Raven the Trickster in one poem seems to illuminate the namings in other poems, as Yeats intended for his works. In "Raven and the Fear of Growing White," for example (from *Songs for the Harvester of Dreams*), Niatum transforms an item of North Coast trickster lore into a powerful prophetic image of the death of the Native world for those who were born of it in modern times. It is, if you will, an authentic instance of "retroactive prophecy," imaginatively continuous with such prophecies in early contact-era narratives—

When the legends cannot feed the fire,
When mother spruce answers no child in the dark,
When hawk fails to reach his shadow on the river,

When First Woman beats hummingbird to the earth,
And salmon eats the rapids until his bones shatter,
When otter steals the long-awaited promise of stars,
And blue-jay stops naming each new storm,
It will end its fear of growing white.[17]

The allusions of the Wasco poet and artist Elizabeth Woody are less programmatic than Niatum's or Ortiz's, but in her writing the traditional stories of her people are vividly *there,* hinted at, deferred to, like the hidden but informing strands and knots in a weaving. Many of Woody's poems have urban, "inner city" settings, in the midst of which mythic characters and episodes suddenly appear with startling effects of irony and humor, as in "Speelyay Thoughts in Seattle" (*speelyay* is Sahaptin for Coyote):

Riding an elevator, my aunties and I, dressed
in fine city clothes, go up in an empty building. Go down.
Talking, laughing, we hear the echo of our happiness.
One aunt says, "This must be how the Huckleberry Sisters feel
inside Coyote's belly, talking of how things go right. Go wrong
when no one listens. . . ."[18]

In one of her stories, "Buckskin," an Indian family living in Portland fondly recall their indomitable '76 Ford Galaxie 500 the way their Plateau ancestors would have cherished the memory of a fine war-horse. The tone of the story includes self-mockery—a Ford is not an Appaloosa steed!—but in the main the author is celebrating the adaptive continuation of old Indian values into the present.[19] On this impulse in her work, Woody has written eloquently:

Through my awareness of my history, tradition is alive. I can take my place
as a responsible link in a dynamic process. My work embodies tradition, not
as static dogma, but as public devotion to the continuation and enrichment
of "the People" . . . We listen, absorbed in the story by blood, by association,
listening with the part that is both one's self and many selves. In the sound
of water, the sheen of river rock—a song, a poem, a story—is faithful to
continuance.[20]

What about Indian *drama?* Given the ferment in Indian writing, one might have expected to find more Native American playwrights by now, but several deterrents may be in effect. One is that the Native theatrical impulse, being traditionally caught up in religious ceremonies (notably among the Southwest and North Coast nations) has not been as adaptable to modern uses as the lyric and narrative traditions have been. Another handicap, surely, is the sheer difficulty of learning how to mount plays: one needs, not just play-scripts, but trained actors, a theater, a receptive audience, and money to guarantee the above! The encouragement of Native playwrights and theater companies ought to hold a high priority for the well-wishers of modern Indian arts.

At least a few gifted playwrights have appeared, notably Tomson Highway, a Canadian Cree based in Toronto, and Hanay Geiogamah, a Kiowa. Geiogamah was first discovered and sponsored by the famous Cafe LaMama group in New York City; his ritual play 49 achieves an extraordinary double vision of traditional and contemporary Indian realities through the staging of a typical Oklahoma Indian drinking fest, or "49," on the site of an ancient Native dancing ground. In the course of the play, the old festivity comes to haunt, vitalize, and *formalize* the new. Near the end, "Night Walker," the ceremonial leader of the play-within-the-play, appears on stage with a *bull-roarer,* surely the first appearance in the history of American theater of that venerable Indian theatrical-religious property! Geiogamah seems to have left off writing plays, in favor of dance (he is the director of the American Indian Dance Theater) but his works mark an auspicious beginning that other Native playwrights, and for that matter, cinema writers, are sure to follow.[21]

Among Indian novelists, to my mind nobody has drawn on Native mythology and narrative tradition with more inventive power and grace than Louise Erdrich (Ojibway), James Welch (Blackfeet/Gros Ventre), and Leslie Silko (Laguna)—three very different writers whose emergence in the '70s and '80s illuminated what has been rightly called an on-going "American Indian literary renaissance."[22] Each is formidably talented and sophisticated in the ways of modern literature—and each has created forms of fiction that are richly continuous with the traditional forms of Native storytelling.

Erdrich's *Tracks,* for example, set in Ojibway country in the dismal final years of the "Allotment" era (1912–24), is wonderfully pervaded with oral stories and storying—gossip, rumor, oral history, myth. One of the novel's two "voices," old Nanapush (named for and a protégé of the great

Ojibway trickster) is an accomplished storyteller, and in fact the overall aim of his tellings in the book is to convey what can survive of traditional Anishinabeg culture to his adoptive granddaughter Lulu, to whom he says, "My girl, listen well." [23]

Welch's *Fools Crow,* arguably the first Indian historical novel, recreates the struggles of the Pikuni band of the Blackfeet nation to carry on in their traditional way against Anglo encroachment, smallpox epidemics, and internal conflicts. On one level, Welch addresses myth and storytelling realistically, letting them appear when and how they would in the lives of his characters, for whom the old stories are at once familiar possessions and full of vital power and mystery. On another level, however, Blackfeet mythology profoundly shapes and informs the novel, as in the way the Blackfeet creation story of Old Man and First Woman seems to charter the basic values of compassion and solidarity that the Pikunis are still trying to uphold against violent change; and in the use Welch makes of his people's myth of Feather Woman, banished from the sky world and her husband Morning Star and her son Scarface and living in a kind of limbo between worlds, which figures as a complex image of the future situation of Fools Crow and his people, living "in exile" in their own land. In effect, the Feather Woman story serves as a resonant mythic subtext for the entire novel. [24]

The same can be said of Leslie Silko's deployment of Keresan mythology in *Ceremony,* except that where Welch incorporates his people's mythology into the design of his novel realistically, in terms of the day-by-day lives of his characters, Silko formally separates her re-tellings of Pueblo myth from her narration of the novel's *fictive* episodes, but does so according to an intricate paralleling and foreshadowing of the latter by the former, so that, again, as in Welch's novel, her fictional story of Tayo, the troubled veteran of World War Two, is literally *underwritten* by her narration of the mythology of his people, the Laguna. [25]

The novel begins, appropriately, with an invocation of Ts'its'tsi'nako, "Thought Woman" or "Spider grandmother," who initiated creation—"She thought outward into space, and what she thought became reality" [26]—and thus stands as a mythic protagonist in Silko's narrative and also as a sacred prototype of the creative artist. The invocation also names Thoughtwoman's two sisters, Nau'ts'ity'i and I'tcts'ity'i, and the former figures crucially in Keresan mythology as "Our Mother," whose eventual anger at human misbehavior causes her to leave the world and withdraw rain and fertility with her, bringing drought and misery to the people, until Hummingbird, Fly, and a few others embark on a long-drawn-out ceremonial quest to regain her favor.[27] Silko is no hidebound traditionalist as an artist, certainly, but nearly every page reveals her loving dedication as a fiction writer to the task of rooting Tayo's story of recovery from personal sterility in the old Laguna stories of Nau'ts'ity'i and the regeneration of the world through the recovery of her goodwill. Indeed, the whole book testifies to the author's commitment to the Native idea of "story" as a symbol, *the* symbol in fact, of the mysterious going-on of life itself. In her own words at the beginning of the novel, "You don't have anything if you don't have the stories. / They are all we have to fight off / illness and death" (p. 1).

Tayo (whose name may derive from a Keresan tale about a young man who after great suffering flew on an eagle to Spider Grandmother's house to be blessed[28]) begins to recover from his catatonia as he remembers visiting as a boy the spring in the narrow canyon, where later he will spend his idyll with the girl, Ts'eh. "Everywhere he looked, he saw a world made of stories, the long ago, time immemorial stories . . . . It was a world alive, always changing and moving, and if you knew where to look, you could see it, sometimes almost imperceptible, like the motion of the stars across the sky" (p. 100).

When Tayo subsequently remembers seeing "a light green hummingbird" on this visit, we recall for him, in keeping with the mythic sub-text of the novel, the heroic role Hummingbird plays in recovering First Mother's goodwill toward mankind, in the origin myth as Silko has already begun to tell it, in advance of the story of Tayo.

The Indian idea of a world full of remembered stories paralleling, impinging on and edifying one's own story is central to Silko's achievement, and I want to conclude by glancing at a wonderful episode in this novel of wonders, which will allow me to sum up, I hope, what I have been saying about the complex interaction of ethnographic scholarship and criticism, and about the remarkable fusion of cultural inheritance and imaginative innovation that writers like Silko are achieving. At the end of Tayo's idyll at the spring with Ts'eh (who I suspect is the old Navajo shaman Betonie's granddaughter), she foresees death for Tayo when he returns to the pueblo, and begins to weep. When Tayo asks why she is crying, she replies: "The end of the story. They want to change it. They want it to end here, the way all their stories end, encircling slowly to choke the life away. The violence of the struggle excites them, and the killing soothes them. They have their stories about us—Indian people who are only marking time and waiting for the end" (p. 243).[29]

In an audacious move, the author here seems to turn directly on us as Anglo readers, accusing us through Ts'eh of enjoying the story of Tayo's ordeal even as the Anglo aesthetic to which we subscribe is preparing the way in our imaginations, not unpleasantly, for the eventual tragic outcome of Tayo's entrapment and death. It is, of course, a just and telling comment on the tradition of novels about Indians by Anglo writers, and on the cultural convention, still very much alive, of "the Vanishing Red Man"; but I think it is more than that. I fancy that it is Silko's declaration of independence, at least for this one novel, from the whole Western tradition of tragic fictions, ending in the heroic death in isolation of the protagonist: "the rest is silence." I imagine Silko to be saying, "The rest is *not* silence. If this is what you are expecting and wanting, reader, I am hereby refusing to gratify you, for I know a different literary tradition, an endless story whose episodes are still unfolding for people like Tayo, sustaining and healing them."

It is hard to imagine a more compelling instance of the freedom of the individual talent, discovering and realizing itself in and against the diverse narrative traditions with which American Indian writers, like all writers in our language, must work. As scholars and teachers, as stewards of a truly expansive and expanding American literature, we must be prepared to learn what we can of the old traditions, Indian as well as Anglo, in order to be able to recognize and appreciate the free play of such talents, and what they create and re-create, and continue.

NOTES

Introduction

1. *Chinook Texts* and *Kathlamet Texts* appeared in Bulletins 20 and 26, respectively, of the U.S. Bureau of American Ethnology. The dialects of Lower Chinook are Shoalwater and Clatsop; those of Upper Chinook are Kathlamet (sometimes considered as a separate language), Clackamas, and Wasco-Wishram. For a complete classification and geography of Chinookan, see Dell Hymes, *"In Vain I Tried to Tell You": Essays in Native American Ethnopoetics* (Philadelphia: University of Pennsylvania Press, 1981), pp. 4–5, 15–23.

2. T. T. Waterman's "The Explanatory Element in the Folktales of the North American Indians," *Journal of American Folklore* 27 (1914):1–54. Waterman's study and Robert Lowie's "The Test Theme in North American Mythology" (*Journal of American Folk-lore* [1908]:97–144), are especially valuable and should be better known today. Paul Ehrenreich's books from this period include *Die Sonne in Mythos* (1910) and *Die Allgemeine Mythologie* (1915).

3. In particular, Stith Thompson's literary anthology, *Tales of the North American Indians* (first published in 1928 and still the best collection of Indian narratives in print), Paul Radin's incomparable works on the Winnebago literary heritage, including *The Trickster* and *The Road of Life and Death,* and Melville Jacobs's equally monumental contributions as editor and interpreter of the Clackamas Chinook

repertory (*Clackamas Chinook Texts, The Content and Style of an Oral Literature,* and *The People Are Coming Soon*) should be mentioned; all are indispensable. Twenty-eight years of solitary labor elapsed between Jacobs's transcription of the Clackamas material in 1929–30 and the publication of volume one of *Clackamas Chinook Texts*! Both volumes are out of print.

4. A list of Anglo poets and writers who are knowledgeably, accountably "in touch" with Native American and Canadian literatures might begin with Gary Snyder, William Stafford, W. S. Merwin, David Wagoner, Don Berry, Jerome Rothenberg, Ted Hughes, Dee Brown, James Reaney, George Ryga, Brian Swann, Frank Herbert, Ursula Le Guin, Howard Norman, Thomas Sanchez, William Heyen, Craig Leslie. An incomplete list of important Native American writers would include N. Scott Momaday (Kiowa-Apache), Leslie Silko (Laguna), Simon Ortiz (Acoma), Duane Niatum (Klallam), Marnie Walsh (Sioux), Ray Young Bear (Mesquakie), Gerald Vizenor (Ojibwa), James Welch (Blackfeet), Vine Deloria (Sioux), Lance Henson (Cheyenne), Hanay Geiogamah (Kiowa), Paula Gunn Allen (Laguna-Sioux), Louise Erdrich (Ojibway), Michael Dorris (Modoc), Sherman Alexie (Spokane), Joy Harjo (Creek), Diane Glancy (Cherokee), Elizabeth Woody (Wasco), Luci Tapahanso (Navajo), Linda Hogan (Chickasaw), Maurice Kenny (Mohawk), Ofelia Zepeda (Papago). See essay 15, this volume.

5. Theodore Roethke, "The Longing," in *The Collected Poems of Theodore Roethke* (Garden City: Doubleday, 1968), p. 189. Like Thoreau at the end of his life, Roethke at the end of his was projecting some sort of formal engagement with Indian lore.

6. Jarold Ramsey, *Coyote Was Going There* (Seattle: University of Washington Press, 1977).

7. See Hymes's many essays and his landmark study, *"In Vain I Tried to Tell You"* (1981); Dennis Tedlock's edition of Zuni literature, *Finding the Center* (1978), and his essays in *The Spoken Word and the Work of Interpretation* (1983); and J. Barre Toelken's "Poetic Retranslation and the 'Pretty Languages' of Yellowman," with Tacheeni Scott, in *Traditional Literatures of the American Indian,* ed. Karl Kroeber (Lincoln: University of Nebraska Press, 1981), pp. 65–116. The ethnopoetics journal *Alcheringa,* founded by Tedlock and Jerome Rothenberg, is also recommended.

8. Or shall we follow the outlandish procedure advertised for Ruth Beebe Hill's novel *Hanta Yo,* whereby her English text was supposedly translated into archaic Lakota Sioux and then back into something like English?

9. See Hymes, "Discovering Oral Performance and Measured Verse in American Indian Narrative," originally published in *New Literary History* 8:431–57; revised and reprinted in Hymes, *"In Vain I Tried to Tell You",* chap. 8.

10. Laura Bohannon, "Shakespeare in the Bush," in Allan Dundes, *Every Man His Way* (Englewood Cliffs: Prentice-Hall, 1968), pp. 477–86.

11. See Karl Kroeber's stimulating comparative essays "Deconstructionist Criticism and American Indian Literature," *Boundary 2,* 7 (1979):73–92) and "Poem, Dream, and the Consuming of Culture," *Georgia Review* 32 (1978):266–80.

Kroeber's work as the founding editor of the *Newsletter* of the Association for the Study of American Indian Literatures (ASAIL) has contributed much to the academic growth of the field.

12. Archie Phinney, *Nez Perce Texts,* Columbia University Contributions to Anthropology, vol. 25 (1934), p. ix.

13. Edward Curtis, *The North American Indian* (Norwood, MA: Plimpton Press, 1911), vol. 8, pp. 145–46. As a petroglyph, Tsagiglálal still stands, looking south across the Columbia River at the head of the Long Narrows, just above the site (now inundated by a dam) of 10,000 years of continuous Native habitation.

1 / Creations and Origins

1. Edward S. Curtis, *The North American Indian* (Norwood, MA: Plimpton Press, 1924), vol. 13, p. 210; narrator "Long Wilson."

2. Mircea Eliade, *Myth and Reality* (New York: Harper and Row, 1963), pp. 21–38.

3. T. T. Waterman, "The Explanatory Element in the Folktales of the North American Indians," *Journal of American Folklore* 27 (1914):1–54. Waterman's study, and others from this time by other associates of Boas and by Boas himself, amount to a devastating refutation of then-recent work by German "solar-myth" proponents, especially Paul Ehrenreich. See Richard Dorson, "The Eclipse of Solar Mythology," in *Myth: A Symposium,* ed. T. A. Sebeok (Bloomington: Indiana University Press, 1972), pp. 25–63. Certainly, inasmuch as the Native mythologies present their worlds as basically intelligible, they are involved with explanatory functions, just as any imaginative literature is, to some extent. The work of Lévi-Strauss tends in fact to view myth as a kind of "higher etiology" or "General Theory" of reality. The discoveries consequent on such a view have revolutionized our concept of how "primitive" peoples used their minds, but too often we seem to be asked to forget that those "minds" (like ours) also cherish their traditional narratives for all the idiosyncratic pleasures—clarification of personal identity, love of heightened language, delight in entertainment, and so forth   which literary art can afford.

4. Percy Cohen, "Theories of Myth," *Man* (1969):337–53.

5. Bronislaw Malinowski, "Myth in Primitive Psychology," in *Magic, Science, Religion, and Other Essays* (Boston: Free Press, 1948), p. 77. This essay is a central statement of the social-charter theory of myth, and its importance for the literary study of American Indian myth-narrative is, I think, considerable. Malinowski will not let us forget that myth was and is functional in tribal cultures beyond what we find in our own imaginative literature, and that the forms of myth reflect these functions. See also W. R. Bascom, "Four Functions of Folklore," *Journal of American Folklore* 67 (1954):333–49.

6. Dell Hymes, *"In Vain I Tried to Tell You": Essays in Native American Ethnopoetics* (Philadelphia: University of Pennsylvania Press, 1981), p. 337.

7. Curtis, *North American Indian,* vol. 13, p. 210.

8. Eliade, *Myth and Reality,* pp. 36 ff.

9. See, for example, the wonderfully stately Zuni emergence myth in Dennis Tedlock's "The Beginning" in *Finding the Center* (New York: Dial Press, 1972), pp. 223–98. See also Tedlock's essay on understanding such works, "The Spoken Word and the Work of Interpretation," in *Traditional American Indian Literatures,* ed. Karl Kroeber (Lincoln: University of Nebraska Press, 1981), pp. 45–64.

10. See the personalized creation story of the Paiute "doctor" Sam Wata, in Jarold Ramsey, *Coyote Was Going There* (Seattle: University of Washington Press, 1977), pp. 437–38, which ends "Maybe the white people don't know about the beginning of this earth." The organization of *Coyote Was Going There* was conceived to emphasize the distinctive "imagination of place" of the Northwestern Indians, region by region; no Native group had a more richly "storied" homeland than did the Klamaths.

11. George Bird Grinnell, *Blackfoot Lodge Tales* (1892; reprint ed., Lincoln: University of Nebraska Press, 1962), pp. 137–39. Grinnell was an editor and naturalist, not an academic ethnographer, but his transcripts are generally trustworthy, as can be seen by comparing them with those of Clark Wissler and D. C. Duvall, *Blackfoot Mythology,* Anthropological Papers of the American Museum of Natural History, vol. 2 (1908). I have discussed the ethnographic and literary merits of Grinnell's work more fully in an introduction to a reissue of Grinnell's intertribal collection, *The Punishment of the Stingy and Other Stories* (Lincoln: University of Nebraska Press, 1982).

12. In the Wissler-Duvall version, Old Man undertakes the creation of human life in cooperation with "Old Woman," who allows Old Man "first say" in everything provided that she gets the "second say" (p. 20).

13. In the Wissler-Duvall version, Old Woman says, "It is better for people to die forever, for if they did not die forever, they would never feel sorry for each other, and there would be no sympathy in the world" (p. 20).

14. For example, see Kiowa and Modoc narratives in Alice Marriott and Carol K. Rachlin, *American Indian Mythology* (New York: New American Library, 1972), pp. 223–29.

15. See my discussion of these issues in regard to Orpheus narratives, in essay 4.

16. Samuel Beckett, *Endgame* (New York: Grove Press, 1958), pp. 87–91.

17. It is a striking fact that, in two of our most important collections of Western Indian traditional narratives—from the Wasco-Wishram and Clackamas Chinookan groups—no creation myths exist. It may be an unhappy accident of cultural loss or transcription; or it may be that these Indians simply didn't imagine their beginnings in the accustomed way.

18. The Joshua myth is in Leo J. Frachtenberg and Livingston Farrand, "Shasta and Athapascan Myths from Oregon," *Journal of American Folklore* 28 (1915) 224–28, narrated by Charlie Depoe. A garbled version of the myth was collected in Chinook Jargon by J. Owen Dorsey in 1884: "Indians of Siletz Reservation, Oregon,"

American Anthropologist 2 (1889):58–60. For cultural details, see Philip Drucker, "The Tolowa and Their Southwest Oregon Kin," *University of California Publications in American Archaeology and Ethnology,* vol. 36, no. 4 (1937), pp. 221–99. Drucker blandly notes about the scope of his ethnographic study that "lack of time prevented my collecting mythology. The tales are long and numerous" (p. 268), and he then offers a four sentence abstract of what appears to be the story under discussion here. Even from a strictly ethnographic point of view, such indifference to the literary aspect of a Native culture is deplorable.

There is additional information on the Joshuas, or "Tututnis" as they are called in most of the literature, in Curtis, *North American Indian,* vol. 13, pp. 93–95, including a long, hair-raising autobiographical narrative of contact-era life by a Joshua elder of Charlie Depoe's generation.

19. There are in fact twenty-three references to numbers between 2 and 16: of numbers through 13, only 7 and 11 are left out, as if in deference to (or avoidance of) the main Caucasian cult-numbers.

20. Drucker notes that the "Creator" is a "rather remote" being to the Tututnis—sometimes addressed in prayer, after being offered tobacco-smoke (p. 267). In Dorsey's version from Siletz, the creator ("Old Man") has an assistant, but he is something of a trickster, it appears, in tricking the first woman into sleeping with him rather than the Creator! (The woman is not created: she merely walks in from the south.)

21. For a list of Earth-diver stories across the country, see Motif Index No. A 811; a short list is given by Stith Thompson in *Tales of the North American Indians* (Bloomington: Indiana University Press, 1968), p. 279.

22. In the Siletz version, the Creator likewise sees footprints as soon as land appears, and deplores them—"that is sickness! It is bad!"—but is unable to wash them away.

23. The Midgard serpent was, of course, one of the monstrous creations of the Nordic trickster Loki.

24. Frachtenberg and Farrand, "Shasta and Athapascan Myths," p. 225.

25. Claude Lévi-Strauss, "The Structural Study of Myth," in *Structural Anthropology* (New York: Doubleday, 1967), pp. 209–14.

26. The Australian aborigines believe in the "al-cheringa" or Dream Time of creation.

27. Another ubiquitous American Indian motif is that of the "Star Husbands," Motif Index No. C15, in which young girls "wish on stars" for husbands, and are usually unhappily rewarded. In general, wishing is a potent and by no means idle exercise in Western Indian culture. See a seriocomic example of this, "She Deceived Herself with Milt," from Jacobs's Clackamas collection, in Ramsey, *Coyote Was Going There,* pp. 102–3, and commentary on the story in essay 8.

28. Frachtenberg and Farrand, "Shasta and Athapascan Myths," p. 227.

29. Homer, *The Odyssey, Book One,* trans. Richmond Lattimore (New York: Harper and Row, 1967), p. 32.

30. The extent to which myths serve to expound "lore" per se, often very practically, should not be underestimated. The Nez Perce editors of *Nu Mee Poom Tit Wa Tit: Nez Perce Legends* (The Nez Perce Tribe, 1972) point out, in stressing this function, that one story in their anthology names and specifies the taste of twenty-two plants, another tells "in detail how to fashion good straight arrows," and so on (p. xv).

31. Frachtenberg and Farrand, "Shasta and Athapascan Myths," p. 227.

2 / Coyote and Friends

1. See essay 1, pp. 4–7. Again, I want to acknowledge Percy Cohen's excellent, astringent essay, "The Study of Myth," in *Man* (1969), pp. 337–53; and also MacLinscott Ricketts's "The North American Indian Trickster," based on his doctoral dissertation, in *History of Religions* 5(2) (1966):327–50. Ricketts tends to invest the Trickster with too much intellectuality, I think, but his essay is unquestionably the best comprehensive study of Indian tricksters since Radin, and is indispensable, as is Barbara Babcock-Abraham's survey, "'A Tolerated Margin of Mess': The Trickster and His Tales Reconsidered," in *Journal of the Folklore Institute* 11 (1975):145–86. To my knowledge, no one has yet taken up in earnest what may be the crucial question about the trickster as a global figure: that is, why is he almost invariably male? Or to put it more exactly (given the sexual ambiguities of many tricksters), why do there seem to so few female tricksters in world folklore? Is this remarkable apparent omission merely the consequence of a too narrow, perhaps sexist concept of tricksterhood—or is it an authentic phenomenon? If authentic, it must have important cultural and psychological meanings.

2. Melville Jacobs, *The Content and Style of an Oral Literature* (New York: Wenner-Gren Foundation, 1959), pp. 136–77.

3. A convenient (and mind-boggling) example of a trickster-transformer's career in synopsis is given by Elizabeth Jacobs in her *Nehalem Tillamook Tales* (Eugene: University of Oregon Books, 1959), pp. 198–200.

4. Barre Toelken gives an amusing illustration of the importance of these trickster distinctions to Indians in his excellent *Dynamics of Folklore* (Boston: Houghton Mifflin, 1979). A friend of Toelken's, from the Coos tribe of the Oregon coast, told a Navajo a Coos Coyote story wherein Coyote steals and eats fish. The Navajo responded, "That's not a Navajo story" because the Navajo Coyote would never eat fish! (p.192)

5. See Hymes, "The 'Wife' Who 'Goes Out' like a Man: Reinterpretation of a Clackamas Chinook Myth," in *"In Vain I Tried to Tell You"* (Philadelphia: University of Pennsylvania Press, 1981), pp. 274–308. See also essay 5, this volume, and Frank Kermode's observations in *Nineteenth Century Fiction* 33 (June 1978):152–54.

6. Ella Deloria, *Dakota Texts,* Publications of the American Ethnological Society, vol. 14 (1932); republished in abridged form as *Dakota Texts,* ed. Agnes Picotte and Paul Pavich (Vermillion: Dakota Press, 1978).

7. Claude Lévi-Strauss, "The Structural Study of Myth," in *Structural Anthropology* (New York: Doubleday, 1967), p. 223.

8. W. B. Yeats, *A Vision* (London: Macmillan, 1961), p. 25.

9. Yeats, *A Vision,* p. 189. There is even a certain pawky tricksterish element in the final version of *A Vision,* related to the poet's uneasiness about what people would make of his work—for example, his disguise as "Giraldus" in Dulac's woodcut, the elaborate silliness of the fictive prefatory chapters, and so on.

10. Ted Hughes, interview in *The Listener,* July 30, 1970, p. 149.

11. Paul Radin, *The Trickster* (New York: Schocken Books, 1972), p. 21.

12. Sigmund Freud, "Wit and Its Relation to the Unconscious," in *The Basic Writings of Sigmund Freud,* trans. and ed. by A. A. Brill (New York: Modern Library, 1946). For an exemplary literary application of Freud's view, see C. L. Barber, *Shakespeare's Festive Comedy* (Cleveland and New York: World Publishing Co., 1963). I have drawn in this section from the "Introduction" to my anthology of traditional Native literature from the Oregon Country, *Coyote Was Going There* (Seattle: University of Washington Press, 1977).

13. Sigmund Freud, *The Future of an Illusion,* trans. W. D. Robson-Scott (New York: Doubleday, 1961), p. 18.

14. For example, Wakdjunkaga's final apotheosis. In the literature of the interior Salish of British Columbia, Coyote goes away after his great transforming journey upriver, but it is taken by some as a possibility that he will eventually return. See essays 11 and 12 of this book on adaptations of this belief in response to the coming of the whites. In "Deconstructionist Criticism and American Indian Literature," *Boundary 2,* 7 (Spring 1979), Karl Kroeber explores how, in the case of the Mojave culture hero Mastamho, "The story [of Mastamho's end] helps to construct the Mojave culture by deconstructing its culture hero" (p. 84). Again, I would question whether tricksters are really identifiable with "culture heroes," but Kroeber's witty identification of Coyote and Co. as "deconstructionists" sheds light on them—and trenchantly exposes some of the limits of deconstructionist criticism.

15. Radin, *The Trickster,* pp. 150–54.

16. Élémire Zolla, *The Writer and the Shaman* (New York: Harcourt Brace Jovanovich, 1973), another entry in the apparently endless line of enthusiastic and generally ill-informed misappropriations of Indian culture to our own.

17. E. M. Forster, *Aspects of the Novel* (New York: Harcourt Brace, 1954), p. 55.

18. J. Barre Toelken and Tacheeni Scott, "Poetic Retranslation and the 'Pretty Languages' of Yellowman," in *Traditional American Indian Literatures,* ed. Karl Kroeber (Lincoln: University of Nebraska Press, 1981), pp. 80–81.

19. Géza Róheim, "Culture Hero and Trickster in North American Indian Mythology," in *Selected Papers, International Congress of Americanists,* ed. Sol Tax (Chicago: University of Chicago Press, 1952), vol. 3: *Indian Tribes of North America,* p. 193. In "The Function of Humor in Three Nez Perce Indian Myths," *American Imago* 11 (1954):249–61, Dell Skeels explores three Coyote narratives psychoanalytically in terms of the effects of their humor. Speaking of an audience's likely

identification with Coyote, Skeels argues that "the ego because it never gave up its supremacy through conscious identification has no difficulty in reasserting its control, and the super-ego is served by the punishment of Coyote" (p. 260).

20. Such commentary owes something to the proposition of Otto Rank in *The Myth of the Birth of the Hero* (New York: Vintage Books, 1959) that "the true hero . . . is the ego, which finds itself in the hero, by reverting to the time when the ego was itself a hero, through its first heroic act, i.e., the revolt against the father" (p. 84). One wishes that Rank had seen fit to turn his Freudian attentions to the Trickster, as a logical follow-on to the Hero. For the Hero as follow-on to the Trickster, see Joseph Henderson, "Ancient Myths and Modern Man," in *Man and His Symbols* (New York: Laurel, 1968), pp. 103 ff.

21. Erik Erikson, "Observations on the Yurok: Childhood and World Image," *University of California Publications in American Archaeology and Ethnology,* vol. 35, no. 10 (1934–43), p. 299. See also Erikson's *Childhood and Society* (New York: Norton, 1950).

22. Radin, *The Trickster,* pp. 19–20.

23. In *Content and Style,* Jacobs notes how, in some individual stories, Coyote appears to learn, mature, profit from his experiences in the course of the plot — see, for example, "Badger and Coyote Were Neighbors," pp. 27–36. As will be seen in detail in essay 4, Western tricksters do appear as the protagonists of a few serious, even tragic, narratives, as in the "Orpheus" stories of the Columbia River Chinookans and the Nez Perces, in which their tricksterish natures are subtly modulated but not completely lost sight of.

24. See, for example, the Chinookan version in Katherine Berry Judson, *Myths and Legends of the Pacific Northwest* (Chicago: A. C. McClurg, 1910), pp. 74–76.

25. See the remarks by the Navajo storyteller Yellowman, p. 34; also Maria Chona's memories of Papago stories as pedagogy in *The Autobiography of a Papago Woman,* ed. Ruth Underhill, Memoirs of the American Anthropological Association, vol. 46 (1936), pp. 5 ff.; and Judy Trejo, "Coyote Tales: A Paiute Commentary," in *Readings in American Folklore,* ed. Jan Brunvand (New York: Norton, 1979), pp. 192–98.

26. Bruno Bettelheim, *The Uses of Enchantment: The Meaning and Importance of Fairy Tales* (New York: Knopf, 1976), p. 12.

27. For a convenient summary, see Ricketts, "North American Indian Trickster," pp. 328–34.

28. Radin, *The Trickster,* pp. 168–69. Apropos of such ideas, Cohen remarks, "If myth is a way of anchoring the present in the past, then it will draw to it the symbols and images of primordial awareness which, in most human minds, will be linked with what is infantile and repressed in the unconscious"("Study of Myth," p. 350).

29. Victor Turner, *The Ritual Process* (Chicago: Aldine, 1969, The Lewis Henry Morgan Lectures of 1966 at the University of Rochester), pp. 94–95.; also idem, *Drama, Fields, and Metaphors* (Ithaca: Cornell University Press, 1974), pas-

sim, and his entry on "Myth" in *International Encyclopedia of the Social Sciences*, vol. 10 (New York: Macmillan, 1968), pp. 550–51.

30. Radin, *The Trickster*, p. 160.

31. Aeschylus, "Prometheus Bound," trans. David Grene, *Greek Tragedies*, vol. 1 (Chicago: University of Chicago Press, 1964), p. 81. See also Stanley Diamond's essay "Plato and the Definition of the Primitive," in *Primitive Views of the World*, ed. Stanley Diamond (New York and London: Columbia University Press, 1969), pp. 170–93.

32. See Ricketts, "North American Indian Trickster," pp. 328–29.

33. *Tales of the North American Indians*, ed. Stith Thompson (Bloomington and London: University of Indiana Press, 1968), p. 22.

34. See essay 1, this volume.

35. Again, Yellowman's observations on Coyote come to mind, pp. 34–36.

36. Lévi-Strauss, *Structural Anthropology*, especially pp. 250 ff.; also on brico-lage as a basic myth-making process, see idem, *The Savage Mind* (Chicago: University of Chicago Press, 1973), pp. 16–23.

37. James Teit, "Folktales of Salishan Tribes," in *Memoirs of the American Folklore Society* 11 (1917):82.

38. Gary Snyder, "The Incredible Survival of Coyote" in *The Old Ways* (San Francisco: City Light Books, 1977), p. 81. See also the appreciations of Old Man Coyote in William Bright's well-edited and delightful anthology, *A Coyote Reader* (Berkeley and Los Angeles: University of California Press, 1993). The current wide-spread interest of poets and writers in Coyote lore is more than a literary fad: Snyder, Hughes, and others may be telling us that we are in need of trickster fig-ures suited to our culture, lest we become increasingly vulnerable to their demonic antitypes, the charismatic cult-leaders. One thinks of Charles Manson and his mur-derous cult-family alongside Ken Kesey and his "Merry Pranksters."

39. E. Jacobs, *Nehalem Tillamook Tales*, pp. 198–200; Radin, *The Trick-ster*, p. 39.

40. Charles Olson, "Human Universe," in *Charles Olson: Selected Writings*, ed. Robert Creeley (New York: New Directions, 1966), p. 66.

41. Radin, *The Trickster*, pp. 168–69.

42. In this connection, Dell Hymes has pointed out to me that there is a plu-rality of names for Coyote in Clackamas Chinook.

43. The sources of these narratives are, respectively: Melville Jacobs, *Kula-puya Texts*, University of Washington Publications in Anthropology, vol. 11 (1945), p. 91, narrator: John B. Hudson. (I am using, with his permission, Dell Hymes's verse version of Jacobs's text, as first published in the *Journal of the Folklore Institute* [1981]:148–49); Robert Lowie, "Myths and Traditions of the Crow," *Anthropologi-cal Papers of the American Museum of Natural History* 25 (1918):30–31, narrator: Medicine Crow; Pamela Munro, "Two stories by Nellie Brown," in *Yuman Texts*, ed. Margaret Langdon, *International Journal of American Linguistics*, North Ameri-can Texts Series, vol. 1, no. 3 (1976), p. 48, narrator: Mrs. Nellie Brown.

In the Kalapuya text, Coyote's masturbation would presumably be a sacrilegious act in a sweathouse; his appetite for "news" and the trouble it causes him are vintage Coyote. For commentary on the story, see Hymes, *"In Vain I Tried to Tell You,"* pp. 91 ff. In the Crow text a degree of satire against post-contact dandyism among the Crows is to be suspected; certainly a general theme of *vanita* is present here. The Mojave ethnographic text charmingly suggests how Coyote and his functions survive today, when Indian children may well first encounter him in a "picture book"!

3 / The Poetry and Drama of Healing

1. A. L. Kroeber, *Handbook of the Indians of California*, Smithsonian Institution, Bureau of American Ethnology Bulletin, no. 78 (Washington, D.C.: Government Printing Office, 1925), p. 321.

2. John Bierhorst, ed. *Four Masterworks of American Indian Literature: Quetzalcoatl / The Ritual of Condolence / Cuceb / The Night Chant* (Tucson: University of Arizona Press, 1984).

3. For a summary of Native American metaphysical assumptions that is both incisive and comprehensive, see Paula Gunn Allen, "The Sacred Hoop: A Contemporary Perspective," in *Studies in American Indian Literature: Critical Essays and Course Designs,* ed. Paula Gunn Allen (New York: Modern Language Association, 1983), pp. 3–22. Two useful surveys of Indian traditional medical practice are Eric Stone, *Medicine among the American Indians; Clio Medica: A Series of Primers on the History of Medicine,* vol. 7 (1932; reprint ed., New York: Hafner, 1962); and Virgil J. Vogel, *American Indian Medicine* (Norman: University of Oklahoma Press, 1970).

4. Probably the most vivid and accessible *inside* account of holistic curing practices and "sympathetic magic" as it operates for Indians is given by Maria Chona, Ruth Underhill's Papago informant in *Papago Woman,* Case Studies in Cultural Anthropology (New York: Holt-Rinehart and Winston, 1979).

5. Leslie Marmon Silko, *Ceremony* (New York: New American Library/Signet Books, 1977), p. 132.

6. N. Scott Momaday's personal memoir, *The Way to Rainy Mountain* (1969; reprint ed., New York: Ballentine Books, 1973) focuses on Kiowa belief in the power of language; see especially a passage on "the arrowmaker," pp. 62–3. See also Gary Witherspoon's brilliant study, the best of its kind ever made of a Native language, *Language and Art in the Navajo Universe* (Ann Arbor: University of Michigan Press, 1977).

7. The Tuscaroras, originally of North Carolina, were adopted into the League in the early eighteenth century; hence, one often sees references to "Six Nations."

8. Lewis Henry Morgan, *League of the Iroquois* (1851; reprint ed., Secaucus, NJ: Citadel Press, 1972).

9. See Anthony F. C. Wallace, *The Death and Rebirth of the Seneca* (New York:

Random House/Vintage Books, 1972), especially pt. 2, "The Decline of the Iroquois," pp. 109–236.

10. Throughout this essay, I follow John Bierhorst's text and translation of the *Condolence Ritual,* in *Four Masterworks of American Indian Literature,* pp. 121–68. All quotations are from this edition and are cited as *CR,* followed by the page number.

11. See A. F. C. Wallace, *Death and Rebirth of the Seneca,* pp. 97–8; Morgan, *League of the Iroquois,* pp. 60–1; and Paul A. W. Wallace, *The White Roots of Peace* (Philadelphia: University of Pennsylvania Press, 1946). Repeatedly, even as it moves toward restoration of the League's shaken unity, the *Condolence Ritual* acknowledges that its success may be "for one poor/short day" *(CR,* pp. 155, 161–62, etc.)

12. In a portion of the Founders' Roll Call that interrupts Article Three and directly addresses the dead sachem, the "persons" meant in the ceremony's "you" are explicitly identified: "know that she, *society,* is grieving. / They are mourning in their minds when he / did pass away, he on whom we depended" *(CR,* p. 138).

13. Melville Jacobs, *The Content and Form of an Oral Literature: Clackamas Chinook Myths and Tales,* Viking Foundation Publications in Anthropology, no. 26 (New York: Wenner-Gren Foundation for Anthropological Research, 1959), pp. 27–29; reprinted in Jarold Ramsey, ed., *Coyote Was Going There: Indian Literature of the Oregon Country* (Seattle: University of Washington Press, 1977), pp. 95–99.

14. Bierhorst (1984) quotes J. N. B. Hewitt as saying, "The psychological insight of the framers of this wonderful ritualistic address is without question unsurpassed in any other composition of its kind in any other literature of the world" (p. 117). I would agree—except to make the same claim for the Navajo *Night Chant.*

15. The Requickening sequence is dramatically interrupted after the third article in order that the Eulogy or Roll Call of the Founding Fathers—which itself has been rather dramatically broken off earlier in order for the mourning moiety to welcome the arrived clearminded delegation—can be concluded. After the clearminded orator completes the recitation of each article, the strand of wampum that is its mnemonic text is delivered to the mourners, and *their* orator repeats the text of the article verbatim.

16. See A. F. C. Wallace's "Dreams and the Wishes of the Soul," in *Death and Rebirth of the Seneca,* pp. 59–75, for a full and illuminating account of the importance of dreaming and dream-telling in Iroquoian culture; see especially the summary of observations made by the Jesuit missionary Father Ragueneau in 1649 (pp. 61–62), which seem to anticipate Freud on the language and interpretation of dreams point for point.

17. Cited in Eric Henderson, "Kaibeto Plateau Cermonialists: 1860–1980," in *Navajo Religion and Culture: Selected Views,* ed. David M. Brugge and Charlotte J. Frisbie (Santa Fe: Museum of New Mexico Press, 1982), pp. 164–75. Against the precipitous decline in recent years in the ranks of competent ceremonialists, Henderson notes that a school for medicine men has been established.

18. All quotations from *The Night Chant* are from John Bierhorst's edition in *Four Masterworks of American Indian Literature* and are cited parenthetically as *NC*, followed by the page number.

19. Bierhorst, *Four Masterworks of American Indian Literature*, p. 281.

20. Ibid., pp. 288–89.

21. That the *Night Chant* has apparently attracted to itself this initiation ritual for children (at the beginning of the fifth and seventh days) indicates, as Bierhorst (1984) suggests (pp. 344–55, note 56), how sacred the *Chant* is to the Navajos. All who partake of it—patients, ceremonialists, onlookers, children undergoing a different ritual within its context—will benefit from its unique power.

22. Personal communication in February 1986 from Dr. Stephen Kunitz, University of Rochester School of Medicine. Dr. Kunitz is one of the pioneers of medical research among the Navajos. See his contributions on Navajo culture and health care, Stephen J. Kunitz and Jerrold E. Levy, "Navajos," in *Ethnicity and Health Care*, ed. Alan Harwood (Cambridge: Harvard University Press, 1981), pp. 337–96; and Jerrold E. Levy and Stephen J. Kunitz, *Indian Drinking: Navajo Practices and Anglo-American Theories* (New York: John Wiley, 1974).

23. See Kunitz and Levy, "Navajos"; and Gladys A. Reichard, "Theory of Disease" and "Theory of Curing," in her *Navajo Religion: A Study of Symbolism* (Tucson: University of Arizona Press, 1983), pp. 80–122.

24. Bierhorst, *Four Masterworks of American Indian Literature*, p. 282.

25. Ibid.

26. Ibid., pp. 283–85.

27. Bierhorst notes, with reference to the Matthews text, that although Navajo symmetry and number-magic would seem to call for a *fourth* sand painting to be performed on the Eighth Day, it "is said to have been withheld—or forbidden—by the gods *(NC,* 324).

28. Norman Cousins, *The Healing Heart: Antidotes to Panic and Helplessness* (New York: Norton, 1983), p. 131. In his Introduction, D. Bernard Lown considers "the lethal power of words" (p. 13) in the doctor-patient relationship and observes with concern that many physicians seem to be "abandoning the power of the word as a therapeutic tool" (p. 12). It is worth noting that in curses, the powers of language are aimed at doing just the opposite of what is intended in ceremonies like the *Night Chant:* to invoke evil sprits, confusion, and despair, and to isolate the victim from his communities. See Walter B. Cannon's examination of verbal strategies in cursing in his pioneering study, "'Voodoo' Death," *American Anthropologist*, n.s. 44 (April–June 1942):169–81.

29. Katherine Spencer, *Mythology and Values: An Analysis of Navajo Chantway Myths* (Philadelphia: American Folklore Society, 1957), pp. 155–64.

30. See Bierhorst's diagram of the setup of a longhouse for the Condolence Ritual, *Four Masterworks*, p. 114.

31. As Bierhorst points out, this hair-raisingly expressive action is not given in Matthews' original text: it is incorporated by Edward Sapir and Harry Hoijer in

their *Navajo Texts* (Iowa City: Linguistic Society of America, 1942), pp. 256–57. There is a well known custom among Navajos and other Indians of the West, of formally presenting newborn infants to the sun, as it appears in the east at dawn. Likewise, the patient/subject of a performance of the "Night Chant" would face the dawn as one newborn.

4 / From Mythic to Fictive in a Nez Perce Orpheus Myth

1. A version of this essay was read at the 1976 meeting of the Rocky Mountain Modern Language Association in Santa Fe, New Mexico. The essay originally appeared in *Western American Literature* 13 (August 1978), and has been reprinted, with additions, in *Traditional American Indian Literature: Texts and Interpretations,* ed. Karl Kroeber (Lincoln: University of Nebraska Press, 1981; revised ed. 1996). On the Orpheus theme, see Åke Hultkrantz's very full study, *The North American Indian Orpheus Tradition,* Ethnological Museum of Sweden Monograph Series, no. 2 (Stockholm, 1957); oddly enough, Hultkrantz ignores our text. Also see Anne Gayton, "The Orpheus Myth in North America," *Journal of American Folklore* 48 (July–September 1935):263–93. Gayton's study apparently came out too early for her to consider Phinney's collection. The story has been adapted by Jarold Ramsey and Samuel Adler in a cantata for chamber orchestra, baritone, and dancers, *The Lodge of Shadows* (New York: Carl Fischer and Sons, 1976).

2. Archie Phinney, *Nez Perce Texts,* Columbia University Contributions to Anthropology, vol. 25 (New York: Columbia University Press, 1934), p. vii.

3. Letter, Phinney to Boas, 20 November 1929, American Philosophical Society Library Collection, Philadelphia.

4. Phinney, *Nez Perce Texts,* p. ix.

5. Ibid., pp. 282–85. Phinney presents the story as a "second version" of another Orpheus story, "Coyote the Interloper" (pp. 268–81), but in fact the two are radically different. For reasons unknown to me, Phinney does not give the Nez Perce language text for "Coyote and the Shadow People," as he does for the rest of his stories. Additional versions of Phinney's "Coyote the Interloper" have appeared in Haruo Aoki, *Nez Perce Texts,* University of California Publications in Linguistics, vol. 90 (1979), pp. 50–58; in Allen Slickpoo, Sr., et al., *Nu-Mee-Poom Tit-Wah-Tit: Nez Perce Tales* (Nez Perce Tribe, 1972), pp. 65–69; and Dell Skeels, "Style in the Unwritten Literature of the Nez Perce Indians" (Ph.D. diss., University of Washington, 1949), pt. 2, pp. 229–34. None of these sources gives a version of "Coyote and the Shadow People."

6. In Phinney's collection, for example, see "Coyote Causes His Son to Be Lost," "Bat and Coyote," and "Bears and Coyote," in which (p. 480) a Bear says to Coyote, "Vile you are, Coyote" (nasáwaylu). See Aoki, *Nez Perce Texts,* pp. 3, 57–58.

7. For an account of the event, and photographs of the lodge, see Edward Curtis, *The North American Indian,* vol. 8 (Norwood, MA: Plimpton Press, 1911), p. 40. The appearance of the lodge and the reference to the "conical lodge" (tipi)

that Coyote and his wife use en route home, in connection with the references to horses and a roundup, suggest that the story as we have it dates from not before the middle of the eighteenth century, after the appearance of horses and horseback encounters with Plains culture.

8. Father Blanchet in *Notices and Voyages of the Famous Quebec Mission to the Pacific Northwest,* ed. and trans. Carl Landerholm (Portland: Champoeg Press, 1956), p. 68.

9. See essay 6, this volume.

10. It is a measure of this story's pervasive seriousness that, whereas in other of Phinney's texts Coyote is variously—and comically—married to wives identified as "Mouse" (evidently his favorite), "Lady Bullfrog," "White Swan," and "Flying People," here the wife has no animal or typological identity; she is only "Coyote's wife" and is recognized only by him and by the spirit guide.

11. The Wishram story is in Curtis, *North American Indian,* vol. 8, pp. 127–29. Another Wishram version is in Edward Sapir, *Wishram Texts,* Publications of the American Ethnological Society, vol. 2 (Leiden: E. J. Brill, 1909), pp. 107–17; the same collection contains a Wasco version transcribed by Jeremiah Curtin (pp. 127–29).

12. Text and commentary are given in Jacobs's pioneering study, *The Content and Style of an Oral Literature* (New York: Wenner-Gren Foundation, 1959), pp. 27–36.

13. For another "double-return" Orphic story, see the Klamath "Lululaidi," told by Lulu Lang, recorded by Theodore Stern, in *The Stories We Tell: An Anthology of Oregon Folk Literature,* ed. Suzi Jones and Jarold Ramsey (Corvallis: Oregon State University Press, 1994), pp. 220–24.

14. Phinney, *Nez Perce Texts,* p. 282.

15. For ethnographic commentary see Herbert Spinden, "The Nez Perce Indians," *Memoirs of the American Anthropological Association,* vol. 2, pt. 3 (1908); and Curtis, *North American Indian,* vol. 8, pp. 52–76. Dell Hymes has conjectured (personal communication) that behind Coyote's final situation, sitting alone in despair, stands a "set" of Northwest stories from several tribes in which a person goes off in shame or despair to a lake or some other lonely place, and is transformed. (See essay 5, this volume.) Part of the sense of finality in the end of the Nez Perce story lies in the recognition that Coyote can neither transform nor be transformed; he is "beyond myth."

16. George Bird Grinnell, *Blackfoot Lodge Tales* (1892; reprint ed., Lincoln: University of Nebraska Press, 1962), p. 139. For a view of tricksters as creators of death in some Indian myths, see M. L. Ricketts's essay, "The North American Indian Trickster," *History of Religions* 5 (1966):327–50.

17. In "Serial Order in Nez Perce Myths," *Journal of American Folklore* 86 (1971):104–17, Brian Stross examines "myth initials" and "myth finals"—the opening and closing expressions of the narratives—in relation to other kinds of serial order in them and finds two kinds of myth finals: "Either the audience leaves the scene of action while the actor or actors remain in a state of relative inaction . . . or

else the actor or actors leave the scene of action without a corresponding shift of scene by the narrator." In the second form of ending, "the audience is transported from the world of myth to the world of reality by means of an explanatory connection between the two" (p. 108). In the case of "Coyote and the Shadow People," Coyote's last episode seems to conclude with Stross's first kind of myth final, and yet in effect—our sense of movement from mythic to fictive representation of reality—it seems to correspond to his second kind, albeit without formulaic expression or "explanatory connection." In fact those elements have already appeared at what would be the conventional ending of the story, before Coyote's last quest, when the death spirit tells him, "Only a short time away the human race is coming, but you have spoiled everything and established for them death as it is."

18. William Butler Yeats, "Meru," *The Collected Poems of William Butler Yeats* (New York: Macmillan and Co., 1960), p. 333.

5 / "The Hunter Who Had an Elk for a Guardian Spirit," and the Ecological Imagination

1. I owe the sarcastic abbreviation to Karl Kroeber, who in turn got it from an Indian student of his. A version of this essay was presented at the session of the Association for the Study of American Indian Literatures in conjunction with the 1980 Modern Language Association annual convention, and has been published in *Smoothing the Ground*, ed. Brian Swann (Berkeley and Los Angeles: University of California Press, 1983), pp. 309–22. It has also been excerpted in *Orion* (October 1981), pp. 51–53.

2. William Carlos Williams, *Selected Poems of William Carlos Williams* (New York: New Directions, 1963), p. 108. The recent emphasis on environmental literary study and "ecocriticism" is a welcome sign that teachers and scholars are becoming more accountable to environmental issues in their work. See the publication *Isle*, and for a well-thought-out Native approach to environmental education, see the books by Joseph Bruchac and Michael Caduto, especially *Keepers of Life* and *Keepers of the Earth*.

3. Leslie Spier and Edward Sapir, *Wishram Ethnography*, University of Washington Publications in Anthropology, vol. 3, no. 3 (May 1930), pp. 258–59. Reprinted in Jarold Ramsey, *Coyote Was Going There: Indian Literature of the Oregon Country* (Seattle: University of Washington Press, 1977), p. xxxiii; most of the other Chinookan texts mentioned here are likewise reprinted in this anthology.

4. See in Melville Jacobs, *The Content and Style of an Oral Literature* (New York: Wenner-Gren Foundation, 1959), "Coyote Made Everything," pp. 59 ff.: various springtime foods say, in turn, "Was it not for me and my advent in this season, people would be unable to keep their breath."

5. For example, see a Northern Paiute ethnographic text recorded by Isabel Kelly, "A Hunter's First Kill," in Ramsey, *Coyote Was Going There*, p. 257.

6. Jeremiah Curtin, "Wasco Tales and Myths," in *Wishram Texts*, ed. Edward Sapir, Publications of the American Ethnological Society, vol. 2 (1909), pp. 257–59. In his *Memoirs* (Wisconsin Biography Series, vol. 2 [Madison, 1942]), Curtin notes that he worked at Simnasho and Warm Springs with Pitt and McKay, the latter a mixed-blood who had distinguished himself as a scout in the Modoc War and in recent years had been the star of a snake-oil troupe and the hero of a dime novel!

7. Curtin's text appears to be slightly garbled here and in the next sentence, in that the guardian elk is referred to as a female. Female guardian spirits do in fact appear in Chinookan stories (see note 27 below), but against Curtin's two feminine references here (and the use of *it* in the same paragraph!) I note that the elk is referred to as "master" at the beginning of the story and is clearly perceived as male during the meeting in the lake. Hence I have restored the masculine references in keeping with the rest of the story.

8. All who aim at a literary understanding and appreciation of traditional Indian literature owe much to the heroic forty years' labor of Melville Jacobs as transcriber, translator, editor, and critical interpreter of Northwest repertories, and it is good to see the beginnings of a serious exploitation of his scholarship. But on the question of accessibility, it must be noted with regret that Jacobs did not advance his or his subject's cause by persistently denying, in the dourest terms, that an untutored but literate "Euro-American" reader could ever enjoy and understand in the least degree Native stories like those in his *Clackamas Chinook Texts*. The net effect of such pronouncements is to nullify unfairly what general readers can and do perceive in the stories as imaginative literature, incomplete and inadequate though these perceptions may be.

9. See Spier and Sapir, *Wishram Ethnography*, pp. 238 ff.; also Edward S. Curtis, *The North American Indian*, vol. 8 (Norwood, MA: Plimpton Press, 1911), pp. 100–106.

10. Sapir, *Wishram Texts*, pp. 221–23, The narrator was Louis Simpson.

11. Spier and Sapir, *Wishram Ethnography*, p. 238. The deathbed presentation of elk-skins may also, beyond the special circumstances of the story, have some connection with the fact that the Wishram and Wasco people danced their most sacred dances on elk-skins; hence, the skins would have been inherently associated with spirit-power.

See Dell Hymes's analysis of Wishram guardian-spirit disclosures, based on materials in Spier and Sapir, in "Two Types of Linguistic Relativity," in *Sociolinguistics*, ed. William Bright (The Hague: Mouton, 1966), pp. 114–67, especially pp. 137–41. Hymes argues that for the Wishram people (and almost certainly for their trans-Columbia kin, the Wasco), spirit-transactions, bestowal of names, and myth-recitations all partook of a linguistically based pattern consisting of "a speaker as source, a speaker as addressor who repeats the words of the source, and an audience" (p. 150), and also a strict sense of timing. Space prevents a full discussion of this pattern in terms of the story under analysis here, but there does seem to have been an underlying formal connection between the story as a mythic narrative and the guardian spirit transactions it dramatized in performance. Hymes's essay helps to understand something that any Wishram or Wasco would have known by feeling: that two such "nodes" of their cultural system as spirit-power transactions and myth-tellings were organically related to one another, and together related to the other nodes of the system.

12. Sapir, *Wishram Texts*, p. 289.

13. Melville Jacobs, *The People Are Coming Soon* (Seattle: University of Washington Press, 1960), p. 180.

14. See Jeremiah Curtin, *The Memoirs of Jeremiah Curtin*, Wisconsin Biography Series, vol. 2 (Madison, 1942), pp. 355, 360, et seq.

15. Dell Hymes, "Discovering Oral Performance and Measured Verse in American Indian Narrative," in *"In Vain I Tried to Tell You"* (Philadelphia: University of Pennsylvania Press, 1981), pp. 309–42.

16. See Hymes, "The 'Wife' Who 'Goes Out' like a Man," in *"In Vain I Tried to Tell You,"* pp. 274–98; and Jarold Ramsey, "The Wife Who Goes Out like a Man, Comes Back as a Hero: The Art of Two Oregon Indian Narratives," essay 6 of this volume.

17. In a Wishram tale in Curtis, *The American Indian*, vol. 8, pp. 111–12, Coyote encounters a foolish Myth Age man who is out gathering firewood because his wife is, they think, pregnant; he is carrying the wood in a bundle between his legs, and it becomes clear that neither he nor his unpregnant wife has any understanding of coitus! Lack of other evidence prevents the conclusion that "gathering firewood" during a wife's lying-in may have been a comic act, like our "boiling water" for nervous and useless husbands—but it is a possibility.

18. Jacobs, *Content and Style*, p. 133.

19. See text and commentary in Jacobs, *Content and Style*, pp. 27–36; also essay 4, this volume.

20. Curtin, "Wasco Tales and Myths," in Sapir, *Wishram Texts*, pp. 248–52. There is a Clackamas version with commentary in Jacobs, *Content and Style*, pp. 108–16.

21. Jacobs, *The People Are Coming Soon*, p. 52. To argue that any sensible Chinookan auditor would have condemned the hunter straight off for foolishly heeding his father instead of the spirit guide, is to ignore the evidence Jacobs provides of such familial tensions and conflicts in the culture, and it is to reduce a richly mediative story to the status of a cautionary fable. A similarly reductive interpretation, based on an ethnographically suspect stereotype of a "typical native" (one thinks of similar claims on behalf of Shakespeare's "typical audience"), would deny all sympathy to Coyote in his second Orphic quest at the end of the Nez Perce "Coyote and the Shadow People" (essay 3). No doubt Native listeners would have perceived that the elk hunter and Coyote "should have known better," but then our perception that Othello and Brutus "should have known better" does not negate our sympathy for them, either.

22. Jacobs, *The People Are Coming Soon*, p. 176. In Charles Cultee's story

about his great-grandfather's spirit-power accession, the young hero already has several powers, but is urged to seek ut'unaqan, "the female guardian spirit of your ancestors"; clearly a family connection is meant. Franz Boas, *Chinook Texts*, Bulletin of the Bureau of American Ethnology, no. 20 (1894), p. 214.

23. Jacobs, *The People Are Coming Soon*, p. 179.

24. Hymes, "The 'Wife' Who 'Goes Out' like a Man," pp. 287 ff.

25. Sapir, *Wishram Texts*, p. 235. I have added bracketed clarifications to those in parentheses given by Boas.

26. Melville Jacobs, *Northwest Sahaptin Texts*, Columbia University Contributions to Anthropology, vol. 19 (1934), pp. 5–6.

27. See for example the Coos hero tale, "The Revenge against the Sky People," text and commentary in essay 6 herein. I am indebted to Dell Hymes for suggesting, from the Lower Columbia Chinookan repertory, the story of "How Cultee's Great-grandfather Acquired a Guardian Spirit" as a possible "+ +" hero story in these terms. The young hero manages to acquire the favor of the female ancestral spirit ut'unaqan, as his father has ordered him to do, but upon his return he does not tell his father what he has accomplished, thereby preserving the secret basis of his power. See note 21 above: Boas, *Chinook Texts*, pp. 213–14. In the same volume there is a story—"The Elk Hunter," pp. 236–37—in which a boy successfully acquires and employs elk-hunting power from a female spirit because he is an orphan; hence there is no conflict for him between human father and spirit-guardian, and the story stands outside our bipolar set. A third heroic figure in Chinookan literature—more "+ +" in characterization than in action—is Panther, interestingly enough a successful hunter of elks in the Kathlamet story "Panther and Owl," in Franz Boas, *Kathlamet Texts*, Bureau of American Ethnology Bulletin, no. 26 (1901), pp. 129–41. I am grateful to my colleague Tom Hahn for suggesting Ike McCaslin in Faulkner's *The Bear* as an apt "+ +" analogue from our own literature.

6 / The Wife Who Goes Out like a Man, Comes Back as a Hero

1. Melville Jacobs, *Clackamas Chinook Texts*, pt. 2, text no. 37, Publications of the Indiana University Research Center in Anthropology, Folklore, and Linguistics (1959), pp. 340–41. This essay first appeared in slightly different form in *PMLA* 92 (January 1977):9–18.

2. Melville Jacobs, *The People Are Coming Soon* (Seattle: University of Washington Press, 1960), pp. 238–42; Dell Hymes, "The 'Wife' Who 'Goes Out' like a Man: Reinterpretation of a Clackamas Chinook Myth," *Social Science Information* 7(3) (1968):173–99; reprinted in *Structural Analysis of Oral Tradition*, ed. Maranda and Maranda (Philadelphia: American Folklore Society, 1971), pp. 49–80; reinterpretation and retranslation in "Discovering Oral Performance and Measured Verse in American Indian Narrative," *New Literary History* 8 (1977):345–69; both essays revised as chapters in Hymes, *"In Vain I Tried to Tell You": Essays in Native American Ethnopoetics* (Philadelphia: University of Pennsylvania Press, 1981). Frank

Kermode, "The Structure of Fiction," *Modern Language Notes* 84(6) (1969):891–915, and "Sensing Endings," *Nineteenth Century Fiction* 33 (June 1978):152 ff. Alan Dundes, "Introduction" to *Karok Myths*, ed. A. L. Kroeber and E. W. Gifford (Berkeley and Los Angeles: University of California Press, 1980), pp. xxxvii ff. J. Barre Toelken, *The Dynamics of Folklore* (Boston: Houghton Mifflin, 1979), pp. 217–20.

3. Ruth Underhill, ed., *Papago Woman* (New York: Holt,Rinehart, and Winston, 1979), p. 51. For a thorough and lucid description of the storytelling context of one Western tribe, see Theodore Stern, "Some Sources of Variability in Klamath Mythology," *Journal of American Folklore* 69 (1956):1–9, 135–46, 377–86.

4. I give Hymes's text, as printed in "Discovering Oral Performance" (chapter 9 in *"In Vain I Tried to Tell You,"* pp. 310–12).

5. Jacobs, *The People Are Coming Soon*, pp. 242–43.

6. Hymes, *"In Vain I Tried to Tell You,"* p. 291.

7. In Thomas, *Quite Early One Morning* (New York: New Directions, 1956), p. 27. Morris Freilich has independently identified this polarity in numerous myths from a variety of cultures, calling it "Smart/Proper," in *Current Anthropology* 16(2) (1975):207–26.

8. Ernest Hemingway, *The Short Stories of Ernest Hemingway* (New York: Scribner's, 1953), p. 95.

9. Hymes, *"In Vain I Tried to Tell You,"* p. 285.

10. See J. Barre Toelken and Tacheeni Scott, "Poetic Retranslation and the 'Pretty Languages' of Yellowman," in *Traditional Literatures of the American Indian: Texts and Interpretations*, ed. Karl Kroeber (Lincoln: University of Nebraska Press, 1997). See essay 2, this volume.

11. W. B. Yeats, "The Tragic Theater," *Essays and Introductions* (London: Macmillan, 1965), pp. 240–44.

12. Leo J. Frachtenberg, *Coos Texts*, Columbia University Contributions to Anthropology, vol. 1 (1913), pp. 149–57. Another version is in Melville Jacobs, *Coos Myth Texts*, University of Washington Publications in Anthropology, vol. 8, no. 2 (1940), pp. 235–37.

13. Claude Lévi-Strauss, "The Structural Study of Myth," in *Structural Anthropology* (New York: Doubleday, 1967), p. 213. There are in fact forms of "The Revenge against the Sky People" in the recorded mythology of the Alsea and Tillamook tribes, both from the Oregon coast; and the Quileutes of the Central Washington coast, the Lillooets of the interior of British Columbia, and the Nootka of Vancouver Island have more distant analogues. See Leo J. Frachtenberg, *Alsea Myths and Texts*, Bureau of American Ethnology Bulletin, no. 67 (1920), pp. 141–49; Franz Boas, "Traditions of the Tillamook Indians," *Journal of American Folklore* 11 (1898):136–38; Elizabeth Jacobs, *Nehalem Tillamook Tales* (Eugene: University of Oregon Books, 1959), pp. 24–28; Manuel Andrade, *Quileute Texts*, Columbia University Contributions to Anthropology, vol. 12 (1931), pp. 69–71; *Lillooet Stories*, ed. Randy Bouchard and Dorothy Kennedy, *Sound Heritage 6*, no. 1 (1977); Franz Boas, *Indian Myths and Legends from the North Pacific Coast of America*, trans. Dietrich

Bertz, with introduction by Claude Lévi-Strauss, forthcoming ("The Revenge of the Brothers"). An analogue to the child's unheeded discovery of the intruder appears (in an incest story) in Ella Deloria, *Dakota Texts,* ed. Agnes Picotte and Paul Pavich (Vermillion: Dakota Press, 1978), p. 8.

14. Jacobs, *The People Are Coming Soon,* p. 218.

15. Hymes, "In Vain I Tried to Tell You," pp. 289–90.

16. For another instance of internal conflict dramatized with complete "behavioristic" objectivity, see "Coyote and Badger Were Neighbors," and Melville Jacobs's interpretation in *The Content and Style of an Oral Literature* (New York: Wenner-Gren Foundation, 1959), pp. 27–36.

17. Leo J. Frachtenberg, "Traditions of the Coos Indians of Oregon," *Journal of American Folklore* 22 (1909):25. For additional ethnographic information on the Coos, see Melville Jacobs, *Coos Narrative and Ethnologic Texts,* University of Washington Publications in Anthropology, vol. 8, no. 1 (1939), and Homer G. Barnett, "Culture Elements Distributions VII: Oregon Coast," in *Anthropological Records* 1(3) (1957):155–203.

18. Jacobs, *The People Are Coming Soon,* pp. ix–xi and passim.

19. Frachtenberg, *Alsea Myths and Texts,* p. 145.

20. Jacobs, *Coos Narrative and Ethnologic Texts,* p. 74. Among many California tribes, in fact, headdresses made of woodpecker scalps were an important trade item. See K. Teeter, *The Wiyot Language,* University of California Publications in Linguistics, vol. 37 (1964), p. 227.

21. For example, see the mythic ending of an otherwise highly realistic Wasco story, "A Wasco Woman Deceives Her Husband," in Edward Sapir, *Wishram Texts,* Publications of the American Ethnological Society, vol. 2 (1909), pp. 248–52.

22. Jacobs, *Coos Myth Texts,* University of Washington Publications in Anthropology, vol. 8, no. 2 (1940), p. 129.

23. T. T. Waterman, "The Explanatory Element in the Folktales of North American Indians," *Journal of American Folklore* 27 (1914):1–54. See essay 1, this volume.

24. Hymes, "The 'Wife' Who 'Goes Out,'" p. 197.

25. When, at the end of a Myth Age narrative the raconteur thus directed the story's long-ago action at his listeners, "The people are almost here," what did they feel? Solidarity, a sense of historical continuity, and therefore, perhaps, a sense of responsibility as the People? Ignoring all sorts of obstacles to such a comparison, there is something of this effect at the conclusions of Shakespeare's history plays, notably *Richard III* and *Henry VIII:* the Shakespearian audience was made to see itself as "coming soon," in the accession of Henry VII and in the birth of Elizabeth.

26. Rev. Samuel Parker, *Journal of an Exploring Tour beyond the Rocky Mountains* (Ithaca, 1838), p. 235.

27. See Dell Hymes's "Folklore's Nature and the Sun's Myth," *Journal of American Folklore* 88 (1975):345–69.

7 / Uncursing the Misbegotten in a Tillamook Incest Story

1. Franz Boas, "Traditions of the Tillamook Indians," *Journal of American Folklore* 11 (1898): 34–38.

2. Professor May M. Edel's texts, except for references and abstracts and one short narrative in her article, remain unpublished.

3. May M. Edel, "Stability in Tillamook Folklore," *Journal of American Folklore* 57 (1944): 118–27. See also her "Tillamook Language," *International Journal of American Linguistics* 10(1) (1939): 1–57.

4. Elizabeth Jacobs and Melville Jacobs, *Nehalem Tillamook Tales* (Eugene: University of Oregon Books, 1959; reissued by Oregon State University Press in 1990, with introduction and notes by Jarold Ramsey and appendix by Dell Hymes). Mrs. Pearson's main source was her father; she told Mrs. Jacobs that she "had heard these stories every winter until she was almost forty" (p. vii). She reported the following protocols of Tillamook storytelling: "Tillamooks told myths only in midwinter, approximately during the months of December and January. . . . Only old people were privileged to recount myths. Children and younger persons reclined on mats. . . . Children were cautioned not to sit when listening lest they grow hunchbacked. . . . No tale was considered the property of the raconteur; but it was believed that the same story should not be told by a second raconteur during the same season. One occasion for repetition of myths during the season, which involved a legitimate breach of the rule, was the necessary additional recountings for the purpose of teaching children to tell the stories verbatim; then the child repeated each sentence after the raconteur, and in special sessions for children" (pp. vii–ix).

5. See John Swanton, *The Indian Tribes of North America*, U.S. Bureau of American Ethnology Bulletin, no. 195 (1952), p. 472.

6. Jacobs, *Nehalem Tillamook Tales*, pp. 45–54.

7. D. Demetracopoulou, "The Loon Woman Myth: A Study in Synthesis," *Journal of American Folklore* 46 (1933): 101–28. A good example of this "set" of stories is "The Girl Who Married Her Brother," in Livingston Farrand and Leo J. Frachtenberg, "Shasta and Athapascan Myths from Oregon," *Journal of American Folklore* 28 (1915): 212–14.

8. See Demetracopoulou, "Loon Woman Myth," pp. 109 ff.

9. Jacobs, *Nehalem Tillamook Tales*, pp. 69–70. "I myself, I shall be surf forever. When I am angry I will turn my face to the south. Then it will become rough, this ocean will be very treacherous. When I feel all right I will turn my face to the north. Everything will be quiet then." Nevertheless, Wild Woman's impulses carry on past the Myth Age in the adventures of a set of "Younger Wild Women"; see p. 45 and pp. 157–62. In another story concerning Wild woman per se, after she has seduced another kidnapped "grandson" into precocious copulation with her, a scandal ensues—"Wren has been raping his grandmother"—and when Wild Woman hears of it she decrees, apropos our story, "From now on people will never be able to copulate with a relative without being found out" (p. 62).

10. See Edel, "Stability," pp. 121, 124.

11. Edel, "Stability," p. 125. The issue of "self-censorship" of Indian narratives is vexatious. It seems to have been practiced especially when the transcribers were women, as Ella Deloria notes in her *Dakota Texts* (Vermillion: Dakota Press, 1978), p. 6, and as Wasco Chinookans have reported to me about recitations given to Ella Clark for her *Indian Legends of the Pacific Northwest* (Berkeley and Los Angeles: University of California Press, 1953).

12. Jacobs, *Nehalem Tillamook Tales,* p. 58. In general terms, such an upbeat "moral" figures in many of the best-known Native hero-narratives of the Far West— the "Blood-clot Boy" tales of the Blackfeet and other Plains tribes, for example. And of course the heroes of such stories share something with the low-born, ill-favored, but plucky, and finally triumphant, protagonists of European fairy stories.

13. It might be asked, why not subject this story to the form of structuralist analysis followed in discussing the Chinookan, Coos, and Wasco stories in essays 5 and 6? It could be done, I suppose, but the main polarities of the story seem to be so one-sided, at least as I formulate them, that a bipolar analysis per se seems rather pointless, especially insofar as it would neglect (at least on the level of the English text) the remarkable texture of the story. Certainly it is hard to see how, unlike the stories for which I have attempted a bipolar analysis, this story deals with conflicting goods at all. In that sense, what is being "mediated"?

14. See most of the "Coyote" stories, for example, in my *Coyote Was Going There* (Seattle: University of Washington Press, 1977). The strategy is especially subtle in stories in which the stock Coyote figure must seem to transcend itself, as it does in the Nez Perce and Chinookan "Orpheus" stories discussed in essay 4.

15. The motif of the malevolent "mothering" female with some sort of container is widespread in the West and may correspond to some general ambivalence in these cultures about the purposes and status of women past menopause, as Melville Jacobs suggests in *The Content and Style of an Oral Literature* (New York: Wenner-Gren, 1959), in discussing Wild Woman's equivalents in Clackamas literature, Grizzly Women (pp. 159 ff.). See the At'at'ahlia "Basket-Ogress" in *Coyote Was Going There,* pt. 2. Another more distant kin is the Dzonoqua monster of North Coast tribes.

16. Jacobs, *Nehalem Tillamook Stories,* p. 47.

17. In one of Mrs. Pearson's stories about the transforming character known as "Ice," Ice copulates with a girl from a tribe to which the act is unknown. He is watched by a young boy, who is immediately inspired to try it—with his sister! Ice decrees against incest: "No! No! Do not do that! . . . Never copulate with your mother, your sister, or anyone like that" (p. 7). The tone of the story is wildly facetious, utterly unlike that of our "Wild Woman" story.

18. See essay 6, this volume.

19. Cf. Boas's version, in which, before the spying episode, "The children were playing with shells. They arranged them in couples as husbands and wives" (p. 36)—an even stronger prefigurement than in Mrs. Pearson's version.

20. See J. Barre Toelken's excellent critique of this defect in the Lévi-Strauss-ian method in "Poetic Retranslation and the 'Pretty Languages' of Yellowman" (with Tacheeni Scott) in *Traditional American Indian Literatures: Texts and Interpretations,* ed. Karl Kroeber (Lincoln: University of Nebraska Press, 1981), pp. 65–116.

21. John Bierhorst, Introduction to *The Red Swan* (New York: Farrar, Strauss, and Giroux, 1976), p. 10. Bierhorst speaks of a "self-reiterating tendency in mythic narrative," and notes an analogous tendency in the splitting or doubling of characters within one narrative. The narrative effects of either form of "reit-eration" can be very striking, and if they don't constitute literary art, what shall we call them?

22. If this detail is "etiological" and the Mole is to be seen as the mythic pro-totype of all moles (and I am not convinced that it is), it is the single instance in a myth that is otherwise exclusively concerned not with "explanation" or even "char-tering" but rather with the dramatization of the full course through two generations of a personal and potentially a social calamity.

23. Boas, "Traditions," p. 37.

24. The magical location of a villain's heart in some other part of his body or in an article of clothing is, of course, widespread, not just among Western Indian repertories, but globally. Motif Index No. 2311. On basket-caps, see Jacobs, *Nehalem Tillamook Tales,* p. 52.

25. This female Blue Jay is not identified, evidently, with the male Blue Jay who figures as a latter-day trickster and gossip among the Tillamooks and other coastal tribes. See his Orphic adventures in the Chinookan "The Girl Who Married a Ghost" (Boas), reprinted in Ramsey, *Coyote Was Going There,* pp. 161–65.

26. As the only character left in the story who knows the boy's origins, Wild Woman might have revealed them by calling him Incest Boy or some such, but such sly malice is never her style. Instead the name she does give him is in effect a be-stowal of power, however grudging, underscored by his killing of her soon after. In a story about one of her post-transformation "Younger Wild Woman" successors, a youth copulates with an ogress but refuses to marry her; as a consequence he obtains great spirit power from her—but she kills all of his unprotected relatives (Jacobs, *Nehalem Tillamook Tales,* pp. 157–58).

8 / Generic and Racial Appropriation in Victoria Howard's "The Honorable Milt"

1. Dell Hymes, *"In Vain I Tried to Tell You": Essays in Native American Eth-nopoetics* (Philadelphia: University of Pennsylvania Press, 1981), p. 327.

2. Dell Hymes, "Folklore's Nature and the Sun's Myth," *Journal of American Folklore,* 88 (1975):345–69.

3. Jarold Ramsey, "Introduction" to *Nehalem Tillamook Tales,* ed. Elizabeth and Melville Jacobs (Corvallis: Oregon State University Press, 1990), pp. xi–xxv.

4. Melville Jacobs, *The Content and Style of an Oral Literature* (Chicago: University of Chicago Press, 1959), pp. 120–21.

5. Hymes, *"In Vain I Tried to Tell You,"* pp. 274–98.

6. Hymes, *"In Vain I Tried to Tell You,"* pp. 287 ff.

7. The Clackamas people were living precisely at the end of the Oregon Trail, around what became Portland and Oregon City; hence by the 1870s their culture had been engulfed, and had vanished by the turn of the century—except for the remarkable survival of Mrs. Howard and her repertory. For ethnographic descriptions of the Clackamas and their neighbors, see Melville Jacobs, *The Content and Style of an Oral Literature,* pp. 8–21 and passim, and Stephen Dow Beckham, *The Indians of Western Oregon* (Coos Bay, OR: Arago Books, 1977).

8. In part because of the rigidities of his psychoanalytic approach to literary interpretation, Jacobs is notably insensitive to the distinctly female perspective in much of Mrs. Howard's repertory. For a discussion of this defect in Jacobs's monumental work, see Craig Thompson, "Gender Representation in Two Clackamas Myths," *Studies in American Indian Literatures* 3(1) (1991):19–39.

9. Dell Hymes, "A Theory of Irony and a Chinook Pattern of Exchange," in *The Pragmatic Perspective,* ed. Jef Verschueren and Marcella Berucelli-Papi (Amsterdam and Philadelphia: John Benjamin, 1987), pp. 323–29.

10. Hymes's work on Clackamas texts makes it clear that "The Lordly Milt" ought to be recast as measured verse. But for the purposes of this essay, with no competence in the Clackamas language, I must rely on Jacobs's prose translation, with the title and the Widow's song reworded by Hymes, as noted above. The text is quoted from Jacobs, *Clackamas Chinook Texts,* pt. 1, Indiana University Research Center in Anthropology, Folklore, and Linguistics, Publication 8 (Bloomington, 1958), pp. 359–60.

11. Jacobs's commentary on the Milt story in *The People Are Coming Soon* (Seattle: University of Washington Press, 1960, pp. 243–47) concentrates mainly on the dynamics of Milt's spirit-power relationship with the Widow, noting the story's generic and racial perspectives only in passing.

12. *Motif Index of Folk-Literature,* ed. Stith Thompson, vol. 1 (Bloomington: Indiana University Press, 1928, 1968), p. 489.

13. Jacobs, *Clackamas Chinook Texts,* pt. 2, Indiana University Research Center in Anthropology, Folklore, and Linguistics, Publication 11 (Bloomington, 1959), p. 468.

14. Jacobs, *Clackamas Chinook Texts,* pt. 1, pp. 246–55.

15. Jacobs, *Clackamas Chinook Texts,* pt. 1, pp. 226–40.

16. Melville Jacobs, "Cowlitz and Upper Cowlitz Myths," *Columbia University Contributions to Anthropology,* vol. 19 (1934), pp. 139–40.

17. The Clackamas phrasing for "Oh, that you become a person" appears verbatim, for example, in Mrs. Howard's "Awl and Her Son's Son," "Stick Drum Gambler," and elsewhere in her repertory.

18. Hymes, "A Theory of Irony," pp. 322–24.

19. Jacobs, *Clackamas Chinook Texts*, pt. 2, p. 652.

20. The recording is in the Ethnomusicology Archives of the Melville Jacobs Collection at the University of Washington, #14542 (45), Tape 11, Band 2. I am grateful to Gary Lundell, Archival Specialist, for help in working in the collection.

21. Hymes, "A Theory of Irony," p. 328.

22. Claude Lévi-Strauss, "The Structural Study of Myth," in *Structural Anthropology*, trans. Claire Jacobsen and B. C. Schoepf (New York: Doubleday, 1967), pp. 207–25.

23. Dean and Lucille Saxton, eds. *Legends and Lore of the Papago and Pima Indians* (Tucson: U. of Arizona Press, 1979), pp. 28–44.

24. *Papago Woman,* ed. Ruth Underhill (New York: Holt Rinehart and Winston, 1979), p. 52.

25. Ursula Le Guin, *Always Coming Home: A Novel* (New York: Harpers, 1985), p. 54.

26. Constance Penley, "Feminism, Psychoanalysis, and the Study of Popular Culture," in *Cultural Studies,* ed. Lawrence Grossberg, Cary Nelson, and Paula Treichler (London: Routledge, 1993), p. 484. What Penley calls "this overwhelming media environment we all inhabit" has no exact equivalent in traditional Indian life—but if not "overwhelming," the oral literature of any Native culture was certainly all-pervasive and always subject to "local" appropriations and co-optings, as I have tried to show here.

27. Michel de Certeau, *The Practice of Everyday Life,* trans. Steven Rendell (Berkeley: University of California Press, 1984), p. 29.

9 / *Simon Fraser's Canoe; or, Capsizing into Myth*

1. Alan Dundes, *The Morphology of North American Indian Folktales,* Folklore Fellows Communications, vol. 81, no. 195 (Helsinki, 1964), pp. 59 ff. See also Vladimir Propp, *Morphology of the Folk Tale* (Bloomington: University of Indiana Press, 1958).

2. I am speaking here of radical Native inventions, within a mythology; in the case of contacts with other cultures, both Indian and Anglo, the Western Indian freely incorporated such exotic material as Provencal "Petit Jean" stories and episodes from the life of Jesus Christ. But "freely" is, in itself, misleading; as is developed in essays 12 and 13, such incorporations and adaptations seem themselves to have proceeded according to the "rules" of the receiving mythology. Christ comes to duplicate Coyote as a transformer, for example, not to displace or contradict him.

3. See, for example, Bannock and Chinook "psychic" narratives of this kind in Jarold Ramsey, *Coyote Was Going There* (Seattle: University of Washington Press, 1977), pp. 32, 166.

4. For "volcano stories," see essay 11. For the Paiute myths, see my *Coyote Was Going There,* pp. 247, 253 ff. In the same collection there is a Tillamook story

of traded encounters between the Indians and "people from the other side of the ocean," with details that strongly suggest actual contact with Orientals on both sides of the Pacific—including an unmistakable reference to a bamboo-forest (pp. 167–70)!

5. Bronislaw Malinowski, "Myth in Primitive Psychology," in *Magic, Science, Religion, and Other Essays* (Boston: Free Press, 1948), p. 77.

6. I am persuaded that the work of Lévi-Strauss amounts to the most important, and certainly the most rigorous, consideration of myth-evolution we have.

7. In *Lillooet Stories*, ed. Randy Bouchard and Dorothy Kennedy, *Sound Heritage 6*, no. 1 (1977):42. Narrated by Sam Mitchell sometime between 1968 and 1973—representing, therefore, over 150 years of oral transmission, all in the contact era!

8. *The Letters and Journals of Simon Fraser, 1806–8*, ed. W. Kaye Lamb (Canada: Macmillan Co., 1960), pp. 89–92.

9. *Lillooet Stories*, ed. Bouchard and Kennedy, p. 43.

10. James Teit, *Mythology of the Thompson Indians* (the Jesup Expedition), Memoirs of American Museum of Natural History, vol. 12, no. 1 (1912), p. 414. In another of Teit's Thompson texts, in Boas's *Folktales of Salish and Sahaptin Tribes*, Memoirs of the American Folklore Society, vol. 11 (1917), p. 64, a woman from Spences Bridge, Wa'xtko by name, tells how one of her ancestors, Tcexe'x (the "Spences Bridge chief" in Semalitsa's account) gave a great speech before Fraser and was given a "silver brooch" by Fraser, which was eventually buried with the last of Tcexe'x's sons. On the whole, such oral history has been neglected, both as an invaluable historical source and as an aspect of Native traditional literature.

11. One recalls Edward Sapir's classic anecdote of divergent interpretive opinion within a tribe, "Two Crows denies this," in "Why Cultural Anthropology Needs the Psychiatrist," *Selected Writings of Edward Sapir*, ed. David Mandelbaum (Berkeley and Los Angeles: University of California Press, 1949), pp. 569–77; and also Lévi-Strauss's haunting story (from Boas) in *Structural Anthropology* (New York: Doubleday, 1967), pp. 169–73, about the Kwakiutl shaman Quesalid who disbelieved his own magic. In all of his work on the Thompson Indians, James Teit is at pains himself to avoid what might be called "ethnographic absolutism," usually prefacing ambiguous or disputed details with "Some say . . ."

12. See John Bakeless, *Lewis and Clark: Partners in Discovery* (New York: William Morrow, 1947), p. 83. See also note 10 above.

13. Teit, *Mythology of the Thompson Indians*, p. 416.

14. Franz Boas, "Introduction" to James Teit, *Traditions of the Thompson Indians of British Columbia*, Memoirs of the American Folklore Society, vol. 6 (1898), pp. 11–12.

15. I would conjecture that such a synthesis of parallel or reduplicated elements may have occurred regularly when "reality" touched mythology, as here— a sort of "short-circuiting" of such elements that is. Unlike the well-known tragic interaction of myth and "history" in sixteenth-century Mexico, whereby Cortez

was at first welcomed as a god whose return had been prophesied, there is no evidence in the Thompson mythology of any such prophecy that the myth-persons would return, but the possibility was there, certainly.

16. See Teit, *Traditions of the Thompson Indians*, pp. 45 ff., and idem, *Mythology of the Thompson Indians*, p. 224. Kokwela was the son of a girl who secretly married the "Kokwela" root; the son's heroic career begins, in the familiar pattern first formulated by Otto Rank (in *The Myth of the Birth of the Hero*), with his asking about his father. Cf. essay 1.

17. Teit, *Mythology of the Thompson Indians*, p. 416.

18. Ibid.

19. Such interconnections of Native mythology and history are discussed from the special perspective of "retroactive prophecy" in essay 11. Semalitsa's phrase here, "beings spoken of in tales of the mythological period," intersects with the foreboding cry, as preserved in Clatsop Chinook oral history, of an old lady who saw the first Anglo ship: "The thing about which we have heard in tales is on shore!" See Ramsey, *Coyote Was Going There*, pp. 174–75.

20. Ezra Pound, "Hugh Selwyn Mauberly," in *Selected Poems* (New York: New Directions, 1957), p. 67.

10 / Fish-Hawk and Other Heroes

1. A notable exception to this neglect is the work A. L. Kroeber pursued for more than sixty years on the nonmythological traditions of the Mohave Indians of California. In *A Mohave Historical Epic*, Anthropological Records, vol. 11, no. 2 (1951), Kroeber presents the text of what he calls a "pseudohistory. It is the product of imagination, not recollection; and therefore an effort at literature" (p. 72). What is fascinating is that the story is set up to make the leisurely adventures of Hipahipa and other heroes of a purported Mohave migration sound like oral history! In *A Mohave War Reminiscence 1854–1880* (Berkeley and Los Angeles: University of California Press, 1973), Kroeber and his son C. B. Kroeber present a genuine instance of oral-traditional history, about the last "heroic" generation before the Mohave way gave to Anglo influence.

2. One obvious reason is that although Western Indians cultivated heroes, they did not have the religious-social systems whereby to deify them, as happened in Mexico.

3. See, for example, G. B. Grinnell, *The Cheyenne Indians, Their History and Way of Life* (New Haven: Yale University Press, 1924), 2 vols.; G. B. Grinnell, *Blackfoot Lodge Tales* (1892; reprint ed., Lincoln: University of Nebraska Press, 1962), pp. 242 ff.; G. B. Grinnell, *Pawnee Hero Stories and Folk-tales* (Lincoln: University of Nebraska Press, 1961); Royal B. Hassrick, *The Sioux: Life and Customs of a Warrior Society* (Norman: University of Oklahoma Press, 1964); John Stands-in-Timber and Margot Liberty, *Cheyenne Memories* (New Haven: Yale University Press, 1967).

4. See Grinnell, *Blackfoot Lodge Tales*, pp. 249–50; also L. V. McWhorter,

Hear Me My Chiefs: Nez Perce History and Legend (Caldwell: Caxton Press, 1952), p. 592.

5. *Black Elk Speaks,* as told through John G. Neihardt (New York: Pocket Books, 1972), p. 63.

6. Leslie Spier, *Klamath Ethnography,* University of California Publications in American Archaeology and Ethnology, vol. 30 (1930), pp. 37–38; reprinted in my *Coyote Was Going There* (Seattle: University of Washington Press, 1977), pp. 211–12.

7. Keith and Donna Clark, eds., "William McKay's Journal, 1866–67," *Oregon Historical Quarterly* 79 (Summer 1978):121–71; 79 (Fall 1978):269–338.

8. Edward Sapir, *Wishram Texts,* Publications of the American Ethnological Society, vol. 2 (1909), p. 223.

9. Morris Swadesh, "Cayuse Interlinear Texts," MS, film 373.1, reel 48, Boas Collection, American Philosophical Society Library, Philadelphia.

10. The entire episode is narrated by Gilbert Minthorne with considerable skill as to the dramatic selection and ordering of events; it seems clear that he was an able and enthusiastic raconteur in Nez Perce Sahaptin of Cayuse traditions.

11. Cayuses are in fact something of an ethnic and linguistic mystery. The Kiowas have an origin legend about a quarrel that divided the original tribe as it began to leave the Rockies for the Plains: half carried on to the East, and the other half is said to have gone west. Given the similarity of tribal names and ways, could this lost band be the Cayuses? See N. Scott Momaday, *The Way to Rainy Mountain* (New York Ballantine, 1970), pp. 22–23.

12. A recent attempt to rediscover the Cayuse is Robert H. Ruby and John A. Brown, *The Cayuse: Imperial Tribesmen of Old Oregon* (Norman: University of Oklahoma Press, 1972). The book suffers from a tendency to neglect oral traditions of the sort discussed here.

13. "Fish-Hawk's Raid against the Sioux," *Alcheringa* 3(1) (n.s.) (1977):96–99; reprinted in Ramsey, *Coyote Was Going There,* pp. 25–27; based on Morris Swadesh's transcription and literal translation in "Cayuse Interlinear Texts." The measured verse text presented here was first published in *Coming to Light: Contemporary Translations of the Native Literatures of North America,* ed. Brian Swann (New York: Random House, 1994), pp. 346–56.

14. See Dell Hymes, "Discovering Oral Performance and Measured Verse in American Indian Literature," chap. 9 in *"In Vain I Tried to Tell You": Essays in American Ethnopoetics* (Philadelphia: University of Pennsylvania Press, 1981), pp. 309–43. One hopes that someone fluent in Nez Perce will do for its oral literature what Hymes is doing for the Chinookan repertories and Dennis Tedlock for Zuni and Quiché: that is, work out the Native narrative poetics, and translate and present the texts accordingly.

15. I give the photo in both the *Alcheringa* text, p. 99, and in *Coyote Was Going There* (along with a photo of "All-alighted-on-the-ground"), p. 7.

16. Merrill D. Beal, *"I Will Fight No More Forever": Chief Joseph and the Nez Perce War* (New York: Ballantine, 1963), p. 11. The riskiness of such expeditions is

illustrated in a traditional "morning and evening speech' recorded by Herbert Spinden in "Nez Perce Tales," in *Folk Tales of Salish and Sahaptin Tribes,* ed. Franz Boas, Memoirs of the American Folklore Association (1917), which begins: "People, remember that when we come to the buffalo country, we are in danger of war at all times. Our young men must be alert and guard well the camp. Do not let the enemy get the best of you!" (p. 201). In the same text, there is a myth, "Coyote in the Buffalo Country," which ends with a prediction of a different sort of risk for Nez Perce men: "This country will always be this way. When a man starts back from here with a new wife, he will always lose her before he gets home" (p. 195).

17. Grinnell, *Blackfoot Lodge Tales,* p. 250. The custom is prominent in James Welch's brilliant novel of Blackfoot life in the 1860s, *Fools Crow.*

18. Most of the militant Plains nations had "Dog Societies" among their warrior fraternities. See Grinnell, *The Cheyenne Indians,* vol. 2, pp. 48, 63–69, for details on the "Dog Men" and "Crazy Dogs." Generally, the Dog Soldiers were identified by some canine element of costume, "dog disguised," as here.

19. McWhorter, *Hear Me My Chiefs,* p. 17.

20. See McWhorter, "The Narrative of Red Elk," *Hear Me My Chiefs,* pp. 25–27, and "Two Moon's Narrative," pp. 41–48, 568 ff., in which the young hero escapes the enemy and must return home barefoot, with no food—"when came the morning, snow was above my ankles." Also the story of Five Wounds—"Just 22 of us fought that night with the Snake Indians, who numbered over one hundred" (p. 2). See also narratives in Allen P. Slickpoo, Sr., *Noon Nee-me-poo: Culture and History of the Nez Perces,* vol. 1 (Nez Perce Tribe, 1973), notably the story of Cloud-gatherer (p. 19).

Another "conventional" element in the Fish-Hawk story—the "red jackets" worn by the braves—figures in the remarkable colored-pencil sketches of Nez Perce military and horse-stealing exploits found recently on the Umatilla Reservation (in a house once owned by the Cayuse hero, Capt. Sumkins!) and published by Theodore Stern, Martin Schmitt, and Alphonse F. Halfmoon in "A Cayuse Nez Perce Sketchbook," in *Oregon Historical Quarterly* 81 (Winter 1980):340–76. The coats appear to be long "capotes": the editors point out that during the Nez Perce War, three young warriors dyed their coats red to show defiance and were known as "the Red Coats."

21. McWhorter, *Hear Me My Chiefs,* pp. 589–91, narrator Wottolen, with translation and additional notes by Camille Williams. McWhorter adds a comment by Homer Allen, who saw the six warriors leave and saw them return "many suns later"—"afoot, with moccasins entirely worn away, completely naked except for the breechcloth, haggard from hunger and fatigue" (p. 591).

22. Narrated by Owen Gould in Dell Skeels, "Style in the Unwritten Literature of the Nez Perce Indians" (Ph.D. diss., University of Washington, 1949), vol. 2, pp. 218–22.

23. McWhorter refers to Wottolen (son of the great warrior Many Wounds) as "a noted Native historian," *Hear Me My Chiefs,* p. 3.

24. Slickpoo, *Noon Nee-me-poo*, vol. 1, pp. 15, 18 ff. On page 15, a photo is given of a blanket on which is drawn or painted pictures of "an encounter with the Cheyenne during a horse raid by the Us-ka-ma-tone (The Brothers)." There are also photos of Kool-kool-tami or Kilkiltami, in youth and age (pp. 22–23). See references to him as "Moses Monteith," a Presbyterian preacher, in A. C. and E. D. Morrill, *Out of the Blanket: The Story of Sue and Kate McBeth* (Moscow: University Press of Idaho, 1978).

25. I wonder, for example, about the various wounds reportedly suffered by the participants: were these "shared" in retellings?

26. Slickpoo, *Noon Nee-me-poo*, p. 19. For parallel spirit-power customs among the Wasco and Wishram Chinookans, see essay 4, this volume.

27. In his *Nez Perce Texts* (University of California Publications in Linguistics, vol. 90 [1979]), Haruo Aoki gives a description by Elizabeth G. Wilson of an old-time celebration at Weippe, Idaho, for which many bands converged to dig camas and observe the Dreamer religion and, no doubt, to tell tales like this one. Herbert Spinden records a "Speech before a War-dance" ("Nez Perce Tales," p. 201), which suggests that war dances were also the occasion for celebrating tribal history and heroic tradition: "People, we shall see the garments of our dead men of long ago; so every one must come, because another time we may not be living. People, you will have a chance to tell the tale of your war-adventures after the dance today."

11 / Retroactive Prophecy in Western Indian Narrative

1. Tribal Chairman Roy Wilson in *Mt. St. Helens, the Volcano*, ed. Al McCready and Joseph R. Bianco (Portland: Oregonian Publishing Co., 1980), p. 36. Recent historians of the mountain's eruptions generally begin their chronicle with the 1840s, but a visitor to Fort Vancouver in the 1830s, the Rev. Samuel Parker, reports in detail an eruption in August 1831 (*Journal of an Exploring Tour beyond the Rocky Mountains* [Ithaca, 1838], p. 18).

2. Charles Wilkes, *Narrative of the U.S. Exploring Expedition during the Years 1838–1842*, vol. 4, pp. 439–40 (New York: George P. Putnam, 1851). Wilkes notes the "retroactive" element himself, observing that in fact the Indians "had knowledge of the whites long before the epoch designated." Cornelius had been an early supporter of the missionary Elkanah Walker, who arrived at Tshimakain in 1838, but his enthusiasm for Christianity seems to have cooled. See *Nine Years with the Spokane Indians*, ed. C. M. Drury (Glendale: A. C. Clark Co., 1976).

3. See Hayden White's discussion of "prefiguration" on the part of the historian in *Metahistory: The Historical Imagination in Nineteenth Century Europe* (Baltimore: Johns Hopkins University Press, 1973, 1980), pp. x–xi and passim.

4. *Kalapuya Texts*, ed. Melville Jacobs, University of Washington Publications in Anthropology, vol. 11 (1945), p. 69, narrator: John B. Hudson. It is curious that, to my knowledge at least, there are no extant "prophecies" of what was the worst single disaster to overtake the Western Indians after contact with the whites —

that is, the terrible epidemics, apparently malarial, that destroyed village after village along the Columbia and elsewhere in the 1830s. Perhaps it was a happening too horrible to be assimilated in mythic terms. The general lack of reference to virulent diseases in the mythologies is perhaps one clue, among others, that in their main outlines the narratives predate the contact era, when, besides malaria, smallpox, influenza, tuberculosis, and VD were introduced. A wonderful Kiowa story about how Saynday, the Kiowa trickster, outwitted "Smallpox" (who appears as a Protestant missionary!) and saved the Kiowas is given by Alice Marriott and Carol Rachlin in *American Indian Mythology* (New York: New American Library, 1968), pp. 177–78.

5. *Wishram Texts,* ed. Edward Sapir, Publications of the American Ethnological Society, vol. 2 (1909), pp. 229–31. "The events are supposed to have taken place at the Cascades long before the coming of the whites." In her *Indian Legends of Canada* (Toronto: McClelland and Stewart, 1960), Ella Clark gives dream-prophecies of the coming of the whites from the Ojibwas and the Micmacs (pp. 150–52).

6. The Zunis, *The Zunis: Self-Portrayals* (New York: New American Library, 1972), p. 2. The Mayan Cuceb, dating from the sixteenth century, seems likewise to contain elements of retroactive prophecy and foretellings of the present—which for the Mayans, of course, centered on Spanish occupation. See *Four Masterworks of American Indian Literature,* ed. John Bierhorst (New York: Farrar, Strauss, and Giroux, 1974). A weird extension of the impulse into Anglo counter-culture has appeared recently in the form of a widely circulated bogus "letter" from Chief Seattle of the Duwamish, dated 1854 and based stylistically on his great 1855 speech, but aimed at "prophesying" ecological and moral disaster at hand for late twentieth-century America. The prophecy is sincere and may well have merit, but its vehicle is full of anachronistic howlers—Chief Seattle is made to claim, for example, to have seen carcasses of buffalo from the railroad! Trains were in fact nowhere near Seattle's country in the 1850s, nor did the slaughter of buffalo (on the Great Plains, not in the Northwest) begin until after the Civil War. But what is at stake in the document, clearly, is not historical accuracy, but a kind of mythic truth-in-prophecy. See *Rochester Times-Union* (September 11, 1981), editorial page. Rudolf Kaiser has sorted out some of the tangled strands of the speech in "Chief Seattle's Speech(es): American Origins and European Reception," in *Recovering the Word,* ed. Swann and Krupat (Berkeley: University of California Press, 1987), pp.497–536. See also Albert Furtwangler's fascinating study, *Answering Chief Seattle* (Seattle: University of Washington Press, 1997).

7. H. S. Lyman, "Reminiscences of Louis Labonte," *Oregon Historical Quarterly* 1 (1900):167–88. The text of "the Skookum's Tongue" is in Jarold Ramsey, *Coyote Was Going There* (Seattle: University of Washington Press, 1977), p. 94.

8. Unpublished transcript in the files of the British Columbia Indian Language Project, Victoria, B.C.; narrator, Annie York, November 1973.

9. James Dorsey and A. L. Kroeber, *Traditions of the Arapaho,* Field Columbian Museum Publications, vol. 5 (1903), p. 19; J. R. Swanton, *Tlingit Myths and Texts,* Bureau of American Ethnology Bulletin, no. 39 (1909), p. 129.

10. Sarah Winnemucca, *Life among the Piutes,* ed. Mrs. Horace Mann (Boston and New York: G. P. Putnam and Sons, 1983), pp. 6–7. Sarah recalled her grandfather exclaiming, "My white brothers—my long looked-for white brothers have come at last!"

11. Winnemucca, *Life among the Piutes,* p. 14.

12. Franz Boas, *Chinook Texts,* U.S. Bureau of American Ethnology Bulletin, no. 20 (1894), pp. 278–79, narrated by Charles Cultee. Boas gives a literal as well as a "free" translation, and the former gives evidence that Cultee was performing a story as a self-conscious narrative artist, not just recounting a tribal anecdote.

13. See Dell Hymes's consideration of such patterns or "constellations" on a regional basis in *"In Vain I Tried to Tell You": Essays in Native American Ethnopoetics* (Philadelphia: University of Pennsylvania Press, 1981), especially chap. 8.

14. Dell Hymes, "Folklore's Nature and the Sun's Myth," *Journal of American Folklore* 88 (1975):345 ff.

15. Quoted by Claude T. Bissell, *Humanities in the University* (Legon: University of Ghana, 1977), p. 80.

16. See Cedric Whitman, *Sophocles: A Study in Heroic Humanism* (Cambridge: Harvard University Press, 1951), pp. 10–19 and passim; and C. M. Bowra, *Ancient Greek Literature* (New York: Oxford University Press, 1960), pp. 99 ff. See also Henry A. Myers, *Tragedy: A View of Life* (Ithaca: Cornell University Press, 1956).

17. W. S. Merwin, "Canso," in *The Dancing Bears* (New Haven: Yale University Press, 1954), p. 76. See my essay, "The Continuities of W. S. Merwin," in *Massachusetts Review* 14(3) (1977):569–90.

18. Quoted by Frank Kermode in *The Sense of an Ending* (New York: Oxford University Press, 1967), p. 31.

19. In some Western mythologies, these transformational intervals seem to be clustered together, so as to constitute a separate "Era of Transformations." Elizabeth Jacobs thus speaks of "three successive time-levels" among the Tillamooks of Oregon. "The earliest is the myth age. The next is the era of transformations, when South Wind [the Tillamook trickster-transformer] made the world over as it is known today. The third is the period of true happenings," *Nehalem Tillamook Tales* (Corvallis: Oregon State University Press, 1990), p. ix.

20. Robert Redfield, "Primitive World Views," *Proceedings Of the American Philosophical Society* 96 (1952):30–36.

21. See N. Scott Momaday, *The Way to Rainy Mountain* (New York: Ballantine, 1970), and Elsie C. Parsons, *Kiowa Tales,* Memoirs of the American Folklore Society, vol. 22 (1929).

22. Bronislaw Malinowski, "Myth in Primitive Psychology," in *Magic, Science, Religion, and Other Essays* (Boston: Free Press, 1948), p. 77.

23. Percy Cohen, "Theories of Myth," *Man* (1969):351–52. Cohen does acknowledge that "prophecy and myth may co-exist and even feed on each other," but an even more fundamental interaction is at work in these texts and, I think, in the mythologies of Western Indians generally.

24. See studies by James Mooney, *The Ghost Dance Religion,* Bureau of American Ethnology Annual Report, vol. 14, no. 2 (1896), and Weston LaBarre, *The Ghost Dance* (Garden City: Doubleday, 1970).

25. Hymes, "Folklore's Nature and the Sun's Myth," p. 360.

12 / The Bible in Western Indian Mythology

1. See, for example, Rev. Samuel Parker, *Journal of an Exploring Tour beyond the Rocky Mountains* (Ithaca, 1838), p. 236. This skepticism in a way parallels the reluctance of early folklorists to believe in the African origins of the Uncle Remus stories; the assumption was that blacks must have gotten them from the Indians. See Alan Dundes, "African Tales among the North American Indians," *Southern Folklore Quarterly* 39 (1965):207–19.

2. *The Mission of St. Augustine to England,* ed. Arthur James Mason, D.D. (Cambridge: University Press, 1897), pp. 77 ff.

3. Stith Thompson, "Sunday School Stories among Savages," *Texas Review* 3 (1917):109–16, and idem, *European Tales among the North American Indians,* Colorado College Publications in Language, vol. 2 (1919); Horace Beck, "The Acculturation of Old World Tales by the American Indians," *Midwest Folklore* 8 (1958): 205–16; Richard Dorson, *American Folklore* (Chicago: University of Chicago Press, 1959), pp. 23–25, and idem, "Comic Indian Anecdotes," *Southern Folklore Quarterly* 10 (1945):113–28; Francis L. Utley, "The Bible of the Folk," *California Folklore Quarterly* 4 (1945):1–17. Neither Thompson nor Beck considers the forms of Biblical assimilation; Dorson offers several entertaining instances of eighteenth-century Indians retelling Bible stories, but no interpretive commentary. Utley's essay is rich in suggestions about the general importance of Biblical derivations, but it relegates examination of New World materials to the status of "a valuable subsidiary study" (p. 5) in favor of European and Near Eastern subjects.

4. See, for example, *Kalapuya Texts,* ed. Melville Jacobs, University of Washington Publications in Anthropology, vol. 11 (1945), pp. 275 ff., and Jacobs, ed., *Northwest Sahaptin Texts,* vol. 1, Columbia University Contributions to Anthropology, vol. 19 (1934); also Louise McDonald, "Folklore of the Flathead Indians of Idaho," *Journal of American Folklore* 14 (1901):250–51; and "European Tales from the Upper Thompson Indians," ed. James Teit, *Journal of American Folklore* 29 (1916):301 ff. Other examples of assimilated European tales (and additional instances of Indian Bible stories) are in Stith Thompson's *Tales of the North American Indians* (Bloomington: University of Indiana Press, 1966), chaps. 8, 9.

5. *Notices and Voyages of the Famed Quebec Mission to the Pacific Northwest,* ed. and trans. Carl Landerholm (Portland: Champoeg Press, 1956), pp. 193–94.

6. Rev. Cushing Eells, quoted in Myron Eells, *Father Eells, or the Result of Fifty-five Years of Missionary Labors in Washington and Oregon* (Boston and Chicago: Congregational and Sunday School Publishing Co., 1894), p. 97.

7. Landerholm, *Notices and Voyages,* p. 45.

8. See illustrations in *Notices and Voyages,* and in John Fahey, *The Flathead Indians* (Norman: University of Oklahoma Press, 1974), p. 60. For a detailed account of the use of the Catholic ladder, see Father Blanchet's report of his services on Hood's Canal in 1839; Landerholm, *Notices and Voyages,* p. 63.

9. Landerholm, *Notices and Voyages,* p. 84. See also Kris White and Janie St. Laurent, "'Mysterious Journey': The Catholic Ladder of 1840," *Oregon Historical Quarterly* 97 (Spring 1996):70–88.

10. Clifford M. Drury, ed., *The Diaries and Letters of Henry H. Spaulding and Asa Bowen Smith, Relating to the Nez Perce Mission, 1838–42* (Glendale: Arthur H. Clark, 1958), p. 170.

11. Francis Utley, "The Bible of the Folk," *California Folklore Quarterly* 4 (1945):1–17.

12. Landerholm, *Notices and Voyages,* p. 51; Drury, *Diaries and Letters,* p. 170.

13. Drury, *Diaries and Letters,* p. 108.

14. Ibid., p. 140.

15. A. B. Meacham, *Wigwam and Warpath* (Boston: John P. Dale, 1875), p. 89. Perhaps it was the same skeptic who summarized a sermon on Moses as follows: "Well, he was telling about a man getting lost a long time ago. Got lost and couldn't find himself for forty years. That's a big story, but maybe it is so. I don't know. Never heard it before" (p. 134).

16. In Landerholm, *Notices and Voyages,* Father Blanchet observes that "a number were surprised and provoked when I explained to them the blessedness of heaven: they appeared to like better the sojourn on this earth than to go away to enjoy celestial bliss" (p. 68).

17. Thompson, "Sunday School Stories," p. 109.

18. During his nine years among the Spokane and Flathead Indians, Elkanah Walker contrived a syllabary and printed a translation of the Gospel of Matthew. See Clifford M. Drury, *Nine Years with the Spokane Indians* (Glendale: Arthur H. Clark, 1976), pp. 485–86.

19. I have adapted some ideas here from John R. Swanton's essay on forms of dissemination between Native groups; see "Some Practical Aspects of the Study of Myths," *Journal of American Folklore* 23 (1910):6 ff. On the value of Bible lore for the understanding of acculturation and myth diffusion generally, see Utley, "The Bible of the Folk," especially pp. 15–16.

20. In Swanton's terms, this would be "combination on account of similars."

21. James Teit, *Mythology of the Thompson Indians,* Memoirs of the American Museum of Natural History, vol. 12, pt. 2 (1912), pp. 400–401.

22. On the level of adaptation, Swanton speaks of "ritualization of myths, which takes place when an attempt is made to weave together the borrowed, sacred legends into a consistent tribal, clan, or society story." In *The Death and Rebirth of the Seneca* (New York: Random House, 1972), pp. 242 ff., Anthony F. C. Wallace describes in detail the "adaptations" made by the prophet Handsome Lake of traditional Seneca beliefs and myths to his new Christian-influenced gospel. Ultimately,

one thinks of the New Testament's drastic "adaptation" of the Old Dispensation in the name of a continuity of belief.

23. James Teit, "Folk-tales of Salish Tribes," *Memoirs of the American Folklore Society,* vol. 11 (1917), pp. 80–83. There seems to have been a tradition in some Northwest mythologies of a succession of transformers; for a Creation story in which Jesus as the "Chief Above" sends down first Crow, who is an utter failure, and then Coyote, who is a success, see Melville Jacobs, *Northwest Sahaptin Texts,* in Columbia University Contributions to Anthropology (1934), pp. 238 ff. In *"In Vain I Tried to Tell You": Essays in Native American Ethnopoetics* (Philadelphia: University of Pennsylvania Press, 1981), Dell Hymes gives the text of a Wishram Chinookan "Crier's" speech, which takes a much harder line, urging the people on Sunday to ignore Christian worship, and insisting that "SHuSúgli [Jesus] was a Jew; / he was not Nadidanwit, / and he was not for the Nadidanwit" (p. 204).

24. Teit, *Mythology of the Thompson Indians,* pp. 402–4. For general ethnographic background, see Teit, *The Thompson Indians of British Columbia,* Publications of the Jesup North Pacific Expedition (Leiden: E. J. Brill, 1909), vol. 1, pt. 4. Teit reports that according to a post-contact shamanistic tradition only non-Christians go over the old trail to the spirit-land; those who are Christians must go by a new trail, after a long period of "wandering around from one graveyard to another" (p. 359).

25. Isabel Kelly, "Northern Paiute Tales," *Journal of American Folklore* 51 (1938):437; reprinted in Jarold Ramsey, *Coyote Was Going There* (Seattle: University of Washington Press, 1977), p. 258. A more straightforward adaptation of the Adam and Eve story, from the Klamaths, is given by A. S. Gatschet in *The Klamath Indians,* Contributions to North American Ethnography, vol. 2 (1890), pp. xciii–xciv; reprinted in Jones and Ramsey, *The Stories We Tell* (Corvallis: Oregon State University Press, 1994), pp. 291–92. Here Satan is a shaman who tempts Eve with a sweet berry and then steals all the fruit in the Garden.

26. Teit, "Folk-tales of Salish Tribes," pp. 53–56. For ethnographic details, see Teit, *The Thompson Indians of British Columbia,* vol. 1, pt. 4, pp. 324 ff. For an instance of secular mythopoesis of great power—a dramatization in strictly traditional forms of the disastrous consequences of contact with whites—see Charles Cultee's "The Sun's Myth" (Kathlamet) in Dell Hymes's translation and with his commentary, in *Journal of American Folklore* 88 (1975):345 ff. In this volume, see essays 9 and 11.

27. See Teit, *The Thompson Indians of British Columbia,* pp. 343 ff.

28. Teit, "Folk-tales of the Salish Tribes," p. 53. Compare Francis Utley's brief analysis of Christian and Native elements in a Pima creation myth in "The Bible of the Folk," pp. 14–15.

29. In the modern transcriptions being compiled in the British Columbia Indian Language Project (Victoria, B.C.), there are a number of remarkable tales on Christian and European folk themes. I am indebted to the project's director, Mr. Randy Bouchard, for calling my attention to these unpublished stories.

30. See Sarah Winnemucca Hopkins's poignant account of how her grandfather, the Paiute chief Truckee, ruinously persisted in welcoming the whites to Nevada in the 1840s because of his strict interpretation of the Paiute creation myth, in *Life among the Paiutes,* ed. Mrs. Horace Mann (New York: G. P. Putnam's Sons, 1883), pp. 6–7. See essay 11, this volume. A collection of essays by the distinguished scholar Äke Hultkrantz on some of the issues discussed in this essay has been edited by Christopher Vecsey: *Belief and Worship in Native North America* (Syracuse: Syracuse University Press, 1981). See especially the essays listed under "Persistence and Change."

13 / Tí� Jean and the Seven� headed Dragon

1. See Stith Thompson, *European Tales among the North American Indians: A Study in the Migration of Folk-Tales,* Colorado College Language Series, vol. 2, no. 34 (April/May 1919), and his *Tales of the North American Indians* (1929; reprint ed., Bloomington: Indiana University Press, 1967), pp. 201–60. Thompson's two volumes together provide the fullest bibliography of Indian-European tales in print.

2. Dell Hymes, *"In Vain I Tried to Tell You": Essays in Native American Ethnopoetics* (Philadelphia: University of Pennsylvania Press, 1981), p. 276.

3. **Tlingit:** John R. Swanton, *Tlingit Myths and Texts,* Smithsonian Institution Bureau of American Ethnology, Bulletin 39 (Washington, D.C.: Government Printing Office, 1909), pp. 196–98. **Thompson:** James Teit, "European Tales from the Upper Thompson Indians," *Journal of American Folk-lore* 29 (1916):301–29. **Shuswap:** James Alexander Teit, "Sna'naz and Seven-Heads," in *The Shuswap,* Memoirs of the American Museum of Natural History, vol. 4 (1909; reprint ed., New York: AMS, 1975), pp. 753–55. **Okanagan:** Randy Bouchard and Dorothy Kennedy, "Okanagan Texts," British Columbia Indian Language Project (unpublished, Victoria, B.C., n.d.), unpaged. **Kalapuya:** Melville Jacobs, *Kalapuya Texts,* University of Washington Publications in Anthropology, vol. 2 (Seattle: University of Washington, 1945), pp. 312–21. **Zuñi:** Elsie Clews Parsons and Franz Boas, "Spanish Tales from Laguna and Zuñi, New Mexico," *Journal of American Folk-lore* 33 (1920):50–64. **Nez Perce:** Herbert Spinden, "Nez Percé Tales," in *Folk-Tales of Salishan and Sahaptin Tribes,* ed. Franz Boas, Memoirs of the American Folk-Lore Society, vol. 2 (1917, reprint ed., New York: Kraus Reprint, 1969), pp. 180–201. **Kutenai:** Edward S. Curtis, *The North American Indian,* ed. Frederick Webb Hodge (1911; reprint ed., New York: Johnson Reprint, 1970), vol. 7, pp. 149–52. **Plains Cree:** Alanson Skinner, "Plains Cree Tales," *Journal of American Folk-lore* 29 (1916): 341–67. **Blackfoot:** Clark Wissler and D. C. Duvall, *Mythology of the Blackfoot Indians,* Anthropological Papers of the American Museum of Natural History, vol. 2, pt. 1 (1909; reprint ed., New York: AMS, 1975), p. 163. **Piegan:** Truman Michelson, "Letter," *Journal of American Folk-lore* 29 (1916):409. **Osage:** James Dorsey, "Traditions of the Osage," Field Museum of Natural History (Chicago), Anthropologi-

cal Series, vol. 7, no. 1 (1904), pp. 34–37. **Omaha/Ponka:** James Dorsey, "The Cegiha Language: Myths, Stories, and Letters," *Contributions to North American Ethnology,* vol. 6 (1890), pp. 114–16. **Biloxi:** James Owen Dorsey and John R. Swanton, *A Dictionary of the Biloxi and Ofo Languages,* Smithsonian Institution Bureau of American Ethnology, Bulletin 47 (Washington, D.C.: Government Printing Office, 1912), pp. 33–36. **Ojibwa:** Paul Radin, *Some Myths and Tales of the Ojibwa of Southeastern Ontario, Canada,* Department of Mines, Geological Survey Memoir 48, Anthropological Series, no. 2 (Ottawa: Government Printing Bureau, 1914), pp. 47–49; Alanson Skinner, "European Tales from the Plains Ojibwa," *Journal of American Folk-lore* 29 (1916):330–40. **Mohawk:** F. G. Speck and H. P. Beck, "Old World Tales among the Mohawks," *Journal of American Folklore* 63 (1950):285–308.

4. See Wissler and Duvall, *Blackfoot Mythology,* pp. 53–58.

5. Jacobs, *Kalapuya Texts,* pp. 312–21.

6. In Myron Eells, *Father Eells, or The Results of Fifty-Five Years of Missionary Labors in Washington and Oregon: A Biography of Rev. Cushing Eells, D. D.* (Boston: Congregational Sunday School and Publishing Society, 1894), pp. 96–97. See essay 12, this volume.

7. An exception that would seem to "prove" this rule: the official accusation by Reverend Asa Bowen Smith against his colleague among the Nez Perce and other Sahaptin groups, Henry Spaulding, that Spaulding was "in the habit" of mingling his instruction from the Bible with a good deal of fiction, drawing from *Paradise Lost,* etc. See essay 12, this volume.

8. "White Men Are Snakes," in Jarold Ramsey, *Coyote Was Going There: Indian Literature of the Oregon Country* (Seattle: University of Washington Press, 1977), p. 258.

9. H. S. Lyman, "Reminiscences of Louis Labonte," *Oregon Historical Quarterly* 1 (1900):167–88.

10. *The Golden Woman: The Colville Narrative of Peter J. Seymour,* ed. and trans. Anthony Mattina (Tucson: University of Arizona Press, 1985), p. 14. Mattina's fascinating study of a long story he transcribed in Washington State in the 1960s illustrates the continuation into modern times of the Indian/European stories.

11. Thompson, *European Tales among the North American Indians,* pp. 326–27.

12. Claude Lévi-Strauss, "The Structural Study of Myth," in *Structural Anthropology,* trans. Claire Jacobson and Brooke Grundfest Schoepf (New York: Basic, 1963), pp. 206–31.

13. Marius Barbeau, "5. Ti-Jean, les chevaux, et la bête-à-sept-têtes," in his "Contes populaires Canadiens," *Journal of American Folk-lore* 29 (1916):41–45; told by David Sioui in 1914, in Lorette, Quebec. Barbeau also presents a second, rather anomalous version of the story ("42. La Bête-à-sept-têtes"), collected by Gustave Lanctôt, in which there is no impostor and the monster stands guard in the house of three giants; see "Fables, contes, et formulas," *Journal of American Folk-lore* 29 (1916):142–45. In the second series of "Contes populaires Canadiens," *Journal of*

American Folk-lore 30 (1917): 82–86, Barbeau gives a third Quebec version ("58. Les Trois Frères et la bête-à-sept-têtes"), in which Ti-Jean's killing of the dragon leads into the well-known story of the "Blue Light." Other versions can be found in Emmanuel Cosquin, *Contes populaires de Lorraine* (Paris: F. Vieweg, n.d.), vol. 1, pp. 60–66; Geneviève Massignon, *Folktales of France* (Chicago: University of Chicago Press, 1968), pp. 34–39; Paul Delarue, *The Borzoi Book of French Folk Tales* (New York: Alfred A. Knopf, 1956), pp. 187–200.

14. In Barbeau's primary text (no. 5), Ti-Jean's brothers look in vain for the beast that is eating up their hay, and at last Jean discovers that it is a white horse, a black horse, and a red horse—which become his magical helpers.

15. In Jacobs's Kalapuya text, the magical helper is a talking stick; in Barbeau's no. 42, the helpers are a sash, a wand, and a little dog. Massignon's popular version features three horses, white, black, and chestnut, and this is by far the most popular combination.

16. In Barbeau's no. 5 text, Jean retreats to a little cave; in Massignon, he takes a menial job in the King's stable.

17. In Barbeau no. 5, the impostor is "tested" by being made to ride, unsuccessfully, one of the King's most fractious horses—a detail that is, to my knowledge, unique among French versions and nonexistent in Indian adaptations. In Massignon, the impostor is only one of the King's gardeners.

18. In Barbeau no. 5, the recognition scene per se comes about because of a request from the King for both the impostor and Ti-Jean to tell their stories: "'Comment t'y es-tu pris pour tuer la Bête-à-sept-têtes?'" (p. 45).

19. In Barbeau no. 5, "le charbonnier fut brûlé" (p. 45); a similar end comes to the three conspiring coal-miners in Delarue's version (p. 194).

20. James Teit, "The Making of Languages," *in Mythology of the Thompson Indians,* Memoir of the American Museum of Natural History, vol. 12 (1912; reprint ed., New York: AMS, 1975), pp. 400–401.

21. Jacobs, *Kalapuya Texts,* p. 315.

22. In two summarized versions of the story in Teit, "European Tales from the Upper Thompson Indians," pp. 307–8, the monster has eight heads, as it does in Skinner's Plains Ojibwa version. Whether this would have seemed even more freakish than seven heads to the Thompson and the Ojibwa, I cannot say.

23. See note 3.

24. In Skinner's Plains Ojibwa version, the impostor is a "blacksmith."

25. Bruno Bettelheim, *The Uses of Enchantment: The Meaning and Importance of Fairy Tales* (New York: Alfred A. Knopf, 1976), p. 24.

26. In Dorsey's Omaha/Ponka texts, "Orphan" is the hero of a cycle of stories—one of which happens to be a version of the Ti-Jean tale. For the Kutenai and Osage instances, see Curtis, *The North American Indian,* vol. 8, p. 149, and Dorsey, "Traditions of the Osage," p. 35.

27. Jacobs, *Kalapuya Texts,* pp. 312–14.

28. Skinner, "European Texts from the Plains Ojibwa," pp. 330–31.

29. Jacobs, *Kalapuya Texts,* pp. 320–21.

30. See essay 5, this volume.

31. Archie Phinney, *Nez Perce Texts,* Columbia University Contributions to Anthropology, vol. 25 (1934; reprint ed., New York: AMS, 1969), p. 29. The Nez Perce Ti-Jean story is in Spinden, *The Nez Perce Indians* (1908).

32. Phinney, *Nez Perce Texts,* pp. 26–29.

33. Dorsey, "The Cegiha Language," pp. 114–15; Jacobs, *Kalapuya Texts,* p. 315. On the Kalapuya monster Amhuluk, see Albert S. Gatschet, "Oregonian Folklore," *Journal of American Folklore* 4 (1891):141–43.

34. Dorsey, "Traditions of the Osage," pp. 34–37.

35. Thompson, *European Tales among the North American Indians,* p. 332.

36. See essay 12, this volume.

37. Phinney, *Nez Perce Texts,* p. ix.

38. If anything, some editors have been almost too eager to identify what may well be thoroughly Native narratives as "European-influenced." See, for example, Stith Thompson's inclusion of a Zuñi story about a girl and her turkeys in his section "Tales Borrowed from Europeans," in *Tales of the North American Indians,* pp. 225–31. Transcribing and translating this story directly from the Zuñi language, Dennis Tedlock offers it without apology or explanation as a traditional Zuñi narrative in his *Finding the Center: Narrative Poetry of the Zuñi Indians* (New York: Dial, 1972).

39. See, for example, the French-derived tales in Teit's "European Tales from the Upper Thompson Indians."

14 / Francis La Flesche's "The Song of Flying Crow" and the Limits of Ethnography

1. Margot Liberty, "Francis La Flesche," in *American Indian Intellectuals,* ed. Margot Liberty (St. Paul: West Publishing Company, 1978), p. 99.

2. Alice Fletcher and Francis La Flesche, Papers, #4558/48, National Anthropological Archives of the Smithsonian Institution, Washington, D.C. I am grateful to the National Anthropological Archives and, specifically, to Kathleen T. Baxter, Reference Archivist, for help with this project and for granting permission to publish the text of "The Song of Flying Crow" for the first time.

3. In *The Omaha Tribe,* Annual Report of the Bureau of American Ethnology, vol. 27 (1911), La Flesche is allowed to break into the standard scholarly format (presumably laid down by Fletcher and the BAE) from time to time with short personalized accounts of Omaha rituals, anecdotes about the difficulties of collecting material, and so on—but in agate type! This is his account—relevant to the present text—of recording the songs of the Sacred Pole from an Omaha elder, Yellow Smoke, having been at first refused: "As I listened to the old priest, his voice seemed as full and resonant as when I had heard him years ago, in the days when the singing

of these very songs in the Holy Tent meant so much to each gens and to every man, woman, and child in the tribe. Now the old man sang with his eyes closed, and watching him there was like watching the last embers of the religious rites of a vanishing people" (p. 251). Hardly conventional ethnography!

4. In Norma Kidd Green, *Iron Eye's Family: The Children of Joseph La Flesche* (Lincoln: Johnson Publishing Company, 1969), p. 196.

5. Both pieces appeared in *The Southern Workman:* "The Story of a Vision" (February 1901), pp. 106–9, and "One Touch of Nature" (August 1913), pp. 427–28. "The Story of a Vision" has been recently republished in *The Singing Spirit: Early Short Stories by North American Indians,* ed. Bernd C. Peyer (Tucson: University of Arizona Press, 1989), pp. 69–73. It is, in form and style, a kind of ethnographic sketch like "The Song of Flying Crow," but it lacks the persistent self-consciousness. In *Ke-ma-ha: The Omaha Stories of Francis La Flesche,* James Parins and Daniel Littlefield republish these two stories and add sixteen additional stories and sketches, which apparently La Flesche hoped—around 1900–1901—to publish as a collection of fictional pieces on Omaha boyhood.

6. *American Indian Life,* ed. Elsie Clews Parsons (New York: B. W. Huebsch Inc., 1922), p. 289.

7. See Kroeber's Introduction to *American Indian Life,* p. 13.

8. Francis La Flesche, *The Middle Five* (1900; reprint ed., Madison: University of Wisconsin Press, 1963). La Flesche had "ethnographic" troubles with prospective publishers, who objected that the book did not conform to Anglo stereotypes of "wild" Indian children! La Flesche's pancultural aspiration is asserted in the dedication: "To the Universal Boy." Evidently, as noted above, he also considered publishing his short stories and sketches (possibly including the present text) in a collection for general readers but, again, ran afoul of publishers: "One requested that the stories be told with humor on the order of Uncle Remus" (see Green, *Iron Eye's Family,* p. 189). See also Parins and Littlefield 1995.

9. Alice Fletcher, Francis La Flesche, and J. C. Fillmore, *A Study of Omaha Indian Music,* in Archaeological and Ethnological Papers of the Peabody Museum, vol. 1, no. 1 (1893).

10. In her excellent biography of Alice Fletcher, *A Stranger in Her Native Land* (Lincoln: University of Nebraska Press, 1988), Joan Mark notes the pattern: "Francis had a month's vacation at the Indian Bureau, and he usually went to visit his family on the Omaha Reservation" (p. 252).

11. Green, *Iron Eye's Family,* pp. 192–93.

12. La Flesche eventually retired to Carey's farm, near Macy, Nebraska, and died there on 5 September 1932.

13. Green, *Iron Eye's Family,* p. 188.

14. Liberty, "Francis La Flesche," p. 54.

15. William Butler Yeats, *A Vision* (London: Macmillan, 1965), p. 25.

16. The ritual and symbolic significance of the pipe is described at length in Fletcher and La Flesche, *The Omaha Tribe.*

17. Fletcher, La Flesche, and Fillmore, *A Study of Omaha Indian Music,* pp. 18, 43 ff. About "mystery songs," the authors note that "songs belonging to this subdivision are potent to secure general benefits" (p. 43)—a quality that seems to tally with Flying Crow's hopes for his song's beneficent effect on his friends. In the Omaha musical scheme, Flying Crow's composition appears to be the mirror opposite in intention to the Omaha Funeral Song, which "is for the spirit of the dead; it is to cheer him as he goes from his dear ones left behind on the earth; so as he hears the voices of his friends, their glad tones help him to go forward on his inevitable journey" (Fletcher and La Flesche, *The Omaha Tribe,* p. 593). Elsewhere in *The Omaha Tribe,* describing Omaha initiation ceremonies, La Flesche notes that all the songs pertaining to these ceremonies conform to a special rhythmical norm—and then goes on to say that "a similar rule was observed in the songs connected with any given society or rite—they all conformed to the rhythmic standard peculiar to the society or the ceremonial. As a result, an Indian could classify at once a song by its style . . ." (pp. 502–3). So, apparently, here—but La Flesche's *emic* competency cannot identify for him *whose* "mystery song" it is, or personalize its features.

18. See essay 15, this volume, on the validation of traditional forms by the new talents and purposes of modern Indian writers.

19. Fletcher and La Flesche, *The Omaha Tribe,* 643–54.

20. Ibid., p. 156. The crow seems to have been important symbolically to the Omaha because its presence in the sky often served to indicate that buffalo herds were nearby (p. 300).

21. I am indebted for this information to Professor Robin Ridington, who put me in touch with Mr. Paul Brill, and to Mr. Brill himself, for generously sharing information in his Omaha genealogical files with me.

22. See R. H. Barnes, *Two Crows Denies It: A History of Controversy in Omaha Sociology* (Lincoln: University of Nebraska Press, 1984), p. 25.

23. The Omaha religion heavily emphasized the concept of "a common and interrelated life, a living form that permeates, and is continuous in, all forms and appearances" (Fletcher and La Flesche, *The Omaha Tribe,* p. 588). Hence the trend of Flying Crow's meditation, linking the mutability of human lives with those of all creatures, would be, according to Fletcher and La Flesche, very typical of Omaha thinking.

24. The term "self-fashioning" and the idea behind it were suggested by Stephen Greenblatt's *Renaissance Self-Fashioning: From More to Shakespeare* (Chicago: University of Chicago Press, 1980), and by James Clifford's *The Predicament of Culture: Twentieth-Century Ethnography, Literature, and Art* (Cambridge: Harvard University Press, 1988), especially his essay "On Ethnographic Self-Fashioning: Conrad and Malinowski" (pp. 92–113). Clifford's examinations of the "ethnographics" of our literature and art are invariably stimulating and often illuminating. It is odd that he has not taken up the richly problematic writings of Native ethnographers such as Francis La Flesche, William Jones, Archie Phinney, Ella DeLoria, and others.

25. Dorothy Clarke Wilson, *Bright Eyes: The Story of Susette La Flesche, an Omaha Indian* (New York: McGraw-Hill, 1974), pp. 11, 373. The song's currency among the Omaha is also indicated by Francis La Flesche's brother-in-law, the journalist and politician Thomas Henry Tibbles, who quotes from "An Indian Death Song" as follows: "Where shall I go to live forever? / Where shall I go to live forever?" (see *Buckskin and Blanket Days* [1900; reprint ed., Garden City: Doubleday, 1957], p. 243).

If as suggested above La Flesche wrote his memoir of the mission school days he shared with Flying Crow after writing this piece, why does he omit all reference in *The Middle Five* to his runaway friend? Perhaps because he resolved to focus on instances of acculturation like his own and that of his tragic friend Rush; perhaps because he had written all he intended to write about Flying Crow.

15 / Tradition and Individual Talents in Modern Indian Writing

1. Jarold Ramsey, *Coyote Was Going There* (Seattle: University of Washington Press, 1977)

2. See essays 12 and 13, this volume.

3.Thus the first version of D'Arcy McNickle's *Wind from an Enemy Sky* (titled *The Flight of Feather Boy*) was rejected by a publisher in part because the editors felt that it was "insufficiently Indian"; and Francis La Flesche was advised by several publishers that the content of *The Middle Five* wasn't Indian enough. See Louis Owens, *Other Destinies: Understanding the American Indian Novel* (Norman: University of Oklahoma Press, 1992), p. 78.

4. These issues have been cogently discussed by Karl Kroeber, William Thackeray, Robert Lewis, and Kay Sands in a special issue of the ASAIL Newsletter on *The Death of Jim Loney* 5 (Fall 1981):3–4.

5. Silko's review, in a New Mexico newspaper, has been reprinted in *SAIL* 10(4) (1987):187–94.

6. Simon Ortiz, "Towards a National Indian Literature: Cultural Authenticity in Nationalism," in Richard Fleck, *Critical Perspectives on Native American Fiction*. See Gerald Vizenor's discussion of concepts of tribalism, pan-tribalism, and nationalism in relation to what he calls "the literature of dominance" in *Manifest Manners: Post-Indian Warriors of Survivance* (Hanover and London: Wesleyan University Press, 1994), pp. 59–60.

7. See Vine Deloria's *Custer Died for Your Sins: An Indian Manifesto* (New York: Macmillan, 1969) and *We Talk, You Listen: New Tribes, New Turf* (New York: Macmillan, 1970). Even the pronouncements of American Indian Movement leader Russell Means seem to defer to the concept of regional and tribal differences, and the Native pride founded on those differences.

8. See Leslie Silko's criticism of Gary Snyder and other Anglo writers in "An Old-time Indian Attack Conducted in Two Parts," in *The Remembered Earth: An*

Anthology of Native American Literature, ed. Geary Hobson (Albuquerque: Red Earth Press, 1979), pp. 211–16. Silko's polemic and Hobson's own essay in the same volume, "The Rise of the White Shaman as a New Version of 'Cultural Imperialism'" (pp. 100–108), have plenty to say against current Anglo literary exploitations of Native materials and values, but they leave unconsidered the related question of what Indian writers owe to Anglo language and literature. In denying that Anglo writers should engage Indian materials, they also fail to consider that proposition's equally harsh inverse—that Indian writers should not be free to engage Anglo experience. In my view the denial and its inverse constitute a reductio ad absurdum of all such restrictions. A more cogent statement on the issue is Duane Niatum's "On Stereotypes," *Parnassus* 7(8) (1978):160–66. I have pursued the historical aspects of the Americanist neglect of Indian literature in "Thoreau's Last Words— and America's First Literatures," in *Redefining American Literary History,* ed. A. LaVonne Brown Ruoff and Jerry W. Ward, Jr. (New York: Modern Language Association, 1990), pp. 52–61.

9. *Papago Woman,* ed. Ruth Underhill (New York: Holt Rinehart and Winston, 1979), p. 51.

10. The efforts of a group of distinguished anthropologists to present Indian cultures fictively can be seen in a fascinating experiment entitled *American Indian Life,* ed. Elsie Clews Parsons (New York: B. W. Huebsch, 922). See James Clifford, *The Predicament of Culture: Twentieth Century Ethnography, Literature, and Art* (Cambridge: Harvard University Press, 1988).

11. See Claude Lévi-Strauss's structuralist concept of repetition as a way of marking deep structure, in *Structural Anthropology* (Garden City: Doubleday, 1967), p. 226. For a sensitive and informed analysis of forms of repetition and other Native literary features foreign to Anglo readers, see Paula Gunn Allen, "The Sacred Hoop," in *Studies in American Indian Literature* (New York: Modern Language Association, 1983), pp. 13–37. For general commentary on the style of traditional Indian poetry, see my "Native American Poetry," in *The New Princeton Encyclopedia of Poetry and Poetics,* ed. T. V. F. Brogan (Princeton: Princeton University Press, 1993), pp. 42–44.

12. See Elsie C. Parsons, *Pueblo Indian Religion,* 2 vols. (Chicago: University of Chicago Press, 1939), vol. 1, pp. 455 ff.

13. See, for example, the Saynday or "Sendeh" stories in Alice Marriott, *Saynday's People* (Lincoln: University of Nebraska Press, 1963), and Elsie C. Parsons, *Kiowa Tales,* Memoirs of the American Folklore Society, vol. 22 (1929). It is hard to imagine how, in fact, Momaday could have introduced the Saynday material into his book without doing violence to the tone of reverent discovery he maintains so effectively.

14. In T. S. Eliot, *The Dial,* vol. 75 (1923), pp. 480–83.

15. Ortiz, "Time to Kill in Gallup," in *The Remembered Earth,* ed. Geary Hobson, p. 267.

16. Ortiz, "A San Diego Poem," in *The Remembered Earth*, p. 269.

17. Duane Niatum, "Raven and the Fear of Growing White," in *Songs for the Harvester of Dreams* (Seattle: University of Washington Press, 1981), p. 29.

18. Elizabeth Woody, *Seven Hands, Seven Hearts* (Portland: The Eighth Mountain Press, 1994), p. 52.

19. Woody, *Seven Hands, Seven Hearts,* pp. 21–24.

20. Ibid., p. 16.

21. Hanay Geiogamah, *New Native American Drama: Three Plays,* with an excellent introduction by Jeffrey Huntsman (Norman: University of Oklahoma Press, 1980). See also *Aboriginal Voices: Amerindian, Inuit, and Sami Theater,* ed. Per Brask and Willam Morgan (Baltimore: Johns Hopkins University Press, 1991).

22. Kenneth Lincoln, *Native American Renaissance* (Los Angeles: University of California Press, 1983).

23. Louise Erdrich, *Tracks* (New York: Harper and Row, 1988), p. 32.

24. James Welch, *Fools Crow* (New York: Viking, 1986). See my review of the novel in *Parabola* 12 (Spring 1987): 436–37.

25. See Franz Boas, *Keresan Texts,* Publications of the American Ethnological Society, no. 8 (1925–28). For an extensive and tactful study of mythic elements in Silko's short stories, see A. LaVonne Ruoff, "Ritual and Renewal in Kares Traditions in the Short Fiction of Leslie Silko," *Melus* 5 (1978):2–17. In *Four American Indian Literary Masters* (Norman: University of Oklahoma Press, 1982), pp. 106–21, Alan Velie discusses *Ceremony,* not too plausibly, as a "grail story." Silko mixes personal and oral-traditional elements (rather as Momaday has done in *The Way to Rainy Mountain* and *The Names*) in *Storyteller* (New York: Seaver, 1981).

26. *Ceremony* (New York: New Signet/New American Library, 1977), p. 1. Subsequent references are to this text. For ethnographic context, see Hamilton Tyler, *Pueblo Gods and Myths* (Norman: University of Oklahoma Press, 1964), p. 89.

27. Boas, *Keresan Texts,* pp. 8 ff. Other episodes in the novel that are glossed by myth-episodes in Boas's collection include the story of "The Gambler," Kaup'a-ta (pp. 76 ff.), and Tayo's mystical encounter with a mountain lion during his hunt for his uncle's cows, the mountain lion being a powerful Pueblo spirit for hunting prowess and general masculine well-being. See Boas, *Keresan Texts,* pp. 28–33, 72–76, and Hamilton A. Tylor, *Pueblo Animals and Myths* (Norman: University of Oklahoma Press, 1975), pp. 211–36.

28. Boas, *Keresan Texts,* pp. 146–47.

29. In *Manifest Manners,* Gerald Vizenor emphasizes that authentic tribal consciousness is "comic not tragic," as in the way of the trickster (p. 14).

BIBLIOGRAPHY

Aeschylus. *Prometheus Bound.* Trans. David Grene. In *Greek Tragedies,* vol. 1, ed. David Grene and Richmond Lattimore. Chicago: University of Chicago Press, 1960.

Allen, Paula Gunn, ed. *Studies in American Indian Literature.* New York: Modern Language Association, 1983.

Andrade, Manuel. *Quileute Texts.* Columbia University Contributions to Anthropology, vol. 12, 1931.

Aoki, Haruo. *Nez Perce Texts.* University of California Publications in Linguistics, vol. 90, 1979.

Babcock-Abraham, Barbara. "'A Tolerated Margin of Mess': The Trickster and His Tales Reconsidered," *Journal of the Folklore Institute* 11:145–86, 1975.

Bakeless, John. *Lewis and Clark: Partners in Discovery.* New York: William Morrow, 1947.

Bakhtin, Mikhail. *The Dialogic Imagination.* Trans. Caryl Emerson and Michael Holquist; edited by Michael Holquist. Austin: University of Texas Press, 1981.

Barbeau, Marius. "Contes populaires Canadiens," *Journal of American Folk-lore* 29, 1916.

Barber, C. L. *Shakespeare's Festive Comedy.* Cleveland and New York: World Publishing, 1963.

Barnes, R. H. *Two Crows Denies It: A History of Controversy in Omaha Sociology.* Lincoln: University of Nebraska Press, 1984.

Barnett, Homer P. "Culture Elements Distribution VII: Oregon Coast," *Anthropological Records* 1 (3):155–203, 1957.

Bascom, W. R. "Four Functions of Folklore," *Journal of American Folklore* 67:333–49, 1954.

Beal, Merrill D. *"I Will Fight No More Forever": Chief Joseph and the Nez Perce War.* Seattle and London: University of Washington Press, 1963.

Beck, Horace. "The Acculturation of Old World Tales by the American Indians," *Midwest Folklore* 8:205–16, 1958.

Beckett, Samuel. *Endgame.* New York: Grove Press, 1958.

Bettelheim, Bruno. *The Uses of Enchantment: The Meaning and Importance of Fairy Tales.* New York: Knopf, 1976.

Bierhorst, John, ed. *Four Masterworks of American Indian Literature.* New York: Farrar, Strauss, and Giroux, 1974.

———. *The Red Swan.* New York: Farrar, Strauss, and Giroux, 1976.

———. *The Mythology of North America.* New York: Morrow, 1985.

Boas, Franz. *Chinook Texts.* Bureau of American Ethnology Bulletin 20, 1894.

———. *Indianische Sagen von der Nord-Pacifischen Küste Amerikas.* Berlin: A. Asher, 1895.

———. *Kathlamet Texts.* Bureau of American Ethnology Bulletin 26, 1901.

———. *Folktales of Salish and Sahaptin Tribes.* Memoirs of the American Folk-lore Society, vol. 11, 1917.

———. "Traditions of the Tillamook Indians," *Journal of American Folklore* 11:23–38, 133–150, 1898.

Boas, Franz, ed. *Keresan Texts.* Publications of the American Ethnological Society, no. 8, 1925–28.

Bohannon, Laura. "Shakespeare in the Bush." In *Every Man His Way,* ed. Alan Dundes, pp. 477–86. Englewood Cliffs: Prentice Hall, 1968.

Bouchard, Randy, and Dorothy Kennedy, eds. "Lillooet Stories," *Sound Heritage,* vol. 6, no. 1, 1977.

Bright, William, ed. *A Coyote Reader.* Berkeley and Los Angeles: University of California Press, 1993.

Bruchac, Joseph. *Roots of Survival: Native American Storytelling and the Sacred.* Golden, Colorado: Fulcrum, 1996.

Bruchac, Joseph, ed. *Survival This Way: Interviews with Native American Poets.* Tucson: University of Arizona Press, 1987.

Brunvand, Jan. *Readings in American Folklore.* New York: Norton, 1979.

Burlingame, Lori. "Cultural Survival in *Runner in the Sun.*" In *The Legacy of D'Arcy McNickle,* ed. John Purdy, pp. 137–51. Norman: University of Oklahoma Press, 1996.

Carroll, Michael. "Lévi-Strauss, Freud, and the Trickster: A New Perspective on an Old Problem," *American Ethnology* 8 (2):301–17, 1981.

Clark, Ella, ed. *Indian Legends of Canada.* Toronto: McClelland and Stewart, 1960.

———. *Indian Legends of the Pacific Northwest.* Berkeley and Los Angeles: University of California Press, 1953.

Clark, Keith, and Donna Clark, eds. "William McKay's Journal, 1866–67," *Oregon Historical Quarterly* 79:269–338, 1978.

Clements, William M. *Native American Verbal Art: Texts and Contexts.* Tucson: University of Arizona Press, 1996.

Clifford, James, and George Marcus, eds. *Writing Culture: The Poetics and Politics of Ethnography.* Berkeley and Los Angeles: University of California Press, 1986.

Cohen, Percy. "Theories of Myth," *Man*, pp. 337–53, 1969.

Coltelli, Laura, ed. *Winged Words: Native American Writers Speak.* Lincoln: University of Nebraska Press, 1990.

Curtin, Jeremiah. *The Memoirs of Jeremiah Curtin.* Wisconsin Biography Series, vol. 2. Madison, 1942.

———. "Wasco Tales and Myths." In *Wishram Texts*, ed. Edward Sapir. Publications of the American Ethnological Society, vol. 2, pp. 239–314, 1909.

Curtis, Edward. *The North American Indian*, vols. 8 and 13. Norwood, MA: Plimpton Press, 1911 and 1924.

de Certeau, Michel. *The Practice of Everyday Life.* Trans. Steven Rendell. Berkeley and Los Angeles: University of California Press, 1984.

Deloria, Ella. *Dakota Texts.* Publications of the American Ethnological Society, vol. 14, 1932. (Paperback reprint, edited by Agnes Picotte and Paul Pavich, Dakota Press, 1978.)

Deloria, Vine, Jr. *Custer Died for Your Sins: An Indian Manifesto.* New York: Macmillan, 1969.

———. *We Talk, You Listen: New Tribes, New Turf.* New York: Macmillan, 1970.

Demetracopoulou, D. "The Loon Woman Myth: A Study in Synthesis," *Journal of American Folk-lore* 46:101–28, 1933.

Derrida, Jacques. *Of Grammatology.* Trans. Gayatri Spivak. Baltimore: Johns Hopkins University Press, 1976.

Diamond, Stanley, "Plato and the Definition of the Primitive." In *Primitive Views of the World*, ed. Stanley Diamond. New York and London: Columbia University Press, 1969.

Dorsey, J. Owen. "Indians of the Siletz Reservation, Oregon," *American Anthropologist* 2:58–60, 1889.

Dorsey, J. Owen, and A. L. Kroeber. *Traditions of the Arapaho.* Field Columbian Museum Publications 5, 1903.

Dorson, Richard. *American Folklore.* Chicago: University of Chicago Press, 1959.

———. "Comic Indian Anecdotes," *Southern Folklore Quarterly* 10:113–28, 1945.

———. "The Eclipse of Solar Mythology." In *Myth: A Symposium*, ed. T. A. Sebeok, pp. 25–63. Bloomington: Indiana University Press, 1972.

Drucker, Philip. "The Tolowa and Their Southwest Oregon Kin." University of California Publications in American Archaeology and Ethnology, vol. 36, no.4, pp. 221–99, 1937.

Drury, C. M., ed. *The Diaries and Letters of Henry H. Spaulding and Asa Bowen Smith, Relating to the Nez Perce Mission 1838–42*. Glendale, AZ: Arthur H. Clark, 1958.

Dundes, Alan. "African Tales among the North American Indians," *Southern Folklore Quarterly* 39:207–19, 1965.

———. *Every Man His Way*. Englewood Cliffs: Prentice Hall, 1968.

———. "Introduction" to *Karok Myths*, ed. A. L. Kroeber and E. W. Gifford. Berkeley and Los Angeles: University of California Press, 1980.

———. *The Morphology of North American Indian Folktales*. Folklore Fellows Communications, vol. 81, no. 195. Helsinki, 1964.

Edel, May M. "Stability in Tillamook Folklore," *Journal of American Folk-lore* 57: 118–27, 1944.

———. "The Tillamook Language," *International Journal of American Linguistics* 10 (1):1–57, 1939.

Eells, Myron. *Father Eells, or the Result of Fifty-Five Years of Missionary Labors in Washington and Oregon*. Boston and Chicago: Congregational Sunday School and Publishing Co., 1894.

Ehrenreich, Paul. *Die Allgemeine Mythologie und ihre ethnologischen Gründlagen* (1910) and *Die Sonne in Mythos* (1915). New York: Arno Press, 1978.

Eliade, Mircea. *Myth and Reality*. New York: Harper and Row, 1963.

Erickson, Erik. *Childhood and Society*. New York: Norton, 1950.

———. *Observations on the Yurok: Childhood and World Image*. University of California Publications in American Archaeology and Ethnology, vol. 35, no. 10, 1934–43.

Evers, Larry, ed. *The South Corner of Time: Hopi, Navajo, Papago, Yaqui Tribal Literature*. Tucson: University of Arizona Press, 1981.

Evers, Larry, and Felipe S. Molina, eds. *Yaqui Deer Songs/Maso Bwikan: A Native American Poetry*. Tucson: University of Arizona Press, 1987.

Fahey, John. *The Flathead Indians*. Norman: University of Oklahoma Press, 1974.

Fletcher, Alice, and Francis La Flesche. *The Omaha Tribe*. 27th Annual Report of the Bureau of American Ethnology, 1911. (Reprint ed., University of Nebraska Press, 1972.)

Frachtenberg, Leo J. *Alsea Myths and Texts*. Bureau of American Ethnology Bulletin 67, 1920.

Frachtenberg, Leo, and Livingston Farrand. "Shasta and Athapascan Myths from Oregon," *Journal of American Folk-lore* 28:207–42, 1915.

Freilich, Morris. "Myth, Method, and Madness," *Current Anthropology* 16 (2):207–26, 1975.

Freud, Sigmund. *The Future of an Illusion*. Trans. W. D. Robson Scott. New York: Doubleday, 1961.

————. "Wit and Its Relation to the Unconscious." In *The Basic Writings of Sigmund Freud*, trans. and ed. A. A. Brill. New York: Modern Library, 1946.

Frey, Rodney, ed. *Stories That Make the World: Oral Literatures of the Indian Peoples of the Inland Northwest.* Norman: University of Oklahoma Press, 1995.

Gatschet, A. S. *The Klamath Indians of Southwestern Oregon.* Contributions to North American Ethnography, vol. 2, 1890. Washington, D.C.: Government Printing Office.

Gayton, Anne. "The Orpheus Myth in North America," *Journal of American Folklore* 48:263–93, 1935.

Geiogamah, Hanay. *New Native American Drama: Three Plays.* Edited by Jeffrey Huntsman. Norman: University of Oklahoma Press, 1980.

Green, Norma Kidd. *Iron Eye's Family: The Children of Joseph La Flesche.* Lincoln, NE: Johnson Publishing Company, 1969.

Grinnell, George Bird. *Blackfoot Lodge Tales.* 1892. (Reprint ed., University of Nebraska Press, 1962.)

————. *The Cheyenne Indians, Their History and Way of Life.* 2 vols. New Haven, CT: Yale University Press, 1924.

————. *Pawnee Hero Stories and Folk-tales.* Lincoln: University of Nebraska Press, 1961.

Hassrick, Royal B. *The Sioux: Life and Customs of a Warrior Society.* Norman: University of Oklahoma Press, 1964.

Hemingway, Ernest. *The Short Stories of Ernest Hemingway.* New York: Scribners, 1953.

Henderson, Joseph. "Ancient Myths and Modern Man." In *Man and His Symbols.* New York: Laurel, 1968.

Hobson, Geary, ed. *The Remembered Earth: An Anthology of Native American Literature.* Albuquerque: Red Earth Press, 1979.

Homer. *The Odyssey.* Trans. Richmond Lattimore. New York: Harper and Row, 1967.

Hughes, Ted. Interview in *The Listener,* July 30, 1970.

Hultkrantz, Ake. *Belief and Worship in Native North America.* Edited by Christopher Vecsey. Syracuse: Syracuse University Press, 1981.

————. *The North American Indian Orpheus Tradition.* Ethnological Museum of Sweden Monograph Series, no. 2 , 1957.

Huntsman, Jeffrey. "Native American Theater." In *Ethnic Theater in the United States,* ed. M. S. Seller. Westport: Greenwood, 1983.

Hymes, Dell. "Comment: Problem of Versions," *Journal of the Folklore Institute* 18 (2–3):144–50, 1981.

————. "Discovering Oral Performance and Measured Verse in American Indian Narrative," *New Literary History* 8 (3):431–57, 1977.

————. "Folklore's Nature and the Sun's Myth," *Journal of American Folklore* 88:345–69, 1975.

————. *"In Vain I Tried to Tell You": Essays in Native American Ethnopoetics.* Philadelphia: University of Pennsylvania Press, 1981.

————. "A Theory of Irony and a Chinook Pattern of Exchange." In *The Pragmatic Perspective,* ed. Jef Verschueren and Marcella Bertucelli-Pai. Amsterdam and Philadelphia: Benjamin, 1987.

————. "Two Types of Linguistic Relativity." In *Sociolinguistics,* ed. William Bright, pp. 114–67. The Hague: Mouton, 1966.

Hynes, William J., and William G. Doty, eds. *Mythical Trickster Figures.* Tuscaloosa and London: University of Alabama Press, 1993.

Jacobs, Melville. *Clackamas Chinook Texts.* Parts 1 and 2. Indiana University Research Center in Anthropology, Folklore, and Linguistics, nos. 8 and 11, 1958–59. *International Journal of American Linguistics* 24, no. 2, pt. 2; and 25, no. 2, pt. 2.

————. *The Content and Style of an Oral Literature: Clackamas Chinook Myths and Tales.* New York: Wenner-Gren Foundation, 1959.

————. *Coos Myth Texts.* University of Washington Publications in Anthropology, vol. 8, no. 2, 1940.

————. *Coos Narrative and Ethnologic Texts.* University of Washington Publications in Anthropology, vol. 8, no. 1, 1939.

————. *Kalapuya Texts.* University of Washington Publications in Anthropology, vol. 11, 1945.

————. *Northwest Sahaptin Texts.* Columbia University Contributions to Anthropology, vol. 19, 1934.

————. *The People Are Coming Soon: Analyses of Clackamas Chinook Myths and Tales.* Seattle: University of Washington Press, 1960.

Jacobs, Melville, ed. *Nehalem Tillamook Tales.* Told by Clara Pearson; recorded by Elizabeth Jacobs. Eugene: University of Oregon Books, 1959. (Revised ed., with new introduction and notes by Jarold Ramsey and appendix by Dell Hymes, Oregon State University Press, 1990.)

Jones, Suzi, and Jarold Ramsey. *The Stories We Tell: An Anthology of Oregon Folk Literature.* Corvallis: Oregon State University Press, 1994.

Judson, Katherine Berry. *Myths and Legends of the Pacific Northwest.* Chicago: A. C. McClurg, 1910. (Reprint ed., University of Nebraska Press, 1997.)

Kelly, Isabel. "Northern Paiute Tales," *Journal of American Folk-lore* 51:363–437, 1938.

Kermode, Frank. *The Sense of an Ending.* New York: Oxford University Press, 1967.

————. "Sensing Endings," *Nineteenth Century Fiction* 33:152–24, 1978.

————. "The Structure of Fiction," *Modern Language Notes* 84:891–915, 1969.

Kroeber, A. L. "A Mohave Historical Epic," *Anthropological Records* 11, no. 2, 1951.

Kroeber, A. L, and E. W. Gifford, eds. *Karok Myths.* Berkeley and Los Angeles: University of California Press, 1980.

Kroeber, A. L., and C. B. Kroeber. *A Mohave War Reminiscence 1854–1880.* Berkeley and Los Angeles: University of California Press, 1973.

Kroeber, Karl. *Artistry in Native American Myths.* Lincoln: University of Nebraska Press, 1998.

————. "Deconstructionist Criticism and American Indian Literature," *Boundary 2* 7:73–92, 1979.

————. "Poem, Dream, and the Consuming of Culture," *Georgia Review* 32:266–80, 1978.

————. *Retelling/Rereading: The Fate of Storytelling in Modern Times.* Rutgers: Rutgers University Press, 1992.

————. "Scarface vs. Scar-face: The Problem of Versions," *Journal of the Folklore Institute* 18 (1–3):99–124, 1981.

Kroeber, Karl, comp. and ed. *Traditional Literatures of the American Indian: Texts and Interpretations.* (Essays by Ramsey, Hymes, Tedlock, Toelken and Scott, and Kroeber.) Lincoln: University of Nebraska Press, 1981 (revised ed., 1997).

Krupat, Arnold. *Ethnocriticism: Ethnography, History, Literature.* Berkeley and Los Angeles: University of California Press, 1992.

————. *Turn to the Native: Studies in Criticism and Culture.* Lincoln: University of Nebraska Press, 1996.

————. *The Voice in the Margin: Native American Literature and the Canon.* Berkeley and Los Angeles: University of California Press, 1989.

La Barre, Weston. *The Ghost Dance.* Garden City, NJ: Doubleday, 1970.

La Flesche, Francis. *The Middle Five.* Madison: University of Wisconsin Press, 1963.

Lamb, W. Kaye, ed. *The Letters and Journals of Simon Fraser, 1806–8.* Canada: Macmillan Company, 1960.

Landerholm, Carl, ed. and trans. *Notices and Voyages of the Famous Quebec Mission to the Pacific Northwest.* Portland, OR: Champoeg Press, 1956.

Le Guin, Ursula. *Always Coming Home.* New York: Harpers, 1985.

Lévi-Strauss, Claude. *The Savage Mind.* Chicago: University of Chicago Press, 1973.

————. *Structural Anthropology.* New York: Doubleday, 1967.

Liberty, Margot, ed. *American Indian Intellectuals.* St. Paul: West Publishing Company, 1978.

Lincoln, Kenneth. *Native American Renaissance.* Los Angeles: University of California Press, 1985.

————. *Indi'n Humor: Bicultural Play in Native America.* New York: Oxford University Press, 1993.

Lopez, Barry. *Giving Birth to Thunder, Sleeping with His Daughter.* Kansas City: Sheed Andrews and McMeel, 1977.

Lowie, Robert. "Myths and Traditions of the Crow." Anthropological Papers of the American Museum of Natural History, vol. 25, pp. 30–31, 1918.

————. "The Test Theme in North American Mythology," *Journal of American Folk-lore* 21:97–144, 1908.

Lyman, H. S. "Reminiscences of Louis Labonte," *Oregon Historical Quarterly* 1:167–88, 1900.

McCready, Al, and Joseph R. Bianco, eds. *Mt. St. Helens, the Volcano.* Portland: Oregonian Publishing Company, 1980.

McDonald, Louise. "Folklore of the Flathead Indians of Idaho," *Journal of American Folk-lore* 14:250–51, 1901.

McWhorter, L. V. *Hear Me My Chiefs: Nez Perce History and Legend.* Caldwell, ID: Caxton Press, 1952.

Malinowski, Bronislaw. "Myth in Primitive Psychology." In *Magic, Science, Religion, and Other Essays.* Boston: Free Press, 1948.

Marriott, Alice. *Saynday's People.* Lincoln: University of Nebraska Press, 1963.

Marriott, Alice, and Carol Rachlin. *American Indian Mythology.* New York: New American Library, 1968.

Mason, Arthur James, ed. *The Mission of St. Augustine to England.* Cambridge: University Press, 1897.

Mattina, Anthony. *The Golden Woman: The Colville Narrative of Peter J. Seymour.* Tucson: University of Arizona Press, 1985.

Maud, Ralph. *A Guide to British Columbia Indian Myth and Legend.* Vancouver: Talonbooks, 1982.

Meacham, A. B. *Wigwam and Warpath, or, The Royal Chief in Chains.* Boston: John P. Dale, 1875.

Momaday, N. Scott. *The Way to Rainy Mountain.* New York: Ballantine, 1970.

Monkman, Leslie. *A Native Heritage: Images of the Indian in Canadian Literature.* Toronto: University of Toronto Press, 1981.

Mooney, James. *The Ghost Dance Religion and the Sioux Outbreak of 1890.* 14th Annual Report of the Bureau of American Ethnology, 1896. (Reprint ed., University of Chicago Press, 1965.)

Morrill, A. C., and E. D. Morrill. *Out of the Blanket: The Story of Sue and Kate McBeth.* Moscow: University Press of Idaho, 1978.

Munro, Pamela. "Two Stories by Nellie Brown." In *Yuman Texts,* ed. Margaret Langdon, *International Journal of American Linguistics,* Native American Texts Series, vol. 1, no. 3, pp. 48–50, 1976.

Murray, David. *Forked Tongues: Speech, Writing, and Representation in North American Indian Texts.* Bloomington: Indiana University Press, 1991.

Neihardt, John. *Black Elk Speaks.* New York: Pocket Books, 1972.

Niatum, Duane. *Songs for the Harvester of Dreams.* Seattle: University of Washington Press, 1981.

Olson, Charles. "Human Universe." In *Charles Olson: Selected Writings,* ed. Robert Creely. New York: New Directions, 1966.

Ong, Fr. Walter. *Orality and Literature.* London: Methuen, 1982.

Owens, Louis. *Other Destinies: Understanding the American Indian Novel.* Norman: University of Oklahoma Press, 1992.

Parins, James W., and Daniel F. Littlefield. *Ke-ma-ha: The Omaha Stories of Francis Le Flesche.* Lincoln: University of Nebraska Press, 1995.

Parker, Rev. Samuel. *Journal of an Exploring Tour beyond the Rocky Mountains.* Ithaca, 1838.

Parsons, Elsie C., ed. *American Indian Life.* New York: B. W. Huebsch, 1922. (Reprint ed., University of Nebraska Press, c. 1991.)

———. *Kiowa Tales.* Memoirs of the American Folk-lore Society, vol. 22, 1929.

———. *Pueblo Indian Religion.* 2 vols. Chicago: University of Chicago Press, 1939. (Reprint ed., University of Nebraska Press, 1996.)

Penley, Constance. "Feminism, Psychoanalysis, and the Study of Popular Culture." In *Cultural Studies,* ed. Lawrence Grossberg et al. London: Routledge, 1993.

Phinney, Archie. *Nez Perce Texts.* Columbia University Contributions to Anthropology, vol. 25, 1934.

Pound, Ezra. *Selected Poems of Ezra Pound.* New York: New Directions, 1957.

Propp, Vladimir. *Morphology of the Folk Tale.* Bloomington: Indiana University Press, 1958.

Radin, Paul. *The Road of Life and Death: A Ritual Drama of the American Indians.* Foreword by Mark Van Doren. New York: Pantheon, 1945.

———. *The Trickster.* New York: Schocken Books, 1972.

Ramsey, Jarold. "Coyote Goes Upriver: A Cycle for Story Theater and Mime," *Georgia Review* 35:524–51, 1981.

———. *Coyote Was Going There.* Seattle: University of Washington Press, 1977.

———. "Crow: Or the Trickster Transformed," *Massachusetts Review* 19:111–27, 1978.

———. "Duane Niatum." In *Native American Writers of the United States,* vol. 175, ed. K. Roemer, pp. 198–202. Detroit: Gale, 1997.

———. "Fish-Hawk's Raid against the Sioux," *Alcheringa,* n.s., vol. 3, no. 1, pp. 96–99, 1977.

———. "Fish-Hawk's Raid against the Sioux." In *Coming to Light: Contemporary Translations of the Native Literatures of American,* ed. Brian Swann, pp. 346–55. New York: Macmillan, 1995.

———. "Francis La Flesche." In *Native American Writers of the United States,* vol. 175, ed. K. Roemer, pp. 148–53. Detroit: Gale, 1997.

———. Introduction to *The Punishment of the Stingy,* by G. B. Grinnell. Lincoln: University of Nebraska Press, 1982.

———. "John Campbell's Adventure and the Ecology of Story," *Northwest Review* 29 (2):46–76, 1991.

———. "Native American Poetry." In *The Princeton Encyclopedia of Poetry and Poetics,* ed. T. V. F. Brogan et al., rev. ed., pp. 42–44. Princeton: Princeton University Press, 1993.

———. "Rediscovering Native American Literature," *Humanities* V, 6 (December):20–1, 1984.

———. "A Resource Bibliography for the Study of Native Americans," *Oregon English Journal* 14:62–8, 1992.

———. "A Supplement to Michael Dorris's 'Native American Literature,'" *College English* 41:933–35, 1980.

————. "The Teacher of Modern American Indian Writing as Ethnographer and Critic," *College English* 41:163–69, 1979.

————. "Thoreau's Last Words and America's First Literatures." In *Redefining American Literary History,* ed. A. LaVonne Brown Ruoff and Jerry W. Ward, Jr., pp. 52–61. New York: Modern Language Association, 1990.

————. "'What Escapes Us, We Bring with Us': The Continuities of W. S. Merwin's *The Lice,*" *Massachusetts Review* 14:569–80, 1973.

————. "Word Magic: Indian Poetry," *Parnassus* 4:165–75, 1975.

Ramsey, Jarold, and Suzi Jones, eds. *The Stories We Tell: An Anthology of Oregon Folk Literature.* Corvallis: Oregon State University Press, 1994.

Rank, Otto. *The Myth of the Birth of the Hero.* New York: Vintage Books, 1959.

Redfield, Robert. "Primitive World Views," *Proceedings of the American Philosophical Society* 96:30–36, 1952.

Rice, Julian. *Lakota Storytelling: Black Elk, Ella Deloria, Frank Fools Crow.* New York: Peter Land, 1989.

Ricketts, Mac Linscott. "The North American Indian Trickster," *History of Religions* 5 (2):323–50, 1966.

Robinson, Harry. *Nature Power: in the Spirit of an Okanagan Storyteller,* comp. and ed. Wendy Wickwire. Seattle: University of Washington Press, 1993.

Roemer, Kenneth, ed. *Native Writers of the United States.* Dictionary of Literary Biography, vol. 175. Detroit: Gale, 1997.

Roethke, Theodore. *The Collected Poems of Theodore Roethke.* Garden City, NJ: Doubleday, 1968.

Róheim, Géza. "Culture Hero and Trickster in North American Indian Mythology." In *Selected Papers of the International Congress of Americanists,* ed. Sol Tax. vol. 3. Chicago: University of Chicago Press, 1952.

Rosen, Kenneth, ed. *The Man To Send Rain Clouds.* New York: Vintage Books, 1975.

Ruby, Robert H., and John A. Brown. *The Cayuse: Imperial Tribesmen of Old Oregon.* Norman: University of Oklahoma, 1972.

Ruoff, LaVonne. "Ritual and Renewal in Kares Traditions in the Short Fiction of Leslie Silko," *Melus* 5:2–17, 1978.

————. *American Indian Literatures: An Introduction, Bibliographic Review, and Selected Bibliography.* New York: Modern Language Association, 1990.

Sapir, Edward. *Selected Writings of Edward Sapir.* Edited by David Mandelbaum. Berkeley and Los Angeles: University of California Press, 1949.

————. *Wishram Texts.* Publications of the American Ethnological Society, vol. 2, 1909 (reprint ed., 1973).

Sarris, Greg. *Keeping Slug Woman Alive: A Holistic Approach to American Indian Texts.* Berkeley and Los Angeles: University of California Press, 1993.

Sherzer, Joel, and Anthony Woodbury, eds. *Native American Discourse: Poetics and Politics.* Cambridge: Cambridge University Press, 1987.

Silko, Leslie. *Ceremony.* New York: New American Library, 1977.

————. *Storyteller.* New York: Seaver, 1981.

Skeels, Dell. "The Function of Humor in Three Nez Perce Indian Myths," *American Imago* 11:249–61, 1954.

———. "Style in the Unwritten Literature of the Nez Perce Indians." 2 vols. Ph.D. dissertation, University of Washington, 1949.

Slickpoo, Allen, Sr., et al. *Noon-Nee-Me-Poo: Culture and History of the Nez Perces*, vol. 1. Nez Perce Tribe, 1973.

———. *Nu-Mee-Poom Tit-Wah-Tit: Nez Perce Tales*. Nez Perce Tribe, 1972.

Snyder, Gary. *The Old Ways*. San Francisco: City Light Books, 1977.

Spier, Leslie. *Klamath Ethnography*. University of California Publications in American Archaeology and Ethnology, vol. 30. Berkeley: University of California Press, 1930.

Spier, Leslie, and Edward Sapir. *Wishram Ethnography*. University of Washington Publications in Anthropology, vol. 3, no. 3. Seattle: University of Washington Press, 1930.

Spinden, Herbert. *The Nez Perce Indians*. Memoirs of the American Anthropological Association, vol. 2, pt. 3, 1908.

Stands-in-Timber, John, and Margot Liberty. *Cheyenne Memories*. New Haven: Yale University Press, 1967.

Stern, Theodore. "Some Sources of Variability in Klamath Mythology," *Journal of American Folklore* 69:1–9, 135–46, 377–86, 1956.

Stern, Theodore, Martin Schmitt, and Alfonse F. Halfmoon. "A Cayuse-Nez Perce Sketchbook," *Oregon Historical Quarterly* 81 (4):340–76, 1980.

Stross, Brian. "Serial Order in Nez Perce Myths," *Journal of American Folklore* 86:104–17, 1971.

Stump, Sarain. *There Is My People Sleeping*. Sidney, B.C.: Gray's Publishing, 1970.

Swadesh, Morris. "Cayuse Interlinear Texts." Manuscript, 2 vols. Boas Collection in the American Philosophical Society Library, Philadelphia.

Swann, Brian, ed. *On the Translation of Native American Texts*. Washington, D.C.: Smithsonian Institution Press, 1992.

———. *Smoothing the Ground*. Berkeley and Los Angeles: University of California Press, 1983.

Swann, Brian, and Arnold Krupat, eds. *Recovering the Word: Essays on Native American Oral Literature*. Berkeley and Los Angeles: University of California Press, 1987.

Swanton, John. *The Indian Tribes of North America*. Bureau of American Ethnology Bulletin 195, 1952.

———. "Some Practical Aspects of the Study of Myths," *Journal of American Folklore* 23:6 ff, 1910.

———. *Tlingit Myths and Texts*. Bureau of American Ethnology Bulletin 39, 1909.

Tedlock, Dennis. *Finding the Center*. New York: Dial Press, 1972.

———. "On the Translation of Style in Oral Narratives," *Journal of American Folklore* 84:114–31, 1971.

———. "Oral History as Poetry," *Boundary 2* 23:707–26, 1975.

———. *The Spoken Word and the Work of Interpretation.* Philadelphia: University of Pennsylvania Press, 1983.

Teeter, K. *The Wiyot Language.* University of California Publications in Linguistics, vol. 37, 1964.

Teit, James, ed. "European Tales from the Upper Thompson Indians," *Journal of American Folk-lore* 29:301–10, 1916.

———. "Folktales of Salishan and Sahaptin Tribes." Memoirs of the American Folk-lore Society, vol. 11, 1917.

———. *Mythology of the Thompson Indians.* Memoirs of the American Museum of Natural History, vol. 12, pt. 1, 1912.

———. *Traditions of the Thompson River Indians of British Columbia.* Memoirs of the American Folk-lore Society, vol. 6, 1898. (Reprint ed., Kraus, 1969.)

Thomas, Dylan. *Quite Early One Morning.* New York: New Directions, 1954.

Thompson, Craig. "Gender Representation in Two Clackamas Myths," *Studies in American Indian Literature,* 3:19–39, 1991.

Thompson, Stith. *European Tales among the North American Indians.* Colorado College Publications in Language, vol. 2, 1919.

———. "Sunday School Stories among Savages," *Texas Review* 3:109–16, 1917.

Thompson, Stith, ed. *Tales of the North American Indians.* Bloomington: Indiana University Press, 1966.

Toelken, J. Barre. *The Dynamics of Folklore.* Boston: Houghton Mifflin, 1979.

———. "The 'Pretty Language' of Yellowman: Genre, Mode, and Texture in Navaho Coyote Narratives," *Genre 2,* no. 3, pp. 211–35; revised and reprinted in K. Kroeber, ed., 1997.

Trejo, Judy. "Coyote Tales: A Paiute Commentary." In *Readings in American Folklore,* ed. Jan Brunvand. New York: Norton, 1979.

Turner, Victor. *Drama, Fields, and Metaphors.* Ithaca: Cornell University Press, 1974.

———. "Myth." In *International Encyclopedia of the Social Sciences,* vol. 10, pp. 510–11. New York: Macmillan, 1968.

———. *The Ritual Process.* Chicago: Aldine, 1969.

Tylor, Hamilton A. *Pueblo Animals and Myths.* Norman: University of Oklahoma Press, 1975.

———. *Pueblo Gods and Myths.* Norman: University of Oklahoma Press, 1964.

Underhill, Ruth, ed. *The Autobiography of a Papago Woman.* Memoirs of the American Anthropological Association, no. 46, 1936.

Utley, Francis L. "The Bible of the Folk," *California Folklore Quarterly* 4:1–17, 1945.

Vecsey, Christopher. *Imagine Ourselves Richly: Mythic Narratives of North American Indians.* New York: Crossroads, 1988.

Velie, Alan. *Four American Indian Literary Masters* (Momaday, Welch, Silko, Vizenor). Norman: University of Oklahoma Press, 1982.

Vizenor, Gerald. *Native American Literature: A Brief Introduction and Anthology.* New York: HarperCollins, 1995.

Walker, Rev. Elkanah. *Nine Years with the Spokane Indians.* Edited by C. M. Drury. Glendale: A. C. Clark, 1976.

Wallace, Anthony F. C. *The Death and Rebirth of the Seneca.* New York: Random House, 1972.

Waterman, T. T. "The Explanatory Element in the Folktales of the North American Indians," *Journal of American Folk-lore* 27:1–54, 1914.

White, Hayden. *Metahistory: The Historical Imagination in Nineteenth Century Europe.* Baltimore: Johns Hopkins University Press, 1973 (reprint ed., 1980).

Whitman, Cedric. *Sophocles: A Study in Heroic Humanism.* Cambridge: Harvard University Press, 1960.

Wiget, Andrew, ed. *Dictionary of Native American Literature.* New York and London: Garland, 1994.

———. *Native American Literature.* Boston: Twayne, 1985.

Wilkes, Charles. *Narrative of the University. Exploring Expedition during the Years 1838–1842,* vol. 4. New York: George Putnam, 1851.

Williams, William Carlos. *Selected Poems of William Carlos Williams.* New York: New Directions, 1963.

Winnemucca, Sarah. *Life among the Piutes.* Edited by Mrs. Horace Mann. Boston and New York: G. P. Putnam and Sons, 1883.

Wissler, Clark, and D. C. Duvall. *Mythology of the Blackfoot Indians.* Anthropological Papers of the American Museum of Natural History, vol. 2, 1918.

Yeats, William Butler. *The Collected Poems of William Butler Yeats.* New York: Macmillan, 1960.

———. "The Tragic Theater." In *Essays and Introductions.* London: Macmillan, 1961.

———. *A Vision.* London: Macmillan, 1961.

Zolbrod, Paul. *Dine' Bahane': The Navajo Creation Story.* Albuquerque: University of New Mexico Press, 1984.

———. *Reading the Voice: Native American Oral Poetry on the Printed Page.* Salt Lake City: University of Utah Press, 1995.

Zolla, Élémire. *The Writer and the Shaman.* New York: Harcourt Brace Jovanovich, 1973.

The Zunis. *The Zunis: Self-Portrayals.* New York: New American Library, 1972.

INDEX

Acoma, 260–61

Adaptation: in assimilation of Biblical matter, 160, 215–16

Aeschylus: *Prometheus Bound,* 39–40

Afterlife: Indian conceptions of, 74, 213, 217–20

Alexie, Sherman, xi

Allen, Paula Gunn, 278n.3

Alsea, 109

American literature: relation of Native American literatures to, xxix–vi, 256–57, 266

Anansi the Spider (African): as Trickster, 26

Andersen, Hans Christian: "The Emperor's New Clothes," 101

Appropriation, women's, of stories, 106, 112, 139–41, 145–46

Arapaho, 199

Arrow-chain motif, 106, 215

Artistry, individual, in narratives, 67, 202–3

Assimilation, mythic, of historical events, 161–70, 171–72, 224–36 passim

Augustine of Canterbury, 208

Avidity of tricksters, 27, 41–42. *See also* Trickster

Badger, 77–78, 90

Bandelier, Adolf: *The Delight Makers,* 238

Barbeau, Marius, 228

Beal, Merrill, 184

Beckett, Samuel: *End Game,* 12–13, 18

Bettelheim, Bruno: *The Uses of Enchantment,* 37–38, 230–31

Edel, May, 116, 127

Eells, Rev. Cushing, 210–11, 225

Ehrenreich, Paul, xx

Eliade, Mircea, 4

Eliot, T. S., 260, 266

Elk, 84–85, 92–93

Ellison, Ralph: *Invisible Man*, 26

Empathy: between protagonist and audience, 108

Empirical situation/social norm: conflict of, in Indian stories, 101, 106

Endings, formulaic, 39, 111, 204–5; in Anglo stories about Indians, 265–66

Epithets, 176, 185

Erdrich, Louise, 255, 263–64

Erikson, Erik, 36

"Essence Precedes Existence": in myth, 13

Ethnocentric perspective in myths, xxv, 6–7, 23, 192–93

"Ethnographic novel," 239

Ethnography: place of, in study of Native literatures, 6, 85, 257–63, 307n.24

Ethnopoetics, xxiii–xxiv, 268n.7, 283n.21

Etiological elements in myth, xx, 5, 78, 111, 269n.3

Evangelism: impact of, on Indian imagination, 208–21 passim

Falstaff, 33

Fate: in Chinook narrative, 86–87

Faulkner, William, 25, 256; *The Bear*, 94, 284n.23

Fictive elements in myth narratives, 78–80

Fish, Stanley, 147

Fish-Hawk (Cayuse), 177–93

Fletcher, Alice, 240

Foils: Trickster figures as, 28–29

Foreshadowing: as element of Indian narrative art, 75–76, 93, 108, 129–30

Forster, E. M., 34

Fox, 31

Frachtenburg, Leo J., 103

Fraser, Simon, 161–69

Fraser River, 161, 166

French folktales, 223, 228–29

French Prairie (French/Indian community in Oregon), 226–27

Freud, Sigmund, 27, 32, 36

Functionalism, 6, 42–43, 161, 205, 269n.5. *See also* Malinowski, Bronislaw

Geiogamah, Hanay, 263

Genesis, Book of, 4, 8, 13–14

Ghost Dance, 207, 213

Gopher, 3, 7–8

Grimm, Jacob, 37–38

Grimm, Wilhelm, 37–38

Grinnell, George Bird, 270n.11

Gros Ventre, 39

Guardian spirit: among Chinookans, 85–87, 89–91. *See also* Spirit guardians; Spirit-power

Healing ceremonies, 47–64 passim

Hemingway, Ernest: "Indian Camp," 101

Hermes: as Trickster, 26

Hero stories, 5, 38, 94, 103–12, 126, 137–38, 170–93 passim, 223, 230

Hewitt, J. N. B., 277n.14

Highwater, Jamake, 255

Highway, Tomson (Cree), 263

History: conceptions of, 38, 112, 204–5

Homer: *The Iliad*, 175; *The Odyssey*, 22, 151

Homosexual: character as killer, 28, 100, 142

Howard, General O. O., 174–75

Howard, Mrs. Victoria (Clackamas Chinook), 97, 140–42, 144, 146–49, 151

Milt, 142–43

Minthorne, Gilbert (Cayuse-Umatilla storyteller), 174–76

Misconceptions of Native American myth, 3–4

Modoc, 47

Mohave, 46, 293n.1

Mole, 134–37

Momaday, N. Scott: *The Way to Rainy Mountain*, 253, 258, 260

Monsters in Native tales, 232–33

Motifs: conventional narrative, 144–48, 271n.27

Mount St. Helens, eruptions of: and oral tradition, 194–95

Myth: definition of, 6

Myth Age: in Western mythology, 111, 204–5, 298n.19

"Mythbody," xxvi, 48

Mythopoesis: in Native repertories, 5, 159–69, 201–3, 217–20

Naming ceremonies: Wasco/Wishram, 82–83

Native American Church, 221

Navajo, 34, 56–65 passim

New Criticism: disdain of regional and Native literatures, xxi

New Testament, 213

Nez Perce, 69–80, 174–93, 233

Niatum, Duane (Klallam), 261–62

Night Chant (Navaho), 47–66 passim

Nordic mythology, 20, 26, 102

Oedipal conflicts: in Chinookan stories, 89–91

Ojibway, xxv, 230

Okanagan, 236

Old Man (Blackfeet), 9–12

Old Testament, 203, 212, 214. *See also* Genesis, Book of

Olson, Charles, 42

Omahas, 230, 237–51 passim

Ontogeny/phylogeny: in myth, 22, 38–40

Oral narrative: as literature, xxiii–xxiv

Origin myths, 3–24

Orphic narratives, 69–80, 280n.13. *See also* Death

Ortiz, Simon (Acoma), 256, 260–61

Osage, 230, 234–35

Paiutes, Northern, 199–200, 217

Papagos (Tohono O'Odham), 152

Parallelism: as narrative principle, 53, 135. *See also* Counterpointing

Parker, Rev. Samuel, 113

Parsons, Elsie Clews, 238–39

Pearson, Mrs. Clara (Tillamook storyteller), 116, 127, 130, 140

Pedagogy: in Native myths, xxvi–xxvii, 5, 24, 35–37

Penley, Constance, 154

Persephone, 56. *See also* Orphic narratives, 78

Phinney, Archie (Nez Perce scholar), xxvi, 69–70, 235

Place, sense of: in myths, 8, 19, 23–4, 258–59, 270n.10

Plurality of functions: in myths, 25–26, 42–43

Poetic drama: as analogue to oral/ traditional narrative, 87, 109

Point of view: manipulation of, 93–94

Polarities in Native stories, 29–30, 88–89, 93–94, 284n.27, 288n.13

Pound, Ezra, 169

Primal scene, 131

Progenitors: search for, in myths, 20–21

Prometheus, 40

Prophecy, 196–98, 297n.6. *See also* Retroactive prophecy

Racial innuendoes, 147

Radin, Paul, 31, 34, 39, 41–43

Raven, 40, 42, 102, 261–62
Redemption, 52–53, 213, 216. *See also*
   Evangelism
Repetition: in Indian narratives, xxv,
   258, 309n.11
Roethke, Theodore: *North American
   Sequence,* xxi
Retroactive prophecy, 194–207 passim
Ricketts, M. L., 272n.1
Róheim, Géza, 35, 102

Sand painting, Navajo, 59–60
Sapir, Edward, 83
Satire: in traditional narratives, 33, 217
Schwerner, Armand, 237
Scriptures: influence of, on Indian oral
   tradition, 148, 195, 208–21 passim,
   226, 235–36. *See also* Evangelism
Seal, 28, 96–103, 107, 201
Self-censorship: by storytellers, 288n.11
Self-consciousness: tribal and ethno-
   centric, in myths, xxv–vi, 6, 21,
   23, 39, 94, 129, 137–38, 191–93, 205,
   286n.25. *See also* Ethnocentric
   perspective in myths
Semantic field: concept of, 93–94, 106,
   284n.27
Sexual differences: and versions of
   stories, 106, 112, 139, 141, 145–46.
   See also Appropriation
Sexual innuendo, 130, 147, 153
Shaker Church. *See* Indian Shaker
   Church of the Pacific Northwest
Shakespeare, William: *All's Well That
   Ends Well,* 29; *As You Like It,* 172;
   Hamlet, 102; *Henry V,* 53; *Henry
   VIII,* 286n.25; *King Lear,* 113, 197;
   Macbeth, 11, 25, 110; *Richard II,* 102;
   Richard III, 286n.25; *Timon of
   Athens,* 30; *The Winter's Tale,* xxvi,
   25, 128–29
Shamanism and tricksters, 33
Shame culture, 32, 213

Sherzer, Joel, 139
Sidney, Sir Philip: *The Arcadia,* 172
Silko, Leslie, 255, 259, 264–66
Simpson, Louis, 174–75
Skeels, Dell, 187
Skinner, Alanson, 231
"Smart/Proper," 106–7, 142
Smith, Rev. Asa B., 212
Smoking: as spiritual exercise, 19
Snyder, Gary, 42, 275n.38
Solar myth theories, xx, 159
Sophocles: *Oedipus the King,* 203
Sore Back, 129
Spalding, Rev. Henry, 212
Speculum Mentis: Trickster as, 38, 42
Spirit guardians, 85–88, 90–91, 191–
   92, 284n.27. *See also* Guardian Spirit
Spirit-power: acquisition of, 79, 85–
   87, 135, 284n.27
Spokanes, 195, 206
Star-husband tales, 144, 148, 151
Star Trek, 154
St. Clair, Harry Hull, 103
Stern, Theodore, 295n.20
Stevens, Wallace, 203
Storm, Hyemeyohst, 255
Storytelling: circumstances of, xxv, 29,
   97, 226–28, 287n.4; adaptive varia-
   tions in, 228–31, 235; characteriza-
   tion in, 27, 232
Stross, Brian, 280n.17
Structuralism: limitations of, 133, 139–
   40, 288n.13, 288n.20
Sun, 201–2
Surf, 127
Swadesh, Morris, 175–76
Syncretism: in Indian religions and
   narratives, 220–21. *See also* Ghost
   Dance

Taboo, Orphic, 76–77
Tautology in mythology, 10–13, 77
Tedlock, Dennis, xxiii